ENCOUNTERS WITH A RADICAL ERASMUS

Although Erasmus is now accepted as a harbinger of liberal trends in mainstream Christian theology, the radical – even subversive – aspects of his work have received less attention than they merit. Beginning with a redefinition of the term 'radicalism,' Peter G. Bietenholz examines the radical aspects of Erasmus' writings and their effects on sixteenth- and seventeenth-century readers.

In this study, Bietenholz explores the more controversial Erasmus scholarship on the New Testament and the ways in which it influenced prominent thinkers, including John Milton and Sir Isaac Newton. Turning to other challenges to orthodoxy in Erasmus' writings, Bietenholz shows how Erasmus' opposition to war inspired radical manifestations of pacifism over the centuries. Bietenholz also describes how Erasmus' forthright statements on freedom of thought and religious tolerance elicited both warm approval and fierce rejection, and demonstrates his role in fostering the early modern culture of Scepticism.

Based on a fresh reading of original sources and reactions of contemporary readers who were demonstrably familiar with Erasmus' works, *Encounters with a Radical Erasmus* makes an important and a unique contribution to the intellectual and religious history of the sixteenth and seventeenth centuries.

(Erasmus Studies)

PETER G. BIETENHOLZ is a professor emeritus in the Department of History at the University of Saskatchewan.

ENCOUNTERS WITH A RADICAL ERASMUS

Erasmus' Work as a Source
of Radical Thought
in Early Modern Europe

PETER G. BIETENHOLZ

UNIVERSITY OF TORONTO PRESS
Toronto Buffalo London

© University of Toronto Press 2009
Toronto Buffalo London
utorontopress.com

Reprinted in paperback 2019

ISBN 978-0-8020-9905-1 (cloth)   ISBN 978-1-4875-2510-1 (paper)

Library and Archives Canada Cataloguing in Publication

Title: Encounters with a radical Erasmus : Erasmus' work as a source of
radical thought in Early modern Europe / Peter G. Bietenholz.
Names: Bietenholz, Peter G., author.
Series: Erasmus studies.
Description: Series statement: Erasmus studies | Reprint. Originally published:
2009. | Includes bibliographical references and index.
Identifiers: Canadiana 20190141638 | ISBN 9781487525101 (softcover)
Subjects: LCSH: Erasmus, Desiderius, –1536 – Influence. | LCSH: Erasmus,
Desiderius, –1536 – Criticism and interpretation – History. | LCSH: Radicalism
– Europe – History – 16th century. | LCSH: Radicalism – Europe – History –
17th century. | LCSH: Authors and readers – Europe – History – 16th century.
| LCSH: Authors and readers – Europe – History – 17th century.
Classification: LCC B785.E64 B48 2019 | DDC 303.48/4094–dc23

This book has been published with the help of a grant from the Canadian
Federation for the Humanities and Social Sciences, through the Aid to Schol-
arly Publications Programme, using funds provided by the Social Sciences and
Humanities Research Council of Canada.

University of Toronto Press acknowledges the financial assistance to its publishing program of the Canada Council for the Arts and the Ontario Arts Council,
an agency of the Government of Ontario.

 Canada Council Conseil des Arts
for the Arts du Canada

 ONTARIO ARTS COUNCIL
CONSEIL DES ARTS DE L'ONTARIO
an Ontario government agency
un organisme du gouvernement de l'Ontario

Funded by the   Financé par le
Government   gouvernement
of Canada   du Canada

Contents

Introduction / 3

1
Sebastian Franck Scrutinizes Erasmus' *Annotationes*
to the New Testament / 13

2
Mining Antitrinitarian Ore from Erasmus' New Testament / 33

3
Peace and War According to Erasmus and Sebastian Franck / 69

4
The Castellio Circle: Religious Toleration and
Radical Reasoning / 95

5
Erasmus, His Mistress Folly, and the Garden of Epicurus / 109

6
Doctoring the Truth: Cardano's Erasmian Physic
for the *Libertins* / 141

7
Epicureanism, Scepticism, and Libertinage in Early
Modern France / 157

8
Radical Echoes of Erasmus in Seventeenth-Century England / 171

9
The Taste of Erasmian Spice in Some Classics of Early Modern Literature / 189

Conclusion / 227

Notes / 245

Works Repeatedly Cited / 307

Index of Biblical References / 313

General Index / 319

ENCOUNTERS WITH A RADICAL ERASMUS

Introduction

This study is concerned with some early modern authors who developed radical ideas of a religious or political order and can be shown to have read the works of Erasmus of Rotterdam. Two questions arise: Did reading Erasmus help to foster their radical ideas? And if so, was this outcome intended by him? The second question is the more difficult to answer, though it must vastly intrigue anyone fascinated by Erasmus' work and his phoenix-like personality; it will be dealt with in the concluding section. The first question will be examined in the bulk of this book. It too is not easy to answer, especially when the lapse of time permits a writer to depend on others who had read Erasmus before. At least to the historian it is of greater significance than the first, as it is apt to reveal the broad impact of Erasmus' writing in the intellectual formation of modern society.

'Radical' is a term in common use since at least the nineteenth century, but few have paused to define what is meant by it. One who did is Jonathan Israel, who engaged in examining concepts of a 'distinctly radical character, that is, totally incompatible with the fundamentals of traditional authority, thought and belief.'[1] Erasmus did not, to my knowledge, use the term *radicalis*. It is not classical Latin, but was used, and perhaps coined, by Augustine, who meant by it 'having roots, rooted.'[2] For what follows, Augustine's meaning should be borne in mind along with Israel's definition. The way I propose to use the term, it also means to be conscious of the roots and eager to remain true to them, prepared to cut out the foliage that conceals the base, but also willing to ignore evidence that is opposed to the conclusion reached.

One might perhaps distinguish two ways of advancing radical thought. One is sceptical, the radical questioning of commonly accepted values and institutions. Atheists and anarchists will fit this category. The other way is affirmative and constructive, as when existing structures undergo a radical overhaul. An example around the turn of the nineteenth century is the advance from the classical notion that four elements were basic to the composition of all structures to the identification of some sixty chemical elements that could no longer be split into simpler substances. Whatever the theoretical merit of such a distinction, in practice it is often ignored, especially when radical thought generates radical action. In England's Glorious Revolution (1688) demolition and reconstruction went hand in hand. The principle of hereditary monarchy was retained, but the institution was radically changed, as its basis became the constitution rather than divine rights.

Opinions are subject to change; this also applies to the assessment of radicalism. Manifestos like Luther's Ninety-five Theses or the *Déclaration des droits de l'homme et du citoyen* by the French Revolutionaries (not to mention Olympe de Gouges' *Déclaration des droits de la femme et de la citoyenne*) were undoubtedly radical when issued, but would no longer be radical to a society that had implemented their postulates. On the other hand, a radical concept can form its own tradition. Within an entire system of thought radical notions can be enduring. Given humankind's propensity to some form of religion, atheists have always been seen as the quintessential radicals. Epicurus will always be a radical within the parameters of Greek and Roman theology and natural philosophy, and the Socinian theologians will always be radicals within Gospel-based Christianity.

Was Erasmus radical in the sense of the above definitions? Not really, I think. He was very much aware of the complexity of issues, and as a result he frequently impresses us as a master of ambiguous language. While often determined to go to the root of a matter, he could also be playful, even shallow, aiming for easy rhetorical effects. On the other hand, he valued a number of traditions and held on to a core of fundamental beliefs, but was not a 'fundamentalist' in the sense that a revealed 'truth' must be accepted at face value, unquestioningly and indiscriminately. The freedom to choose, to approve or reject, was essential to him; no revelation could get in the way of that freedom. Also, he did indeed form a number of new concepts that were radical in the early modern period, and some that still are radical. What is more, he tended to defend, rather than abandon, these radical concepts. He often attempted to 'sanitize' radical statements, to strike a balance by reminding the reader of the context in which he had made them or, indeed, modifying that context.

Radical strands in Erasmus' legacy have occasionally been investigated; not often enough, I think. When Silvana Seidel Menchi discovered that to mid-sixteenth-century Italians Erasmus had been a substitute for the outlawed Luther and a stimulant for radical views, she saw herself in fundamental disagreement with the predominant direction of contemporary Erasmus study. The latter, she said, was obsessed with the *via media* and driven 'by ecumenical Catholicism [that] has orchestrated around Erasmus a wide-flung operation of historical self-legitimation.'[3] Bruce Mansfield explored 'a liberal interpretation' of Erasmus in the nineteenth century, an Erasmus who was 'affable, sceptical, "*unparteiisch*," indeed a subversive Erasmus.' While this was an 'isolated Erasmus,' Mansfield insisted that he must be 'mixed in with the theologian, the writer of *spiritualia* and the devoted Catholic Christian,' that is to say, 'the Erasmus of the great consensus.'[4] It is worth noting that Mansfield found that liberal view of Erasmus expressed primarily in the nineteenth century, when liberalism could indeed lead to radical action. Carlos Gilly dealt with Erasmus' legacy in the sixteenth and early seventeenth centuries in the Radical Reformation and among heterodox Spaniards.[5] His survey of radical reactions to Erasmus includes the attacks upon him by the Jesuits Roberto Bellarmino and Antonio Possevino, his influence upon the early Anabaptists and Spiritualists and, subsequently, a group of German Pietists, sometimes called Radical Pietists, and, finally, upon some heterodox Spaniards. Gilly's rich documentation features many little-known testimonies to Erasmus. He equates radicalism with heterodoxy but, sensibly, does not equate heterodoxy with manifest estrangement from a mainstream church.

Reading Gilly will also draw attention to the selective nature of the present study. Where precisely is one to draw the line between radical and middle-of-the-road? I have not included in my treatment Wolfgang Capito, Johann Valentin Andreae, and Stephanus Curcellaeus (to mention just these), although they made much use of Erasmus' work and held for some time at least some views that I would qualify as radical. Nor have I included Giordano Bruno, whose views were radical by any standard and caused him to end in 1600 on the stake. He never mentions Erasmus in his writings, yet told the Venetian inquisitor that as young monk he had used

Erasmus' editions of John Chrysostom and Jerome in copies with Erasmus' name blackened out. Presumably he continued to read Erasmus' books throughout his life[6] and might indeed have found there cautious and qualified support for some of his views and concerns, although others were utterly un-Erasmian.[7] Yet to aim for completeness would have rendered this study unmanageable. Apart from generally excluding the mass of radical testimony whose debt to Erasmus can be sensed rather than documented, I have chosen not to deal with numerous hostile assessments of Erasmus' orthodoxy that can clearly be labelled as 'radical.' His earliest, and unsparing, opponents were conservative Catholic theologians, and later the critique of leading reformers like Luther, Beza, and Calvin was perhaps only by degrees less radical than that of the controversialists of the Catholic Reformation. In the long run these negative assessments did far less than the positive ones to keep Erasmus' legacy alive. The Anabaptists formed a principal constituent of the so-called Radical Reformation, and all of them, even the largely orthodox seventeenth-century Mennonites, took positions that can be called 'radical' and associated with Erasmus' views, especially on baptism. Again this is a topic that the present study will not take up except in the conclusion. All of these aspects have been studied more thoroughly by other scholars than might have been done in these pages.

The end of the early modern period is commonly identified with the close of the seventeenth century. This was also a convenient point to end the present investigation. With Le Clerc's great Leiden edition of Erasmus' *Opera omnia* (1703–6), almost all of his works became readily available and interest in him was rekindled. At the same time, however, as the distance from Erasmus' own lifetime grew, the likelihood of his ideas having been passed on through secondary sources increased and that of a demonstrable influence decreased.

This book examines five major issues. On each of these the views of Erasmus can be considered as radical, and even more so the views that others formed, at least in part, under his influence. The issue presented in chapter 1 deserves to be dealt with first. It is at the centre of Erasmus' life; none other was given so much of his time and energy as his critical work on the New Testament. The notes to his consecutive editions reflect his desire to see the Greek text correctly translated and understood. The task he had set himself was new and often led him to radical conclusions, especially so when he thought that the mistakes that required correction were the result not merely of insufficient knowledge but of deliberate misrepresentation intended to grind an axe. Sebastian Franck was chosen to show how an appreciative reader – and one who would himself have a large following among other radicals of the early modern period – could expose and reinforce Erasmus' radical points. While Erasmus' own critique is radical mostly in a questioning way, chapter 2 deals with a specific issue where his comments were used constructively to form, and subsequently defend, a theology that was largely new and in the eyes of contemporaries daring, if not blasphemous. At issue was the doctrine of the divine Trinity that the papal church had developed over centuries, in particular the part of it that dealt with the two natures of Christ. Often drawing on Erasmus, a succession of Antitrinitarian writers rejected the traditional doctrine of the Trinity. In its place they formulated their own Unitarian teaching.

Chapter 3 brings a move from the sphere of religion to a concern primarily associated with politics, although, to Erasmus at least, politics should answer to a moral code based on the Gospel. In the Gospel he found support for his radical views in the political spectrum, especially the issue he was most emphatic about, the advocacy of peace and the condemnation of war. I have attempted to summarize his views on war and peace, and, in order to analyse them, I have turned again to Sebastian Franck. Franck serves as a mouthpiece for Erasmus' position, discreetly adjusting it to his own yet more radical standard. In times of traumatic conflict the voices of both continued to resonate through the centuries. Erasmus also held radical views on other aspects of governance; however, these were expressed more casually and elicited far less comment than his pacifism. The higher the rank of ecclesiastical and secular leaders, the greater was, together with their powers, the danger of abusing them. Erasmus used fierce language to expose this danger. It was not eliminated by innate qualities of leadership that were, he seems to have believed, hereditary in the princely dynasties of Europe. He also believed that the citizenry should have some responsible part in government, both secular and ecclesiastic, and in the making of decisions that lay in the public domain. Sadly, traditional democracy (*vetus democratia*) was waning in his native Netherlands, but it was of better health in the Swiss cantons. The Bohemian Brethren were solidly grounded in the tradition of the church when they had priests and bishops elected by the congregations.[8]

Chapter 4 introduces the third of my major themes, Erasmus' manifold assertions of freedom of conscience and his persistent pleas for religious toleration. His ideas in this matter arguably gained the highest profile in the long-raging battle for religious toleration that Sebastian Castellio and his friends engaged when Michael Servetus was burnt in Geneva. To Erasmus freedom of conscience and independent decision-making were tied to the assertion of free will, which in turn was an integral component in the process of obtaining salvation. Castellio's affirmation of free will, presented methodically in a rational argumentation, was considerably more radical than that of Erasmus, but was certainly inspired by the latter. Since to Erasmus salvation involved, to a modest degree at least, the exercise of free will, nobody, he believed, was irrevocably excluded from reaching paradise. Here it was Castellio's friend and colleague, Celio Agostino Curione, who conspicuously took up Erasmus' argument, developing it in a millenarian direction.

Chapter 5 presents a fourth theme; the central argument is an investigation of some aspects of Epicurean philosophy, as viewed by Erasmus in the *Moriae encomium* or *Praise of Folly*. Mistress Folly's spirited oratory is unparalleled in Erasmus' oeuvre and so is, as comparisons will show, her approach to Epicureanism – an approach, however, visibly influenced by Lorenzo Valla. Like Valla, Folly ridicules Stoic tenets, using them as a foil against which to offset the merit of Epicureanism. Erasmus is generally known to admire such Stoics as Seneca and Plutarch; in the *Moriae encomium*, however, the onslaught on Stoicism would still deserve the epithet 'radical', even if nothing else Folly says would.

Another strand of Erasmus' radical thought, and the last of my five major issues, is taken up in chapter 6. It concerns Erasmus' defence of simulation and dissimulation and his doubts about the value of unhedged veracity. When he was preparing the first edition of his New Testament, he found instances of pious deception that left him puzzled and pondering. Later it was Luther's radical exposure of the failings of Rome that provoked Erasmus to warn again and again that telling the whole truth could lead to calamitous excesses. His scepticism had limits, however; there existed truths that were beyond questioning. Initial reactions to his statements about lying and truthfulness were critical. He seemed to have no defenders, but as the century progressed that changed, as the example of Girolamo Cardano will show. Cardano praised

Erasmus as one who had mastered 'the art of telling and not-telling' and even criticized him for being too cautious in his defence of deception. Cardano also deserves a close look on account of the impact his writings had in the seventeenth century, especially in France.

In chapters 7 and 8 the focus shifts from Erasmus' writings and coeval reactions to the seventeenth century. While seventeenth-century Holland had been mentioned earlier on account of Sebastian Franck's popularity and the Socinian presence in Amsterdam, a closer look at France and England in the seventeenth century will show how some adroit new steps were taken in advancing Erasmus' radical legacy. Chapter 7 deals with manifestations of scepticism among the French *libertins érudits* and in the *Essais* of their great precursor, Montaigne. Erasmus' encounters with Epicurus come into play, as one of the *libertins*, Pierre Gassendi, brought about a momentous revival of interest in Epicurean philosophy. The trends pursued in this chapter lead by the end of the century to Pierre Bayle and Jean Le Clerc, both living in Holland, both denounced by exponents of a Calvinism more rigid than their own, but linked to one another in their literary activities, though becoming estranged in later years. While they caught on to the radical strands of Erasmus' legacy in quite different ways, together they laid the groundwork for the prominent place that Erasmus was to occupy in the eighteenth-century Enlightenment.

As Chapter 8 will show, English intellectuals of the seventeenth century seized upon rather different facets of radicalism in Erasmus' work, although the scepticism of the French *libertins* invaded England too. In the circle that met at Lord Falkland's estate of Great Tew a subliminal scepticism naturally led to professions of freedom of conscience, while Erasmus' Christian humanism was kept alive amid fulsome attacks upon the Popists. The Erasmus prominently present in seventeenth-century England was the critical New Testament scholar. As might be expected, his radical remarks were popular with some English dissenters, for instance with some (but by no means all) erudite Quakers and, especially, with the English Socinians (in so far as they deserve that name). But echoes of Erasmus were not confined to the Socinian fringe. In a stunning development, three of the brightest lights of that age, Milton, Locke, and Newton, turned to him for help in their quandary about the doctrine of Trinity.

The reader who has straggled along with me thus far deserves a reward. My last chapter presents an attempt to lift off from the arid ground of pamphlets, commentaries, and controversies and rise to the lofty heights of world literature. Although Erasmus' name is never present, credible traces of his radical thought, especially in the *Moriae encomium*, are found in some of the period's classic works of fiction and drama – solid traces in the case of Thomas More, Rabelais, and Ben Jonson, slight ones in the case of Cervantes and Shakespeare. Thanks to them, millions of unsuspecting readers through the centuries have taken part in the encounter with a radical Erasmus. The conclusion of this work, as was mentioned earlier, addresses the question of intent. Did Erasmus mean to do what he did when he raised points that his readers might consider radical or even subversive?

For some parts of this book I could draw on my previously published research: chapter 1, 'How Sebastian Franck Taught Erasmus to Speak with His Radical Voice,' *Bibliothèque d'Humanisme et Renaissance* 62 (2000): 233–48; chapter 2, 'Fausto Sozzini and the New Testament Scholarship of Erasmus,' in *Faustus Socinus and His Heritage*, ed. Lech Szczucki (Cracow 2005), 11–28, and 'Erasmus en het zeventiende-eeuwse antitrinitarianisme: Het geval Daniel Zwicker en Daniel de Breen,' *Doopsgezinde Bijdragen* n.s. 30 (2004): 103–24; chapter 3, 'Un guerriero della pace: Sebastian Franck e il suo *Krieg Buechlin des Friedes*,' in *Guerra e Pace nel pensiero del Rinascimento*, ed. Luisa Rotondi Secchi Tarugi (Florence 2005), 637–45, chapter 5, 'Felicitas (*eudaimonia*) ou les promenades d'Érasme dans le jardin d'Épicure,' *Renaissance and Reformation / Renaissance et Réforme* 30, no. 1 (2007): 37–86 (this is a special issue dedicated to 'le bonheur selon Érasme' and edited by Brenda Dunn-Lardeau).

Two libraries, the Universitätsbibliothek Basel and the Library of the University of Saskatchewan, and especially the librarians in charge of acquisitions and interlibrary loan services, have vitally contributed to the completion of this book. I would also like to acknowledge the help in a number of tricky questions of my friend Robert D. Sider. The transformation from manuscript to book was accomplished smoothly and efficiently thanks to the expert team of University of Toronto Press, especially Terry Teskey, Richard Ratzlaff, Anne Laughlin, and Ron Schoeffel. Behind all my personal encounters with Erasmus over the last thirty years looms benignly the shadow of that wonderful scholar and man, the late R.A.B. Mynors.

Finally, it should be noted that when quoting Latin, German, and English texts from earlier centuries, I have set 'u' and 'v' according to the current practice.

ONE

Sebastian Franck Scrutinizes Erasmus' *Annotationes* to the New Testament

In the vast and sustained labour he devoted to the New Testament Erasmus saw the culmination of his commitment to scholarship. It was work he did mostly in his prime, in his forties, and he worked harder than was good for his health. It was work, he believed, he owed his Creator, who had so generously endowed him to do it. And nothing else he wrote, not even the *Moriae encomium*, was to have so great an influence on posterity.

The first edition of the New Testament appeared in 1516 and was followed, in his lifetime, by four more (1518/19, 1522, 1527, 1535), each newly revised. Each consisted of the Greek text, Erasmus' translation thereof, and a copious apparatus of notes, published as a separate volume. Beginning in 1517, he also published a Paraphrase of all parts of the New Testament, save Revelation. Written in smooth and comprehensible Latin, it was usually fuller than the original text. It offered his own interpretation, but often avoided the provocative statements found in the Annotations. From the outset the translation, the Annotations, and, to a lesser degree, the Paraphrases drew criticism, originally from conservative theologians who found heresies in his humanist philology, but soon also from Lutherans and Catholics who denounced him for departures from their respective doctrines. Erasmus usually published detailed answers to his critics, and these apologies proved afterwards to be a convenient shortcut to most of the controversial positions he had taken. While much of this criticism levelled at him might certainly be termed radical, it was the positive reactions of a radical nature that proved momentous for later currents of European intellectual history, and among the constructive respondents attention is due in the first place to Sebastian Franck.

During his short life (1499–1542), Sebastian Franck was for brief periods a Catholic priest, a Lutheran pastor, and associated with a circle of Anabaptist anarchists before forming his own, strictly personal religious and political views. He left an impressively large body of writings, almost all of them in the vernacular. Franck's German, tinged with Swabian dialect, is rendered doubly difficult by the wealth of his vocabulary and unexpected imagery. Throughout the sixteenth century no other German, Luther excepted, has expressed himself with such originality. This is all the more remarkable as Franck frequently claimed that he was only transmitting, often translating, the findings of others, and that he did so with a fittingly neutral, non-partisan stance. *Unparteiisch* is what he wanted to be; in fact, he introduced that term to the German literary vocabulary. He believed that his role was to present and to instruct; to judge would be up to his readers.

Franck's most important work, the *Chronica* or *Geschichtbibel*, was first published in 1531. It follows the concept of the medieval world chronicle, covering the entire span of historical time from Creation to Doomsday. Taking cues from St Augustine and Otto of Freising, Franck splits his work into a chronicle of secular events down to Charles V and a chronicle of the church. The latter is subdivided into several sections. A chronicle of consecutive popes is followed by one of consecutive councils and the one that concerns us here, the *Chronicle of the Roman heretics and all those whose teachings and articles are now banned and condemned as heretical by the Roman Church*. In compiling his chronicle of the heretics, Franck found it convenient to follow an alphabetical catalogue of the heretics of all ages by the inquisitor Bernard of Luxemburg (published in 1522). Many of Franck's heretics are those so branded by Bernard. Some apparently did hold beliefs that were abstruse and unsavoury by any account, but often Franck was left with the nagging suspicion that his source was not to be trusted.

Already in the introduction he distances himself sharply from the verdict of the Roman Church. To him the popes and the councils represent the 'world,' which is diametrically opposed to the teachings of Christ. Often the church execrates those it ought to canonize, and vice versa. Thus Franck's heretics include not only the likes of Wycliffe and Huss, Luther and Zwingli, but also St Augustine and many other orthodox church fathers, who had expressed some specific views that the Roman Church of Franck's own day should have been expected to anathematize. Franck's heretics also included

Erasmus, and while basically Franck would profile him with the censures of his Catholic critics, Erasmus did not quite fit the above categories of dissenters either condemned or condoned by the church. He comes to mind, however, when Franck, in a concluding essay on the wrongs of persecution, offers his own definition of heretics:

> Hereticus [means] ... a separatist, an eccentric, a chooser, who chooses for himself his own meaning of scripture and holds fast onto it, insisting that it is God's meaning; one, who with his faith and teaching sets himself apart from God's congregation in the church and sets up a sect of his own ... a domestic enemy in God's house, a wolf in sheep's clothing.

The end of that quotation sounds impeccably orthodox. We must consider, however, that to Franck the 'house of God,' the established church, is usually wrong. The true church is 'a spiritual, invisible assembly,' based on faith alone, governed by the Word.[1] Moreover, it is nonpartisan, *unparteiisch*; it wants to serve all and rejects none. Erasmus is called to witness that the Gospel prescribes no religious practices and ceremonies.[2] When Franck wrote his *Chronica*, Erasmus had just moved to Catholic Freiburg, ending his residence in Basel in the wake of the city's reformation. In Franck's sight, Erasmus at Freiburg was indeed a 'wolf in sheep's clothing,' usually intent on cloaking his fair criticisms of the Roman Church – criticisms that begged to be bared of their clothing. But Erasmus was also the prototype of the chooser, the individualist, the *homo sui generis*. Ultimately it is that latter capacity that earned him his long article in Franck's *Chronicle of the Heretics*.

Among the factors that left their mark on Franck's work were his habit of penning his writings in a fast, animated flow and his great familiarity with Erasmus' work. Franck liked to write with a single source under his eyes – in this case he may have had two books by Erasmus before him on the table, while referring to others as well, sometimes from memory, without consulting the text and, as a result, quite unreliably. On the other hand, when a point mattered to him, he was prepared to use diligence and circumspection. Here his principal source was Erasmus' *Apologia ad monachos quosdam hispanos*, a reply to one hundred 'objections' to things he had written, composed by a commission of Spanish theologians representing the major religious orders. Erasmus gave his answer in the autumn of 1527, and it was published the following spring. Franck accompanied the Spanish monks through their hundred objections, more or less in sequence, translating or summarizing. Often, however, he omitted parts of their argument, and sometimes he included parts of Erasmus' answer. A number of the objections he ignored completely; his reasons for doing so were normally practical, such as avoiding excessive repetition or scurrility. Moreover, he frequently went beyond the text of an objection, either adding references from memory or checking and utilizing Erasmus' original text, usually his notes to the New Testament, that had provoked the monks to formulate their objection. In the last and boldest part of Franck's list, his points, with some exceptions, are no longer based on the *Apologia ad monachos*. Rather, he seems to have selected the texts himself, often again from Erasmus' Annotations to the New Testament. At the end of his list he did, however, refer the reader to the whole series of apologies, in which Erasmus had answered his critics, ending with the one against the Spanish monks. Already at the outset he had encouraged his readers to go directly to Erasmus' writings. The bits Franck had 'stolen' from him should animate them to read what came before and after. The discourse around the selected quotations was like the gold setting around precious stones, crafted by an incomparable master.³

Franck, a one-time Catholic priest, belonged to the first generation of Protestants, and though he soon parted company with Luther, he remained fiercely critical of the Roman Church. Of the inquisitors or *Ketzermeister* he wrote with special animosity. Choosing the *Apologia ad monachos* as his base permitted him to present many passages that showed Erasmus in flagrant disagreement with official Catholic dogma, or at least with views held dear by conservative theologians steeped in traditional scholasticism. That was what Franck wanted to drive home in the first place, and often he could do it by rendering Erasmus' point without manipulation, although we shall also find many places where, in rendering Erasmus' point, he sharpened it. As well, the Church of Rome was not his only target; he likewise managed to claim Erasmus for views that were heterodox in the judgment of the Lutheran and Zwinglian churches.

To begin with the anti-papal variety, here are some of Erasmus' 'heresies' regarding the Catholic hierarchy. To support their charge that 'Erasmus seems to assign priestly authority to all people at large,' the Spanish monks had cited the Annotations and the Paraphrase of Matthew 16:16–19 (and also Erasmus' *Ratio*).[4] In reply to Peter's avowal that Christ was 'the son of the living God,' Christ proclaimed: 'You are Peter (Πέτρος), on this rock (πέτρα) I will build my church ... I will give you the keys to the kingdom of Heaven.' Franck expressed Erasmus' 'heresy' in one lapidary sentence: 'The Christian church is not built on Peter but on Christ (Annot. on Matthew, ch. 16).'[5] This is a radical and somewhat misleading reduction of Erasmus' argument, as adduced by the Spanish monks. Citing, as usual, some church fathers, Erasmus pointed out that the rock on which the church was to be built was not Peter, but his avowal of Christ's divinity, proclaimed here on behalf of all Christianity, and that Christ, when conferring the power of the keys, addressed himself to all and not to Peter alone. One can see that the Spanish monks were reminded of Luther's 'common priesthood of all believers'; however, the individualist Franck had no use for this thought. For his radical rendering that the church was built on Christ, not Peter, he could have claimed some support from Erasmus' note, according to which Augustine himself had said as much. Cautiously Erasmus went on:

> Indeed, I am puzzled how some can deflect [Christ's] words toward the Roman Pontiff, whom they doubtless fit since he is the leader of the Christian religion. But not only him do they fit, but all Christians, as Origen elegantly shows.[6]

So, tersely, with Franck's help, Erasmus had found his radical voice.

Without guidance from the Spanish monks Franck tackled two of Erasmus' notes to the Gospel of John. His reporting is fair, but zest was added through succinctness. With regard to John 20:22–3, Erasmus emphasized that the reborn Christ authorized his disciples to forgive sins, but not before he had infused them with the Holy Spirit. Erasmus concluded: 'Respect authority, but be sure that the Spirit is present, through whom [Christ] assigns authority,' while Franck in a marginal note deftly stated: 'Without the Holy Spirit the church's power is nothing.' In John 21:15 Christ instructs Peter: 'feed my lambs.' Franck reduced Erasmus' note to one point: 'He fiercely opposes those, who obtain their cure and episcopacy solely with money and mischief (*gelt und geylen*).[7] Understandably, the Spanish monks had also looked for passages that would align Erasmus with the Lutheran doctrine of salvation by faith alone. To Franck this was clearly an important tenet. He copied what they had indicated, but he was also reminded of similar passages and in two places added references to Erasmus' paraphrases of Romans and Galatians.[8]

The Spanish monks had dedicated a lengthy section (objections 75–85) to things Erasmus had written about Mary, the mother of Christ – appropriately so, for she was of abiding interest to Erasmus. His statements concerning her had repeatedly been criticized before, and he had been induced to make some modifications in his notes to Luke 1:28–9.[9] Franck uses the monks' objections and elements from Erasmus' replies to produce a powerfully succinct statement, in which Erasmus is seen to reduce the Virgin Mary to the status of common humanity. Her permanent virginity could not be safely deduced from the Gospel. Although she had conceived Jesus in a unique way, she later gave birth like any other woman. On occasion she wavered in her faith. This issue mattered sufficiently to Franck to turn from the monks' objections to Erasmus' own text in the Annotations and perhaps also the Paraphrases. He thus could further enhance the most incisive point the monks had made. In the Paraphrases Erasmus rendered Luke 1:28: *Ave, gratia plena* with *Ave et gaude, virgo gratiosa*, thus causing Mary's conversation with the visiting angel to be less hallowed and more humanly loving. In his notes Erasmus had indeed used the term 'a lover's greeting (*salutationem amatoriam*)' to describe the angel's words. As Franck put it: 'He made Mary in grace, charm and feeling (*im anmût und affect*) somewhat equal to other women.'[10] This no doubt made Erasmus' departure from Mariolatry appear more radical than it actually was. Franck concluded with a summary of his own, claiming that 'in many places' Erasmus had said that prayers were best directed to Christ rather than the Virgin and that to honour the saints, one should follow their example rather than adore them.[11]

Turning to the teachings of the Church of Rome, Franck lists some that, he says, Erasmus considered as adiaphoric. They were not articles of faith. No one should kill, or get killed, for their sake; no one should be persecuted. The topics are listed in the form of questions: Does the primacy of the Roman bishops derive from Christ? Are the cardinals a necessary institution of the church? Was auricular confession instituted by Christ? Is free will instrumental to salvation? Can human works ever be called good? Can the mass, in its various forms, be called a sacrifice? Franck here follows the

Spanish monks, but whereas he does not choose to identify a source, they do. It is in this case not the Annotations, but Erasmus' *Spongia* against Hutten. In his answer to the monks Erasmus explains the context. He had listed these points not worth dying for in reply to Hutten's challenge that one must be prepared to die for the Gospel truth. Erasmus had agreed, but added that the listed questions, no matter how emphatically the Lutherans wished to deny them, were really adiaphoric and had no part in the truth worth dying for.[12] Franck follows the Spanish monks in turning Erasmus' argument around. What was primarily said against the Lutherans now appears to be said uniquely against the Catholics. By concealing the source and the context, Franck gives the statement a categorical validity.

The issue of auricular confession, which is an essential part of the Catholic sacrament of penance, exercised the Spanish monks; four of their objections (29–32) are devoted to Erasmus' improprieties in this matter. Franck reduces the charges to two points. When rendering objection 29, he also checked and used Erasmus' note on Acts 19:18. Erasmus claimed that individual auricular confession had developed from the private counselling of bishops. Originally confessions had been voluntary and made to the whole congregation. So it still had been in Jerome's time (objection 31). The second point also speaks for Franck's spiritualist outlook. Talking of sin in his *Exomologesis*, Erasmus had warned lest the rigid division of sins into diverse categories and a painstaking attention to minute circumstances detract the mind from God's charity and cause hatred and despair (objection 32).[13] The Spanish monks next turned to Erasmus' lapses concerning the sacramental character of the mass (objections 33–7). Franck again picked out two issues. The first was Erasmus' remark about the absence of scriptural proof that Christ himself had spoken and acted exactly as did the priest in the Eucharistic consecration.[14] Franck developed a second point more fully: communion under both species, as it was being freshly reintroduced by the Protestants. He literally translated Erasmus' argument (response 37) that at Augustine's time and even later small children had been served the Eucharistic chalice. Hence it was unconvincing when Catholic authorities now claimed that it could not be served even to an adult congregation because a drop of the sacramental wine might be spilled.[15] Franck also made sure that Erasmus' concerns about the sacrament of matrimony were voiced, in this case, however, briefly and not in full measure. According to Erasmus' proposals, a church-approved separation should be more accessible and place fewer restrictions on the subsequent lives of divorcees. If here he argued for greater lenience, he demanded, on the other hand, that the church refuse to recognize mere oral consent as a valid marriage. Franck only mentioned this latter point but, like the monks, he referred the reader to Erasmus' 'seven folio leaves long note on 1 Corinthians 7:[39]'.[16] Following the monks, but adding another reference, he also stated that Erasmus 'favoured matrimony above virginity.'[17]

A considerable number of the Spanish objections were directed to Erasmus' philological scrutiny of the Bible text, an exercise that was met with great hostility by the Catholic theologians of the old school, but was generally approved and taken up in the Lutheran camp. Franck translated a good deal of the corrections and critical comments that the monks had gathered from Erasmus' New Testament. Receiving the Holy Ghost did not prevent the apostles thereafter from erring (response 49); after all, they were human and their memory could be faulty. The New Testament authors had picked up their Greek from street parlance. Paul, in particular, thought in Hebrew and had trouble expressing his thoughts in Greek. Therefore he obtained the assistance of Titus, whose Greek was better.[18] Independently, Franck adds a pointed challenge to the claims in Acts that the apostles had the gift of speaking in diverse languages. Franck said it was possible – Erasmus had even said it was more likely – that by dint of miracle diverse listeners would all understand what the apostles spoke in Hebrew. At any rate, the gift of tongues was not permanent; it would only come to pass when a miracle was required.[19]

The Greek original as well as the Vulgate translation of the New Testament left much to be desired. Some texts were ridiculous and liable to do harm, unless they were understood allegorically. Moreover, the texts had suffered through multiple copying; no two manuscripts were in full agreement. There was also deliberate tampering to bring the texts in line with Trinitarian theology formulated later on. Erasmus felt free to challenge both Paul's words and the interpretations some fathers had given to them.[20] Franck also reproduced a passage from Erasmus' reply to objection 60, giving it a radical twist. Erasmus had said that it was not for him to decide whether the church could alter any wording in scripture; Franck had him say that doubtless the church could not.[21]

On occasion Franck presented statements that the Spanish monks had understood as attacks upon their church in a way that should have raised suspicion among the mainstream reformers as well. Smartly linking separate quotations, the monks accused Erasmus in objection 55 of claiming that nothing concerning ecclesiastical ceremonies was to be found in the Gospel and then stating that the sacraments too were mere ceremonies. Franck went beyond Erasmus' defence when he summed up: all ceremonies of the church might be called sacraments and all sacraments are ceremonies, that is, external things that do not advance salvation.[22] In a Protestant city like Strasbourg, where Franck lived when he wrote the *Chronica*, readers might pause when he paraphrased Erasmus to the effect that Christ, like the sun, belonged to all and did not want to be locked into the walls of a given city.[23] There are also cases where Franck, rightly or less so, presented Erasmus in direct opposition to Luther. Ingeniously expanding on some of the monks' objections, Franck quoted independently a statement that, he believed, showed Erasmus in opposition not only to Augustine but also to Luther, in that he was denying Christ's real presence in the Eucharist. But that Erasmus had never done, though his position was subtle and somewhat ambiguous.[24] Franck also made him take a position directly opposite to Luther's when he had him state that in the Lord's Prayer 'we ask for supernatural (*übernatürlich*) bread.' Erasmus' note to Matthew 6:11, to which Franck referred, was far less unequivocal.[25]

Erasmus' views on coercion and toleration in matters of faith were condemned by the Spanish monks under the heading *Contra Sanctam Haereticorum Inquisitionem*. By the time Franck wrote his *Chronica* in Strasbourg, the Anabaptist Melchior Hoffmann had had to flee that city to escape arrest, and Zurich had become the first Protestant city to execute an Anabaptist. The issue of coercion versus toleration had become ecumenical and a major concern for Protestant magistrates. Franck saw it that way; he did not repeat the reference to the Holy Inquisition, but rather offered his own conclusion that Erasmus 'in many places opposes all human legislation in matters of faith, intent on burdening the conscience.'[26] A little later Franck dramatized Erasmus' despairing exclamation (in a note on John 20:21) that were Christ to return right then, he would be treated worse by the contemporary Pharisees than he was by those of his own time. To this Franck added, on his own: 'and more cruelly martyred.'[27] Franck likewise raised the stakes when he translated a phrase the monks had found in Erasmus' prologue to the Paraphrase on Matthew:

> Perhaps it is advantageous not to coerce [the heretic], but to leave him to his conviction until he might come to his senses, nor to inflict any penalty beyond exclusion from the sacraments.

Unlike the Spaniards, Franck had no use for Erasmus' premise that the above advice was a last resort. First 'everything must be tried, lest any one strays from his original faith.'[28] At the beginning of their polemic, the Spanish monks, like others before them, had attacked Erasmus' exposition of the parable of the tares (Matthew 13:24–30, 36–43). Here Franck merely remarked that Erasmus had written 'against those who believe that heretics ought to be reduced to the faith by force of clubs and various forms of execution.' Franck also drew attention to the concluding section of his *Chronicle of the Heretics*, where he translated several pages from Erasmus' long response to this particular objection.[29] Franck's own view on this matter must be further discussed in chapter 4.

Franck knew well that some other heresies attributed to Erasmus were bound to antagonize the reformers at least as much as the Catholics. By the time he wrote his *Chronica*, Anabaptism was widespread and uniformly condemned by the leading Catholics, Lutherans, and Zwinglians. In this climate some of Erasmus' statements were apt to assume a new, and for their author embarrassing, relevance, especially when summed up the way Franck did so. The Spanish monks quoted a sentence from Erasmus' note on 1 Corinthians 15:31 that questioned the swearing of an oath in civil matters. Erasmus, however, as the rest of his note made clear, did not think that the prohibition applied to religion. Seemingly unaware of that specific objection, Franck simplified Erasmus' position generously to 'how in all matters (*aller ding*) one should not swear.' He referred to Erasmus' notes on Matthew 5:33–7, but there too Erasmus said unambiguously: 'In matters of faith and devotion, however, the apostles too and Christ did swear.'[30] In short, Franck attributed to Erasmus the radical position taken by the Anabaptists, and later by sects like the Quakers.

With regard to baptism, Franck eagerly reported the incriminating point that the Spanish monks had pried from Erasmus' preface to the Paraphrase of Matthew. They stated succinctly that

Erasmus 'in a certain fashion taught the repetition of baptism.' With the help of Erasmus' response, Franck rendered that proposal more adequately. Erasmus, he said, spoke of a renewal ceremony tied to catechization that might be repeated several times through the youth of a Christian. On the other hand, he ignored Erasmus' emphatic denial *quod iterari videatur baptismus, id quod non fas est*. On the contrary, Franck insisted on the term 'to baptize frequently' and added another line, on which the Spanish monks had also pounced: 'Some think it suffices to be immersed in a little water, and presto one becomes a Christian.'[31] Franck also picked up a point Erasmus had made in one of his responses to the Spanish monks:

> There are countless things that the ancient fathers did not dare to define, although without pronouncing on them, they revered them. Of this sort are ... whether infants should be baptized; whether they should be given the Eucharist.

In Franck's translation Erasmus' point is sharpened. 'Without pronouncing on them, they revered them' is given as an afterthought and rendered in a way that makes it almost incomprehensible.[32]

To imply Erasmus' complicity with these Anabaptist tenets was a grave matter, but it was not the ultimate charge that could be levelled against his orthodoxy. Erasmus sensed that in the eyes of his Catholic critics his worst heresy was deviation from the doctrine of the Trinity. He opened his *Apologia* to the Spanish monks with his own catalogue of eighty places, mostly from the Annotations and Paraphrases, that could demonstrate the orthodoxy of his Trinitarian theology. Following that, he covered at disproportionate length the monks' first twenty-one objections to things he had written about the Trinity, especially the divinity of the Son. An example that Franck felt went to the heart of the matter and warranted a full translation was objection 2, copied from Erasmus' long note on 1 John 5:7:

> Perhaps we should strive with devout zeal to become one with God rather than sort out with zealous curiosity how the Son differs from the Father, and from both the Holy Spirit. I, for one, can simply not see how that which the Arians deny can yet be taught, unless it were through sophistry (*ratiocinatione, mit bewerlichen argumenten*). Finally, seeing that the

whole passage is obscure, it cannot be much help in defeating the heretics.[33]

Franck translated a good deal of the Spanish objections, including a number that would become standard arguments in the ongoing Trinitarian debate.[34] He also added lines from Erasmus' responses, seeing that they were every bit as likely to give offence as the texts quoted by the monks.[35] But for once Franck did not use his incendiary devices; on the contrary, he frankly admitted that Erasmus did not oppose the doctrine of the Trinity. He had only pointed out that it was not found in the New Testament. We shall return to this point later. Despite Franck's uncustomary reserve, the wide circulation of the *Chronica* certainly helped to keep Erasmus' comments alive amid the motley crowd of sceptics with regard to the Trinity down to Newton, Locke, and beyond. Admittedly, Franck here was one channel among many others that kept Erasmus' radical voice resonant.

Hell as a place of eternal punishment became closely related to the doctrine of the Trinity in the seventeenth century when both were rejected by the Polish Socinians and the English 'Arians.' The concept of infinite retribution for finite trespasses seemed both unethical and irrational. From Origen to the revival of Origenism in the Renaissance it had left some otherwise sincere Christians uneasy – among them Erasmus, who held Origen in exceptionally high esteem. Erasmus' pronouncements on hell were intensely scrutinized and widely censured. The Spanish monks incriminated a statement from *Hyperaspistes I*. In it Erasmus had asked two questions: whether the souls of the reprobate would suffer retributive torment from the hour of death or only from the Day of Judgment; and whether the fire of hell was material (or, as the monks put it, natural). Neither point questioned either the existence of hell or, as Origen had done, whether it was everlasting. In fact, in fairness to Erasmus the Spanish monks had begun their quotation of Erasmus' two queries with his orthodox premise, referring to scripture: 'when we read that the wicked are consigned to the fires of hell after this life, the question is asked.' Franck suppressed that premise, and thus taken out of context, Erasmus' words sound decidedly subversive.[36]

To question the immediacy of retribution seemed to align Erasmus with the advocates of what, since Calvin, has been termed psychopannychism, that is to say, sleep or death of the soul from the moment of physical decease to doomsday. Luther had for a while embraced this concept, since it provided potent ammunition against the Popish purgatory. The Catholics, of course, rejected it, and so later did Calvin. On the other side, Michael Servetus took up the idea, and it remained popular among Anabaptist and other radicals, especially the Socinians, for whom it became the logical prelude to an even more radical concept, namely permanent annihilation. Only the elect resurrected; the reprobate, rather than facing the traditional fires of hell, simply disappeared.[37] Erasmus' other suggestion, that the fire of hell might mean mental rather than physical torment, was equally ominous. Franck translated the 'natural fire' of the Spanish monks with *ein marterlich, natürlich feür*, thus implying the notion of a physical pain, such as was suffered by the victims of the Inquisition burned on the stake. Franck likewise translated the monks' last objection. In the *Enchiridion* Erasmus had said that the flames that burned the rich man in Luke 16:19–31, and also the other torments of hell, 'of which poets have written at great length, are nothing other than the perpetual anxiety of mind that accompanies the habit of sinning.'[38] Erasmus' rejection of a material fire, as elaborated by Franck, was an important step towards the complete demise of hell, or at least towards a revival of Origenism among the circles of English Platonists and by that great Erasmian, Jean Le Clerc.[39]

The Spanish monks were not overly concerned with Erasmus' views on the secular state and society. Not until near the end of their list of objections did they move beyond the ecclesiastical sphere and produce two statements that they deemed to be scandalous. Franck translated them and also added three more references, but he can hardly be said to have shifted the balance. Earlier in the *Chronica*, in his preface to the *Chronicle of the Emperors*, he had presented the political Erasmus at his radical best, but here, dealing with Erasmus' 'heresies,' he too stuck overwhelmingly to the religious order. This is not to say that Erasmus' sociopolitical 'heresies' lacked momentum. Indeed, Franck made him speak out more forcefully than he had meant to do. The monks reported a passage from the *Enchiridion*:

Christian charity knows no exclusivity (*proprietatem, eygenthumb*) ... Did you think it was only to monks that private possessions were forbidden and poverty imposed [Franck adds: and forgiveness of all things extended]? You were wrong. Both rules were meant for all Christians.

It may be noted that in his response to the monks Erasmus boldly reaffirmed his position, bolstering it with additional quotations from his own works and references to Aristotle, Paul, and Augustine. He did admit, though, that contraventions of these rules were punishable by divine only and not by human law. Franck preferred not to mention this crucial restriction.[40] Erasmus was far less affirmative in his response to the other objection, which Franck translated as follows:

> All that the Gospels and the Apostolic Letters state about rents and tolls and about honouring and obeying the kings pertains to the pagan princes. A Christian, however, owes nothing to a fellow Christian except extending to him brotherly love.

Erasmus protested that the monks tried to rile the emperor and the Christian rulers against him. In fact, quoting from the *Institutio principis Christiani*, they had omitted to say that their statement was 'referring to pagan princes, since at that time there were not yet any Christian princes.' Moreover, the second sentence in the doctored quotation was taken from another source, namely Erasmus' note to Romans 13:8.[41] Franck too, when he spoke in his own name, was cautious. In the *Chronica* his account of the German Peasant War emphasized over and over again that all rebellion was godless. There was no question but that the 'poor' peasants were oppressed in ways that scripture had never licensed and that the harsh retaliation that followed the revolt hit the guilty and the innocent alike. But first and last, Christianity meant suffering; the peasants ought to have remembered that the Christian was a sheep, not a wolf.[42]

Not content with the quotations adduced by the Spanish monks, Franck also translated a passage from Erasmus' notes on Ephesians 6:5–7: 'Slaves, obey your earthly masters ... give the cheerful service of those who serve God, not men.' Commented Erasmus:

> It seems hardly Christian, when Christian lords do not concede to their serfs what was conceded to slaves by the [Mosaic] law which is much harsher than Christ's [namely,

manumission after seven years]. Indeed, it seems shameful that the names of 'lord' and 'serf' are heard at all among Christians. Since baptism makes brothers of all of us, how can it be that one brother calls another 'serf'?

Franck chose to translate this one part of Erasmus' argument. The rest was more ambiguous. Erasmus had also cited Augustine's comment that these verses taught the slaves not to press their Christian masters for freedom. Although he did not like it, said Erasmus, Augustine was correct. The Roman law too insisted on submission, but not the Gospel law.[43]

The Spanish monks did not find enough fault with Erasmus' pleas for peace to raise this issue. Franck, by contrast, did raise it. Nowhere else was his own position more germane to that of Erasmus. His summary of two important notes (on Luke 22:36–8 and John 20:21) is such that even Erasmus himself would have had no grounds to feel upset:

> He denies the Christians all armed resistance and demonstrates with many lines from Ambrose, Augustine, and Origen that Christians ought to be directed to peace and patience, not war. Neither war nor self-defence was conceded to the Christians by the ancient fathers. Nevertheless, he says that this is not to deprive the princes of their right.[44]

Our survey so far has shown how Franck strove to present Erasmus as the champion of antiauthoritarian positions – positions, for the most part, that Franck himself advocated. Indeed, in a number of cases we have seen him streamlining and aggressively restating Erasmus' arguments. Here the question must be asked: did he unfairly distort what Erasmus was saying, or did he rather help Erasmus state what he really meant, in cases where Erasmus himself had succumbed to equivocation? Did Franck grind his own axe, or did he sincerely endeavour to bring out what to him was the essential message of a revered master? If we attempt to answer this question, we might first look at some issues where Franck turned his back on the otherwise so convenient guidance of the Spanish monks. He parted company with them in an effort to set the record straight, to be fair to Erasmus, when they were being unfair to him.

Erasmus continued to be accused of Pelagianism by orthodox theologians of all stripes, but the Spanish monks' only sally in that direction was ignored by Franck – and deliberately so. Their objections 73 and 74 charged that in his notes on Romans 5:12–14 Erasmus had abetted the Pelagians, who denied original sin. He had sided with the heretic Jovianus against Jerome and berated the orthodox doctors in support of the Pelagians. Perhaps oblivious of his role as a pro-forma inquisitor in his *Chronicle of the Roman Heretics*, Franck must have thought that the charge was groundless. Erasmus had merely corrected a wrong translation of the Greek text. Paul said 'death pervaded the whole human race, inasmuch as all men have sinned,' and not 'in him, or due to him [Adam], all men have sinned.' The doctrine of original sin could indeed be defended, said Erasmus, but this was not the way to do it, even though Jerome in his battle with Jovianus had been carried away to twist the meaning of scripture, as were others from time to time. Franck here had no use for the Spaniards.[45]

In three places the Spanish monks accused Erasmus of playing down the importance of free will. On the basis of their objection 98 Franck summed up:

> [Erasmus] does not accept the doctrine of the free will as an article of faith. In *De libero arbitrio* he says that the ancient fathers had written about it a great deal and at great variety, of which, he says he does not so far have a perfectly complete understanding and explanation, except that he believes that there is yet a measure of force in free will.[46]

An equally fair but even more revealing assessment of Erasmus' uneasy pondering is found already on Franck's preceding page (including a line from response 54):

> Free will [Erasmus] defends half and half, and he says that this term is to be found neither in the Greek nor in the Latin manuscripts. However, he is more for than against free will, but not so as many believe.[47]

Obviously here Franck is far from making Erasmus sound like a radical or fair prey for inquisitors.

As mentioned earlier, Franck was likewise unable to retain his role as spokesman for the prosecution when he turned to Erasmus' statements on the Trinity. In one instance Franck began to quote from the Spanish monks' long objection 6. At issue was the meaning of Matthew 1:23: 'He shall be called Emmanuel, a name which means "God is with us."'¹ The monks considered it a pernicious heresy that Erasmus could not see here an explicit assertion of Christ's divinity. At this point Franck lost patience with the monks and offered the following defence of Erasmus:

> Some monks, who ... are supposed to be *inquisitores heretice pravitatis* twist this and charge that he denies, racks, tortures and bends every authority and every passage of scripture which pays tribute to the divinity of Christ. This Erasmus does not do, nor is his topic in this place whether or not Christ is God. That he is God, Erasmus acknowledges in eighty places, which he himself adduces [at the beginning of his *Apologia*] ... In this way Erasmus wants to stir up many, to chase them to the source and the defence, and to reveal the source of the correct text, what it is able [to teach us] in its essence and original language, what is added or deleted ... Afterwards many take this amiss, as if he had written about the faith, asserting this or that.[48]

Although Franck may not always have been able to stick with such a detached analysis, his concern here clearly was for Erasmus' true position. In this sense too we must understand an otherwise puzzling statement. It must mean that Franck again wanted to assert Erasmus' insistence that the tradition of the early church warranted belief in Christ's divinity and certain other key doctrines, although scriptural support for them was scant or altogether missing.[49]

In the cases just mentioned Franck was able to present Erasmus' views fairly because this is what he wanted to do. And he also wanted to do this, I think, in the many cases where he helped Erasmus sound uncompromising. He believed that many of Erasmus' arguments contained a radical core that perhaps could not be readily discerned. Making sure that this core would not be overlooked was to render a service to the reading public as well as to Erasmus himself. Now, did he do Erasmus a service? Erasmus most certainly decided he did not. Even before he had set eyes on Franck's *Chronica*, just being told about it caused him to undertake frantic attempts at limiting the perceived damage.

On 5 September 1531 the printed *Chronica* was ready for distribution. On 14 December Erasmus wrote to a friend that he had learned about it that very day by way of a letter from the chancellor of King Ferdinand, Cardinal Bernhard von Cles.[50] The Habsburg court had apparently taken a particular interest in Franck's preface to the *Chronicle of the Emperors* and decided that Franck was slandering the imperial majesty.[51] As that preface was replete with citations from Erasmus, the latter obviously ought to be warned. Erasmus lost no time; King Ferdinand was a patron and his host in Freiburg. He wrote several letters, including a denunciation addressed to the Strasbourg council. Similar steps were undertaken by the archbishop of Mainz, Albrecht von Brandenburg, and on 18 December Franck was jailed. On 2 March 1532 Erasmus wrote to the Strasbourg reformer Martin Bucer.[52] He chalked up some earlier sins of the Strasbourg printers and then said that he had heard from Franck directly:

> The tone in which he wrote me! He wrote from his prison, but I should rather have thought it was a bistro. Not that he would beg forgiveness for his offence; he rather seems to expect me to thank him for the honour he has done me. Such brazenness does not come from other cities. Yet, how guilty is that man, when he had submitted his manuscript to the censors and published it with their permission? Even before I had seen the book, I wrote the cardinal a letter exonerating your council, and I wrote again, more explicitly. The cardinal answered that nothing as yet had reached the ear of the king Ferdinand.[53]

When Erasmus wrote this, Franck had been expelled from Strasbourg. It is clear from his subsequent translation of the *Moriae encomium*[54] that his admiration for Erasmus had survived the latter's denunciation of the *Chronica*. Already what Erasmus said about Franck's letter from prison confirms that Franck thought he deserved Erasmus' gratitude. Whether or not Erasmus liked it, Franck did vastly contribute to his popularity in early modern Europe.

Franck's preface to the *Chronicle of the Emperors* did induce Erasmus to make some changes in a new edition of his *Adagia*, published two years later, but in the long run what caused the greatest stir was not Franck's presentation of Erasmus' political stance, but Erasmus' place among Franck's 'heretics.' As we have seen, a good deal of the provocative quotations in that section were derived from Erasmus' *Apologia ad monachos hispanos*, a writing that was reprinted three times the year after its first publication in 1528. After that, it never again appeared in print except in the huge *Erasmi opera omnia* of 1540 and 1703–6, nor was it ever translated. By contrast, Franck's complete *Chronica* had by the year 1600 been printed sixteen times in German and seven times in Dutch.[55] From the second half of the sixteenth to the first quarter of the seventeenth century, perhaps no foreign author was reprinted more often in the Dutch language than Franck.[56] Franck was in his early forties when he died in 1542. He has left us with a stunning paradox. It is reasonable to assume that he himself was profoundly influenced by Erasmus' spirituality, his morally founded piety. But what he passed on to posterity in his *Chronica* and his translation of the *Moriae encomium* was primarily the rational, critical, even subversive side of Erasmus, and it was heard loud and clear. Erasmus' rancour was premature; Franck understood how Erasmus could best contribute to the growth of the European mind. Western society has become more rational since the early sixteenth century. Whether it has also become more ethical and more pious is, to say the least, doubtful.

TWO

Mining Antitrinitarian Ore from Erasmus' New Testament

MICHAEL SERVETUS

When a group of Spanish theologians met in 1527 at Valladolid to investigate Erasmus' alleged lapses from orthodoxy, the doctrine of Trinity stood at the centre of their concerns. Accordingly, when Erasmus answered their charges, the Trinity filled the foremost place in his *Apologia adversus monachos hispanos*.[1] Right to the end of the period covered in this book, no other issue in his writings would draw so much radical interpretation. Erasmus could hardly have foreseen this development; debates on issues related to the Trinity had been dormant for centuries. By the time he published his New Testament he had formed the conviction that the elaborate doctrine of the Trinity, as articulated by Athanasius and the Council of Nicaea (325),[2] had no foundation in the Bible and that only unsound exegesis or even tampering with the text would allow later interpreters to find scriptural support for that doctrine. That conclusion only strengthened his desire for a spontaneous spiritual encounter with the Son of God on the basis of a common humanity. With an awareness rooted much deeper than reasoning, though not averse to reason, Erasmus believed that for Christ to be the exemplary model of humankind he had to be seen as insecure at times and capable of suffering. By comparison with the human Jesus, the Christ, second person of the Deity and humanity's redeemer from original sin, would need to pale. Erasmus' frequent avowals of Christ's divinity notwithstanding, a number of his statements continued to cause unease even among his friends. One to voice such a concern even before the publication of the New Testament was John Colet, while Jacques Lefèvre d'Étaples did so immediately after the first edition of 1516.³ From that time onward, Erasmus' statements on Trinitarian issues were those most likely to cause controversy. As the momentum grew, the discussion unfolded along a characteristic pattern also to be found in controversies on other issues. Catholic critics passed on their findings to one another, enlarging their stock of objections as they progressed, and Erasmus would answer every attack. Protestant radicals were perhaps not likely to turn to the Catholic pamphlets and books, but might find in Erasmus' answers a convenient guide to statements of his that could serve their case against the Trinity and other causes – though some, of course, would be sufficiently well versed in his writings to find their munitions without, or beyond, such guidance. So did, as we have seen in the preceding chapter, Sebastian Franck. Once Erasmus' points were integrated into a standard arsenal of Antitrinitarian argumentation, they were again passed along from one writer to the next.

In the later Middle Ages the concept of the Trinity figured prominently in the debates between Christian theologians and their Jewish and Muslim counterparts, but among the Christian heretics a rejection of the Catholic doctrine of the Trinity was not noteworthy. The dubious honour of moving Erasmus to the fountainhead of modern Antitrinitarianism belongs to Edward Lee. While studying in Louvain, Lee, a future archbishop of York, reacted to the first two editions of the New Testament by raising concerns that were evidently shared by other conservative theologians. In 1520, when after much to-ing and fro-ing his censures finally appeared in print, they highlighted already many of those *Annotationes* to Erasmus' New Testament that were to become the common stock-in-trade of early modern Antitrinitarianism.⁴ Above all, Lee was the first to zero in on what is known today as the *Comma Johanneum*. This refers to a clause in the First Letter of John (1 John 5:7–8) that was commonly found in the Latin Vulgate. There the Father, the Son, and the Holy Ghost are described as being one. Erasmus did not find this clause in any of the Greek manuscripts at his disposal and accordingly omitted it from his Latin translation. He suspected that copyists had added it at the time of the Arian controversies. In fact, if authentic, it was in all of scripture the only unambiguous testimony to a common bond uniting the three divine persons. The conservative camp reacted with outbursts of horror and confronted Erasmus with a Greek manuscript that actually contained the clause. He then lived up to a promise he had made and, in the third edition of the New Testament (1522), restored the clause. In the accompanying note, however, he aired his suspicion – justified, as we know now – that the manuscript was recent and the Greek text had been retranslated from the Latin. He also insisted that, contrary to the intentions of its devisers, the *Comma* was not suited to prove the heretics wrong. The reference was to consensus, mutual help, and uniformity of witness, not to unity of nature or substance, analogous to what Christ said in John 17:21: 'May they [my disciples] all be one; as thou, Father art in me, and I in thee, so also may they be one in us.'[5] As we shall see, Erasmus' treatment of the *Comma Johanneum* remained a *cause célèbre* throughout the period covered in this book.

The father of sixteenth-century Antitrinitarianism was Michael Servetus (ca. 1510–53). Single-handed he set an unexpected and new accent for the history of Christianity in early modern Europe, for while Lee was taken to task and even mercilessly lampooned by some of Erasmus' admirers, the leading Protestant theologians showed initially little appetite for a Trinitarian controversy. Servetus changed that. In the course of his highly unusual life he had repeatedly turned up on the periphery of Erasmus' sphere. In 1527, still a teenager, he attended the Valladolid conference as secretary to Juan de Quintana, who later became the confessor of Charles V. A memorandum by Quintana is preserved and shows that he had examined Erasmus' texts with serious attention. With the traditional heresies of the early Christian church in mind, he too paid special attention to the Trinity and Christ's divinity. On both these issues he found that Erasmus had raised doubts bound to stimulate heterodoxy. Quintana's probe of Erasmus may well have started his secretary on the way to his own first book, the inflammatory *De Trinitatis erroribus*. To quote Carlos Gilly:

> Many passages in *De Trinitatis erroribus* sound so much like a reaction to Quintana's arguments that it is easy to imagine how the young Servetus might have assisted him in the composition of his memorandum as a kind of *advocatus diaboli*.[6]

Soon after Valladolid, Servetus and his master parted company, but remembering his former secretary, Quintana later said that the book's argument could well point to Servetus' authorship, although he did not expect him to be so well versed in the Bible. By 1530 the young Spaniard had arrived in Basel in search of a publisher for his book and, as we shall see, of Erasmus himself. Julia Gauss assumed that Erasmus' defence against his censors at Valladolid, the already mentioned *Responsio ad monachos hispanos*, rekindled Servetus' interest in the sage of Rotterdam.[7] We know that others used it as a convenient guide to Erasmus' sundry pronouncements about the Trinity.[8] Thus it may well have led Servetus to Erasmus' New Testament notes. Although in Servetus' three theological works Erasmus is mentioned only twice by name,[9] Gilly has shown that the Spaniard had definitely learnt from Erasmus' Annotations and in a number of verses followed his translation.[10]

In *De Trinitatis erroribus*, discussing Philippians 2:6–7, for instance, Servetus was well aware of Erasmus' note, since he uses some identical key terms. Erasmus said that he did not see how this passage would help to disarm the Arians, and this is probably what alerted the Spanish monks to the thought that Erasmus actually armed them, in case they would surface again. Servetus, like Erasmus, argues that Paul's words emphasized the humility of the human Jesus: 'though he was in the form of God, he did not think to snatch at equality with God, but emptied himself, assuming the form of a servant.' Both also agree that the concept of Christ's two natures was far from Paul's mind – a point that Servetus makes again and again. Erasmus states his disagreement with Augustine and other fathers who had understood that Christ did not need to snatch at equality because he was indeed equal to the Father. Paul, he said, 'speaks of Christ as a man' who, being a man, was bound to reject the thought of equality with God. Servetus agreed, although he was not prepared to give up the notion of the Son's equality altogether, especially in view of John 5:19–23. He was at pains to define how Christ himself had understood his equality with God, of which he here refused to take advantage. The Spaniard had to part company with Erasmus, though, when the latter made it clear that he did not question the eternity of the Son, although Servetus himself continued to struggle with a concept of some form of pre-existence of Christ before the Son became flesh.[11]

In John 7:39, Erasmus translated 'The Holy Spirit (*Spiritus sanctus*) did not yet exist,' but in his note he suggested – in fact, correctly – that *sanctus* was an addition that went back to Greek copyists, while in the Vulgate this had been changed to *Spiritus datus* so as to avoid any suggestion that the Spirit was not eternal – needlessly so, because John spoke not of the substance of the Holy Spirit, but of the empowerment of the apostles that had not taken place by then. Erasmus' argument led Servetus to the radical conclusion that the Holy Spirit did not exist before men were empowered by it and did not exist independent of being given to men.[12] More than such direct borrowings, however, it was Erasmus' constant tendency to humanize Christ that assisted Servetus in forming his conviction that it defied logic to posit an eternal Son and an incarnated second person of the Deity. To become a mediator and the saviour of man, Jesus Christ had to be a concrete human being, though indeed begotten of the Father and thus sharing his substance, eternal as the Word but not as the Son.[13] It was the Son, the deified man who, in a formula perhaps inspired by Erasmus, became Christ, the king, the priest, the prophet, the saviour.[14] But in a final step, more reminiscent of the Neoplatonists than of Erasmus, the Son, the deified man, achieved the deification of all mankind.[15] In light of our definition, Servetus was an exemplary radical. In his stubborn thinking there was no room for Erasmus' many hesitations and ambiguities. He took points from Erasmus, but what was lost in his abstract theology was the vibrant, affectionate *philosophia Christi* of the great humanist.

The only occurrence of Erasmus' name in *De Trinitatis erroribus* regards the *Comma Johanneum* (1 John 5:7–8). One might have expected Servetus here gleefully to adopt Erasmus' rejection of the much-taunted endorsement of the Trinity, but this he did not do, and his position set the course for most in the Antitrinitarian movement.[16] Both in *De Trinitatis erroribus* and the later *Christianismi restitutio* Servetus never as much as hinted at the dubious authenticity of the *Comma*, but his own argumentation was, nonetheless, directly inspired by Erasmus' annotation. In order to render his scepticism about the clause less subversive and his decision to restore it less pregnant, Erasmus had stated that even if it were retained it would fail to provide 'a potent projectile' to combat the Arian heretics, and he cited several fathers who had maintained that consensus and cooperation was meant, but not unity of substance. Servetus followed suit; he started out by repeating Erasmus' references to John 17:21 and 10:30, that is to say, verses where the unity of Son and Father meant oneness of mind and authority, and thus harmony, setting an example for the entire flock, but could not possibly be understood theologically in the sense of an identical nature (*homoousia*).[17] In these latter cases, the authenticity of the scriptural testimony was not in doubt, and the *Comma*, when retained and interpreted analogously, would reaffirm distinctness in the case of the Son and also of the Spirit. Here, as elsewhere, Servetus usually stuck to the Vulgate; he could often call up a verse from memory and knew that, unlike Erasmus' new translation, it had a homely ring for his readers. Moreover, when Servetus wrote, Erasmus had already reinstated the familiar clause.

Whether Erasmus ever read much of *De Trinitatis erroribus* may be doubted. What is certain is that Servetus would have liked him to. When he arrived in Basel in July 1530 he may have been disappointed to find that Erasmus had left for Freiburg. So it was thither that Servetus travelled to present Erasmus with a copy of the newly printed book, but the latter apparently 'would not lend him an ear.' In a letter to the Strasbourg reformer Martin Bucer he referred to what can only be Servetus' *De Trinitatis erroribus*. He had been told, he wrote, that the book was printed in Strasbourg with the wholesale approval of Wolfgang Capito, indeed, that Oecolampadius would permit a new edition in Basel if a few corrections were made.[18] To suggest that the reformers of Strasbourg and Basel sympathized with Servetus' ideas was malicious, but not entirely unfounded. The brilliant young Spaniard had encountered much encouragement in the Rhenish cities. Martin Borrhaus and Wolfgang Capito, who befriended him, were not only staunch Erasmians but also casual strayers from the path of orthodoxy. After Servetus' burning in Geneva, a circle of religious exiles in Basel, all with radical tendencies, spearheaded a protest movement that initiated the modern history of religious toleration. Its leading figure, Sebastian Castellio, was increasingly influenced by Servetus' Antitrinitarian positions.[19]

Servetus' sparkling intelligence was surpassed perhaps only by his self-confidence. He had freely talked about his views with his host in Basel, who was none other than Oecolampadius, the head of the newly reformed church. Whereas his publisher preferred to remain anonymous, the Spaniard himself did not hesitate to put his name on the title page of *De Trinitatis erroribus*. In seeking contact with Erasmus, Servetus likely expected him also to acquiesce with the cogency of his arguments. In the end he may even have hoped to convince John Calvin of his views. Calvin, a personal friend from student days in Paris, then faced serious opposition in Geneva. Did Servetus think that that made him vacillate? Did he think that, anyway, doomsday was imminent?[20] When Servetus resolved to go to Geneva, the chances are that he hoped to engage Calvin. Instead he was burnt.

Worthy of his namesake angel saint, Michael Servetus had set out to slay the dragon of the Trinity. Erasmus became his helper in that combat, probably without realizing it, and certainly against his will. He did not share Servetus' conviction and, as we can say in retrospect, Servetus was uncongenial. He was passionate in his beliefs and his search for truth, but his books do not show passion. They were not reprinted, except for three partial re-editions of the *Christianismi restitutio* in the 1560s, one in Latin and two in Polish.[21] Among the later Antitrinitarians he was revered as a torchbearer, but not often consulted. It is in his death that he came to life. The radical refugees, who vigorously protested against his execution, found the way back to a spontaneous language and a resonance worthy of Erasmus, the champion of toleration.

LELIO SOZZINI

An often-reproduced print of the early eighteenth century shows the genealogical tree of early modern Antitrinitarians. At its roots figures Lelio Sozzini (1525–62), identified as follower (*assecla*) of Servetus.[22] While studying in Padua and Bologna, this Sienese patrician had come in contact not only with Anabaptist ideas, but also with Antitrinitarian ones that had infiltrated the Anabaptist circles in northern Italy from the time of Servetus' early writings.[23] At that time the writings of Erasmus still were widely available there. A few years later Giulio Basalù, a member of the circle Lelio had frequented, told the Venetian inquisitors how he and his mentor had turned to Erasmus' annotations on verses like John 1:14 and 10:30, and Philippians 2:6. There, said Basalù, they had found defiance of traditional patristic exegesis and confirmation of their belief that Christ was not God.[24] By October 1548 Lelio had fled from Bologna where he had been threatened with the stake,[25] to begin an itinerant life that would take him repeatedly to Geneva, Basel, and Zurich, where he eventually died. He journeyed to France, the Netherlands, England, Germany, and twice to Poland. In 1552 and 1556 he returned to Italy. In Basel he frequented the circle of radicals around Celio Secondo Curione and Sebastian Castellio. In Geneva he became acquainted with Calvin, in Zurich with Bullinger. Especially in his correspondence with the latter two he developed an astute technique of raising tricky theological problems. With seeming innocence and thirst for enlightenment he asked questions that were really designed to bare the faults in the fabric of orthodox theology and ecclesiology.

An example is his exchange of letters with Bullinger regarding the sense of Matthew 16:20: *Tunc praecepit discipulis suis, ut nemini dicerent quia ipse esset Iesus Christus* (Vulgate). In a terse note Erasmus had clarified the meaning: Jesus did not want his disciples to tell anyone that he was the Messiah, 'the Christ.' In the text *Iesus* was a later addition and contrary to the intended meaning. As Servetus had done before him, Lelio accepted Erasmus' point. Moreover, in referring to Origen's distinction between a time when it sufficed to preach Jesus and a time when it was necessary to preach the Christ, Erasmus had given another lead that Lelio now developed. Although the apostolic mission was thus subject to change, the church retained the view that it was necessary for salvation to acknowledge and proclaim Jesus Christ the Saviour. How then, Lelio asked Bullinger, could the disciples be instructed to conceal this crucial truth, although previously they had been instructed to preach that the Messiah's kingdom was at hand (Matt. 10:6–7)? According to Antonio Rotondò,[26] Lelio here launches nothing less than a covert attack upon the very idea of a confession of faith, such as the orthodox churches required it (and Bullinger would three years later exact from Lelio).[27] Lelio's question could also be related to selective dissimulation, as advocated by Erasmus, practiced by Protestants in Italy, and defended by Lelio. Clearly, Lelio here demonstrates his method of subjecting the Gospel to a pointed rational scrutiny, and his question left Bullinger waffling in his search for answers.[28]

Lelio's propensity to this form of private dialogue may in part explain his reluctance to lay down his views in writings addressed to a wider public. Probably the only work that he passed on to his friends in manuscript form is the *Brevis explicatio in primum Iohannis caput,* an exposition of John 1:1–14, brief but of seminal importance for the development of Antitrinitarian thought.[29] Whereas Servetus and others who followed in his wake retained in some form or other the notion of a Christ extant before the incarnation, Lelio sets a radically new standard in that he denies any form of pre-existence prior to Mary's miraculous conception and virgin birth.[30] At first glance the *Brevis explicatio* does not reveal any debt to Erasmus. Lelio argues that the beginning of John does not refer to a pre-existent divine Christ incarnated in the man Jesus and, accordingly, that 'through him all things come to be' does not refer to the creation of the world, but to a 'new creation' or reconciliation and regeneration of humankind through Jesus Christ.[31] Erasmus has no truck with this argument, untenable as it is. He was worlds away from arguing, as Lelio did, that 'In the beginning was the Word' referred to the beginning of Jesus' preaching. In turn, Lelio was indifferent to the preference of *sermo* over *verbum* that had stirred up so much trouble for Erasmus.

On closer inspection, however, one finds amid the plethora of scriptural references used by Lelio in presenting his case some telling impulses that come, directly or indirectly,[32] from Erasmus' New Testament. Lelio quotes 2 Corinthians 5:17–19 with the relevant departures from the Vulgate to be found in Erasmus' translation. 'When anyone is in Christ, he is a new creature (or: creation; *nova creatura*; καινή κτίσις); the old has passed away; behold, all has been made new (*vetera praeterierunt; ecce nova facta sunt omnia*)' Lelio quotes this passage in support of his claim that by analogy John 1:3, *Omnia per ipsum facta sunt*, also speaks of the *nova creatura*. Erasmus would have approved of the methodology of using a verse in scripture to explain another, but not of the – invalid – conclusion. Lelio also retains the characteristic features of Erasmus' translation with his next quotations in pursuit of that same argument, Ephesians 2:15 and 3:9, and later on when quoting 1 John 4:2–3, one of the many places where Erasmus suspected that the Vulgate text had been manipulated in order to thwart the early heretics.[33] Finally Lelio again follows Erasmus' version when quoting 2 Corinthians 8:9, 'He was rich, yet for your sake became poor (*pauper*).' His context stresses Jesus' destitution and humility[34] in a way that is reminiscent of Erasmus' persistent emphasis on Christ's willingness to share the weaknesses of the human condition, although Erasmus was far from agreeing with Lelio's predictable conclusion. While stressing the substantial novelty of Lelio's explanation that 'In the beginning was the word' refers to Jesus' preaching, Antonio Rotondò suggests that Erasmus' annotation on John 8:25 might have been foremost among the stimuli that encouraged the Sienese to deny Christ's pre-existence. Jesus told his disciples he was 'even what I have told from the beginning,' or as Erasmus translated: 'first of all, I am what I have told you before.' According to the opaque Vulgate text, Christ was calling himself 'the beginning,' and the patristic commentators had laboured to explain how that was meant. For, said Erasmus, only the Father can be called the 'beginning' *simpliciter et absolute*.³⁵ While Lelio himself does not seem to refer to that verse, it figures, as we shall see, prominently in subsequent Antitrinitarian appeals to Erasmus' exegesis.³⁶ Erasmus was prominent in defining the Christ's threefold office as priest (*sacerdos*), king (*rex*), and enlightened prophet (possessing *plenitudinem gratiae divinae*) – a formula that, beginning with Lelio's *Brevis explicatio*, would become standard with the Socinians but was used as well by others. For a reader of Erasmus it is not difficult to find a radical understanding of Christ as a model and a teacher rather than the saviour, and this is likely how the Socinians read Erasmus.

It seems safe to assume that Lelio was greatly influenced by Erasmus' approach to the New Testament, his methodical reliance on philology, and his rational discussion of interpretative options. Erasmus realized that the New Testament authors often did not describe Jesus as fully divine, but he was also aware of the undeniable mystery of divinity that accompanied Jesus, especially in the accounts of John and Paul. In any event, his profound appreciation of Christ's humanity went far beyond the exercise of sound philology. Lelio understood both the value and the limits of the support Erasmus could give to his own radical theology. Prudence made them congenial, and so did, ultimately, their loving faith in Jesus Christ.

VOICES FROM POLAND AND TRANSYLVANIA

When Lelio Sozzini travelled in Germany and twice, in 1551 and 1557–8, visited Poland, central and eastern Europe harboured quite a number of Antitrinitarians – often scattered in small groups and dissonant among themselves, but vigorous and, in the eyes of the orthodox surrounding them, troublesome. Those among them who recorded a debt to Erasmus are far too numerous to be surveyed here; suffice it to mention Francesco Lismanini (1504–66), a one-time Franciscan, born on the Venetian island of Corfu, who also had intensive contacts with Lelio Sozzini in both Switzerland and Poland. 'Seeds of Erasmus' were credited with helping to bring about his conversion to Antitrinitarianism, while he himself invoked Erasmus's testimony in a curious manner.³⁷

We must leave it at that and turn to a collection of writings published under the joint authority of the Unitarian ministers of Transylvania and Poland: *De falsa et vera unius Dei Patris, Filii et Spiritus Sancti cognitione libri duo*.³⁸ As the title suggests, the book's foremost intent is twofold, namely to assert the Unitarian doctrine, as developed by Lelio Sozzini, and to repel the opposing arguments of orthodox Trinitarians. Lelio's own *Brevis explicatio in primum Iohannis caput* is the most notable piece of the anonymous collection. The principal author, however, appears to be Ferenc Dávid, while organization and editing were the work of Giorgio Biandrata. The importance of *De falsa* is underlined by the unusually large number of copies printed as well as the existence of partial versions in Hungarian and Polish. Nowhere else is Erasmus placed so squarely at the centre of the sixteenth-century Unitarian argument as in chapter VII of the first book of *De falsa*. This offers a succinct list of many of his New Testament annotations with the explicit goal of demonstrating the confusing diversity of past exegesis and the traditional proclivity for twisting the meaning in support of the Trinitarian cause. The cited notes are chosen to show either the correctness of a Unitarian interpretation or the fallacy of a Trinitarian one, often fabricated by manipulating the text. In stressing that Erasmus shows the 'variety and inconstancy' of translations and comments, the unknown authors of this chapter appear to admit that Erasmus' support for their own view is often far from obvious. He may stress that more than one understanding has merit; or he may indicate interpretations that militate against the Trinitarian orthodoxy, but at the same time distance himself from them; or he may 'balance' his endorsement of an Antitrinitarian interpretation with pledges of his personal orthodoxy. In their concluding remarks the authors warn that anyone trying to find fault with Erasmus' judgment had better produce solid arguments or he would face ridicule. They also state that they could have produced many more annotations in which Erasmus exposes 'the laughable tricks of Trinitarian philosophizers,' while at the same time defending him against the slanderers that accuse him of favouring 'Arian trifles.'[39]

Unacknowledged this time, Erasmus comes to word again in the fourth chapter of the first book treating of abominable Trinitarian fetishes, complete with illustrations. Over a full page Girolamo Cardano is quoted describing a magical procedure centred upon a head with three faces. Cardano, however, had acknowledged that he copied this text from one of Erasmus' early letters.[40] An incident of magical practice, duly punished by the authorities, does of course not suggest that Erasmus or for that matter Cardano questioned the Trinity; on the contrary. Yet it shows what the Transylvanians cared to read, and elsewhere in

De falsa the claims for Erasmus' complicity with Antitrinitarianism are, as we shall soon see, repeated, this time less discreetly.

An original and important accomplishment of the Transylvanians was to add a historical dimension to the Antitrinitarian cause, and again the impulses received from Erasmus were considerable. In three substantial and very public letters[41] (as well as elsewhere) he had dealt, unsystematically but consistently and lucidly, with the beginning and progress of Christian theology. To begin with, he noted an essential change in the proclamation of Jesus' message as the New Testament moves from Matthew, Mark, and Luke on to John and Paul – a point that will be discussed later in this chapter.[42] Next and more significantly, he noted a development in the interpretation of that message that occurred in the first four centuries of the Christian era, from the age of the apostles to the Council of Nicaea and the generation of fathers after that. In a crucial departure from the tenor of the earlier three gospels, the evangelist John was induced 'to commit to writing certain mysteries concerning the divine nature of Christ.'[43] He was driven to do so in view of the errors disseminated by the sects of the Cerinthians and the Ebionites. Moving on from John to the earliest fathers of the church, Erasmus concluded:

> Thus it was the foolhardiness of heretics that drove the apostle into more openly claiming divine nature for Christ, just as the boldness of the Arians drove the orthodox Fathers to lay down some more definite principles on the same subject when they would have preferred to refrain from defining the kind of thing that far surpasses the capacity of the human mind and cannot be defined without great peril.[44]

That 'kind of thing' was the often controversial details of Trinitarian theology, culminating in the dispute over 'the matter of ὁμοούσιον and ὁμοιούσιον.'[45] In the third letter he added more details and names, and emphasized that the forging of the theological definitions was due to heresies developed from Platonic philosophy – clearly for him a necessary development, but a regrettable one too. Among the new heretics were

> Simon. He held that the world was not created by God but by angels, a misconception he seems to have borrowed from Plato ... [and] the strangest[46] of them all, Valentinus, a student

of Platonic philosophy, and despite his shortcomings, a man of some considerable learning and eloquence.[47]

These points, unsystematically advanced by Erasmus, were taken up in Transylvania and formed into a coherent theory, most remarkably so in the first three chapters of the *De falsa*. The third chapter is titled 'On the origin and progress of the Triad, and on the beginning of sophistry and of various opponents to it.' First came, again, the Evangelist John who knew the truth about Jesus and warned of opposing machinations of pseudo-prophets. Then at the time of Ignatius, based on Greek philosophy, the idea of Trinity developed. Cerinthus and Ebion preached the eternal Christ. From the time of Origen, the Antichrist, who had masterminded the Trinitarian deception from the onset, became even bolder. Under his impact there followed generations of fathers bedevilled by controversies. The author of this chapter, perhaps Dávid, mentions many names in reasonably chronological order. Gradually a shift occurred. It was no longer the heretics that promoted the Trinity, but the orthodox fathers themselves. Origen had remained uncontaminated, but not so Basil, Chrysostom, Jerome, Augustine, and others. Chapter 6, the one preceding the Erasmus catalogue, lists with remarkable fairness a series of quotations from Augustine's *De Trinitate*, 'so that the impartial readers may notice his diligence in interpreting scriptures, his sincerity too, and may take heed lest they overestimate human ability.' A subsequent chapter, however, endeavours to wring from the same orthodox fathers statements in support of the Unitarian cause in order to demonstrate that it was never quite defeated.[48] To return to chapter 3, Constantine, the great emperor, recognized the fallacy of the Trinitarian teaching and turned to Arianism. Later the Trinitarian doctrine caused the entire East to defect from Christianity. While the Jews, of course, had always adhered to a strict monotheism, suras from the Quran are quoted as proof that the Muslims did likewise.

The reader is then invited to leap forward to the Middle Ages. Satan caused the Sorbonne to be founded, and thus the scholastics began to invent new and more hair-splitting definitions, which the author sums up in a long quotation from the preface of Beatus Rhenanus' censured edition of Tertullian. For the last part of chapter 3 the author switches back to opposition against the Trinity. Apparently a new start was made in the twelfth century with Joachim of Fiore, who took on Peter Lombard and was condemned.[49] The author offers specific references to show that even the scholastics themselves, amid their cavils, could not always quell their own doubts. A contemporary Paris theologian, Gilbert Genebrard, confirmed that the Trinitarian doctrine had been entirely unknown until the time of Tertullian, when it began to take shape under the impact of the heresies then circulating.[50] Pierre d'Ailly plainly stated that it was unscriptural. With another leap forward, we reach Erasmus, Servetus, Henricus Cornelius Agrippa, Bernardino Ochino along with others, and finally Lelio Sozzini. In a subsequent chapter Erasmus' place is elaborated upon:

> There came forward Erasmus Roterodamus, who was the first one in our time to remove that [stumbling] stone and teach the One God the Father, and that not obscurely, while hinting (*carpens*) at the rest rather than state it openly. After Erasmus, Michael Servetus came forward ...[51]

The distinction accorded to Erasmus in *De falsa* ought to be seen in the context of the stunning number of works by Erasmus present in the libraries of Hungary and Transylvania in the early modern period.[52]

Johann Sommer (c. 1540–74), a Saxon, who migrated to the Saxon townships in Transylvania, married Dávid's daughter, and eventually became the master of the school at Cluj, was especially indebted to Sebastian Castellio and Jacopo Aconcio and their radical pursuance of the tolerant and rational aspects of Erasmus' programme. Erasmus' annotations to the New Testament also were an important tool to Sommer. In his controversy with Péter Károli he explained 1 Timothy 3:16 with specific reference to Erasmus, whose note was particularly attractive to the Antitrinitarians. According to Erasmus, the simplest interpretation of the puzzling verse was to assume that it was neither God nor Christ but the Gospel, which through Jesus 'was manifested in the flesh ... preached among the nations, believed on in the world, taken up in glory.'[53]

In the wake of his Transylvanian predecessors, Sommer pursued the quest for the historical roots of Antitrinitarianism with unsurpassed zeal. He is most original when he tries to show that the doctrine of the Trinity in all its aspects derived from Platonic philosophy. The New Testament writers used the Greek language, with which they were not really familiar, because they wished to accommodate gentile readers who had no Hebrew. Unfortunately these readers approached the Gospel with their own grounding in Greek philosophy. The result was a compilation of errors that gave rise to the dogma of a Christian Trinity. Sommer became almost obsessed with his theory; in support of it he scoured Plato, especially the *Timaeus*, but also Aristotle and the Neoplatonists.[54] As we have seen, Erasmus too had earlier given some thought to the possibility that Platonic concepts had derailed the simple and sound understanding of the Gospel message. He avoided, however, the seemingly logical conclusion that John and Paul themselves, rather than only the heretics of the apostolic age, had been influenced by the Greek philosophers. Sommer did likewise; moreover, like the authors of *De falsa*, he did not suggest a continuous presence of Antitrinitarian thinking. Rather he perceived a new, but as yet inconsequential, beginning at the dawn of the sixteenth century with Paulus Riccius, a German Jew converted to Christianity.[55]

FAUSTO SOZZINI

The dominating figure of the early modern Antitrinitarian movement is Fausto Sozzini (1539–1604), Lelio's nephew. In 1562–3 Fausto was in Zurich, where he took possession of the papers of his recently deceased uncle, and also in Basel. He thus came to know the *Brevis explicatio* of the first chapter of John that Lelio had written shortly before his death. Fausto reacted by writing, then and there, his own first work of importance, entitled *Explicatio primae partis primae capitis Evangelistae Ioannis* (first published in Alba Iulia, 1568), an elaboration of and complement to Lelio's *Brevis explicatio* but, as will be seen shortly, setting new accents. Fausto was again in Basel from 1575 to 1578, writing there his influential treatise *De Iesu Christo servatore*. He then travelled to Transylvania and in 1579, ending his migrations, he settled in Poland.

While in Basel, Fausto also edited Castellio's posthumous *Dialogi quatuor* on predestination and free will, not without some adaptations where his own views differed from Castellio's text. At the beginning of his preface Fausto inveighs against a concept of predestination, which he traces back to Augustine and blames for the absurd conclusion that God is the author of all sins. Among the opponents of predestination, the pride of place goes to Erasmus, the champion who battled Luther to a definitive rout.[56]

This enthusiastic declaration for Erasmus stands at the beginning of Fausto's long list of publications, and there is no reason to think that his feelings ever changed. It cannot, however, be said that he played a key role in the transmission of Erasmus' ideas, although he turned to Erasmus' writings rather more often than one might have expected. His own work is preserved in less than perfect condition, sometimes pieced together by editors long after his death or, as in the case of the important commentary on Matthew, incomplete and unrevised. Often formulas like 'I seem to recall' point to the absence of relevant books at the time of writing. As far as the Bible is concerned, he follows the Antitrinitarian tradition of quoting the Vulgate, but feels free to replace words that he finds inadequate. He had regular access to one of Beza's Bibles, but after Beza, the largest number of his references concerning the New Testament may well be to Erasmus' annotations and paraphrases. These seem to be more numerous than the references to the Latin New Testament of Castellio, who greatly influenced his intellectual development.

It is beyond the scope of this study to analyse the full range of Fausto's theology and socio-religious thought, or even the evolution of these in the course of his life. To show the impact of Erasmus it is enough to discuss some key New Testament references in Fausto's collected writings, usually without regard to specific works, for often the same verses are discussed in several places.[57] Looking first at a number of passages on Trinitarian issues, as well as some others that reveal a debt to Erasmus, will eventually permit us to reach some conclusions on their respective approaches to exegesis and to the role of Erasmus in the work of the man whose importance caused all subsequent Antitrinitarians of early modern Europe to be called Socinians.

As mentioned at the beginning of this chapter, the earliest and for a time most momentous attack upon Erasmus' New Testament concerned the *Comma Johanneum* (1 John 5:7–8), the unique reference in the Vulgate to the three persons of the Trinity bearing witness in heaven and 'being one.' Starting with Servetus, the Antitrinitarians could not fail to get involved in this controversy. They found two points in Erasmus' long note particularly relevant to their own case, and Fausto repeatedly referred to Erasmus when he discussed these. The first was that the clause about the three witnesses in heaven was likely fabricated in a later age preoccupied with combating the Arian heresy. To Fausto, as to most others minded like him, this first point was unimportant in view of the second, concerning the unity of the three witnesses. The Greek should be translated, not *hi tres unum sunt*, 'these three are one,' but *in unum sunt*, which ought to be taken to mean 'agreeing with each other about their witness.' This was how John expressed himself elsewhere. While advising his readers to consult Erasmus' annotation as well as his responses to Lee and the theologians of Louvain, Fausto formulated the classic Antitrinitarian exposition of the *Comma*.[58]

In the indispensable – and in Fausto's case multiple – discussion of the first chapter of John, Fausto follows, above all, the pioneering interpretation of his uncle Lelio. John 1:3 and 1:10 did not refer to the creation of the universe. The 'world' made by the 'Word' was the 'new creation,' man saved through his faith in Christ. While this was not Erasmus' understanding of John's words, it is noticeable how little he had to say in this context about the genesis of the universe, while the emphasis he generally placed on Paul's 'new creation' may well have impressed the Socinians.[59] In his *Explicatio* of the beginning of the Gospel of John, Fausto does not mention Erasmus, but Juliusz Domański in a seminal paper indicates two passages that almost certainly are based, one on Erasmus' annotations, the other on his paraphrase.[60] Moreover, Erasmus' extensive notes on John 1:1–3 led Fausto to an argument that is not to be found in Lelio's commentary. Erasmus notes that the Greek text adds to 'God' the definite article in 'the Word was with God,' but omits that article in 'and the Word was God.' 'God' with the article, he explains, is the Father, and the Word that is with him is the Son. But the Word itself, which is the Son, is 'God' without the article. Fausto repeats Erasmus' argument, but of course avoids his conclusion that this was John's awkward way to point to the common divine essence in the different persons of the Trinity.[61] Fausto also breaks new ground with a further elucidation, and here Erasmus is mentioned. According to Fausto, 'God' in 'the Word was God' does not refer to a person but is designative (*appellativum*). Men too are often called divine. A note refers to Erasmus' adage I i 69: *Homo homini deus*, which states that the ancients tended to apply the notion of divinity to benefactors of any kind, for instance even the geese on the Roman Capitol.[62] Less conspicuously, Fausto also endorsed Erasmus' preference for *sermo* over *verbum* as a translation of λόγος, which he found better suited to his own understanding of John's term as manifestation of the Father's will.[63]

Erasmus' noticeable unease with his own Trinitarian explanation of John 1:1–3 encouraged Fausto to leap to the Antitrinitarian one that the Son is not equal to the Father, a sentiment that Erasmus in fact shared to a point.[64] The notion of the Son's incarnation was repugnant to the Antitrinitarians. Following Servetus and Lelio, Fausto insisted that those who (like the Vulgate and Erasmus) translated the Word 'became flesh, *caro factum est*' (John 1:14) were quite wrong. Rather one should translate (as Lorenzo Valla had done): 'was flesh, *caro fuit.*' While the Greek justified both versions, the former and the act of incarnation it insinuated were ruled out by the context.[65] He also declared – in a significant step beyond his uncle's model – that it was due to Satan's dissemination of Platonic philosophy among the early Christians that the timeless word (*verbum fuit*) began to be understood in a false Trinitarian sense. Even at the time of the apostles the false as well as the correct beliefs concerning Jesus Christ were in circulation, but John did not write his gospel in reaction to Ebion and Cenrinthus, since they had never embraced the correct (Socinian) belief, nor had later Arius. Although Fausto does not attempt to chart the historical genesis of Antitrinitarianism, his argument bears some resemblance to views held by Servetus and, especially, later the Transylvanians, and with regard to these we have noted the Erasmian parallels.[66]

In all Trinitarian debates the extent, and perhaps the limits, of Jesus' divinity were of central importance. Erasmus' note on John 17:3 was often recalled both by fault-finding Catholics and appreciative Antitrinitarians. Erasmus explained that in John's *te solum Deum verum,* 'the only true God' referred to the Father alone, and not also to Jesus Christ, who was mentioned in the same sentence. But Erasmus found it prudent to add that John's *solum* was meant to exclude not Jesus but the pagan deities. The verse, Erasmus said, invited an Arian interpretation, and Augustine had laboured to no avail to prove it wrong. Fausto repeatedly mentioned Erasmus' note, contrasting its argument with Beza's ambivalent translation that could be taken to refer to the Father and the Son alike. Fausto insisted that John had no truck with the nature of either Father or Son, but stressed the obedience and gratitude due to both – a point that was germane to Erasmus' paraphrase.[67]

Erasmus' note on Romans 9:5 was the target of many Catholic attacks and as a result underwent many amendments in the course of the successive editions of his New Testament. Understandably, the Antitrinitarians were fascinated by two issues Erasmus had raised concerning the Vulgate text, which reads: *Christus secundum carnem, qui est super omnia Deus benedictus in saecula*. Erasmus had noted that some of the earliest fathers had not found the word *Deus* in this verse. His second point was that, even if one accepts the reference to 'God,' one might not want to relate his being praised for ever to Christ, but treat it as an independent doxology referring to the Father. Thus both of Erasmus' points do away with a witness for the divinity of Christ. Fausto was not content with simply affirming their validity; he also added a new argument. Even the reading that Christ was 'God over all, *super omnia Deus*' would merely affirm that the human Christ would eventually (after his death and resurrection) receive from the Father authority over everything.[68]

The orthodox dogma claimed that the Son was both eternal and equal to the Father. This prompted Fausto to propose two highly original expositions of New Testament verses, both of which owned inspiration to Erasmus. John 8:58 reads enigmatically: 'Before Abraham was, I am.' Erasmus translated 'before Abraham was born (*antequam Abraham nasceretur*),' to emphasize, with Augustine and Chrysostom, that John here thought of two different forms of existence, temporal in Abraham's case, eternal in Christ's. Servetus, in line with his tortuous notion of a pre-existence, adopted Erasmus' *nasceretur*, while Lelio actually opposed the verse to those who held that Christ was eternal. The Gospel, he said, used 'figures and tropes' to show that from the beginning of the world Christ was 'defined and expected,' before Abraham was 'promised.' Fausto proposed a radically new approach, albeit taking clues, it seems, from both Lelio's emphasis on premonition and Erasmus' conjecture that the Vulgate's *antequam Abraham fieret* might be a copyist's error for *foret*. The assumption of a future tense suited Fausto, who suggested *fiat*. He pointed out that in Hebrew 'Abraham' meant 'father of many people,' and with a vast sweep of imagination explained that what Jesus meant was: 'I tell you, Jews, that you must accept me as the Christ, and must do so before "Abraham," that is the Gentiles, will acquire God's kingdom and you will lose it.'[69]

A radical reinterpretation of Erasmus' comments is also found when we turn to John 3:13. Erasmus retained the Vulgate translation: 'No one ascends into heaven but he who descends from heaven: the Son of Man who is in heaven.' But according to Erasmus' notes the

Greek states '*did* ascend into heaven,' and thus Jesus alive on earth, who speaks these words, cannot refer to his future ascension. Likewise instead of 'the Son of Man who is in heaven,' one could translate 'who was in heaven,' that is to say, before he had descended, and discover here an allusion to the two simultaneously held natures of the eternal Son. Not deterred by the orthodoxy of Erasmus' notes, Servetus had availed himself of the choice of translations offered therein and posited 'who is now in heaven' – only now, after his resurrection and ascension. Fausto preferred the option 'who did ascend,' as had Beza, also following Erasmus' lead. But where they had found figurative speech pointing to Christ's two natures, Fausto boldly insisted on a literal understanding: John, and John alone, did indeed report that Jesus in the course of his earthly life had once been raised to God's presence in ecstasy. The same, after all, had previously happened to Elijah and would later happen to Paul.[70]

Underlying the just-mentioned argument is also Fausto's aversion to the dogma of Christ's redeeming death on the cross. To state that through his death Jesus had offered the Father satisfaction for our sins was, in Socinian view, utterly wrong. Only with his ascension to heaven did Christ become the divine Redeemer, while it fell to the man Jesus to teach us how to emerge from the state of sin. It was important for Fausto to present a pertinent interpretation of Romans 3:25, and he did so repeatedly, adopting Erasmus' translation, according to which Jesus Christ was the one God had designated to reconcile us to himself through faith, by means of his blood (*quem proposuit Deus reconciliatorem per fidem, interveniente ipsius sanguine*). At the same time Fausto blamed Castellio for translating, as the Vulgate had done: 'putting faith in his blood,' which suggested atonement through Christ's death on the cross.[71] In a related attack against the orthodox dogma Fausto referred to Acts 20:28, a verse that, I think, had not formerly been used in the Antitrinitarian camp. It instructs the ministers 'to feed the church of God [modern versions read: of the Lord] which he won with his blood.' Fausto called Erasmus' *Apologia ad Sanctium Caranzam* to witness that there was nothing absurd in the Father calling the blood of his Son his own blood. Erasmus, however, ended his argument by saying that he was content if the verse was read as a reference to the Son, who here exceptionally would be called 'God,' as he deserved according to the true faith. And that latter point Fausto did not care to mention.[72]

Fausto's high regard for Erasmus and a certain affinity of their positions were of course not restricted to the discussion of Trinitarian issues. Both stressed the efficacy of faith that manifested itself in good works and lightened the burden of predestination. Fausto's comments on 1 Peter 2:8, source of the proverbial *petra scandali*, are interesting not only for his view on predestination but also for the circumspection on which they were grounded. Here too Erasmus' New Testament proved helpful to him. Erasmus translated: 'they stumble because they resist the word, and what they were taught they disbelieve.' In his notes and his paraphrase he specified that the Jews resisted the Gospel and ignored the Mosaic Law that should have prepared them for the Gospel. He thus was a long way from the traditional predestinarian understanding of the Vulgate text: 'they disbelieved the word, as they were destined to do.' Fausto somehow found his own interpretation. It was not that they were destined to disobey, but 'they gravely hurt themselves and, because they reject the word, promote their own ruin.' Their disobedience, thus, is only the inevitable consequence of their (voluntary) rejection of the Gospel. He then turned to Beza and Castellio: 'Both pervert this passage, the former insisting on his predestination, the latter because he totally rejects predestination. But even Erasmus, whom Castellio has followed, erred in his interpretation of this verse.'[73] While he anticipated modern translations in rejecting Erasmus' understanding of that verse, Fausto was searching for a balanced solution to the conundrum of predestination, and so was also Erasmus.

Fausto was certainly more radical in his rejection of original sin, and this is shown in his accounting for Erasmus' extensive and controversial comments on Romans 5:12–18. It is true that Erasmus here broke down a scriptural pillar of the doctrine of original sin by showing that the Greek text repudiates a traditional exposition of the Vulgate version in this sense. As Erasmus pointed out, Paul did not suggest that sin, and through sin death, had come into the world because of one man, Adam, in whom all men sinned. Rather, Paul said that death spread to all men because all men sinned – not *in quo [Adamo] omnes peccaverunt*, but *quatenus omnes peccaverunt*. In his paraphrase Erasmus specified that no one had avoided imitating Adam's example in sinning. But after a thorough review of patristic expositions, he cautiously refused to admit that Paul's words negated original sin; he merely maintained that they were of no use to prove that doctrine to sceptics. As others had done before him, Fausto adopted Erasmus' reading, but was unreserved in his rejection of original sin.[74] He was even bolder in his treatment of Romans 6:6: 'We know that our old self was crucified with him so that the sinful body might be destroyed and we might no longer be enslaved to sin.' When Fausto examined this verse he noted the different translations of Beza and Erasmus. To define the condition of the neophite's sinful body, Beza used the verb 'to weaken (*enervare*),' Erasmus used 'destroy (*aboleri*).' 'Weakening' of the sinful body allows for the continued effect of original sin, and accordingly Beza referred the preceding 'Walking in the newness of life' to the future beyond earthly existence. Erasmus, by contrast, opened the way for Fausto's own interpretation. To Fausto the believer's death to sin and newness of life occur now and here, and afterwards the spiritually reborn will no longer be crushed by sin. Although not immune to sin, through the mercy of God they will easily be able to cope with the temptations.[75]

The examples discussed so far show, I think, that Fausto's judgment of Erasmus was favourable, though not uncritical. In fact, it could be remarkably balanced and fair, as when he called upon Erasmus to witness his assertion that in John 20:28 the disciple Thomas did quite properly call Christ – that is, the risen Christ, who ought to be worshipped – 'my God.' Erasmus, Fausto wrote:

> who in such matters is always most diligently informed and who in all passages where Christ appears to be called 'God' weighs and probes the words with care, with the result that the Trinitarians not unjustifiably suspected him of Arianism, while the Antitrinitarians counted him among those who somewhat cryptically (*subobscure*) were opposed to the Trinity; and yet he admitted candidly that in this verse Christ is openly called 'God,' although elsewhere he may say that there is reason to hesitate.[76]

Fausto again invoked Erasmus' example, quoting from the *Apologia adversus monachos hispanos*, in support of his assertion that one could reject the doctrine of the Trinity and still admit that the New Testament in a given context might refer to Christ as God.[77] Not often in Fausto's time was Erasmus read so perceptively.

Fausto and Erasmus were united in their sober search for the precise meaning of words and an exposition based on sound reasoning, but on occasion Erasmus displayed a sense of psychological complexity that was lost on Fausto. Such was the case when Fausto insisted that Paul, after his conversion had set him 'free from the law of sin and death,' could impossibly say of himself that sin deceived and killed him (Romans 7:11, 8:2) There had to be another person. Speaking in first person singular (Romans 7:7–25), Paul 'lends his person to those not yet reborn.' Erasmus, who knew the ambiguities of the human mind only too well, understood that it was of himself that Paul spoke so harshly.[78] Given the inspiration Fausto undoubtedly drew from Erasmus in a great many places, one should also be aware of some substantial differences in their common approach to exegesis that have been analysed by Juliusz Domański.[79] He noted that Fausto's exegesis was based on a principle Erasmus had found in Augustine: that the sense of confusing text passages should preferably be clarified by looking at other Bible texts that used the same words.[80] However, Erasmus made far less use of the *textus-ex-textu* method than did Fausto and, in fact, all Antitrinitarian writers, starting with Servetus. On the other hand, Erasmus usually turned to a succession of Christian fathers in order to demonstrate a variety of possible expositions. Fausto's purpose, by contrast, was not to offer the reader choices, but to establish the meaning of a text in no uncertain terms. On the whole he did not refer to patristic commentaries unless they lent support to his exposition.

Both had little taste for allegorization and philosophical speculation in the approach to the Gospel. Erasmus believed, however, that in reading the Old Testament an allegorical approach was indispensable. He was also open to its use in the New Testament, although with noticeable restraint and never at the risk of ignoring the literal sense. To 'play' with allegories was permissible for the sake of moral edification, but not in order to ascertain the truth of a doctrine.[81] This approach was bound to appeal to the Antitrinitarians since allegorization had been used liberally by Christian theologians of all ages in order to find scriptural proof for the dogma of the Trinity. The majority of Fausto's pickings from Erasmus concerned the precise meaning of a Greek word and were thus germane to a sober investigation of the literal sense, since that was most likely to satisfy his quest for rationality.[82] An example is his understanding of the entreaty for the daily bread in the Lord's Prayer (Matthew 6:11, Luke 11:3). While both had here an open mind about the options of literal and figurative interpretation, Erasmus thought primarily of spiritual sustenance, the 'heavenly bread,' whereas Fausto stressed the need to ask for actual food to support the body.[83] Colossians 2:20–3 deals with Mosaic regulations of daily conduct that Christ's disciples no longer ought to observe. While Erasmus and Fausto both found the passage obscure, Erasmus boldly concluded that the difficulty was that the Greek text did not express what Paul had meant, whereas Fausto clung to a literal interpretation at the price of a tortuous construction.[84] Fausto's unwillingness to depart from the letter of the text also shows when he compared Matthew's and Luke's versions of the Sermon on the Mount and after some hesitation concluded, in view of some differences in their rendering of the Beatitudes, that both could not be referring to the same sermon[85] – a thought that does not seem to have crossed Erasmus' mind.

Fausto's approach to the Sermon on the Mount shows how far he was from asking the questions that would begin to occupy Bible scholars in the seventeenth century – questions about the interdependence of New Testament writers, about the likelihood of a common source, in short, questions about the history of the canon. It deserves attention, however, that he had studied a section of Erasmus' writing that addressed the problem of divine accommodation, a problem we have touched upon before.[86] In his *Ratio* Erasmus examines at length the uses of language in scripture, most eminently Christ's similes and parables, as a model for the Christian preacher. Pious precepts would be communicated more effectively if the allegories used in either Testament were employed. Christ's *sermo propheticus* frequently challenged, indeed deceived, his disciples by hinting at truths that they would not understand until later.[87] The Jews fancied through many centuries the concept of a Messiah ruling as a powerful worldly king, until Christ's humble appearance showed how mistaken they were. In between the examples of the purblind apostles and Jews Erasmus fits, lightly, as if in passing:

> Thus the eternal Wisdom has – why, I don't know – chosen allusive imagery in order to both inculcate itself to the pious minds and deceive, so to speak, the profane.

It is this sentence that Fausto remembered and quoted in a different context and in slightly different form. A supporter had formulated a series of troublesome questions. Given the inspired character of scripture, how could the correct teachings (in the Socinian sense) disappear so completely after the time of the apostles? How was one to avoid the absurd conclusion that God wanted people to err and to perish? Fausto answered that any problems encountered in scripture did not stand in the way of its proclaiming, clearly and rationally, what was necessary to salvation. The only question in the end was obedience or disobedience towards God's mandates. He quoted the last verse of Hosea: 'The Lord's ways are straight and the righteous walk in them, while the sinners stumble.' This reminded him of

> a perfect statement by the great Erasmus of Rotterdam, when he talked of the figurative mode of expression in scripture: 'I don't know why the eternal Wisdom has chosen allusive imagery in order to both inculcate itself to the pious minds and deceive, so to speak, the profane.'[88]

Erasmus' attempt to clarify the specific purpose of a Bible author with regard to his audience meant a first step, albeit small, towards a critical comparison of the authors among themselves. Accommodation in the progress of *Heilsgeschichte* initiated the push towards a critical history of the Bible canon. But this was not the context in which Fausto read Erasmus' statement. To him it became a conclusive assertion of theodicy. Whereas Erasmus often suggested that readers could now find in the Gospel allegorical allusions to the Trinity and Christ's two natures, Fausto's chief example of veiled Gospel language is the promise of eternal life. Sincere believers can understand this and live so as to earn it; others cannot.[89]

FROM POLAND TO HOLLAND

From 1601 the centre of Socinian intellectual activity, including a school and a printing shop, was located at Raków, but as Polish Catholicism rebounded, Raków was doomed. In 1638 it was destroyed, and the leading minds of the movement began to move to the diaspora. Between 1658 and 1661 all Socinians were banned from the kingdom, unless they converted. At that time Amsterdam became prominent among the centres of Socinian emigration. The Socinians were never numerous in Holland, but thanks to their writings Socinianism came face to face with the new intellectual trends of the seventeenth century, and thanks to their publishing it came to be widely known and exhaustively refuted in Germany and England as well as the Netherlands. The beginning of the seventeenth century also marked a revival of interest in Erasmus' work, and, indeed, both trends shared major points of appeal. Both promoted the supremacy of morality in religion, the ascendancy of free will over predestination, the abolition of a physical hell, and the plea for religious toleration. Erasmus continued to be consulted by the leading Socinian authors of the two generations following Fausto Sozzini, although perhaps less frequently than Fausto himself had done. As time progressed, a good deal of Erasmus' findings had been taken up, appreciatively or critically, by more recent Bible scholars. Despite this, Benedykt Wiszowaty frequently referred to Erasmus in his notes to the final edition of the Raków Catechism,[90] thus in a way enshrining his importance for the Antitrinitarian movement. A glance at two lesser lights that were, however, characteristic representatives of Socinianism in Holland may bring this chapter to its conclusion

Daniel Zwicker (1612–78)

Zwicker was the most prolific author among the Socinians hailing from Danzig (Gdańsk), but throughout his life he remained in the shadow of distinguished correligionists. In Danzig he was outshone by his own mentor, the cosmopolitan Martin Ruar, a former head of the Raków school and a correspondent of Grotius and Mersenne. Later, as an exile, he was eclipsed by such lights of the Polish emigration as Samuel Przipkowski and Jonasz Szlichtyng. Zwicker was bent on arguing and, in doing so, used the traditional devices of scholastic logic. As a physician, he had received a scientific training, but in Danzig and to a lesser degree in Königsberg (Kaliningrad), where he had studied, all education was imbued with the culture of German humanism, in which Erasmus continued to be conspicuous.[91] Ruar, in particular, was quick to consult his New Testament and to advise inquirers to read his works.[92] Erasmus is featured in Zwicker's first book-size avowal of Socinianism, written in German and published before he was expelled from Danzig and moved to Amsterdam. In this work, with the Latin title *Revelatio Catholicismi veri*, Zwicker criticizes a statement of the Jesuit Denis Petau (Petavius) by comparing it to a sentence of Erasmus that he calls a

Köhler-rede ('bit of bunk').[93] In his long note on Romans 9:5 Erasmus probed whether Paul here calls Jesus Christ 'God' or even refers to the whole Trinity, or whether he ends his argument with a doxology referring alone to the Father. Erasmus decided that the Greek text did not permit the problem to be solved, though his comparisons with other texts – he probably meant such as 2 Corinthians 1:3 – showed him inclining towards that last option. But amid many demonstrations of his own Trinitarian orthodoxy he also said that if the church should teach that Christ was called 'God' here, one ought to defer to the church. That was what Zwicker branded as a *Köhler-rede*, but then he also quoted Erasmus' following statement that since Paul's words were ambiguous, they were no help in proving the Arians wrong.

In its noticeable ambivalence this early passage is, I think, symptomatic of a stance towards Erasmus that resembled that of Zwicker's Socinian mentors and would continue to find expression in Zwicker's own writings. He was of course aware that he had an affinity with Erasmus in such major topics as the quest for religious toleration and an end to warfare.[94] He also resembled Erasmus in that he found great value in the witness of the Christian fathers, at least the ante-Nicene ones, whom he studied intensely and with endurance. Following the trend we had witnessed in Transylvania, he turned to the early history of the Christian church to find evidence for both the correctness of the Unitarian position and the tragic slide into the Trinitarian abyss.[95] Here he distanced himself from Rakovian Socinianism, which had usually looked to scriptural exegesis alone for proof of the truth of its doctrine. As a result, Zwicker had to ward off suspicions that his reliance on tradition smacked of Catholicism.

His principal debt to Erasmus lay undoubtedly in the field of New Testament exegesis. At the time of his death he owned a number of books by Erasmus, including the New Testament Annotations and Paraphrases and at least one copy of Erasmus' New Testament translation.[96] There were also Greek and Latin Bibles by Arias Montanus, Beza, Curcellaeus, Osiander, and Tremellius-Du Jon.[97] One of Zwicker's pamphlets offers a precious glance at the regular gatherings of a small study group in his own house. We can take it for granted that Erasmus had his place among the variety of Bibles that were placed on the table.[98] Zwicker's *Irenicum Irenicorum* (1658) includes a fourteen-page long index of scripture references, appropriately entitled *Parva*

Biblia. Here, he says, he has chosen Tremellius for the Old Testament and Beza for the New, although he never seems to follow any translation slavishly.[99] As always, editions and commentaries that had become available after Erasmus' death might carry forward points Erasmus had made. When Zwicker turns to Erasmus himself, phrases like *Jam Erasmus in suis Annotationibus ... monstravit*, flow readily from his pen.[100] Erasmus is seen as the initiator of a new exegetical tradition that all along its progress remains heavily indebted to him. When Zwicker refers explicitly to him it is, predictably, most often to enlist him for the unremitting war against the Trinity. In the *Novi Foederis Josias* (1670), Zwicker gives the following list of Bible verses whose Trinitarian exposition 'already Erasmus had shown to be lame and unsound,' namely Isaiah 7:14, John 10:30, Acts 20:28, Romans 9:5, Philippians 2:5–6, Colossians 2:9, Titus 2:11–13, Hebrews 1:7–9, and 1 John 5:7, 20.[101] Many of these had already been berated by Erasmus' early Catholic critics and all had then been picked up by Zwicker's Antitrinitarian predecessors. Perhaps more revealing yet of Erasmus' continued voice among the seventeenth-century Dutch radicals is Zwicker's next reference, which directs the reader to Sebastian Franck's *Chronica,* specifically to the section on Erasmus in the *Chronicle of the Heretics*.[102] In some intriguing arguments against the Trinity Zwicker shows himself indebted to Erasmus' annotations without actually saying so. Erasmus' comments on Romans 1:3–4 had earlier aroused the suspicion of Edward Lee and the interest of some Antitrinitarian authors, including Servetus and Fausto Sozzini. When discussing this text in his *Novi Foederis Josias,* Zwicker insists that Jesus' 'coming into existence from the seed of David' ought to be understood in the light of Galatians 4:4, 'issued from Mary' (*factus ex semine David – factus ex muliere*), whereas the following verse, 'designated the Son of God in power according to the Spirit of holiness by his resurrection,' meant 'not until his resurrection.'[103] Zwicker refers to 'Beza, Grotius and other experts of the Greek language.' Beza actually acknowledges Erasmus and follows his translation in the critical points, but both insist that Paul had meant to express that the Son's divine nature was timeless and here conjoint with the human one.[104] Zwicker uses their corrections of the Vulgate text and ignores their conclusion.

In the same book Zwicker examines at some length 1 John 5:20 and, predictably, argues that the concluding *verus Deus* refers to the Father rather than the Son. He repeats Erasmus' point of grammar in support of this interpretation, but mentions him only when adducing the analogy with Romans 9:5, a verse that has been mentioned above. Erasmus had often had to defend his repeated claims that it was untypical for Christ to be named God in the New Testament but, unlike Zwicker, he never denied that there were exceptions,[105] and here left open whether this might be one. Unlike the authors of *De falsa*, Zwicker chooses to ignore his expression of doubt.[106]

Zwicker vigorously advocates the rejection of original sin. Like Fausto Sozzini,[107] he must have read Erasmus' very long note on Romans 5:12 with special attention and a will to radicalize its tenor. Erasmus had shown that Augustine, among others, had read and interpreted the text incorrectly. It did not say that Adam's sin was passed on to all humankind. Ignoring Augustine was no crime, as Erasmus showed with the example of a tenet that Augustine had believed to be necessary for salvation, whereas the church now deemed it heretical. Zwicker quoted this argument in a polemical exchange with an Antwerp Jesuit.[108]

To conclude, reading Zwicker is rarely a pleasure. He is harsh and quarrelsome, and his writing lacks lucidity. His references to Erasmus are not enthusiastic; no doubt he was annoyed by Erasmus' countless assurances of orthodoxy. In short, one might hesitate to call him an 'Erasmian.' Posterity has remembered him primarily for a single page of his *Irenicum Irenicorum*. There he asserts that he is not a member of any church, but is indebted to all of them for some precious insight. The Bohemian Brethren and the Lutherans taught him, he says, the need for reform, the Calvinists rational exegesis, the Remonstrants freedom of conscience, the Greeks esteem for their church fathers, the Roman Catholics the indispensability of good works, the Socinians critical thinking in general, and the Mennonites Christian morality. Church reform, freedom of conscience, reason, esteem for the patristic tradition, a faith that shows in daily conduct and works of charity: one can argue that these together sum up the religion of Erasmus and that, in this sense, Zwicker was indeed an Erasmian.

Daniel De Breen (1594–1664)

There is so far no evidence of direct contacts between Zwicker and Daniel De Breen (Brenius), although during the seven years

(1657–64) both lived in Amsterdam they may well have met at gatherings of the Collegiants, to whom both had strong ties. The Collegiants were a radical religious group with Remonstrant (Arminian) and Mennonite roots, dedicated to tolerance and spiritual and intellectual freedom.[109] In the wake of his contacts with Martin Ruar, who was later to become Zwicker's mentor, De Breen developed a strong sympathy with Unitarian theology, although unlike Zwicker he was never a professed Antitrinitarian. The defining aspect of his religion was the chiliastic expectation of a millennial reign of righteousness, in which Christ will govern souls from on high rather than being physically present on earth. This millennium would be ushered in by the conversion of all Jews.[110] Turning to De Breen's debt to Erasmus, it must be stated right away that his chiliasm owed little to the sage of Rotterdam. De Breen's end-of-the-world expectations were utterly un-Erasmian, even though he must have looked favourably to Erasmus' Pelagian tendencies and his faith in a liberal access to salvation. Also De Breen would find little support in Erasmus' writings for his conviction that the holding of a public office was contrary to the spirit of Christ. On this issue too Zwicker took an analogous, but more radical, position. Whereas he held that Christianity and magistrature were totally incompatible, De Breen was content to assert that a Christian magistrate was as a Christian lacking in faith.

In two other regards, however, Erasmus' influence on De Breen was considerable. One was Christian ethics, the pious conduct of daily affairs, governed by an accurate understanding of virtue and vice. Here Erasmus was readily acknowledged by De Breen; not so, however, in the other issue, which was his aversion to the doctrine of the Trinity. Although one can assume that De Breen was well acquainted with standard Socinian literature, he argued his rejection of the Trinity cautiously and with a wise regard for evidence pointing in an opposite direction. Exactly in this respect Erasmus was apt to become his guide and mentor. De Breen's familiarity with Erasmus' work is evidenced in his *Compendium theologiae Erasmicae*, a work of his youth that seemed lost for a while and was eventually published thirteen years after his death.[111] The *Compendium* is an intriguing blend: some texts are copied from Erasmus' writings, some are De Breen's summaries of texts by Erasmus, while others are visibly inspired by him but offer De Breen's own words and frequently his own extensions, modifications, and perhaps distortions of Erasmus' thoughts. All of this is fused together without markings.¹¹² De Breen has a remarkable command of a number of Erasmus' writings. He runs through them forwards and backwards, sometimes adopting just a few words. There is no theology to speak of in De Breen's *Compendium*; it is a treatise on Christian ethics. Taking his clues from Erasmus' *Enchiridion*, he monitors the growth and gradual perfection of piety. Among the virtues that a Christian must aim for, a peaceable disposition is important, and so in particular is prudence. Guided by prudence, a Christian will progress on the path to spiritual freedom and tolerance. In remarkable fashion De Breen emphasizes an important strand of Erasmus' thought that we shall find otherwise more typically taken up in Italy and France. Prudence entails caution in the use of truth. 'We need a sort of holy cunning; we must be time-servers,' De Breen repeats after Erasmus.¹¹³ Paul used dissimulation; Christ remained silent.

> If the personified Truth ordered that truth to remain untold for a while, on whose knowledge and profession a person's salvation depends, what then would be new about me saying that the truth in some place ought to be suppressed?¹¹⁴

Later De Breen quotes a passage from the dedicatory preface to Erasmus' paraphrase to Corinthians:

> This Paul of ours is always skillful and slippery, but in these two Epistles he is such a squid, such a chameleon – he plays the parts of Proteus and Vertumnus ... Always Christ's business is his main concern; always he thinks of the well-being of his flock, like the true physician leaving no remedy untried which may restore his patients to perfect health.¹¹⁵

Already in the *Compendium theologiae Erasmicae* De Breen had made much use of Erasmus' New Testament Annotations and Paraphrases. The place where he takes stock of Erasmus' theology, however, is his *Breves in Vetus et Novum Testamentum annotationes*.¹¹⁶ What is relevant here is the part of the New Testament, a selection of short scripture texts that De Breen gives in Greek and comments on in Latin. Most of his notes are explanatory paraphrases, edifying rather than text-critical. Usually he offers just his own interpretation and, unlike Erasmus, does not discuss divergent opinions. He shows no taste for controversy. Citing the

Christian fathers, which with Erasmus was the rule, is with De Breen the exception. Explicit references to modern exegetes are also rare, but Beza, Pistorius and, especially, Grotius are named more often than Erasmus. The familiarity he had gained in the course of compendiarizing Erasmus shows, however, in the casual way in which he used Erasmus' paraphrase of 2 Timothy 3:15–16, partly quoting, partly rephrasing. All of scripture, says Paul, is inspired. Erasmus pointedly remarked that this included the Old Testament as prophetic overture to the message of the New. Erasmus' emphasis on the Old Testament in the eschatological context of Paul's chapter clearly appealed to De Breen's chiliastic approach.[117] Writing, as he did, a continuous commentary of the Old and New Testaments together is unusual among authors inclined to Socinianism.

On the other hand, De Breen resembles the major Socinian authors in his constant efforts to clarify the meaning of one verse through comparison with others. A substantial number of De Breen's New Testament annotations prove right J Trapman, who had pointed out that De Breen adopted essentials aspects of Socinian theology, especially with regard to the person and divinity of Christ.[118] De Breen's comments on the beginning of the Gospel of John are clearly influenced by the Socinians. When John (1:1) says that the Word was 'in the beginning,' he does not refer to the creation of the universe, as in Genesis, but to the 'new creation' preached by the man Jesus and his harbinger, John the Baptist: 'the new creation and restoration of all, to be accomplished by Christ in the final age.'[119] In remanding the 'new creation,' to the Millennium, De Breen set himself apart from Lelio and Fausto Sozzini. Like other Socinians, however, he exploited Erasmus' point about the absence of the definite article before 'God' in 'the Word was God.' De Breen adopted the usual Unitarian argument that the verse confirmed the uniqueness of the Father. Likewise, commenting on John 1:14: 'the Word became flesh,' De Breen gladly followed Erasmus (and Beza) who had stated that 'flesh' simply referred to Christ's humanity and not to any divine nature incarnated in the human body. Turning to Paul's elusive words in Philippians 2:6, we have seen earlier how Servetus and other Antitrinitarians used Erasmus' annotation. To quote Erasmus: 'the whole verse, it seems to me, gets brutally distorted when related to Christ's nature.' That Christ was said to be *in forma Dei* and *aequalis Deo* did not refer to his divine nature, which he still concealed at that time, but to his conduct. He was setting an example. 'He was God and he was man. The God he concealed, the man he demonstrated until his entombment.' De Breen echoed Erasmus' subtle distinction, without Erasmus' nod to orthodoxy. Μορφή, the Greek for *forma*, said De Breen, refers not to 'substance' but to 'status' and 'condition,' to the 'image of divinity' exhibited by Christ. His remarks are sober and brief, if compared to the elaborations of other Antitrinitarians who had followed Erasmus' lead.[120]

Romans 5:12 was used, as we have seen, by other Antitrinitarians to question the doctrine of original sin. In commenting on Romans 5:12–19, De Breen is close to Erasmus' paraphrase. Both saw Adam as the type of the Christ to come – Adam, the founder of a generation mired in sin, and Christ, the founder of a new generation that had the potential to overcome sin, both setting an example that humanity was free to follow, Adam the example of disobedience and Christ of obedience.[121]

To fully appreciate the quality of De Breen's Socinian exegesis, one must be aware of the restraint that he imposed upon his penchant. Here he appears as a true disciple of Erasmus, while the contrast to the unrelentingly doctrinaire Zwicker could hardly be greater. Rather than twisting words, De Breen will freely admit the existence of Christ as a divine concept, everlasting as the omniscient Father himself, but not as a divine person waiting to be incarnated.[122] Erasmus had stated that the disciple Thomas, finally convinced of Christ's resurrection, had called him 'my God' (John 20:28), 'the only place in which the Evangelist attributes to Christ the term "God."' De Breen agrees, but with a Socinian twist. Thomas, he says, recognized Jesus as his God, namely 'the Messiah promised to the Jews.' And in order to distance himself from any Antitrinitarian dimwit, he adds: 'in these words there is no invocation of the Father, as some want to believe,' echoing thus Fausto Sozzini, who had been outraged about the clumsy argument of a fellow Socininan, who in fact wanted to believe that.[123]

De Breen's *Annotationes* offer one more, and truly exceptional, testimony to what he clearly believed was the essence of Erasmus' legacy, namely his prudence as opposed to any unilateralism, a sense of tolerance derived from his ability to approach issues from different perspectives. We have already mentioned De Breen's radical conviction that tenure of a magistrate's office was irreconcilable with the true following of Christ. In the *Annotationes* this conviction finds expression when he reaches Acts 17:34. The verse reports how Paul's speech brings about the conversion of Dionysius, a member of the Areopagus court. De Breen points out that nothing is said about Dionysius laying down his office. Thus the question whether a Christian may hold an office, especially in a heathen state, is not addressed.[124] 'Anyhow,' continues De Breen, 'that question must not be decided in the light of a single incident. Rather the complete teachings of the gospels must be considered.' At this point De Breen drops his argument and on impulse – *non pigebit his adscribere*, he says – starts quoting a text by Erasmus that is nearly a folio page long, by far the longest quotation anywhere in De Breen's book. The text that so impressed him (and had already been quoted in his *Compendium* at similar length) is taken from Erasmus' *Ecclesiastes*.[125] It offers a detailed and careful analysis of Paul's speech on the Areopagus. Prudence is the guiding theme as Erasmus reflects on Paul's ingenious massaging of the facts that always stays this side of actual lying. Paul's motive is not fear of persecution, but his desire to reap a profit for Christ. He does not upbraid his audience for their idolatry; he politely calls their idols 'σεβάσματα, objects of veneration.' He refers to their altar dedicated 'to the unknown God,' to imply that they already worship the god he is going to announce, his God, the creator of the universe, whom he describes by quoting their own poet Aratus. Most important, he does not confuse the Athenians by talking about Christ, his divine nature or his cross. 'He only calls him "a man," whom God has brought forth in order that through him the truth will be made plain and the contrite will find grace and forgiveness for all crimes.' It is true that with this part of his long quotation De Breen also adds a new provision to the storehouse of Antitrinitarian argumentation. What really matters, however, is his refreshing move beyond an Erasmus used and abused exclusively for sectarian purposes.

By now we can see, I hope, what Erasmus meant to De Breen, what De Breen did to Erasmus, and what that did to De Breen's contemporaries. De Breen belongs in this chapter because he accepted Erasmus' guidance, offered intentionally or not, as the case may be, towards Antitrinitarian positions, but in his reading of Erasmus, theology commanded far less attention than spirituality and Christian ethics – an order of priorities that Erasmus himself could not have failed to approve. And then there is that extraordinary prominence given to Erasmus' calls for prudence. What is so remarkable about that emphasis on prudence and restraint is that De Breen himself knew how to blend it with bold forays to radical positions: his millenarianism, his radical pacifism and exclusion of office-holding, his Socinianism – positions towards which, millenarianism apart, Erasmus had offered some encouragement. In short, De Breen showed unusual empathy with the core of Erasmus' convictions – a degree of empathy, in fact, that his Dutch contemporaries might have found matched only in Hugo Grotius and the various editions of Sebastian Franck's books.

The purpose of this chapter was to show how some representative figures of early modern Antitrinitarianism sought and found support for their beliefs in turning to Erasmus' New Testament. It is reasonable to assume that others of a like mind did so too. In fact, two more important cases will be discussed in chapter 8. It is worth stating again that Erasmus himself was not an Antitrinitarian. In an age, however, when the Protestant world, at least, would cling to the scriptural foundation of its religion, Erasmus' well-documented claim that the concept of the Trinity could not be grounded on the New Testament was truly consequential. No other insight his exegesis had yielded had such lasting importance.

THREE

Peace and War According to Erasmus and Sebastian Franck

FRANCK'S APPROACH AND HIS SOURCES

In chapter 1 we have seen how Franck developed and publicized some radical views deduced from Erasmus' scrutiny of the Gospel, and here we shall turn again to Franck for guidance. The search for peace and opposition to war was to him, as it was to Erasmus, the most vibrant concern in the field of political governance – so important indeed that both, in tune with their priorities, came to evaluate the political problem in religious terms. For the short period of their direct contacts, however, politics was the dominant factor.

As mentioned earlier, Erasmus' ire about Franck's *Chronica* or *Geschichtbibel* was primarily directed at the introduction to the *Chronicle of the Emperors*. To be associated with heterodoxy, as he was in the *Chronicle of the Heretics*, was bad enough, though hardly new to Erasmus, but to become suspect of insolence towards the imperial house of Habsburg was calamitous. Yet this, Erasmus feared, would be the impression created by Franck's introduction to the *Chronicle of the Emperors,* and that at a time when Erasmus was King Ferdinand's guest in Freiburg. Franck's introduction draws inspiration from judiciously selected texts by Erasmus, above all from the adage *Scarabaeus aquilam quaerit* (The dung-beetle hunting the eagle).[1] This adage presents Aesop's fable amid a selection of curious animal lore, derived from Pliny's *Naturalis historia* and other ancient sources, but the whole is permeated with pungent criticism of brutal autocrats and their insatiable thirst for power. A number of such passages are translated or paraphrased in Franck's preface and attributed to Erasmus by name. The eagle, rapacious, bloodthirsty, murderous to its own kin, hated and feared by other animals, is Erasmus' symbol for the monarchs of the world, both ancient and contemporary, though none of the latter is named. Franck not only resumes Erasmus' biting satire, but he also ties it more closely to the imperial office both by positioning it at the head of a chronicle about the emperors from Christ's birth to Charles V, and by adding a demeaning reference to Charles' ancestor, the Habsburg emperor Frederick III.[2] As mentioned earlier, Erasmus' harsh reaction landed Franck in jail. Moreover, in a revised edition of the *Adagia*, two years after the appearance of Franck's *Chronica*, Erasmus reworded some passages so that they no longer referred specifically to contemporary monarchs.[3]

Although Franck is at pains to distance himself from any thought of insurrection or revolution (especially in his revised preface for the second edition of the *Chronica*), he yet paraphrases a push in support of democracy which is representative of the core of Erasmus' political creed. In Franck's words, the eagle 'is also in conflict with the cranes, perhaps because they like democracy, that is the rule of many in a state, which the princes abhor.'[4] The eagle-princes succumb to an indomitable desire for expansion of their power, and a prominent means to achieve this is war.

In the *Chronica* Franck's enthusiasm for Erasmus found its most pregnant and, given the number of reprints, most effective expression. It is surely proof of an admirable generosity that Erasmus' bitter and mean reaction failed to dampen that enthusiasm. Not only did Franck later translate the *Moria* into German,[5] towards the end of his life he enlisted Erasmus once again in pursuit of a radical cause – in Franck's discourse more radical yet than in that of Erasmus. The issue, a specific and enduring concern of both Erasmus and Franck, was the denunciation of war. In 1539 Franck published his *Krieg Büchlin des Friedes* (Peace's War Manual – a title obviously inspired by another 'manual,' Erasmus' *Enchiridion militis christiani*).[6] The *Krieg Büchlin* is a late work, and in the years preceding its publication Franck had experienced much hardship and harassment. Having been expelled from Strasbourg, he had gone to Ulm, but after two distressing trials was again sent packing. In the summer of 1539 he moved to Basel, but since he was not made a citizen until two years later, he could hardly feel secure there. By the end of 1539 the death of his loyal wife would leave him a widower in charge of five children. In the light of these harrowing experiences we must be prepared to find that the *Krieg Büchlin* is written in a more sombre mood than the *Chronica*. In fact, one notes throughout the work that the eschatological portions of the Old and New Testaments are never far from the author's mind. The last chapter is imbued with the Apocalypse, and here this is no longer the traditional closure of an account of all human history from beginning to end, as it was in the *Chronica*. In the *Krieg Büchlin* the title of that last chapter announces doomsday, Christ's second coming, and his judgment for the 'not distant' future,[7] but compared with the shrillness of many preceding sections, its language is rather measured, nor is it really a doomsday scenario. What Franck appears to preach is not that the apocalypse is traumatically imminent, but rather that it is at all times immanent in the human existence. There is still time for Christians to see the light, and Franck, as always, is engaged in helping them to do so.

Franck's discourse in the *Krieg Büchlin* is, as usual, saturated with a multitude of biblical reminiscences and guided by the work of the authors that he quotes and paraphrases. For this war on war, so he says in the preface, he has armed himself, as with shield and armour, with the testimony of scripture, of course, and ancient and recent teachers, of whom he lists the principal ones: Augustine, Ambrose, Jerome, Cyprian, Bernard of Clairvaux, Tertullian, Origen, Gregory I, Gratian, Denis the Carthusian, Wessel Gansfort, Erasmus, Luther, Henricus Cornelius Agrippa, and Oecolampadius.[8] 'These I shall let do the fighting; I will stay behind them and watch.' The readers must decide whether or not 'warriors can be Christians,' for Franck says he won't. He starts out by assuring them that of the entire book 'only two or three little leaves' are his own work. While this is an obvious exaggeration, it does state his intent. It would, however, be equally true to say that every word in the book is his own, for what he translates, paraphrases, and summarizes is always his peculiar understanding of the texts he presents. Whether it is also the author's opinion remains to be seen; Franck seldom encourages such a distinction. Although he usually names his sources, he rarely bothers to mark where the paraphrase stops and his own discourse resumes.

Franck's procedure calls for some comments. He yields liberally to his penchant for amplifying the texts he reproduces. On the other hand, when it suits him he may also contract them. Both techniques, amplification and contraction, can serve to clarify an author's statement and to reinforce his point; or they can modify the text in ways that range from subtle to drastic. Bruno Quast collated the original texts by Agrippa with Franck's paraphrases and found that at first Franck rearranges, freely but fairly, some passages picked from chapters 79 and 80 of Agrippa's *De incertudine et vanitate scientiarum* (1530). This book caused trouble, and Agrippa had to defend himself with an *Apologia* (1533) in answer to the attacks of the Louvain theologians. Franck also offers a close paraphrase of some sections of the *Apologia*, but he regularly omits the modifying asides with which Agrippa had laced his text. While Agrippa attempted to strike a balance between condemnation and justification of war, Franck's mission is to defend Agrippa against his own second thoughts.[9] This is the technique we have frequently found when discussing the presentation of Erasmus' 'heresies' in the *Chronica*. There Franck made Erasmus speak more boldly and radically than he himself had cared to do; in the *Krieg Büchlin* Franck does the same service, if such it is, to Agrippa.

Franck uses yet another device to manipulate the witness of the champions he has engaged to fight for him his war for peace. Following a precedent set already in the *Chronica*, he cites Luther, quoting passages (*haec ille ad verbum*) that brand the bestiality of mercenary warriors and condemn Mosaic reliance on the sword and the war against the Turks. But on other pages, even in close proximity, Franck attacks some unnamed theologians who spur the princes to attack heretics and infidels and rate warfare to be an honest craft. According to these theologians, orders must be obeyed as long as there is no flagrant proof that the cause is unjust, and, anyhow, a loyal soldier must always assume that he is fighting for a just cause. Indeed, it can be sinful not to go to war. Franck's formulations are sufficiently close to some passages in well-known works by Luther to reveal to contemporary readers the identity of at least one of the unnamed theologians.[10] Thus Luther, using his name, is pressed into service to attack, anonymously, his own considered and generally known position. The technique that Franck here pioneered would be used many times in the ensuing debates of the Reformation age, for instance by Sebastian Castellio and Mino Celsi.[11]

Erasmus, of course, was no stranger to ambiguity, and his statements on war and peace are no exception. Franck, however, cared too much for Erasmus to have exploited his ambiguities the way he was doing with Luther. Take, for example, Erasmus' preface to the 1518 edition of the *Enchiridion*, often known as the 'letter to Volz.' Erasmus here combines a pious wish to see the war against the Turks conducted with spiritual weapons only with an acceptance of the concept of just wars and the mandate of secular princes to conduct them.[12]

Although Franck certainly knew this text, he does not mention it. His many Erasmian quotations and paraphrases in the *Krieg Büchlin* are accurate, but sensibly selected to enhance his own radical conclusions. Erasmus is easily the most important among the sources of the *Krieg Büchlin*. While Franck was familiar with a variety of his statements on peace and war,[13] he concentrates his attention on the two of Erasmus' pacifist writings that one would rate the most important. We must look at these before we can analyse the use Franck made of them.

ERASMUS' ADAGE *DULCE BELLUM INEXPERTIS*

Dulce bellum inexpertis (From the sidelines war seems pleasant) belongs to a small number of adages that Erasmus developed into proper essays and assigned a key function when he revised his *Adagia* for the all-important edition of 1515.[14] It has the form of a treatise, is comprehensive, well constructed, and – by Erasmus' standards – systematic. And – again by Erasmus' standards – it is uncompromising, perhaps the most uncompromising of his many denunciations of warfare. A sentence right at the beginning shows just how far he was prepared to go: 'If there is any human activity that should be approached with caution [– setting a bottom line and then raising the stakes –] or rather that should be avoided by all possible means, resisted [or 'cursed,' *deprecari*] and shunned, that activity is war.'[15]

In a first section Erasmus discusses the nature of humankind in relation to war. Erasmus' argument, stripped of his edifying eloquence, runs like this. All other animals have been equipped by nature so as to assure their survival; only humanity in its natural state is bare, unarmed, and made for laughter and tears, for love and friendship, as befits humans, being in some ways the image of God. How then could the spectre of war take hold of humankind? Erasmus traces a sinister progression from killing wild animals in self-defence to hunting and raising domestic animals for slaughter to finally turning on fellow humans – in sad contrast, he claims, to all other animals that would never harm their own kind. At first the need to eliminate violent individuals provided some legitimation, but when armed struggles between whole tribes developed, war had arrived. Even war was at first controlled by rules and conventions, but under the impact of hysterical propaganda it degenerated into indiscriminate slaughter. There is indeed a red thread running through Erasmus' account of the genesis of war: it is the brutalizing effect of shedding blood. Humanity's divine spark is threatened with extinction: *ubi nam Diaboli regnum est si in bello non est?*[16]

In the following section[17] Erasmus offers an eloquent juxtaposition of the horrors of war and the blessings of peace, but it is the third section, on the impact of war on the church and Christian society, that calls for a closer look. Having earlier traced the genesis of war in human society, as it were, anthropologically and with no regard for the biblical Genesis, Erasmus now looks to history for an explanation as to how war infiltrated Christianity, which had been founded on the principle of complete unity under its head, the prince of peace. When the ancient heresies began to sponsor pagan philosophy and rhetoric, the early church, in defence, had to do likewise, and a taste for disputation (*ambitiosa rixandi libido*) developed. 'Finally things went so far that the whole of Aristotle was accepted into the heart of theology, and accepted to the extent that his authority was almost more sacred than that of Christ.'[18] Gospel teachings were twisted so as to conform to Roman law. With that came titles and honours, first freely conferred, then claimed as a prerogative. The pursuit of wealth came next, first sought as a means for dispensing charity, then craved for personal use. Honours and riches combined led to a quest for power. Bishops usurped secular rule; abbots lorded it over their subjects. Christian princes fell below the standards of their pagan predecessors who had followed strict rules of combat and combined conquest with a civilizing mission.[19]

The next section[20] discusses a number of arguments that were usually presented in attempts to justify war. A refutation is added unless the fallacy is deemed to be self-evident. The Israelites, says Erasmus, had fought by divine appointment and hardly ever among themselves. For Christians the precedent of Old Testament warfare has little validity, as is shown by comparison with circumcision and other Mosaic practices that have been abandoned. Christians should understand Old Testament warfare allegorically as an admonition to do battle with vice. Likewise in the New Testament Peter offers no valid precedent for his successors in Rome to claim 'the two swords.' When Christ ordered Peter to sheathe his sword, he forbade all warfare and – the reader will infer, though Erasmus does not say it here – he also disowned the popes' secular authority. Erasmus then tackles what he calls 'rabbinical' arguments, such as the claim that a soldier merely exercises an honest craft like a butcher – one slaughters animals, the other men; what is the difference? – or that clerics can participate in wars and issue orders as long as they do not touch arms. Claiming to fight a 'just' war was meaningless, for 'who does not think that his own cause is just?' Erasmus admits that self-defence is permitted under natural law as well as common law, but against that he holds the higher authority of the Gospel that commands us to requite evil deeds and words with good ones.[21] He may well be speaking for himself when he concludes: 'A doctor who is truly Christian never approves of war; perhaps he admits it is permissible sometimes, but with reluctance and sorrow.'[22] It is true that some popes and some Christian fathers attempted to legitimize warfare, but they belonged to a more recent time when Christ's own vigour had begun to be abandoned.[23] There is no valid comparison between the criminal law punishing individual perpetrators and collective warfare where, again, both parties will claim to have the right on their side. Erasmus is at his boldest and best when he argues that proprietary rights of princes are not above questioning, for instance, on historical grounds.

> What nation has not at some time both been driven out of its homeland and driven others out? ... The Paduans should try to recover the site of Troy because [their mythical city founder] Antenor once was a Trojan ... In addition, what we call 'rule' (*dominium*) is administration. Rights over men, free by nature, are not the same as rights over cattle. This same 'right' (*ius*) that you have was given by the consent of the people, and the people who gave it, if I am not mistaken, have the power to take it away.[24]

Even assuming that a city could be owned like a field or herd of cattle, is defending it worth the cost? If a prince cannot muster magnanimity, he might at least follow the example of the shopkeeper who knows when to cut his losses. One excuse for war that may sound rather well is that one is coming to the rescue of the church. But again this assumes that what needs to be defended is the wealth of the clergy, as if that were the church and not rather the people (*quasi vero populus not sit ecclesia*).[25] The final resort should be to negotiated settlements that could be parleyed by responsible prelates, nobles, and councillors.

There follows a section[26] that radically questions the justification of a crusade against the Turks. The ultimate goal must be gaining souls for Christ, and warring, even if victorious, does not make converts. It is not from any moral high ground that we attack the Turks. Take the ensign of the cross away, and you have Turks fighting Turks. Better to fight with spiritual weapons, and for this purpose send in the armies of the beggar monks – if only they were still willing to go. Erasmus' conclusion is ambiguous only in that he limits his protest to denouncing offensive war.

> I say these things not because I would entirely condemn an expedition against the Turks if they attack us on their own accord, but in order to ensure that we prosecute the war, which we claim to wage in the name of Christ, in a Christian spirit and with Christ's own protection (*praesidiis*). Let them feel that they are being invited to be saved, not attacked for booty.

The *praesidia* of Christ are a moral conduct worthy of the Gospel and preaching our faith with apostolic simplicity.

In his final section[27] Erasmus again turns to the princes, often addressing his stern rhetoric directly to them. Nearly all their warring is either dumb or vicious. Often it is undertaken on the bad advice of lawyers, theologians, and bishops. Whatever the pretences, the true motives are thirst for glory, lust for gain and, on the home front, an excuse for replacing democratic institutions with tyranny. If the army is victorious, glory will be reaped by the general, often a *condottiere*, rather than the prince, and the ruinous cost of war will be born by the people. Next comes a last admission that war is sometimes inescapable 'because of general perversity.' When you, the rulers have 'left no stone unturned in your search for peace, then the best expedient will be to ensure that, [war] being an evil thing, it is the exclusive responsibility of evil people, and settled with a minimum of bloodshed[28] – advice taken to heart, it seems, by Thomas More's Utopians, who prefer the assassination of an enemy leader to general warfare and, if unavoidable, have the latter conducted by mercenaries. That somewhat problematic advice is followed, however, by an eloquent appeal to the Christian conscience. If we succeed in being innocent, charitable, and patient, then, looking down from this moral high ground, every reason for going to war must inevitably look petty. With that Erasmus trains his focus again on the current events of 1515 and ends with extravagant praise for Pope Leo X and his diplomatic efforts to secure a lasting peace among all Christian rulers. There was an irony, however, that was hardly lost on Erasmus, although he kept silent about it. One goal of Leo's peace among the Christian princes was that it would free them for a collective crusade against the Turks.

ERASMUS' *QUERELA PACIS*

The *Querela pacis*, unlike *Dulce bellum inexpertis*, was written in response to a specific request. Erasmus responded to an appeal by Jean Le Sauvage, chancellor to Duke Charles of Burgundy, the later Emperor Charles V, who was also Erasmus' sovereign. At the Burgundian court Le Sauvage was a leading proponent of a policy of appeasement with France; his request for a rhetorical tribute to peace was politically motivated, and to a modest degree Erasmus was prepared to play Le Sauvage's game.[29] In recent years he had repeatedly broached the topic of war and peace, especially with the *Dulce bellum inexpertis*. He had carefully collected relevant material and now could set to work expeditiously, completing the *Querela* probably at some point between the Peace of Cambrai, March 1517, and the court's departure for Spain in September. He employed again the brilliant literary device he had recently used in his *Moria encomium*.[30] Like Mistress Folly, Mistress Pax speaks to an audience, but unlike Folly she never really comes to life as a person and her audience too remains shadowy. Letting her eloquence flow freely, she is not afraid of occasional repetitions or contradictions and in general takes little care to arrange her arguments in an orderly fashion.[31] Primarily she wants to arouse emotions, to speak to the heart, and the success of the work, which went through many editions and translations, shows that she has been at least heard, if not heeded. In what follows here we shall do her some injustice as, with Franck's reaction in mind, we attempt to correlate some of her discrete remarks on important issues.

The guiding principles of the universe according to which nature has fashioned all beings are harmony and concord. The heavenly bodies, also all living creatures of the same species, indeed many of different species, and even the wicked demons respect and help each other. Humans, in particular, helpless at birth and ever dependent on some form of assistance from fellow humans, were so fashioned by nature that they would create the strongest bonds of mutual sympathy. Yet they developed an insatiable lust for fighting each other on every possible turf. Erasmus asks pointedly how this change came about, but that question, crucial though it may seem to us, to him is only rhetorical. He does not pause to answer it. Even the rudimentary answer given in *Dulce bellum inexpertis* is not taken up here; we are merely referred to the appearance of a Fury and the calamitous magic of Circe's wand that deprives men of their humanity.[32]

The Christian religion tries to restore the sense of concord that nature has infused in humans but humans themselves have suppressed. The example of Christ's life, from the song of the heavenly host at his birth to his words on the cross, teaches nothing but peace, love, and reconciliation. And here Erasmus makes an important distinction. What Christ teaches his followers is total concord modelled after the oneness of the Trinity. This is not to be confused with collaboration on a single issue, presumably dictated by self-interest. Christ 'said not that they should be of one mind but that they might be one, and not just in any way, but, as he said, we are one who are united in the most perfect and inexpressible way.'[33] Christ's church, from the time of his Ascension and Pentecost, took his teaching to heart and reflected it in her sacraments.[34] To little avail; Christian society is teeming with strife. Spouses, families, the inhabitants of the same city – all keep on quarrelling. Petty rivalries among the nations are deliberately kindled by powerful agitators. The princes too, and also the lawyers, scholars, and theologians who egg them on – all clash and fight with each other; and so do the monastic orders and even the bishops and their canons.[35]

Suffice it to recall the events of recent years. No justification for contemporary warfare could be derived from a comparison with the Jews of the Old Testament, who had conquered 'by God's command,' or with other ancient nations who had conquered barbarians in order to civilize them. Now wars are conducted for such trifling reasons as 'the interception of an intended spouse' (meaning Anne of Brittany) or the discovery of 'some mouldering, obsolete title' (as by the French kings in order to justify their claims to the kingdom of Naples). Pope Julius II, who is mentioned by name, is repeatedly criticized for his martial exploits. He is a fine butt for comparison with the Roman emperor Vespasian who, mindful of his oath as Pontifex maximus, kept 'his hands clean of all blood.'[36] As he did in *Dulce bellum inexpertis*, Erasmus reserves some of his harshest censures for the militancy of unscrupulous priests, monks, bishops, cardinals and, indeed, popes, though now without mentioning names. 'What has a mitre to do with a helmet, a crozier with a sword?' In a memorable passage he excoriates the crosses on banners and the Eucharistic communion offered to soldiers readying for battle. How dare they repeat the Lord's Prayer? One by one, Erasmus exposes the absurdity of each petition in the mouth of a combatant: '"Thy kingdom come." Is this how you pray when you are planning so much bloodshed to get a kingdom for yourself?'[37]

The crusade against the Turks is handled here more ambiguously than it was in *Dulce bellum inexpertis*. The Turks, it is said, sacrifice to demons; now the Christians do exactly the same when, to the Turks' delight, they fight among themselves. And while they are fighting each other, some Christians even 'have a treaty with the Turks.'[38] In view of such fratricidal savagery, why should the Turks ever want to convert to Christianity? But then, in an awkward retreat to pragmatism, Erasmus does not rule out a military alliance against the Turks. 'But perhaps it is the fatal malady of human nature to be quite unable to carry on without wars. If so, why is this evil passion not let loose upon the Turks?'[39] If, however, the Christian rulers were to join forces for a crusade against the Turks, this would present exactly the kind of collaboration on a single issue that, Erasmus had said, was not to be confused with the concord taught by Christ.

Turning again to the princes, Erasmus offers some thoughts to ponder for any ruler eager to go to war. War is never worthwhile, no matter how just the cause or how victorious the outcome. There is the economic cost to the treasury, the cities, and the peasantry in terms of military expenditure and lost commerce and production. And there is the moral cost of lost respect for law and decency. The worst are the mercenaries; they are a bane to the prince's own people and to his dignity. He must put up with the corruption of his own captains while he is trying to bribe the enemy's *condottieri*.[40] Thus a ruler should keep the peace out of concern for the welfare of his people. The wars of the recent past 'were all started in the interests of princes and carried on with great suffering of the people, although they were in no sense the people's concern.' Wars should never be undertaken 'except by the consent of the whole people' (as pledged by Mary of Burgundy in the *Grand Privilège* of 1477, and practised by the Swiss). 'Any grounds for starting a war should be a fully public concern,' not 'some personal grievance between princes.' After all,

> it is the humble and despised populace which founds noble cities, administers their foundations considerately, and enriches them in doing so. Then the rulers slip in, and like drones steal the products of other men's industry.[41]

So Christian folk must work together and 'show how the combined will of the people (*multitudinis concordia*) can prevail against the tyranny of the powerful.'[42] If thus peace is the better bargain, what must a ruler do to maintain it? He should avoid alliances – one recalls the contrast between selfish pacts and Christ's true concord as it comes to life in honest arbitration. Alliances (such as those of Julius II) often commit the contracting parties to go to war.[43]

Written to serve the diplomacy of its sponsor, the *Querela pacis* frequently alludes to the politics of the day, often in a veiled fashion. Some such hints have been identified above; repeated barbs also aim for Cardinal Matthäus Schiner, a future patron of Erasmus, but also a prominent opponent of Le Sauvage's engagement for reconciliation with France.[44] Presumably Erasmus meant the chancellor's antagonists at the Burgundian court when he referred to people 'avid for war; with perverted zeal they seek occasions for dissension, they tear France apart,' at least with their verbal salvos.[45] A eulogy of France had appeared earlier in the *Querela pacis*, awkwardly wedged between paragraphs scourging the frenzy of warfare. There Erasmus attributes to domestic concord (rather than the victory on the battlefield of Marignano) that France, 'the unspotted flower of Christendom,' had emerged 'supremely powerful.'[46]

Erasmus' Mistress Pax returns to her political agenda in the peroration of her speech. She metes out measured praise to each of the principal rulers. Pope Leo X in his love of peace sets an example for lay folk and clergy alike. Next King Francis I of France is singled out for praise on account of his unselfish conduct in the peace negotiations, but when Erasmus says that Francis is 'ready to buy peace,' he ignores that it rather was his own ruler, Charles, who made concessions to the French in the Treaty of Noyon (August 1516).[47] Charles also receives some few words of praise in the peroration, while Henry VIII of England is at least mentioned. Emperor Maximilian, however, the principal – and recently humiliated – enemy of France, is paid the dubious compliment that he does not loathe peace.[48] The *Querela pacis* ends on a note of ambiguity. When concord reigns among the Christians, they will be 'dear to Christ, in pleasing whom is the sum of happiness,' but the 'enemies of the cross,' that is to say, the Turks, will have more reason to fear them – obviously not on account of their peaceful resolve. In fact, before long the Treaty of Cambrai of March 1517 would pledge their monarchs to a joint crusade.

These were Erasmus' texts that Franck had under his eyes when writing much of the second chapter of the *Krieg Büchlin*. He moved from one page to the next, picking out what he wanted but becoming gradually more selective – tired, perhaps, or impatient – as he progressed. On the whole he renders Erasmus' thoughts correctly; thus our attention must be directed primarily to what he added or omitted. As we set out to accompany Franck on this journey, we may perhaps anticipate a conclusion that will impose itself at the journey's end. Here Franck does not poke Erasmus' fire to burn more brightly, as he did in the *Chronicle of the Heretics*. Here, as in the *Chronicle of the Emperors*, Erasmus supplies Franck with the fuel to light a fire of his own, and the flames come in hues that differ markedly from those of Erasmus.

The *Querela pacis*, being Erasmus' best-known anti-war pronouncement, is what Franck took up first. It guided him through seventy-two pages (folios 31r–67r). Folios 67v–70r were inspired by Erasmus' letter to Antoon van Bergen (Ep 288, a prelude to much of his subsequent pacifist argument), and folios 70r–104v, or sixty-eight pages, by the adage *Dulce bellum inexpertis*. Our comparison of Franck's texts with those of Erasmus needs to be focused on some key issues.

Notions of Peace

To Erasmus peace exceeds the sphere of the individual. He often uses the term *pax* concurrently and almost interchangeably with the terms *concordia, unanimitas, amicitia,* and *necessitas.* Nature herself has designed humans to live in concord and to knot the ties of friendship that flow from it. It ought to hold sway – but sadly often doesn't – throughout human society in couples, families, cities, nations, monasteries, and the entire church. Indeed, concord in the highest degree is what Christ himself demands of his flock.[49] Franck summarizes Erasmus' vision of peace as the founding principle of the universe and all living species,[50] but otherwise Erasmus' emphasis on the collective nature of peace had little appeal to him. To Franck peace can never be comprehensive, at least not until the end of time, because it is subject to a dichotomy. There is a true peace, a peace of God, that only true Christians can attain, while the ungodly 'world' has a peace of its own, a peace devised by Satan. In that sense Franck proposes to understand John 14:27: 'Peace is my parting gift to you, my own peace, such as the world cannot give.' By contrast, the world's peace, short lived, as it is, is

> a poor peace that can be ruined by an old crone with words alone ... All of [the world's] visible worth, happiness and honour lies in such a shallow grave, indeed at the wayside of the open road, that rust, moths, and thieves can get at it, steal it and loot it. Such a wretched peace! This is not the one Christ grants; his peace lies buried and locked deep down in God, the true treasure-chamber, and no mishap, no peril, no death, and no enemy can get at it.[51]

While the world's peace holds out a specious promise to end suffering, God's peace sublimates suffering. Paraphrasing the *Theologia Germanica*, Franck explains:

> Those who complain about having neither peace nor rest in the world, but only much temptation, affliction, and suffering, should be told that the Devil too and also the wolves and the bears can have peace, provided things turn out the way they want. These [sufferers] should discover delight *(letze)* and peace in God ... the inner peace that breaks through and penetrates all oppression, misery, and suffering, so as to leave one patiently enjoying an eternal peace in God himself.[52]

Franck's shift from societal concord, as stressed by Erasmus, to inner peace also connotes individualization. As the reader is shown again and again, peace to Franck is ultimately a spiritual solace to be found in silence and separation.

The Genesis of War

War is the Devil's domain. Erasmus mentioned that in passing, while Franck states over and over again that war was contrived by Satan and the warrior is a *vermenschter Teuffel*, a devil wrapped in human flesh.[53] Following Erasmus' guidance, Franck emphasizes that peace is a constituent principle of the nature of man modelled in God's own image.[54] But then 'the enemy of man, the old snake and its seed in us,[55] [interfere] and in defiance of all God's commandments tear up everything that was sown into our hearts by the woman's seed and the peace of God.' Seduced by Satan, we shed blood, we go to war, although grace can through Christ restore us to Adam's original perfection prior to the Fall. In this restoration, which is a bedrock conviction with him, Franck anchors his hope that war is not invincible.[56] Franck follows Erasmus in tracing the genesis of war in anthropological terms, with homicide crowning a crescendo of bloodshed that began with primeval man's combat with predatory wild animals. Franck enlarges on Erasmus' progression, but as a result it gets even more muddled. He is not ready to ignore that Genesis places Cain's murder of Abel at the very beginning of human history. Following Agrippa, he sees in Cain's fratricide a first watershed in human history. But echoing classical notions of a Golden Age, he also states that for 1666 years, from Adam to Noah, mankind was strictly vegetarian.[57] From Cain hailed the *kriegsvolk*, which he equates with the nobility (although not as explicitly as does Agrippa), while the *friedvolk*, descended from Abel, equals the commoners who get reduced to serfdom.[58] The historical prospect that comes into view here, arching from Adam and his sons to the end of time, corresponds with the chronological frame of Franck's *Chronica*, which, true to its title, also spans from creation to doomsday. For Erasmus such a concept of history based on the Bible had little relevance. He never thought of turning to Genesis for an explanation of the origins of war. Ultimately, however, Franck's religious grounding provided a clear and simple answer to the question how war had come about – a question that Erasmus with his anthropological musings had not answered adequately. To Franck war is the Devil's doing, and no more needed to be said about it.

It is true that neither Erasmus nor Franck ever discussed the causes of individual conflicts in terms of strategic, economic, industrial, or mineral resources. To theorists from the seventeenth century onward Erasmus' claim that wars were uniformly caused by princely greed and the self-interest of ecclesiastical and secular courtiers and Franck's claim that all wars were Satan's doing would have to sound naive. Yet both authors continued to be reprinted and translated, especially at times like the Thirty Years' War and after the two world wars of the twentieth century. Their protests against war flowed from a sense of morality based on religious conviction – an impulse that would never lose its strength throughout the history of modern pacifism.

War and the Christian Conscience

In his adage *Dulce bellum* Erasmus, having traced the appearance of war in the evolution of humans, appropriately goes on to ask: 'Where did it creep in from then, this plague that has infected the people of Christ?'[59] Franck has no time for Erasmus' explanatory sequence beginning with the early Christian heretics who infected the church with the Greek taste for philosophical controversy. To Franck the Devil is perfectly capable of acting single-handed. (Also, as he had shown in the *Chronica*, to blame the heretics for corrupting the church was mostly a cheap excuse.) On the other hand, he dwells at length on the arguments that might justify war to the Christian conscience, especially the testimony of the Old Testament. Franck's evident concern may be due to the fact that he wrote in the thick of the Protestant Reformation when all scriptural evidence, and the eschatological books of the Old Testament in particular, had gained greater weight than was the case a quarter of a century earlier with Erasmus and the politicians sponsoring his *Querela*. There Erasmus is content to stress the extolment of peace in Isaiah and the Psalms, while 'the Lord of hosts and vengeance' must be understood allegorically. In the adage *Dulce bellum* the argument concerning the Old Testament filled a paragraph and ran like this: the ancient Israelites engaged in war by God's command and never for selfish or trifling reasons. They hardly ever fought among themselves. Even so, when many of their other practices, circumcision for instance, are frowned upon, why should their warfare now be worthy of imitation? Clearly their example must not be followed *ad litteram*. A

Christian's Philistines and Moabites are the vices and the fear of death.[60] Franck, by contrast, is thorough. He amplifies all that Erasmus has said and sometimes sharpens the points. The Old Testament generally prefigures the Gospel, and so, he argues, the wars of Israel were necessary in order to prefigure the true wars of the Christians against the enemy within.[61]

How seriously Franck is taking the precedent of Old Testament wars can be seen in a long-winded, intersecting sequence with the heading: 'How and why the Old Testament goes to war' (161r–185r). He lists six conditions that must be fulfilled if a warrior is to be recognized as God's servant. First, for every single move in the operations one has to ascertain that it conforms with God's will. To Israel God's will was announced by word of its prophets, but prophecy has long ceased to exist and without it Franck, for one, cannot see how warfare might be legitimated (161v–162v). The second and third conditions state that wars must not be undertaken for selfish or trivial reasons. God's hand is commonly seen in a conflict when he supports the weaker side and sees to it that those who started the war for no good reason 'get boxed on the mouth' (164v, 172r). The soldier, no less than the ruler who has launched the war, must examine his conscience. Against Luther[62] Franck argues that an unjust cause removes the duty to obey orders, although he does not want to go so far as Wessel Gansfort and justify subjects who rebel against a despotic ruler. Gansfort's argumentation could not legitimize the German Peasant Rebellion (165r–169r). Conditions four and five re-emphasize the need for a clean conscience. War must be the last resort when all means for a peaceful settlement have been exhausted; also the army's moral discipline must be impeccable. For those who fight truly in God's cause numerical strength does not matter, as Israel's triumphs over stronger enemies showed.

> Moreover, God ordered Moses to so arm [his people] as if everything was to be conducted and achieved by their own might, in the manner of the other pagans, so that the hidden God would not be found out (*unversucht bleibt*) and, indeed, could accomplish his victory under disguise. (178r–v)

The enemy may be fooled, but the righteous warrior himself must, like David did, always remember that God alone is the source of his strength. With all that, to let oneself be guided by the precedent of scripture, especially the Old Testament, creates problems, even for Franck himself. On the one hand, he bitterly denounces allegorization as a tool that permits the advocates of war to 'twist scripture at will' (176v) to their own advantage. Yet, seemingly unaware of the dilemma, unresolved as he moves on to condition six, he emphasizes that the Mosaic law, indeed the whole Old Testament, is valid, but only as a figure of the truth to be revealed later. The Jews who lived by these laws were playing with dolls, as it were. When a young woman gives birth to a real child, her dolls can rest (*Feierabend haben*) (180v–181r). Yet, a literal following of biblical examples, as practised by the Münster Anabaptists, is even worse (179r–v, 182r). Franck's conclusion is that to be permissible for Christians, a war would have to respect the six conditions imposed by God in the Old Testament, and this clearly was not feasible. It would be 'rare like storks in the winter.'[63]

> But I believe that were we to have peace until someone would take up arms with troops carrying the six conditions as their livery, mark of distinction (*hoffart*), and ensign, we would not have many wars but rather long, indeed everlasting peace. (184v–185r)

The intensity of Franck's discussion of the Old Testament precedent suggests that he saw here the greatest obstacle to the total rejection of war. As to the New Testament, Franck like Erasmus found that, given its indisputably pacifist tenor, any potential incentive for armed conflict was easily dealt with. When Peter drew his sword he was 'still half a Jew,' and Christ's reaction was unequivocal. Franck harangues the reader:

> Wait for the Lord's word and order; then you may go to war. But I'll say that after God through Christ has suspended the wars until the end of the world (Psalm 46), you would have to wait a long time until God will send you in the New Testament a prophet and his message as to how, when and with whom you should engage in bodily fight, as he had figuratively layed out for Israel in the Old Testament.[64]

'Just War' and the Christian Tradition

Franck follows Erasmus in his scrutiny of Greek and Roman authors and, with his propensity to humanism (which is often underrated by Franck scholars), he adds classical texts of his own selection, such as a fine quotation from Lucretius.[65] But the writers of Greece and Rome never developed a comprehensive concept of peace and war in their antithesis to each other. Christianity, however, faced a new and troublesome perspective. Jesus' message in the New Testament, above all in his Sermon on the Mount, is unquestionably and radically pacifist. In the Old Testament, however, the Jews often engage in war on explicit orders from God. The problem was exacerbated when the church, especially in the West, began to be involved in politics. It became imperative to specify situations in which war was justified, and the post-Nicene fathers, the canon lawyers, and the scholastic theologians all set themselves to the task of doing so. Generally speaking, their arguments proceeded along two lines: War was just when it was unselfish, defensive, or restorative. Moreover, even in a just war not everybody could engage in actual fighting. Clerics likely could not, while mercenaries and criminals might jeopardize the justness of the cause. When writing on peace and war, Erasmus and Franck showed considerable familiarity with the relevant patristic and medieval sources. They were thus aware of these issues, but even Erasmus was hardly prepared to take them up systematically. He did not reject the concept of just war, but he found it suspect. In his note on Luke 3:14, he reacted to Augustine's theory of just war: 'I think it is permitted to prefer the teachings of Christ and the apostles to the views of Augustine.'[66] Erasmus usually touched upon the subject when countering objections to his own pleas for peace. The other side, he claims, attempted to draw justification for warfare from the fathers, the canon law, the law of nature, and even the Roman law. But the stark fact is that in a conflict every party will claim that its cause is just, that the 'right' is on its side. A war is just when the ruler decrees it is just.[67] No matter how just a war is, the damage it causes is always greater than the gains; thus an unjust peace is preferable to a just war.[68]

Franck hardly seems to share even the modest interest Erasmus had shown in the theories of just war. It is true that he repeats many of Erasmus' arguments and aptly summarizes his critique of post-Nicene justification of war by saying that it was devised *bei dem abnemendenn Christo* when Christ was waning.[69] His own, more radical, approach is the one we have described above. It led him to the conclusion that while a war sanctioned by God (and therefore obviously just) was always possible in theory, in practice it could come to pass no longer. Christ's words in the Gospel had made the occurrence of just war impossible. Consequently he ignores Erasmus' *De bello Turcico*, written in the wake of the Turkish conquest of Hungary and siege of Vienna (published in March 1530). Here Erasmus had gone much farther than ever before (but not as far as Juan Luis Vives)[70] in justifying, even advocating, concerted military action against the Turks, while continuing to insist that war must be the last resort when all else fails.

Two Approaches to Pragmatism

Neither Erasmus nor Franck could ignore that warfare was solidly embedded in the fabric of their society and that no recent peace treaty had changed that. The lessons, however, that both derived from such a realistic assessment were quite different, which in part was due to their different perceptions of the readership they wished to address. The *Adagia* were intended for educated members of the general public eager to add lustre to their Latin writing style and receptive to Eramus' own socio-political criticisms that were adroitly mixed in with the ancient lore. The *Querela pacis* and the *Institutio principis christiani* offered a twofold and balanced appeal, on the one hand to Europe's ruling class, on the other hand again to the general public. They all should come to see that warfare was monstrously immoral, but also that it did not make sense, either politically or economically or sociologically. His appeal was directed to the Christian conscience, but also to reason. There was no point in holding out hope for a universal, everlasting peace – for that mankind was too imperfect – but a peaceful propensity inherent in human nature could perhaps be awakened and strengthened.

Remembering the events of his own time, one should not blame Erasmus when he failed to see the usefulness of interstate alliances as a safeguard for peace. Likewise the arbitration he recommended could not succeed, as we know today, without an enforcement mechanism. The arbitrators that Erasmus envisaged were worthy individuals drawn from prelates and lay courtiers – classes that collectively he tended to describe as unworthy. Even his astonishing calls for a plebiscite to sanction any military intervention somehow seem too good to be true. More typically he seemed to assume that war and peace depended exclusively on the whims of a ruler. What did it mean to have a rightful claim to some territory? 'What nation has not at some time both been driven out of its homeland and driven others out? How many migrations have there been from one place to another?' Such is the state of human affairs; the suggestion Erasmus made in another place that wars might be avoided by fixing the boundaries of territories once and for ever is understandable, indeed logical, but hardly realistic.[71] He did not suggest concrete mechanisms or legislation; nor did he foreshadow the debates on limitation and regulation of warfare as they became popular with the political theorists of the seventeenth century.

Even so Erasmus offered a fair measure of constructive pragmatism that Franck generally chose to ignore. His own sense of realism perceived a mankind lost in sin and ruled by the Devil. The 'world' would never listen to his admonitions, least of all when he urged an end to war. Individuals, however, were redeemable and, from the humanist perspective, instructible. They could be, or become, Christians in a restrictive (but not sectarian) sense of the term. Through Christ they could return to the state of innocence and peace that Adam had enjoyed before his fall. In eschatological times all mankind that was to survive the onslaught of Antichrist would be truly Christian, and then peace would be perfect and everlasting. Some puzzling formulations notwithstanding, a sober assessment right at the beginning of the *Krieg Büchlin* makes clear how Franck views his readership. He offers his service

> to all children of peace and the light. As [if they were] limbs of my body they will want to suffer with me the cruel blessings of the truth and transfer Christ's death from his body to my body. The others, however, will for ever go on warring. They won't get anything out of me and won't stop warring on account of my writing because inside them their warlord, Satan, can never stop to lie, to deceive, to war, also to bend scripture.[72]

Not for these Franck wrote the *Krieg Büchlin*; they will never accept it. He wrote for those 'who in their simplicity hang between the sky and the earth, suspended in doubt.' And, yes, among these pious souls there are some soldiers, 'who still belong to the pen of Christ, as do the lost sheep of the house of Israel,' and also some lords and princes. That such defectors from the 'world' to the flock of Christ exist at all casts an important light on Franck's intent. All his emphasis on suffering and *Stille* does not preclude that he too wants to provoke action, that he wants to recruit soldiers to his war for peace. Furthermore, Franck's disillusioned and in this sense pragmatic restriction of his audience saves him from the yet greater disillusionment that Erasmus suffered, at least momentarily. In 1523 Erasmus published a *catalogue raisonné* of his works in the form of a very long letter. In it he recalls the genesis of the Mistress Pax's *Querela*, ending on a note of deep resignation:

> And so on instructions from Jean Le Sauvage I wrote the *Querela pacis*. By now things have come to such a pass that one ought to compose her epitaph, for there is no hope of her recovery.[73]

In this moment, at least, Erasmus was prepared to admit that his *Querela* was a cry in the wilderness,[74] doomed to fall on deaf ears. Not so Franck. For him – we have seen it[75] – the 'world's' peace is, like war itself, the doing of Satan. Here Franck has no business and therefore no reason to lament a lack of resonance. He knows that the sheep in Christ's pen that he wants to console and edify are few and far between. For greater effect he often chooses to address them individually in second person singular. This is most noticeable in his extraordinary last chapter with the title: 'That the pervasive warring and shouting is a sign of doomsday and the second coming of the Lord, that the last judgment and the deliverance of the just are not far away.'[76] While Franck here deals at length with the apocalyptic war and the momentary triumph of Antichrist – the judgment day itself, he says, is not his subject – it is a foregone conclusion that in the end God will subdue Satan, which means that the faith of the just, after having been sorely tried, at last will triumph.[77] Antichrist's seeming victory will come at the end of time, but it occurs also here and now; it concerns each reader willing to listen to Franck:

> If here you see nothing than flagrant overpowering (*verhergenn*), boasting, and victory on the side of Antichrist, and consequently nothing but defeat, wailing, and suppression on the side of God and his people, then consider of which kind and party you yourself are. Here you don't hear that Christ goes to war or wins, but that he suffers and is subdued ... [Ostensibly the triumph is Antichrist's], but the truth is Christ's, in the spirit, inside and for ever.[78]

It is debatable how much Erasmus contributed to the avoidance of military confrontations between states; Franck clearly contributed less than Erasmus, but his approach and his language were bound to have a strong appeal for the radical wing of early Protestantism and therewith for churches that even today stand out in their commitment to pacifism.

It remains to offer some conclusions on the stimuli that Erasmus contributed to Franck's thinking and writing about war and peace. When Franck wrote his *Krieg Büchlin*, few monographs on that topic were available in print and most were by Erasmus. It can be assumed that these latter prompted Franck to attempt a monograph of his own and that he also used German translations of Erasmus' pieces.[79] Usually his rendering of Erasmus' points is straightforward, but some cases are more complex. At the end of his final chapter on apocalyptic warfare Franck returns abruptly to his polemic against Luther and Bucer.[80] He now offers his definitive answer to 'a little question (*eyn kleynes fraeglin*)' that had come up in that debate, namely whether a soldier who did not serve as mercenary, but carried out the orders of his own sovereign, would be absolved from personal responsibility for his actions. The resumption of this argument at the very end of the whole work indicates that the 'little question' greatly mattered to Franck. He says he could perhaps agree, provided the war were defensive and not undertaken for 'ambition, glory, envy, revenge, wanton thirst for blood or tyranny'[81] and met the six conditions (which he had formerly said could impossibly be met at the time). He then applies to the soldiers themselves the argument Erasmus had used for dismissing the notion of just war. But while Erasmus had usually[82] seen justness as a question that only concerned the rulers (and that they would predictably answer in their own favour), Franck took Erasmus' point and, with Luther in mind, applied it to the individual soldier:

> Thus the soldiers on every side are just when they serve their master. The king of France, the Roman emperor, the Venetians and the pope – all have their confederates and each has a sworn-in soldiery. Now if each soldier rallied behind his lord, and if the four all wage war against each other (as had happened at the time of Maximilian), so there are on

every side thoroughly pious soldiers and mercenaries! Yet, God knows how dishonourable and despotic the quest of each party is. In this fashion even the servants of Herod are excused ... This is where we must come to if we accept obedience as a sufficient divine authorization for waging war. But one precondition dissolves that argument, [namely] that no oath, alliance, pledge or allegiance is valid against God.

Here, using Erasmus' argumentation, is Franck's final reaction not only to Luther but also to Erasmus' own compromises.[83]

In another case Franck distances himself from Erasmus more directly. In the *Krieg Büchlin* he never refers to Erasmus' *De bello Turcico*, no doubt because he disliked Erasmus' endorsement, qualified though it was, of a crusade-like campaign against the Turks. Franck often fails to mark the point where a paraphrase ends and his own discourse resumes. In the following case his explicit attribution of the statement to Erasmus can be read as a silent caveat, lest the readers assume that Franck shared his view:

The Turks ought to be enticed to embrace the Christian faith through teaching, good deeds, and a blameless conduct rather than assaulting and molesting them, weapon in hand. Although, if one ever wanted to wage a war, it would be more acceptable to target this enemy of our faith and salvation, and it would create a better impression (*schein*) of responsibility, or so says Erasmus. Also [the war] should be a common concern of all, and all ought to know why one needs to wage it.[84]

Franck renders accurately the point Erasmus made in the *Querela pacis*,[85] but having repeatedly insisted that his readers ought to judge for themselves, he puts them here to the test. After all, they could hardly have failed to realize that he himself did not approve of Erasmus' excuse for fighting against the Turks and had no use for Erasmus' point that a move to war should require public consent.

Franck's most distinctive mark is the line he draws between the true Christians who might, he hopes, take his pleas for peace to heart and the Satanic 'world' that he knows will not. It is obvious that for Franck the principal rulers of Europe, praised in the peroration of Erasmus' *Querela*, also belong to this godless world, and along with them the institutional churches. As we just quoted, all were involved in 'dishonourable and despotic' politics. Both Franck and Erasmus know and accept that an end to warfare is not in sight. But while for Erasmus this knowledge leads to an unhappily conceded compromise, Franck can afford to be radical. Erasmus, addressing the rulers and the public at large, must bring himself to find minimal conditions for the legitimation of warfare while doing all he can to help reduce it. Franck, addressing only the pious few, can boldly state conditions for divinely authorized warfare that, if they were ever met, can no longer be met now; to true Christians war is anathema. Reading Erasmus leads Franck to where Erasmus himself did not see fit to go.

FOUR

The Castellio Circle: Religious Toleration and Radical Reasoning

DE HAERETICIS, AN SINT PERSEQUENDI

Religious toleration became an issue of intensive public debate with the trial and burning of Michael Servetus in 1553 in Geneva. Heresy and ways to end it had, of course, been a concern much earlier. The Christian fathers, both Greek and Latin, had dealt with the subject in writings that exercised great influence later on; but not before the age of printing and the new wave of persecution brought about by the Reformation did the debate about religious dissent achieve the climactic prominence that it was to retain to the end of the seventeenth century. Also, the pamphlets and books occasioned by the burning of Servetus propelled Erasmus' thoughts to a central position in the toleration debate.

The key document is the anonymous *De haereticis, an sint persequendi ... multorum tum veterum tum recentiorum sententiae*, a selection of arguments in support of toleration by authors past and current, gathered together by Sebastian Castellio (1515–63) and, presumably, some helpers, all like himself members of a circle of religious exiles living in Basel.[1] First published in 1554, the small volume was soon translated into German and French, later also into Dutch. It has been studied intensely by modern scholars;[2] here we are concerned primarily with the prominent place it gave to testimonies by Erasmus. Castellio, who had already published a series of Latin dialogues for the schools and his Latin translation of the entire Bible, soon to be followed by a French one, was thoroughly familiar with Erasmus' work. As will soon become clear, he knew precisely what to select for his collection. It is true that before it was Erasmus' turn, *De haereticis* presented Luther and

Johann Brenz, all three of them receiving about equal space, but Luther and Brenz, the reformer of Württemberg, both dealt with specific aspects. Luther's point was that secular authorities had no mandate to judge consciences, Brenz's that Anabaptist heretics should not be prosecuted as long as they were peaceful. By 1554, when *De haereticis* was published, both statements were for the record. Castellio's readers, Protestants for the most part, could hardly fail to realize that the two German reformers were now advocating harsh measures of suppression. Similarly, two short excerpts calling for moderation, by none other than Calvin, in this context would be seen above all as an insult to the Genevans. Erasmus, by contrast, was quoted addressing the issue more broadly. Since he replied to Catholic critics, he stood apart from the polemics inside the Protestant camp.

Following the Erasmus texts, Castellio reproduced some short statements by Protestant liberals – 'Erasmians,' as Roland Bainton not unfairly called them, among them Celio Secondo Curione. A new level of intensity is reached with the more substantial contributions of Sebastian Franck and Castellio himself, both having their identity thinly veiled under pseudonyms. Franck often echoes Erasmus and even refers to him in the two passages from his *Chronicle of the Heretics*[3] that the editors of *De haereticis* had newly translated from the German. In keeping with the plan of his *Chronicle*, Franck mentioned individual heretics, especially Jan Hus, whom the church, being a part of the wicked 'world,' had condemned, often slaughtered, and their writings suppressed. Had more such writings been preserved, as were exceptionally those of Hus, one would likely find them sound and saintly. The 'world' inverted all true values (as Erasmus had shown in the adage *Sileni Alcibiadis*). Therefore Christ often spoke 'in parables and obscure words,' incomprehensible to the world, while the church stepped up the persecution as it became progressively more corrupt through the centuries.

Erasmus, to turn now to his own testimony, had criticized the persecution of heretics primarily in brief comments scattered through his work and correspondence. There is no writing from his pen entirely devoted to the topic of toleration, such as we have found devoted to his protests against war. Castellio selected three samples of some substance, the most representative anyone could have found. He also edited them, cutting bits that repeated points made earlier, but also might have reinforced them. In fairness to the tenor of Erasmus' texts, he included a passage that seemed to deny the contemporary relevance of the parable of the tares, which was the proof text most commonly cited in support of toleration.[4] If *De haereticis* enhances the radical tenor of Erasmus' words, this is not due to Castellio's editing, but to the context in which they are placed. Had Erasmus been alive at the time *De haereticis* was published, he might not have reacted as angrily as he did to Franck's *Chronicle of the Heretics*, but might still have felt uncomfortable. The persistent advocate of discretion and balance was here placed, as it were, at the vanguard of a noisy protest march.

Erasmus' three pieces were not presented in proper order. The text that had triggered the attacks answered by Erasmus in the other two pieces comes last and, moreover, is not given under his name, but under that of Conradus Pellicanus, a Zurich professor who in his own Gospel commentary had copied Erasmus' paraphrase of the parable of the tares (Matthew 13:24–30, 36–42) word for word.[5] The other two pieces were written later when Erasmus answered the attacks of Catholic critics, namely the Paris theologian Noël Béda (1527) and the Spanish monks (1528),[6] and in the course of doing so came to expand his interpretation of Christ's parable. In his paraphrase Erasmus adopted the exposition given by John Chrysostom in one of his homilies, which had set a standard for the subsequent patristic exegesis and was likewise reproduced in *De haereticis*.[7] According to Chrysostom, the tares in the parable were the heretics, and Christ's purpose was to prevent the war and bloodshed that would inevitably follow if they were put to death. Other forms of restraint, however, could be used and might succeed in reclaiming many heretics to orthodoxy, that is, turning the tares into wheat. This, and also the danger that some ears of wheat would be pulled together with the tares, is why the servants were forbidden to weed the field. Those tares that proved incurable would be sent to hell when Christ sits in judgment.

In his defences Erasmus ridiculed Béda's interpretation (later to be repeated by Calvin and Beza) that the tares connoted not just the heretics, but also the common criminals whom no one wanted to exempt from punishment. Therefore, when it could be done without endangering the wheat, the tares should be rooted out. Erasmus also seemed to anticipate a predestinarian objection that was later formulated by Beza: a species cannot change. The tares that Satan sows will always be tares; nothing can turn them into ears of wheat. According to Erasmus, however, the Lord's seed was the evangelical doctrine and the tares were the teachings of the heretics, not the heretics themselves, who would thus retain the capacity of changing their mind.[8] Two other points argued by Erasmus would later be resumed regularly in the debate on religious toleration. Erasmus insisted that Christ had addressed the parable to his disciples only, and by extension to the ministers of the church. It would thus in no way deprive civil authorities of their right to suppress criminals, including seditious heretics who were disturbing the public peace. Also Erasmus warned lest coercion push heretics to simulation and a feigned practice of orthodoxy. He commented savagely on the judicial procedures of the Inquisition, but he also stated repeatedly that when he rejected the death penalty for non-violent heretics, he did not therewith rule out milder forms of coercion.[9]

Toleration to Erasmus was the inevitable consequence of his conviction that the essence of Christianity was charity and mercy, not severity. Mutual toleration was also indispensable for Christian concord. He never abandoned the notion of an invisible universal church that included all true Christians, regardless of dogma, even though late in his life he came to accept the inevitability of different confessions coexisting in political states like Poland and the Empire. Secular authority had always had a mandate to preserve religious peace. As Castellio quoted him: 'If riots ensue and each side claims to be the Catholic Church, and the question has not been sufficiently aired, the prince should curb both sides.' As early as 1521 he had proposed that the dispute between Lutherans and Catholics be settled by a board of arbiters appointed by the major princes of Europe.[10]

As usual, Erasmus' pronouncements were not free from ambiguity. Beza later argued that the defenders of toleration had better not count on Erasmus' support. Gleefully he cited from the texts chosen by Castellio what seemed to be one of Erasmus' typical equivocations:

> I say this not because I favor the heretics. I hate them, if anyone does. I will not favor a milder treatment of anyone I know to be a heretic, that is, one who errs maliciously, who is factious and incurable.

In this case, however, Erasmus was vindicated by another religious exile in Basel, Mino Celsi, who countered Beza by pointing out that the first of Erasmus' three conditions was hard to prove, while the third one was plainly impossible to meet. While alive, a heretic was never incurable. In fact, a little later in Castellio's excerpt Erasmus added (after Augustine): 'Who can teach those who have been killed? Who can raise up the slain?'[11]

The texts selected by Castellio date from 1527 and 1528, a time when little had remained of Erasmus' initial sympathy with the Protestant reformers. But neither then nor, indeed, at any time did he falter in his willingness to plead the cause of peaceful individuals and groups suffering persecution on behalf of their beliefs. Roland Bainton has gathered examples of his pleas and protests that stretch from an incident in 1500 when Erasmus was in Orleans to a passage written in 1532, recalling the savage execution of a gifted surgeon. It is true that in 1529 he joked in rather bad taste about the burning in Lucerne of an enraptured simpleton, but in the same breath he spoke with great warmth of the plight of the Anabaptists in general, who had high moral standards and did not attempt to subvert the state. A year later, however, when Erasmus began to learn about the experimental Anabaptist state of Münster, his condemnation was unequivocal.[12]

It is time to turn to the texts in *De haereticis* that were written by Castellio himself. He certainly does take up Erasmus' leads, but the subsequent execution of Servetus created a new and powerful rallying point: the pleas become more strident, the protest more caustic. While editing the New Testament, Erasmus had often encountered issues that he could not settle because the text or the meaning was not clear. This point returns with a new emphasis in Castellio's piece, presented under the German name of Georg Kleinberg, that deals predominantly with the plight of the German Anabaptists: 'talking about the understanding of Scriptural passages, the sense of which is not yet clear. If they were not obscure controversy would have ceased, for who is so demented that he would die for the denial of the obvious?'[13] In an excerpt from the dedicatory preface of his Latin Bible, inserted in *De haereticis* under his own name, Castellio describes the dire consequences when hesitation and doubt give way to bull-headed judgment. 'We are bloodthirsty through zeal for Christ, who, rather than shed blood, poured forth His own.'[14] In the dedicatory preface to *De haereticis* Castellio vows to do all he can to staunch

> the blood of those who are called heretics, which name has become today so infamous, detestable, and horrible that

there is no quicker way to dispose of an enemy than to accuse him of heresy ... [If only the princes were to listen to him.] Then we should not have so many fires, so many swords dripping with the blood of the innocent, and we should not now be eating fish fattened on the blood of those for whom Christ gave his own.

There is no heresy that can be objectively defined and lawfully persecuted. Castellio adds: 'After a careful investigation into the meaning of the term heretic, I can discover no more than this, that we regard those as heretics with whom we disagree.'[15]

Scripture, such as it is, can be cited by the persecutors in their own sense, and refuting them avails nothing. 'The persecutors persevere and listen to no one unless he is also a persecutor.'[16] This is how Castellio starts the section presented under the French name Basile Montfort and devoted to refuting the arguments proffered in Geneva and elsewhere in support of Servetus' condemnation, especially Calvin's *Defensio orthodoxae fidei* that was already in print. Castellio strives valiantly to demonstrate flaws in the scriptural base of the case in favour of persecution; he shows, for instance, that the heretics of his time must not be equated with the false prophets and blasphemers put to death according to the Old Testament.[17] But he knows that his exposition of scripture will not stop the inquisitors and their Protestant counterparts; at best he can hope to persuade an unbiased public. He relies more broadly than Erasmus has done on the record of history. Augustine's eventual advocacy of compulsory observance of Catholic rites only led to 'a feigned profession which lasted as long as the coercion and the fear of punishment.' When the Vandals, who were Arians, swept the region, Catholicism collapsed. With the recent ascendancy of a Catholic queen in England Protestantism had a similar fate, although it had been embraced freely, or so at least it had seemed. 'Little wonder that measure is given for measure and that those who do violence suffer violence.'[18] Castellio's major shift, however, is from marshalling evidence to causing his readers to view religious persecution with a sense of moral outrage. His rhetoric rises to apocalyptic pitch: 'there is no end to this slaughter until the Lord, at His coming, overtakes us gory, battened, and fat with the blood of our brothers,' and culminates in a prayerful dialogue: 'Dost Thou, o Christ, command and approve of these things? Are they Thy vicars who make these sacrifices? Art Thou present when they summon Thee to such butchery (*viscerationem*) and dost Thou eat human flesh?'[19] A further remark, finally, points to another way in which Castellio intensified Erasmian impulses. Exclaimed Montfort: 'Nothing is too monstrous to teach the people when to doubt is prohibited, since if you doubt or do not believe, you are put to death.'[20] More will have to be said soon about the exigencies of doubting.

A few years after the publication of *De haereticis*, the object of its pleas, including Erasmus' part in them, was broadened to include a category of victims that he likely would rather not have seen included. The Netherlander Johannes Wier (Weyer, 1515–88) was a personal physician to the dukes of Cleves and thus a member of a court that had for some time endorsed a uniquely liberal form of Catholicism, open to many Lutheran influences and often hailed for its unprecedented implementation of Erasmian ideas in religion and education. Wier joined the court in 1550; by that time Cleves had moved closer to the Habsburg camp, but the intellectual climate remained conducive for Wier to compose his monumental and immediately controversial book on witchcraft and its imaginary nature. *De praestigiis daemonum* was published in 1563, not surprisingly in Basel. The printer, Johannes Oporinus, had once been Paracelsus' famulus and had earlier published Andreas Vesalius' anatomical *Fabrica*, along with *De haereticis* and other revolutionary works.[21] Such was the demand for Wier's book that Oporinus and other printers could launch seven more Latin editions, three enlarged by the author, until 1583. The work contains two chapters dealing with heretics rather than witches. The first reproduces some texts by church fathers opposed to the death penalty for heretics, including two excerpts from John Chrysostom, precisely as they had previously appeared in Castellio's *De haereticis*. The other chapter resumed, literally, two thirds of Erasmus' long reply to the Spanish monks concerning the treatment of heretics, identical in part with the portion appearing in *De haereticis* but fuller than the latter.[22] Wier hardly bothers to explain why the treatment of heretics is relevant to his probe on witches, but he does quote the title of a section in the Spaniards' attack on Erasmus: 'Against the Holy Inquisition of Heretics,' and in the text he does insert the term 'inquisitor' where Erasmus had avoided it. The point is that when tried, witches and heretics are exposed to the same senseless and ruthless treatment. Erasmus wrote nothing that would have supported Wier's linking the predicament of witches to that of heretics. He loathed all forms of superstition and probably was more sceptical about reports of magic and superstition than he usually cared to show in his letters,[23] but on the whole his compassion was reserved for the victims of religious coercion.

Pleas for religious toleration multiplied in the ensuing age of Confessionalism. For the time being, Basel, its exiles and its printers, remained in the forefront and Erasmus' testimony continued to resonate. It was prominent in the substantial book of Mino Celsi (1577), the most comprehensive appeal for toleration published in the sixteenth century;[24] and also in the German treatises of a little-known dissident Lutheran, Georg Mayer (or Meyer), published posthumously at Basel in 1595 and 1596.[25]

BROADENING THE REACH OF SALVATION, AND OF DOUBT

Religious toleration was not the only concern of the circle around Castellio; looking at some others will show, once again, how Erasmus encouraged radical advances, and here simultaneously on two quite different fronts: towards confidence and towards doubt. To promote toleration in the face of intransigence Genevan-style and the Catholic Inquisition, however, was always paramount. It created the bond between the members of the circle and represented a centre from which they could branch off in different directions.

De haereticis, an sint persequendi includes two short texts by Celio Secondo Curione (1503–69), who had fled from Italy with the Inquisition on his heels and now taught classics at the University of Basel. The two quotations were taken from his book *Pro vera et antiqua ecclesiae Christi autoritate* (1546/7), written and published after his arrival in Switzerland. *De haereticis* quoted Curione referring to Anabaptists, who were justly suppressed because they were violent. As long as they were peaceful, one must conclude from this short sentence without context, they should be tolerated.[26] This, however, was certainly not the interpretation of Heinrich Bullinger, the head of the Zurich church, who had nothing but praise for Curione's book when it was published, and later supported the Genevans during Servetus' trial and after his execution. The other excerpt attacked ecclesiastical claims to secular jurisdiction, but concealed that Curione's target was not Calvin, but the pope. During his last years in Italy he had launched unusually bold and frank attacks upon the Church of Rome. Implicitly his book opposed Erasmus' constant calls for moderation and reconciliation between the feuding religious camps. In fact, it can be read as a sequel to Curione's vicious attack on Erasmus, which will be discussed in another context.[27]

This attack by Curione is directed, however, to one specific attitude of Erasmus and actually confirms the Italian's intensive occupation with his thought, which rarely ended in disagreement.[28] In Italy Curione had belonged to Evangelical circles that were much attracted to Erasmus' work. In Basel he was a close friend of Castellio's, and the Genevans had good reason to suspect his collaboration in the launching of *De haereticis*. Only his affinity to the Calvinist concept of predestination presented a marked contrast with the other members of the Castellio circle and, of course, with Erasmus too. That being said, Curione's positive response to another aspect of Erasmus' philosophy of Christ deserves investigation; it breaks new ground and also comes with some curious twists.

In his Italian years Curione was profoundly impressed by one of Erasmus' writings, although he did not then know, and perhaps never knew, that it was Erasmus' work. *De immensa Dei misericordia concio* (1524) proved highly popular. Two editions were published within months from each other; a German translation followed in 1525, an English and a Dutch one in 1526, a Spanish one in 1549. An Italian translation acknowledging Erasmus' authorship appeared in 1551. Already in 1542, however, Erasmus' sermon was available in Italy as *Trattato divoto et utilissimo della divina misericordia*, published in Brescia under the name of the Carmelite Marsilio Andreasi. That Andreasi's book is for the most part a faithful translation of Erasmus' *Concio* totally escaped attention until Silvana Seidel Menchi showed it to be so.[29] To understand the popularity of Erasmus' sermon is not difficult. Amid an abundance of uplifting Bible verses, it drives home its consoling message that God's goodness has opened the way to salvation to each and every one. No sin is grave enough to block that way irremediably. Humans can be indulgent out of fear or self-interest – not so God, who showers upon all his *felix diluvium misericordiae*.[30] It is true that God's promise of salvation calls for an active human response; a path of repentance and charity must be trod between the dual pitfalls of arrogant self-assurance and black despair. Humankind can indeed embrace God's goodness; the excellence of the human soul surpasses everything else in the universe he created.[31]

To accommodate objections raised by his friend, the bishop of Basel, Erasmus had made some changes in his manuscript, but the text as printed still offered a bold endorsement of justification by faith alone, followed by a barb against the sale of indulgences.[32] Although Andreasi suppressed this specific passage, his rendering of Erasmus' work was still bound to gratify Italian circles sympathetic to the Reformation. He retained the original's pastoral, benignly moralizing tone, and by eliminating Erasmus' mythological lore adapted it to the taste of those who were educated but not learned, such as the Evangelical-minded duchess of Mantua, to whom he dedicated his piece. Among those touched by it was Curione, then still in Italy. He discussed its subject with his friends and, in doing so, drew the initial inspiration for his own *De amplitudine beati regni Dei dialogi* (published in 1554).[33] In the latter he recalled his first reaction to Andreasi's work: 'Reading it impressed me; it bowled me over, carried me away in admiration of God's goodness, so much so that I almost dissolved in tears.'[34] In Basel he had his sixteen-year-old son Orazio translate the work into Latin, and so it was published in 1550 by the Basel printer Johannes Oporinus, without a mention anywhere of Erasmus and that other Latin text, his *Concio*.[35]

Celio secondo's basic theme in *De amplitudine* is God's ample mercy that causes the elect to outnumber the reprobate. Departing from the homiletic style of his models, he raises a number of precise questions that were the subject of theological debate and finds the form of dialogue better suited to do so. He respects Calvin's double predestination, together with the concept of an everlasting hell and, generally, the principal dogmas of the Swiss reformers. He avoids any challenge to the Trinitarian doctrine. What raises doubts, nevertheless, about his loyalty to the official churches is his emphasis on spirituality. To give an example, he insists that it is not any public act of observance that marks the true Christian, but a secret commitment, not physical ablution, but 'the baptism of the heart which is the baptism undergone by the spirit.' If it were otherwise, Hymenaeus, Alexander, Ananias, and Sapphira (1 Tim. 1:19–20, Acts 5:1–11) and many other baptized reprobates would be in Paradise, and not in hell. It is true that Curione here directly contradicted Erasmus, who in his *Concio* had insisted that the physical destruction of Ananias and Sapphira was not tantamount to eternal damnation.[36] On the other hand, Curione's tolerance for Christian faith *in occulto* favoured the simulation of Evangelicals-at-heart in Catholic countries, who concealed their beliefs in order to remain unmolested. Such 'Nicodemites,' as Calvin branded them, Curione had already defended in his *Pro vera ecclesiae autoritate*.[37]

Without much of an explanation Curione moves from his affirmation of Erasmus' wide-open gates of heaven to a concept dear to the radical spiritualist wing of the Reformation. Often in terms of rapture, he announces an intermediate coming of Christ between his human life on earth and his return on the day of judgment, a 'second coming' that ushers in his millennial reign over a world united in faith. For, and here is the link with the principal theme, the magnitude of grace extends not only to the Jews and the Muslims, but also to the heathens in the newly discovered parts of the globe.[38] If Curione left open whether the Millennium should be understood literally as well as allegorically, he was explicit in applying to it the classical myth of the Golden Age. This was not, of course, the Golden Age at the dawn of human history that Hesiod had praised, nor was it Virgil's and Erasmus' Golden Age Returning after prolonged corruption. Curione's Golden Age at the end of time was unprecedented and climactic; implicitly it depreciated the claims that the Protestant Reformation was a unique turning point. The view that Christ would return to assume his millenarian rule had been condemned already in the Lutheran 'Augsburg' confession of 1530.[39] No wonder, thus, that the blatant manifestation of heterodoxy in Curione's book raised grave concern, even among his friends in Zurich and Basel. Bullinger, who had read the manuscript, objected to Curione's millenarian concept and specifically to the image of the future Golden Age that, incidentally, had been evoked three years earlier by Castellio in similar terms of exaltation.[40] In Basel Curione could not obtain permission to publish his book, so that it had to be printed in the obscure Poschiavo. The objections were clearly similar to the ones raised by Bullinger, for the confidence that grace was obtainable for all did not seem to raise problems here. It had previously been expressed by both Erasmus and Andreasi in their books published in Basel.

With his insistence on the amplitude of grace Curione followed in large measure an Erasmian inspiration, and with his millenarian accretions he pursued it to the point of heterodoxy. This was the only occasion on which the highly respected Basel professor and author exposed himself to public controversy, but we clearly face here the proverbial tip of an otherwise invisible iceberg. Curione had left Italy as an intrepid champion of a Calvinist-oriented reform and, consequently, as a critic of what he perceived to be Erasmus' vacillation. As he became acquainted with certain radical views held in the circles of religious exiles, his loyalty to the official Swiss churches became superficial at best. He was in touch with Lelio Sozzini and other Antitrinitarians, such as Matteo Gribaldi. Indeed, with due prudence he showed his interest in Servetus' writings and probably met the arch-heretic when he came to Basel.[41] Not only did he come to defend Italian Nicodemism, he himself became well versed in the techniques of simulation and dissimulation. At least when defending his *De amplitudine beati regni Dei*, he could publicly, and rightly, claim that the 'greatly learned and widely famous *herr Erasmus Roterodamus*' was first and foremost on his side.[42]

To return to Castellio, for him too there were other issues than religious toleration that held him in the gravitational compass of Erasmus' work. In their critique of scholastic theology one notes almost inevitable similarities, even verbal ones, for instance in conjunction with the conundrum of Trinitarian doctrine.[43] Also, both famously championed the cause of free will, Erasmus against Luther, Castellio against Calvin. Here too verbal affinities were bound to occur, although Castellio strikes out more boldly than Erasmus, who in the end almost apologizes for the necessity to retain the concept.[44] Castellio turns against the entire exegetical tradition, including Erasmus, when he insists that faith is not a gift of God, imparted as he sees fit. The way Castellio explains Ephesians 2:8, God's gift is not faith itself, as commonly assumed, but our salvation, effected by faith, and faith lies within the compass of our will.[45]

Erasmus' work on the New Testament did, we have seen it already, set inevitable standards for those who after him engaged in the same pursuit. Theodore Beza, Castellio's nemesis in Geneva, constantly mentioned Erasmus in the notes of his Latin New Testament (1556), and his comments ranged from acknowledged debt to furious polemic. In Castellio's Latin New Testament, by contrast, the less frequent notes rarely refer to a source; Erasmus is not mentioned,[46] but in the defense of his translation against Beza's critique Castellio mentions Erasmus a number of times, usually taking his side against the Genevan.⁴⁷ It is unthinkable that while translating the Greek text into Latin, Castellio would not have had Erasmus' New Testament close at hand, if only to respond to the challenge he had set himself of finding words that were comprehensible, elegant, and had not been used before in this place. There is, in fact, some evidence for his following Erasmus' lead,⁴⁸ and a careful comparison would certainly yield more. Erasmus and Castellio agree that scripture, while divinely inspired, still is written by men and therefore ought to be approached with the human tools of rational criticism, but both see that even sound methods of interpretation have their limits. Erasmus frequently offers his readers choices by quoting different explanations given by various fathers; Castellio, set on avoiding ambiguity, does not do this. Erasmus examined the place of figurative speech in the Bible at length, and Castellio echos his conclusion that in many places a literal understanding is absurd, but unlike Erasmus he presses for a precise rule of interpretation.⁴⁹ Whereas Erasmus is not averse to deciding that some verses convey both a literal and a figurative meaning, Castellio holds that on each occasion only one sense is applicable and, like the Socinians later, he has a marked preference for the literal sense.⁵⁰

Two of Castellio's writings present the most mature, and provocative, formulations of his religious thought and could not be published in his lifetime. *Dialogi quatuor*, an elaborate affirmation of free will, was published in 1578 in Basel under a fictive imprint, edited by none other than Fausto Sozzini; *De arte dubitandi* had to wait much longer before it became available in print.⁵¹ Both approach theology and scriptural exegesis with an increased concern for method and a heightened emphasis on rational inquiry. Erasmus too was inquisitive and sometimes sceptical, but to elevate doubting to the rank of an *ars*, a branch of scientific inquiry based on its own method, would not have occurred to him. Now this is indeed what Castellio did or, at least, tried to do. Without quite doing away with revelation and the guidance of the spirit, he reached a point where only sense perception and reason remained as tools for the understanding of scripture.⁵² These were the tools that allowed one to penetrate to the core of the divine message: 'Finally, taking everything into account, I find that Christ never did or said anything that would have been contrary to the senses or to intelligence.'⁵³ Would that all were to use these tools! Castellio recognized – more so than later the Socinians – that even the rationally most convincing explanation of Bible verse would not persuade a biased interpreter,[54] just as the most lucid scriptural arguments in support of toleration were lost on the closed mind of the persecutors.

Erasmus and Castellio both belonged to a growing tradition in Christian theology that was intent on using a distinction between essential beliefs and non-essential ones (*adiaphora*) to ease dogmatic controversies. Both would not define the essential beliefs in terms of dogma, nor would they look for them outside scripture, although Erasmus, much more so than Castellio, also found merit in the opinions of the Christian fathers.[55] Both avoid declaring that specific beliefs, including the un-biblical dogma of the Trinity, were necessary onto salvation. Castellio invents a now famous dialogue between an anonymous inquirer and Athanasius, who insists that holding, or ignoring, the *fides catholica*, and specifically his own doctrine of the Trinity, will make the difference between going to heaven or to hell. The other speaker remarks that in this case the robber, who was crucified with Christ and came to believe in him, would contrary to Christ's words have to be in hell. 'But it is not for you, Athanasius, to change the times so as to make them accord with your own time (*mutare tuo tempore tempora*), to the effect that what previously was not held to be necessary, after you will be necessary.' In the end the inquirer says that he would defend Athanasius if he could but, really, he can't. He then states his own belief, as Erasmus had done so often, in simple terms reminiscent of the Apostolic creed.[56]

Castellio's emphasis on methodical doubt opens prospects to the future. Parts, at least, of *De arte dubitandi,* in manuscript and in print, were known in the Netherlands around the turn of the seventeenth century,[57] amid a marked 'Castellio renaissance.' At no other time was he read there so much in new editions and translations, although he also met with considerable interest in seventeenth-century England. He was admired (and vilified by others) as a champion of liberal theology and religious toleration, while his role as a forerunner of enlightened scepticism was little recognized before the twentieth century. Hugo Grotius and his Arminian friends were saddened by the injustice he had suffered so often in his life, and Michel de Montaigne, who visited Basel seventeen years after Castellio had died there, called his death in destitution *une grande honte de nostre siecle*.[58]

FIVE

Erasmus, His Mistress Folly, and the Garden of Epicurus

IN THE GARDEN OF EPICURUS

Through the centuries Epicureanism was seen by its critics as a source of misconduct and unbelief; in fact, whether or not it was understood correctly, it did usually invite radical attitudes. An examination of Erasmus' changing views of Epicureanism must primarily rely on statements by himself that refer to Epicurus or indicate awareness of, and perhaps affinity with, some aspects of his philosophy. This is a narrow gate, and as we strive to enter by it, we should not entirely lose sight of the many intermediate sources on Epicurus' system, critical or appreciative or both, with which Erasmus was familiar, such as some pages in the works of Christian fathers, especially Clement of Alexandria, Origen, Arnobius, Lactantius, Ambrose, and Augustine, even some catchwords in the Bible, and many more pages by Greek and Latin authors, among whom Virgil, Horace, Seneca, Plutarch, and Lucian should be noted, and in particular Cicero, Lucretius, and Diogenes Laertius, the great purveyors of Epicurus' authentic thought.[1]

Epicurus' principal tenet, that we should strive to live in an enduring state of pleasure, meant a radical departure from preceding strands of Greek philosophy. To live pleasurably also meant to live in accord with nature. Making good use of Aristotle's work on animals and plants, Epicurus discerned an order of nature that valued organic over inorganic life and terrestrial over celestial accidents.[2] The choice of a garden as the seat of his academy is symptomatic. Erasmus too considered gardens as an infallible source of pleasure and intellectual inspiration. Gardens thus are where we shall begin this study. Thereafter we shall proceed chronologically, examining first the early traces of Erasmus' acquaintance with Epicurus and next his years in Italy. Italy had recently experienced a marked revival of interest in Epicurean thought, leading to a positive revaluation. Here Erasmus' familiarity with the work of Lorenzo Valla acquires a crucial importance. Valla turned Erasmus, to put it boldly, into a sort of convert to Epicureanism, as will be shown by a fresh look at his *Moriae encomium*. After the *Moria* Erasmus' statements relevant to Epicureanism tend to be more casual and inconsistent. In the end, however, we notice a reawakening of concern and almost a return to his initial position, although the loop is not quite completed. Finally, we will want to glance at a wider perspective. The history of Epicureanism is an ongoing, often radical, quest for enduring felicity, although not always proceeding from the same intellectual premises. In a rudimentary fashion, at least, we must try and assign Erasmus his modest place in that history.

The *Antibarbari* is one of Erasmus' earliest works, begun, he says, before he was twenty and very likely completed in the first version that concerns us here by 1499.[3] The writing presents a conversation between Erasmus himself and four of his friends in a setting that is described as follows. Since the passage is well known, it may be quoted selectively:

> But seriously, my friends, since we have happened by chance on such a splendid subject, why should we not set up an academy here on the model of Plato's? No matter if we have not a plane tree like the Platonic or Ciceronian ones ... I am offering you real trees instead ... a whole orchard, which you can see near our house on the left, bordered by noble oaks and the clearest of streams. What if we water this place too with our discussions, so that it will never dry up at any future time? And under that great pear tree, practically in the middle of the garden, there are some very comfortable seats ... If so weighty a philosopher as Socrates could be allured (as in the *Phaedrus*) by the pleasantness of the place to lie down in the grass and converse beside the little spring, why should we not be tempted to sit down here, by these gardens which Epicurus himself might praise?[4]

It was by his readings in the ancient authors that the young Erasmus was guided to this orchard; still, the pear tree likely came from his Holland rather than Plato's single reference to pears or young Augustine's theft of them,[5] and Erasmus' fondness of gardens, real as well as literary, lasted all his life.

To be sure, the pleasures afforded by an unspoiled countryside and by skilful horticulture were known north of the Alps and well before the Renaissance, but it still is in Renaissance Italy that they found emphatic expression in hitherto unknown manner;[6] witness Dante's description of the *Paradiso terrestre,* Petrarch's retreat in the wilderness of the Vaucluse, or Boccaccio's escape from the plague-stricken city to the *giardini meravigliosi* of a Florentine villa.[7] Reminiscences from classical and Renaissance authors join the memories of gardens Erasmus had visited in Italy and the daily experience of the gardens of Basel to help him lay out the most elaborate of his literary gardens in his colloquy *Convivium religiosum.* There are several gardens, among them an orchard with 'many exotic trees,' says the host, 'that I'm gradually training to accustom themselves to our climate.'[8] There is also an atrium garden that reminds one of the visitors to the garden of Epicurus, while later the luncheon seems to him 'Epicurean, nay Sybaritic.'[9]

According to Pliny the Elder, Epicurus' garden in Athens was the first one to be laid out inside a city.[10] Erasmus, in turn, enjoyed in Basel the walled gardens adjacent to the complex of dwellings and business premises of his printer and friend Johann Froben.[11] In particular he liked another garden at a short walk's distance that Froben had purchased on his advice in 1526. Weather permitting, he went there every afternoon to walk, read, and write letters.[12] After his move to Freiburg in 1529 he promptly had occasion to thank a new friend for liberal access to a fine garden. In return he sent a literary 'garden' of his own.[13] Earlier in the decade, when the Reformation controversy was heating up, he wrote disarmingly in a dedicatory preface:

> I would rather be a gardener, enjoying the tranquillity of a Christian and rejoicing in the simplicity of the gospel spirit, than the greatest of theologians three or four times over who must be involved in this kind of strife.[14]

When Erasmus in the *Antibarbari* paid his first furtive visit to the garden of Epicurus, he may not as yet have known Diogenes

Laertius, the major source on Epicurus then available,[15] but by 1500 he definitely knew Seneca's letters that he would later edit.[16] Thus he would likely remember a passage on the garden of Epicurus. The guests entering it, says Seneca, were greeted by an inscription. These are the words of welcome to Epicurus' garden: *Hospes, hic bene manebis, hic summum bonum voluptas est.* And the meal that awaits the guests is frugal indeed.[17]

EARLY TRACES OF AN ACQUAINTANCE WITH EPICURUS

Perhaps the earliest indications of Erasmus' acquaintance with Epicurean thought[18] are found in *De contemptu mundi epistula*, written, it seems, even earlier than the *Antibarbari* and published reluctantly in 1521, with a preface dismissing the piece as 'trifling' and composed 'for practice in writing,'[19] to wit, arguing for and also against, but mostly for, the desirability of a life spent in the monastery. Chapter XI is entitled 'The Pleasures of a Secluded Life.' In the view of some scholars it is the last chapter of the original composition; in any event it offers the crowning arguments in favour of the monastic way of life. 'Pleasure in monasteries?' the fictitious author, a young monk, raises the question. 'Yes,' he answers, 'we live wholly by the rule of Epicurus.'[20]

According to Erasmus' monk, 'Epicurus says that pleasures entailing troubles in uneven measure must be rejected.' For this reason the monks stay sober at all times and avoid immoral conduct as well as public office. 'Epicurus also teaches that one must sometimes undergo pain for the sake of avoiding greater pain, similarly, that one must always pass up some pleasures to obtain greater ones.'[21] Near the end of chapter XI Erasmus displays a sort of Eden with bright green meadows sprouting all sorts of flowers, with shady glades and various fruit trees, and with a crystal-clear stream. But here the delights of nature are simply a metaphor for the assorted joys the monk finds in his scriptural and patristic readings.[22]

When he emphasizes Epicurus' differentiating view of pleasure our monk is on solid ground, and his reference to monastic vigils, fasts, silences, and abstinence is well taken. But what are we to say when he goes on to discourse on the spiritual pleasures?

> First of all, the pleasure of being free from that horrible pain caused by a bad conscience (*sordida conscientia*). According to Epicurus (and let us not abandon him), this is the greatest

pleasure, for he who is free of pain feels no small pleasure. Secondly, is it not pleasurable to contemplate the heavenly, the eternal delights that we hope to enjoy, God willing? ... Can anyone be so dejected, brought so low by mental anguish, that he will not be elated, exhilarated, and eager to leave his mean body behind when he thinks of that life in heaven? ... Although moments of such delight are rare (as St Bernard says) and usually of brief duration, they are nevertheless so intense as to make all pleasures of the world combined into one seem mean and despicable by comparison.[23]

Clearly, Epicurus has no truck with St Bernard's rare moments of religious ecstasy, nor did he, or for that matter Plato or Aristotle, know of any equivalents to the Christian notions of *peccatum* (sin) and *conscientia*.[24] Epicurus' tranquillity of mind bears little resemblance to the relief of a bad conscience that the Christian obtains through the sacrament of penance. Even to mention Epicurus in the context of the monk's argument amounts to perversion. In his preface Erasmus claims that *De contemptu mundi* was written *alieno stomacho*, ignoring his own view on the matter. The least we can deduce from this is that what he had written thirty years earlier by 1521 no longer corresponded with his opinion. This is true of his overwhelmingly favourable judgment of the advantages of monastic life;[25] we shall see later that it is also true of his assessment of Epicureanism.

How much then did Erasmus know about the 'rule of Epicurus' by the time he wrote *De contemptu mundi*? He was familiar with Seneca's moral letters and essays, such as *De beneficiis*; he also knew Cicero's *De finibus* and *De divinatione*, and probably his *Academica*.[26] These sources would allow him to form the correct assessment of Epicurus' moral philosophy that we have found in *De contemptu mundi*. Here he could learn that the pleasure that constituted the supreme good for Epicurus was really absence of pain and tranquillity of mind. But here he was also bound to encounter Epicurus' notions of the finality of human existence and of gods that were indifferent to human affairs, that should be worshipped but not feared, in other words, a denial of divine providence. *De finibus* would also permit a first glance at Epicurus' atomic physics – a subject for which Erasmus would never show much interest. On the other hand, he knew Cicero's *De officiis* and there was bound to find a demeaning assessment of Epicurus' advocacy of pleasure-seeking. Such a blithe approach to Epicureanism was reinforced by Erasmus' familiarity with Horace, who cheerfully called himself a pig from Epicurus' herd.[27] In his convent years Erasmus had had ample opportunity to read the Christian fathers. In Jerome's letters and polemical pieces like *In Rufinum* he would find an Epicurus who commendably urged frugality, but condoned a sordid gratification of the senses and denied providence. Lactantius would endorse such an understanding of Epicurus, and in Augustine's *Confessiones* Erasmus must have read that great doctor's famous admission: 'Debating with my friends Alypius and Nebridius the question of the supreme good and the greatest evil, I would in my mind give the palm to Epicurus, if he had not refused to believe in the soul's life after death and the efficacy of merit, whereas I do believe in them.'[28]

In his preface to *De contemptu mundi* Erasmus also claims that he had as yet 'no equipment of solid reading' when he wrote the piece. This may be true of Greek philosophy in general. With regard to Epicurus' system, nothing Erasmus had written by 1500, so far as we can tell, betrays any knowledge of the principal sources: Diogenes Laertius,[29] Lucretius, or even Cicero's *De natura deorum*. On the other hand, he was at that time familiar with the letters of Francesco Filelfo and Leonardo Bruni,[30] some of which were well suited to provide him with an early glimpse at the philosophical inquiries conducted by Italian humanists and, in particular, a fairly sympathetic revision of the medieval view of Epicurus.[31] Yet in what we know of Erasmus' early writings the impact is minimal. Despite its limitations, the approach of *De contemptu mundi* is more enlightened than that of the *Antibarbari*, where one of Erasmus' speakers equated 'the Epicurean way of life' with 'taking incredible care to escape work, embracing sloth and a sheltered life,' and another quoted Jerome's imprecation of authors 'who with Epicurus had never learnt letters.'[32] But his endorsement of a Christian Epicureanism still is exceedingly awkward. It deliberately ignored Epicurus' denial of an immortal soul and of providence. Erasmus later did acquire his 'equipment of solid reading' in Greek philosophy, but that did not happen until his Italian years.

But what about Platonism? Did not Erasmus owe a considerable debt to Ficino, Pico, and the Platonism of Renaissance Italy in general? And did he not accumulate that debt in Paris, Oxford, and London years before he would set foot on Italian soil? Ficino, in particular, was well known to his friends at that time.[33] If Erasmus too read him, could he have failed to notice Ficino's evident liking for Lucretius?[34] Scholarly opinion on the significance of these influences is divided;[35] Erasmus himself, as far as we can tell, is almost silent.[36] What we do know is that his visits to England led to a thorough acquaintance with Lucian, as Erasmus and More vied with each other translating Lucianic dialogues and More ventured to christianize Lucian,[37] much as Erasmus had christianized Epicurus. Lucian knew all about the Greek schools of philosophy, but rather than imparting solid knowledge of the various systems, he was for the most part content to poke fun at philosophers of every stamp. On occasion, however, he expressed passionate agreement with a specific teaching or attitude. His *Alexander or the False Prophet*, which Erasmus translated, presents Epicureanism as society's prime bulwark against religious fraud and gullible fanaticism.[38] In translating Lucian, Erasmus may have picked up snippets of Greek philosophical thought, but would probably feel discouraged from studying it seriously. Not until he was in Italy did he become familiar with the Greek philosophers and the efforts undertaken by Italian humanists who had translated and edited the Greek texts and taken up their themes. And here, we may assume, he became properly acquainted with that Epicurean revival that, when fully investigated, according to Walter Kaiser, 'should reveal one of the great subversive movements in the history of ideas.'[39]

ERASMUS IN ITALY

Erasmus spent nearly three years in Italy, arriving in September 1506 and departing in July 1509. His correspondence during these years, such as it has been preserved,[40] is very meagre and not particularly significant. In November 1506, when he was in Bologna and the papal troops were attacking the city, he had reason to be gloomy:

> I came to Italy mainly in order to learn Greek; but studies are dormant here at present, whereas war is hotly pursued, so I shall look for ways of hastening my return.[41]

Perhaps unduly tilted by such statements, the balance of scholarly verdict on Erasmus' stay in Italy is negative. One author noted early 'signs of disillusion' and concluded that 'Erasmus had not enjoyed his stay.'[42] But how can anyone who likes gardens not enjoy Italy?

At the time of Erasmus' visit 'l'Italie restait le pays de la vie joyeuse.' Moreover, 'l'esprit italien avait depuis plusieurs siècles acquis une maturité qui pouvait assurer le développement et la vigueur d'une incroyance résolue et systématique.'[43] Augustin Renaudet, who wrote these lines reminiscent of Jacob Burckhardt, was quite aware of the danger of generalizations and assiduous in noting aspects of Italian life that pointed in other directions. It still needs to be maintained that Erasmus encountered in Italy a measure of intellectual and moral freedom and experimentation that did not exist in London, Paris, and Louvain. North of the Alps there were no Borgias and no Machiavellis. We should also remember the extravagances in Italian religious thought and practice that were soon to cause alarm at the Fifth Lateran Council – a fermentation that would continue for a century before it succumbed to resolute suppression.[44] Erasmus himself recalled in later life sarcastically how Italian preachers had tried to enlist Aristotle among the defenders of an immortal human soul.[45] Whatever the balance of unhappy and happy hours Erasmus spent in Italy, I think we can say that the experience emboldened him to write the *Moriae encomium* and the *Julius exclusus*.

When Erasmus arrived, the leading lights of humanistic and philosophical thought that had shone upon fifteenth-century Italy were gone. Philosophical pursuits, with the possible exception of Padoan Averroism, had become the turf of epigones. Erasmus' visits to the university cities of Turin, Padua, Ferrara, and Siena, also to Florence, were short. At Bologna, where he stayed for a year, unenthusiastically supervising the sons of an English court physician who attended the university there, philology outshone philosophy and Erasmus, anyhow, concentrated on the preparation of his *Adagia*.[46] His experiences in Rome gave rise to many critical echoes scattered through his writings from the *Moria* to the *Ciceronianus*. Nonetheless, Rome had also its attractions. For a long time he remembered the congenial kindness with which great dignitaries like Cardinal Domenico Grimani had received him and the preferment he was promised if he were willing to stay.[47] Through many years he expressed a wish to return to the Roman libraries and even to die in the Eternal City, and sometimes that wish was sincere.[48] The ten months Erasmus spent in Venice were enormously significant[49] because of his association with the publishing house of Aldus Manutius, which launched in September 1508 the second edition of the *Adagia*. In comparison to the slim volume of 1500, the text had been increased fourfold. Erasmus' knowledge of classical literature, especially of the Greek authors, had grown to a breadth that very few contemporaries could match. This is how he described his experience in a section added to a later edition of the *Adagia*:

> When I, a Dutchman, was in Italy, preparing to publish my books of *Proverbs*, all the learned men there had offered me unsought authors not yet published in print who they thought might be of use to me and Aldus had nothing in his treasure-house that he did not share with me ... I was bringing nothing to Venice with me except the confused and unsorted materials for a book that was to be, and that material was confined to published authors. With the greatest temerity on my part, we both set to work together, I to write and Aldus to print.[50]

Many Greek authors, among them some on whose Aldine editions Erasmus must have collaborated, are frequently quoted in the Venice *Adagia*, and so is now Diogenes Laertius. In addition to Ambrogio Traversari's Latin translation Erasmus used a Greek manuscript – apparently his own, for it still served him many years later for the revised *Adagia* of March 1533[51] – just before Froben's editio princeps of the Greek Diogenes Laertius became available. Thanks to Traversari's Latin translation, awareness of Diogenes' *Lives* had intensified substantially during the second quarter of the fifteenth century, at least in Italian humanist circles. As a result of this Diogenes renaissance, acquaintance with Epicurus' thought and the study of Greek philosophy in general gained a new dimension. Works like Cicero's *De natura deorum* and *De finibus* that were more readily available came also to be studied with renewed interest, but while Cicero's dialogues provided – inevitably biased – information on the principal tenets of the various schools, their conflicts and convergences, they offered no trace of a historical framework. Diogenes, by contrast, created history by discussing the different schools, and particularly the members of each school in chronological order. It cannot be said of him that he wrote a history of philosophical ideas, but he facilitated and encouraged such an approach. It can be argued, and it was, that the history of philosophy began with the quattrocento humanists.[52] Valiant attempts were made to pin down what separated the ancient Epicureans from the Stoics, Sceptics, and Cynics, who all in one way or another seemed to advance similar concepts. It is safe to assume that echoes of these debates still reverberated when Erasmus was in Italy. Unfortunately we know nothing about the conversations he had with contemporary Italian scholars and not a great deal more about his readings in the works of their great predecessors.

Epicurus' greatest admirer among the Romans and the faithful interpreter of his teachings in Latin verse was Lucretius. He had been rediscovered by Poggio Bracciolini[53] in 1417, that is to say roughly a decade before Diogenes Laertius began to be read more widely. Both together generated a good deal of interest in the Epicurean tradition. In the ensuing debate enthusiastic advocacy of Epicurus' teachings was a rare exception, but the standard medieval denigrations were laid to rest. The Epicurus of Italian humanism was no longer the despicable promoter of filth and glut. His denial of providence and immortality no longer prevented a certain measure of sympathy. Sober, serious, and modest, he relied on human reason to reject greed, fear, superstition, and seemingly heroic asceticism. The pleasure that he claimed was the highest good, while never quite detached from physical sensation, was ultimately serene tranquillity of mind. His atomism and his doctrine of an infinite universe were noted with interest rather than shock and horror. It is again in the Venice *Adagia* that we find Erasmus' earliest references to Lucretius. He also refers to Lucretius in *De pueris statim ac liberaliter instituendis* (1529), which he says was written during his stay in Italy.[54] From another Greek source found in Venice and used for the *Adagia* Erasmus translated a saying by the Epicurean Metrodorus of Lampsacus that ended with the cheerful assertion that 'life is good every way.'[55]

LORENZO VALLA'S APPROACH TO EPICUREANISM AND ERASMUS

His years in Italy led Erasmus to produce two works of lasting importance. The *Adagia* in the Aldus edition became a showcase of 'Herculean' scholarly engagement and erudition.[56] The other great testimony to Erasmus' Italian experience is the *Moriae encomium (Praise of Folly)*. It needs to be closely examined here because it exhibits a profound change in his perception of the Epicurean tradition. To find the right key for our approach to *Moria*, we must, however, first investigate Erasmus' debt to

Lorenzo Valla, the Italian humanist who has influenced him the most. Valla frequently stands apart from his contemporaries among the Italian humanists and is unmatched in the – often wilful – originality of his purpose. All he ever wrote became almost immediately a subject of controversy. There can be no doubt of Erasmus' abiding interest in Valla. As early as about 1488, when he was a monk at Steyn, he paraphrased Valla's *Elegantiae* for the benefit of a friend,[57] and in Paris he borrowed Robert Gaguin's copy of Valla's *Dialecticae disquisitiones*.[58] In 1504 he found a manuscript of Valla's *Adnotationes* on the New Testament and published them the following spring in Paris with a spirited introductory letter that both notes and defends Valla's 'temerity.'[59] A great many references scattered through Erasmus' writings suggest that he always had the *Elegantiae* as well as the New Testament notes close at hand. Annotating the New Testament also created a strong bond between Erasmus and his predecessor Valla in that conservative theologians who rejected their approach were eager to anathematize them both in one breath. Valla was responsible for such novel 'heresies' as claiming that the Apostles' Creed did not date back to the apostles and that Seneca's correspondence with Paul was spurious.[60] On both these issues Erasmus was to side with Valla. In his controversy with Luther he was aware of Valla's superficial affinity with Luther's position, but also of his efforts to reconcile free will with God's foreknowledge.[61] He also referred or alluded to Valla's vicious controversy with Poggio and his attacks on legal authorities. Obvious echoes of Valla's *De falso credita Constantini donatione* can be found in Erasmus' *Moria* as well as in the *Julius exclusus*.

By contrast, in so far as we know Erasmus never referred or alluded to *De voluptate*, Valla's first major work and by far the most interesting treatment of Epicurean ethics to originate in the quattrocento. Originally written in 1431 and attacked without delay, the work went through more than a decade of revisions, in the course of which the title was changed to *De vero bono*.[62] Although we have no references to Valla's treatise, in the course of his movements Erasmus came intriguingly close to some men who played leading parts in its dissemination. In December 1484 Alexander Hegius, the master of the Deventer school that Erasmus had just left, wrote to his friend Rodolphus Agricola: 'I have been reading Valla's book on the True Good, and have become quite an Epicurean.'[63] In 1503 one Pietro Marino Aleandro obtained a manuscript of *De voluptate* and wrote about it excitedly. He attempted to have it published, but apparently did not succeed. Pietro was a second cousin to Girolamo Aleandro and evidently well known to the latter. Both were attached to Cardinal Domenico Grimani, one of Erasmus' great patrons in Rome.[64] In Venice Girolamo Aleandro was, like Erasmus, a member of Aldus' team of scholarly editors. For much of 1508 the two shared room and board, and indeed the same bed,[65] in the house of Aldus' father-in-law, Andrea Torresani. They were obviously on the best of terms and shared many likes and dislikes. When Aleandro left for Paris towards the end of that year Erasmus recommended him warmly to his friends there. In 1521, when their relation had turned into a bitter animosity, Erasmus recalled those days: 'I respected his scholarship and found his character congenial, though he is not like other people; and the two of us seemed by nature to get on very well.'[66] A letter by Aleandro of 1512 clearly shows that by then his affection for Erasmus, their sense of congeniality, and their habit of sharing jokes were still intact. The following passage must surely echo the banter and philosopher-bashing in which they had indulged in Venice:

> If you look in my treasury you will find there only spiders' webs. You are, it will be said, a philosopher, and it is not really becoming for you to bother about such things. Indeed I admit to being a philosopher and a Christian, and hence a mortal man, subject to anxieties and illness, to age and death; and if you lack money for such contingencies as these, literature will bring you no succour save a vain and arrogant faith, like that of the Stoics; to whom I myself, in agreement with the judgment of the ages, greatly prefer Aristotle, who held that riches should be sought before philosophy, though that rascal, your friend Lucian, has most maliciously dubbed this great man 'the most cunning of flatterers' – out of spite, I suppose, because he failed to achieve success like Aristotle's, while he himself was both flatterer and prattler.[67]

Two or so weeks after Aleandro had written this letter from Paris, the humanist printer Josse Bade dated the preface of his edition of Valla's *De voluptate*, and again we are tantalizingly close to matters that concerned Erasmus directly. Bade was one of his chief publishers; no fewer than forty-three of his productions included works written by Erasmus. It was Bade who in 1505 had published Erasmus' edition of Valla's notes to the New Testament, and in 1512, four months after *De voluptate,* he produced the second edition of *Moria.*[68] Aleandro too had much contact with Bade, who dedicated to him in 1514 an edition of Plutarch's *Parallel Lives*. Bade's edition of *De voluptate* cannot, of course, have influenced *Moria,* which was composed three years earlier. But Erasmus himself had been in Paris in the summer of 1511, and only he can have been responsible for the rather thorough revision of *Moria* for Bade's edition.[69] Whatever Erasmus, or Aleandro, may or may not have had to do with Bade's publication of *De voluptate* and *Moria* at such close intervals, no one who has compared the two books can, I think, question that their conjunction in Bade's publishing program was timely and appropriate.

Let us retain three points. First, even before Erasmus in 1509 composed his *Moria* he was keenly interested in anything Valla had written. Second, less than a year before he conceived the plan for *Moria,* in which the Epicurean notion of pleasure plays a conspicuous role, Erasmus had been in constant and congenial contact with Aleandro, in whose circle *De voluptate* was greatly appreciated. Third, Aleandro and Erasmus collaborated with Bade, and before the latter published *De voluptate* and *Moria* both were in Paris, albeit at different times. These factors, taken together, make it difficult to assume that Erasmus never set eyes on *De voluptate*. If he did in fact know it, quite possibly he may also have known other quattrocento treatments of Epicureanism, although again no reference to them is found in his writings. Even without a concrete proof for Erasmus' knowledge of *De voluptate,*[70] comparing it to the *Moria* will greatly help us to understand the latter and Erasmus' new appreciation of Epicurean thought.

An alternative title for *De voluptate* was *De vero bono.* Valla's book deals with the theme of the supreme good – a theme that was extensively debated in antiquity and also vigorously taken up in fifteenth-century Italy. Valla chose to present his argument in the form of a conversation, in which three of his personal friends are presented as advocates for Stoicism, Epicureanism, and Christianity, respectively.[71] The venerable Leonardo Bruni, who speaks for the Stoics, had in fact offered models for this form of philosophical dialogue in his *Dialogi ad Petrum Histrum* (1401–5) and *Isagogicon moralis disciplinae* (1421–4). The principal formal model for both Bruni and Valla, however, was Cicero's *De finibus bonorum et malorum*. Cicero, and also Seneca and Lactantius, were likewise Valla's sources on Epicurean doctrine. Lucretius is cited twice;[72] a direct influence of Diogenes Laertius is not discernable.

We need not examine here how serious and how intentional the distortions were to which Valla subjected both Stoic and Epicurean doctrines. At times he made a sport of professing the contrary of what he had found in Cicero, especially when the latter criticized Epicurean positions.[73] We cannot, however, altogether avoid the thorny question of how Valla's own beliefs corresponded with the pious elaborations of the spokesman for Christianity, who wins the contest. *De voluptate* is also an exercise in rhetoric, and we must always be prepared to find Valla stating the opposite of what he thinks, even when he speaks for himself rather than through the mouths of his dialogists. In his proem to the first book he rails sanctimoniously against those who say that virtuous pagans, both ancient and contemporary, should not automatically be consigned to hell. 'Paganism,' exclaims the author of the *Elegantiae*, that paean on Rome and Latinity, 'has done nothing virtuously (*cum virtute*), nothing rightly.'[74] In Book III, when the advocate of Christianity orates his way to victory, his panegyric on the joys of paradise is suspiciously close to irony and even cynicism. Or how else can we appreciate such flowers as: 'the body and blood of our Lord and King, Jesus Christ, will be ministered to us, even from his very hands, in that most honorable, celebrated, and in truth Godly banquet.' Or again, the Virgin Mary 'will clasp you to her virginal breast, on which she suckled God; and she will kiss you (*libabitque oscula*).'[75] No wonder that the Epicurean advocate of soul mortality mocks that 'Elysium' as 'a place of great happiness, filled with sports, dances, music, banquets and other amusements.' Although these words are directed to his Stoic opponent, the reader cannot fail to see that Christianity too is targeted. If there were Elysian Fields either in the nether world or the world above, they would have to be an abode of pleasure; however, 'as it is plain that there are no rewards for the dead, certainly there are no punishments either.'[76] Can we go wrong when we count Valla among those Italians of whom Burckhardt said: 'It is probable that most of them wavered inwardly between incredulity and a remnant of the faith in which they were brought up, and outwardly held for prudential reasons to the Church?'[77] Valla's religion, fideistic and cynical at the same time, is, I submit, very much part of that culture of alterity that

Erasmus came to experience in Italy, and so is the Epicureanism of Valla's *De voluptate* that Erasmus came to rival in his *Moria*.

Valla's spokesman for Christianity concurs in some points with the Stoic and finds the Epicurean's speech 'more adapted to the perversion of souls.'[78] In fact, the Epicurean is blunt in asserting the indifference of the gods and denying human immortality. Not only are there no souls after death, there are obviously no bodies either; so we had better cling to bodily pleasures while we have our bodies.[79] On balance, however, the Epicurean's views are treated as the lesser evil by the Christian. He says: 'although I disapprove of both sides, I make my decision in favor of the Epicureans.'[80] Valla is unambiguous about one point: 'all three of these books' he says in his introductory remarks 'aim to destroy the race of the Stoics.' And he adds:

> In Books I and II ... I have interspersed gayer and almost (I would say) licentious material, for which no one will blame me if he considers the character of the matter ... What would be further from defending the cause of pleasure than a sad, severe style and the behavior of a Stoic when I am taking the part of the Epicureans?[81]

Indeed, a heavy scent of rhetorical sensuality is unmistakable throughout Books I and II. The Epicurean rails against chastity and the cult of virginity, which deprives women of a free choice. He finds adultery natural and rape preferable to debilitating restraint. Lucretia, an experienced woman, would have enjoyed her rape but for the fear of public exposure.[82] Even the Christian speaker of Book III agrees that the strongest human passion is that for sex, but not until you have reached heaven is there love without betrayal and jealousy, and the beauty of women pales at the thought of the majestic beauty of angels.[83] Women, says the Epicurean, are best, but the pleasures of wine and music too are not to be detested, as the Stoics do it. Abstinence and deprivation, as opposed to Epicurus' own frugality, are by no means the only Stoic virtues that come under fire. In Book II the Epicurean takes aim at the central Stoic principle that virtue (*honestas*) is the supreme good and its own reward. This is how he has a Stoic general harangue his soldiers:

> Leap into the struggle quickly, comrades; fight bravely! There won't be any pay for you after your victory ... Your very wounds and deaths will be your highest reward.[84]

Not always, however, is the Epicurean content with scoring such easy points. Where the anthropological and political ideals of civic humanism are involved, Valla, despite his constant capers and paradoxes, speaks in earnest. The Epicurean, often supported by his Stoic opponent with a set of self-defeating arguments, has an endearing antidote for the taste of virtue, which, the Stoic admits, may be 'harsh, sour and bitter.'[85] From beginning to end his argumentation is accentuated by smiles, mirth, and laughter – laughter, the gift of Nature, that to the Epicurean is a unique blessing and to the Stoic a compulsive expression of sarcasm and contempt.[86] It is indeed when the debate turns to the crucial issue of Nature that the Epicurean's winning ways are particularly noticeable. To Valla's Stoic spokesman Nature is 'cruel,' a 'stepmother,' not a 'mother.' She is responsible for human vices, indeed for a surfeit of vices in the human existence. She makes 'monsters' of us. The only escape is divorce; Nature's vicious gifts, the passions, must be 'rooted out of us completely.'[87] The Epicurean, by contrast, finds that to value the human condition properly, one must understand Nature, its first cause. Her 'multitude of goods' range from 'the goods of the body,' such as 'health, which cannot be separated from charm and beauty,' to 'serenity of mind.' Valla's Epicurean shows himself worthy of the tradition of Lucretius and Virgil, as he talks of the rich variety of enjoyments Nature offers to us. There are the seas, the mountains, the fields, the clouds, the animals and plants to be admired:

> Thus this variety will yield pleasure, as happens with the alternation of days and nights, of clear and cloudy skies, of summer and winter. At one time, we shall eagerly seek the crowd of the city, at another, the freedom and solitude of country villages; at one time we shall be pleased to go on horseback, at another to go on foot, at yet another by boat, at yet another by carriage. We shall give up dice for a game of ball, the game of ball for singing, the singing for dancing.[88]

If these joys are rather vulgar, so be it. While the Stoics 'choose a solitary, sad life' of heroic *apatheia* and isolation that leaves them as if being 'made of marble,'[89] the Epicurean believes that 'fellowship and equality among men constitute the mother of goodwill and peace.'[90] 'We should not, in fact, fight against the crowd, as the

Stoics do, but go along with it, as with a rapid river.'[91] Pleasure, the goal of the Epicureans, can be understood and shared by all, although animals and children have to be content with its lower forms. 'The common people – that is peasants and that sort of men' do count; 'the great multitude,' which to the Stoic is 'the ignorant multitude,' are all born Epicureans.[92] Says the Stoic: 'We must then completely reject the life of peasants unless, God help us, we want to be Epicureans.'[93] Farmer, fool, Epicurean – to the Stoic it is all the same.

Epicurus himself wanted to leave a message for all men and all seasons. To Valla it is a message of common sense and joyous vitality; it sets men free. By contrast, the Stoics and kindred philosophical sects such as the Cynics[94] are elitist and inflexible; they are also hypocrites in that they know that they are asking for the impossible – they want to be gods and end up as Pharisees.[95] Their philosophy, ultimately all philosophy, is sickness, even madness. Epicureanism, by contrast, is more than a philosophy – it is a healthy, happy way of life.

THE *MORIAE ENCOMIUM* AND VALLA'S *DE VOLUPTATE*

Erasmus wrote the *Moriae encomium* in the London home of Thomas More immediately after his return from Italy, but it was conceived while he travelled to England by way of the Netherlands and whiled away the long days on horseback, recalling, he says, his English friends and their learned conversations.[96] We can be sure, I think, that when the *Moriae encomium* took shape in his mind, his thoughts not only travelled forward to England but also back to Italy, to the Italian rediscovery of Epicurus and, probably, to Valla's *De voluptate*. Moria, the person, is a literary creation of genius. She speaks gaily; she speaks philosophically; she speaks in righteous anger; and she preaches devoutly. Usually her points are complementary, not contradictory like those of Valla's speakers. Whatever she says, she means it. Hence we are far less prompted to ask ourselves whether she speaks for Erasmus; she mostly does. As complex as Erasmus himself, she too is always unmistakably herself, always Moria.

As in Valla's treatise, Moria's references to the Stoics and their teachings are persistently uncomplimentary. Here is the first one:

> And the Stoics, as we know, claim to be most like the gods. But give me a man who is a Stoic three or four or if you like

six hundred times over, and he too, even if he keeps his beard as a mark of wisdom, though he shares it with the goat, will have to swallow his pride, smooth out his frown, shake off his rigid principles, and be fond and foolish for a while.[97]

God-likeness and the goat's beard are commonplaces; they can also be found in Valla,[98] and so can the charges of elitism and hypocrisy, which Moria repeats, combining them in a new twist:

> Even the Stoics don't despise pleasure, though they are careful to conceal their real feelings, and tear it to pieces in public with their incessant outcry, so that once they have frightened everyone else off they can enjoy it more freely themselves.[99]

And so it goes on. The Stoics seek shelter behind 'reason's solitary power'; but reason herself fails to gain a foothold in 'the common life of man,' although 'she shouts herself hoarse, repeating formulas of virtue.' Friendship is greatly esteemed by most philosophical sects, but when the 'Stoic philosopher-gods' practise it, it becomes a 'sour and ungracious kind of relationship.'[100] 'Some wise man dropped from heaven' dishes out some paradoxical maxims of clearly Stoic inspiration: man is inferior to the animals, because he might become a slave to his passions; the death of a beloved one is not to be grieved since death cannot be more miserable than is life; a nobleman who lacks 'virtue, which is the sole source of nobility,' deserves to be called a bastard. What makes these maxims so wrong-headed is that in their 'misplaced sense' they ignore common sense experience.[101] Passions are human, but the Stoics shun them 'as if they were diseases, ... that double-dyed Stoic Seneca ... strips his wise man of every emotion,' creating 'a kind of marble statue of a man' (Valla had used the same expression) who in the end might take his own life to escape from his misery. Predictably, Moria echoes Valla's Epicurean in demeaning the heroic suicides of Roman antiquity.[102]

For Erasmus as for Valla Epicureanism is the common-sense philosophy for common people, whereas the Stoics represent the would-be-wise with their lofty contempt for the 'ignorant' multitude. Both quote the same Stoic rule that 'whosoever is not wise, is a fool,'[103] and deduce from it that since nobody is really wise, we all are fools. Moria likes to single out the Stoics, but she makes it clear that their sickly aloofness from real life is shared by all philosophers. And among all philosophers, none resemble the 'Stoic frogs' more than the scholastics of the Middle Ages (and again Valla's Epicurean nods agreement).[104] Scholastics and Stoics rival each other's passion for the silliest syllogisms and other forms of nonsensical reasoning. Moria indulges herself in citing examples of both Stoic and scholastic vintage. She presents scholastic maxims 'which are so paradoxical that in comparison the pronouncements of the Stoics, which were actually known as paradoxes, seem positively commonplace and banal.'[105] In thus presenting the common man's case against the would-be wise, Moria's final witness is Christ:

> There are also some relevant passages in the Gospel where Christ attacks Pharisees and scribes and teachers of the Law while giving his unfailing protection to the ignorant multitude. What else can 'Woe unto you, Scribes and Pharisees' mean but 'Woe unto you who are wise?'[106]

When Moria approaches the mental playgrounds of the Epicureans, she abandons the directness that marked her many references to the Stoics. To delimit, as it were, the parameter of the section that is relevant to our investigation, she mentions, near the beginning, Lucretius and alludes to his wonderful invocation of Venus at the onset of *De rerum natura*. Soon afterwards she borrows Horace's crack at himself as a pig from the herd of Epicurus, and she borrows it again when she turns to her final argument. Epicurus' herd is also Moria's: her 'morons, ... plump, sleek and glossy,' are so totally unlike 'those soured individuals who are so wrapped up in their philosophic studies or some other serious, exacting affairs that they are old before they were ever young.'[107] Taken together, these references to Lucretius and Horace point to an Epicureanism more marked by licence than by abstinence, but Lucretius' poem also exudes a confidence that the essence of humanity is a pure, natural quest for pleasure, although, sadly, that quest can be perverted to produce unnatural greed and uncontrolled passion.[108] Lucretius encouraged a new order of priorities, subtle perhaps but pervasive. For humanists who had taken him to heart, human nature was above all natural. To present it as a receptacle of divine grace and satanic corruption might be sublime, but it was secondary.

Moria may not name the Epicureans, but she never stops mentioning the central notion of their system. 'Pleasure (*voluptas*)' and especially 'happiness (*felicitas*)' and similar terms return incessantly throughout her speech, as she examines the state of society in the various walks of life. Pleasure and happiness, Moria's very own gifts, are everywhere the goal of human existence. Everybody seeks them, with the sole exception of those committed to the souring quest for wisdom:

> Those who strive after wisdom are the furthest from happiness; they are in fact doubly stupid simply because they ignore the fact that they were born men, try to adopt the life of immortal gods, and like the giants, would rebel against Nature.[109]

Disregard of the common human condition equals rebellion against Nature herself. Moria judges human activity in terms of compatibility with, or hostility to, Nature. She herself is so natural that she *is* Nature. And Nature, to Erasmus as to Valla, is the motherly and serene Nature of Lucretius and Virgil rather than the blind Nature that Cicero attributed to Epicurus. Before Nature all humans are equal.[110] Seemingly oblivious of the Christian Creator, Moria calls her *natura parens et humani generis opifex*. In doing so, she happily echoes Lucretius' *natura creatrix*, and like him, she has primeval humankind in what she calls the Golden Age live entirely under the guidance of Nature. So do also the bees, 'the happiest and most marvellous of insects,' and simpletons, who 'have no fear of death.'[111] Much later Erasmus once confessed that originally it was his intention after writing the *Praise of Folly* to follow up with a 'Praise of Nature' and a 'Praise of Grace.'[112] Seeing the prominence of Nature throughout the *Moriae encomium* and of Grace in its last section, one understands that this scheme was never carried out. Also, seeing the prominence of Nature throughout the *Moriae encomium*, the mysterious dating of its prefatory letter 'from the country (*ex rure*)' may gain some meaning.

Like Epicurus, Moria is concerned mostly with *human* nature. Throughout her speech one is reminded of Epicurus' tenet that Nature, acting through sensations and not through reasoning, establishes the norm of truth.[113] She is the source of our instincts, emotions, passions, but the passions and pleasures that she calls forth are not all the same. Moria here follows the lead of Epicurus and Lucretius;[114] she distinguishes between two categories of pleasure. Some are wholesome and innocent, or almost so, while others, fired by greed and craft, are pernicious. About these latter Moria has a good deal to say, but mostly what she says about the harmless pleasures is, it seems to me, of great originality. Is it because Erasmus is steeped in the Christian tradition that even innocent pleasures look so foolish? 'What is there about babies which makes us hug and kiss and fondle them ...? Surely it's the charm of folly, which thoughtful Nature has taken care to bestow upon the newly born.'[115] And so Moria goes on describing the little follies of everyday life, such as that of the father who 'talks about the wink in his son's squinting eye.'[116] Humans, after all, are only human; they are vulnerable, fragile, imperfect, and just because of their imperfection authentic and lovable.

> And so he [Cupid] sees to it that each one of you finds beauty in what he has, and the old man loves his old woman as the boy loves his girl. This happens everywhere and meets with smiles, but nevertheless it's the sort of absurdity which is the binding force in society and brings happiness to life ... It's a true sign of prudence ... to be willing to overlook things along with the rest of the world or to wear your illusions with a good grace.[117]

Here we must mention *Philautía* (Self-love), whom Moria calls her sister.[118] She is present throughout Erasmus' piece and may well be his most original creation. Although the *phílautoi* and *philautía* are the subject of an adage (I ii 92), the terms seem far from common in antiquity. The ancient philosophers seem to have used them rarely. It is true that Valla's Epicurean in a lengthy argument opposes self-preservation to the Stoic virtue of *fortitudo*. Who would ever die for another? he asks.

> I ought to save myself sooner than even a hundred thousand people ... what more perverse idea can be expressed or imagined than that someone should be dearer to you than you yourself (*aliquem tibi esse te ipso cariorem*)?[119]

Thus, any form of altruism would be madness. Now, in the *Moriae encomium* Philautia is substantially different from this sort of brutal, egotistic self-preservation. Asks Moria: 'Can he who hates himself love anyone else (*quemquam amabit qui ipse semet oderit*)?'[120] Her sister Philautia is never entirely innocent, but she is always foolish. She may be calculating, but her actions to the reader, if not to the actor, are always shown to be miscalculated. The *phílautoi* delude only themselves; more often than not the rest of us can smile about their antics.

Moria is an Epicurean of sorts, but she is not a full-fledged Epicurean. Although on occasion she does present the gods as mere spectators of the human scene – 'It's hardly believable how much laughter, sport, and fun you poor mortals can provide the gods every day'[121] – Moria, unlike Valla's Epicurean, believes in providence and human accountability. Hence the long sections of her speech devoted to a harsh critique of actions of selfish folly in all walks of life – self-indulgence that is inexcusable because it does harm to others. Having free access to Erasmus' memories of his stay in Rome, she comments sarcastically on the princes of the church who are far from living up to the challenge of their exalted offices. Of the Roman pontiffs she says:

> All they have left are the weapons and fine-sounding benedictions to which Paul refers (and these they certainly scatter around with a lavish hand) along with interdicts, suspensions, repeated excommunications and anathemas, painted scenes of judgment,[122] and that dreaded thunderbolt whereby at a mere nod they can dispatch the souls of mortal men to deepest Tartarus.[123]

Moria's mercilessly transparent exposure of Julius II contradicts Erasmus' subsequent claims that he had refrained from naming any of his targets: 'my intention was to give pleasure, not pain.'[124] Speaking in a lighter mood, she finds the theologians a 'perfectly happy' lot. Echoing Valla's Epicurean, she says of them:

> They are happy too while they're depicting everything in hell down to the last detail, as if they'd spent several years there, or giving free rein to their fancy in fabricating new spheres [of heaven] and adding the most extensive and beautiful of all in case the blessed spirits lack space to take a walk in comfort or give a dinner-party or even play a game of ball.[125]

While this does not make her an agnostic, Mistress Moria obviously does not encourage excessive preoccupation with the paraphernalia of heavenly beatitude and, especially, the dreaded torments of hell, and in that respect she is a worthy disciple of Epicurus.

As she advances to the last section of her speech (which Erasmus greatly expanded after the first edition), Moria has undergone a change of heart. She has done with jesting. In the place of her Epicurean credentials she now presents her Platonic, on occasion even Stoic,[126] and above all Christian ones.[127] Most definitely she does not repeat the facile line of argument of the young Erasmus who in *De contemptu mundi* claimed that Epicureanism was germane to Christianity.

This last section, amid a final round of classical allusions, is introduced by Moria's second reference to Horace's 'plump, sleek porker from Epicurus' herd.' Thereafter, Moria quotes almost exclusively from the Bible. Some other shifts in her approach are equally significant. For one thing, folly ceases to be presented as the common lot of all mankind; 'true folly' now becomes the exclusive privilege of saintliness. As she begins to shift, Moria still is moved to compliment the author of Ecclesiastes: 'Now don't you think it indicative of exceptional honesty to think that every man is equal?' She still insists that 'all mortals are fools, even the pious' and finds proof for the folly of the Christian religion in

> the fact that the very young and the very old, women and simpletons are the people who take the greatest delight in sacred and holy things, and are therefore always found nearest the altars, led there doubtless solely by their natural instinct.[128]

But then comes an abrupt change as she speaks of the 'vulgar crowd' and points out that

> the common herd of men feels admiration only for the things of the body and believes that these alone exist, whereas the pious scorn whatever concerns the body and are wholly uplifted towards the contemplation of invisible things.[129]

Earlier in Moria's speech human folly has always been a source of pleasures based on self-love and delusion, but now no longer. 'The happiness which Christians seek with so many labours is nothing than a certain kind of madness and folly.' Ultimately it is 'the folly of the cross,' by which Christ offers us redemption.[130]

Christians come very near to agreeing with the Platonists that the soul is stifled and bound down by the fetters of the body, which by its gross matter prevents the soul from being able to contemplate and enjoy things as they truly are.[131]

Moria's parting of company with Epicurus is dramatic and complete. To give in to natural appetites and affections is now seen as the lot of the vulgar crowd, while the truly pious 'strive to root them out from their soul, or at least sublimate them,' focusing their love on God the Father, the *'summa mens ...* which alone they call the *summum bonum.'*[132]

'Perfect happiness' can only be experienced in paradise, but 'some foretaste' may be savoured in the form of mystic rapture, 'when the whole man will be outside himself, and happy for no reason except that he is so outside himself.' However, 'very few have the good fortune' to be granted that foretaste.[133] Moria herself refers repeatedly to St Bernard and Plato as her sources of inspiration, while the Listrius commentary points to passages in Origen,[134] and a modern scholar gave credit to the Platonism of Plotinus and Ficino.[135] Clearly this final argument in Moria's speech is significant and revealing, but it is also traditional and in an important sense it is second-hand.

There can be no doubt about Erasmus' sincere admiration for the long tradition of ecstatic rapture in the Christian devotional experience that began with Christ's transfiguration (Matt. 17:2) and Paul's transport to the third heaven (2 Cor. 12:2). Typically, Moria shares Erasmus' familiarity with the works of St Bernard.[136] After the *Moriae encomium*, this admiration was expressed in other works too, although perhaps not quite so boldly.[137] Yet here it is important to notice a threshold Erasmus did not cross. In 1532 he tells us – and why should we not believe him? – how he saw in a dream St Francis.[138] He is very specific about the saint's appearance and encouraging words, but there is no hint of ecstasy in that whole account. Erasmus himself was not a mystic. Never to my knowledge did he claim that he had personally experienced ecstatic rapture, and while he revered some of the great Christian mystics of the past, the Christians of his own time whom he singled out for praise were no mystics either. The Christian virtues for which he praised a Jean Vitrier and John Colet and also Thomas More in splendid biographical portrait sketches were for the most part of a practical bent.[139] The tradition of ecstatic mysticism did not end with Erasmus' time, but in the subsequent history of Christianity this was not the strand where his legacy bore fruit. The finale of Moria's speech, her praise of the folly of the cross in terms of ecstatic rapture, doubtless presents the climax of her entire argument. To leave it out of consideration would mean to lose sight of Erasmus' plan for the *Moriae encomium* and of his essential message. Yet his true originality, I think, lies elsewhere.

For me the true originality lies in Moria's compassionate approach to the common – and pleasurable – follies of human existence. Here is a concept of human life that owes more than a little to to the social thought of quattrocento humanism, but is really new in its emphasis on human weakness as source of pleasure. When the Stoics 'glory with a loud voice in their virtues,' Valla's Christian preacher reminds them of Paul's self-deprecation.[140] Compunction about one's weakness is not a Stoic virtue; it is a Christian virtue, faithfully practised through the centuries. For Moria, however, our weakness is not a virtue; it is pleasure – and pleasure here and now, rather than a reward to come in heaven, as promised to the poor in spirit and the meek in the Sermon on the Mount.[141]

Here also is tolerance of a new kind. The traditional Christian notion of *tolerantia* does not apply; we cannot *tolerare, suffer with*, someone who is so thoroughly enjoying himself as Moria's fools do. Perhaps we could be expected to *bear with* them, for their happiness is obtained at the price of self-delusion, but then can we help enjoying their illusions and our own smartness? Rather than bearing with them, we are asked to *share with* them; we must realize that their folly, which to us is so transparent, is everybody's folly and thus is ours too, for in our own case *philautía* will prevent us from recognizing it. I must qualify what I just said. Moria gives many examples of egotistic foolish behaviour that is not innocent, but harmful to others and therefore intolerable. Here she is neither amused nor amusing. But in this case too she is following a well-established tradition – a tradition of severe moral censure that had produced such works as Sebastian Brant's *Narrenschiff* (1494).[142] Moria's great discovery is the fairly innocent follies that are inherent in human nature, the foibles that give pleasure to the agent and elicit a sympathetic smile from the observer.

Erasmus' Statements on Epicureanism after the *Moria*: The Loop Is Closing

When Erasmus wrote the *Moriae encomium* in Thomas More's home, he certainly meant it to be tribute to his host and their friendship. In turn, six years later when More wrote *Utopia*, Erasmus was closely associated with its conception and afterwards its publication in Louvain and in Basel. Like Erasmus and More himself, the Utopians are fond of gardens; they are also authentic Epicureans.[143] Nothing in Thomas More's subsequent literary production would resemble *Utopia* even remotely. In Erasmus' oeuvre too the *Moria* certainly stands by itself; however, his response to the challenges of Epicurean thought did not end with the *Moria* although, after Italy, his focus shifted. Greek philosophies now could no longer stand up to his *philosophia Christi*. The work on his edition and translation of the Greek New Testament, interrupted for a while by the editing of Jerome's letters, proved absorbing and led him in due course to the New Testament paraphrases and extensive revisions in the text and the notes, resulting from the consultation of new manuscripts and additional patristic commentaries. He also had to face an unending string of controversies. Occasionally, however, he sought solace in the company of the classics.[144] He continued to edit some of Cicero's moral dialogues,[145] and he translated some bits of Plutarch[146] (1514) and later of Galen (1526). While even before the *Moria* he had occasionally sneered at the Stoics,[147] it rather seems that he was afterwards warming to the long tradition that held that Christians could learn a good deal from the Stoic philosophers. His scattered remarks in *De conscribendis epistolis* (1522), for instance, are all positive.[148]

When Erasmus turned to the Epicureans, he could on occasion fall back on the old cliché and rank them among the epitomes of lasciviousness.[149] Some sentences found in the first, unauthorized edition of *Familiarum colloquiorum formulae* may perhaps date from his student days in Paris. Here Stoic philosophy is called severe and pessimistic. Contemporary theologians are said to argue in Stoic fashion, but their lifestyle is Epicurean in excess. When Erasmus confronted the unauthorized edition with his own, he prudently substituted 'philosophers' for 'theologians.'[150] On the other hand, in 1519 he allowed himself to be dragged into an exchange of letters with the youthful Cardinal Guillaume de Croy whose philosophizing and writing, he reasonably expected, betrayed the help of the young man's tutor, Juan Luis Vives, who was a champion of Stoicism. Erasmus finds Croy's equation of felicity and virtue elitist, and Croy in turn accuses Erasmus of proffering a populist argument that ultimately supports an Epicurean philosophy of unrestrained pleasure. Erasmus replies that, besides virtue, there are physical and worldly blessings that are not automatically dishonourable pleasures.[151]

Erasmus is still prepared to argue that Epicurean ethics are compatible with Christianity, but after the *Moriae encomium* he chooses his words carefully. In the *Paraclesis*, published in 1516 among the preliminary pieces of the New Testament, he states that in the pagan philosophies much can be found that is helpful to Christians. He cites some Stoic, Platonic, and Aristotelian tenets and then continues:

> Even Epicurus teaches that nothing in life can be pleasing to humans, unless it is consistent with a conscience free of guilt which is the fountainhead from which springs true pleasure.[152]

While much of this Epicurean doctrine was also embraced by philosophers like Socrates, Diogenes, and Epictetus, the one to teach and live it most fully was Christ. In *De contemptu mundi* the good Christian was said to be the perfect Epicurean. In the *Paraclesis* he is a selective Epicurean. The passage just cited continues: 'Whatever is more relevant to Christianity, that we shall follow; the rest will leave aside.'

Cautiously reviving the notion of an Epicurean Christianity did not mean that Erasmus was turning his back on the down-to-earth Epicureanism of Mistress Folly. In 1524 and 1529, respectively, he published two new colloquies that feature characters reminiscent of Horace's porkers in the herd of Epicurus. In *Gerontologia* a group of elderly men chance to meet on their way to the Antwerp fair. Decades earlier they had been together at the University of Paris. Now, while travelling in the same coach, they bring each other up on their lives' experiences. One of them, Polygamus, prides himself for having 'no aversion to Epicurus.'[153] He is into his eighth marriage, has fathered numerous children, and is sorry that he cannot have more than one wife at a time. He is a craftsman – seeing the size of the family he supports, apparently a successful one. Like his old friends, Polygamus is a survivor.

Polyphemus, a character of the colloquy *Cyclops, sive Evangeliophorus*, is more colourful and more complex than Polygamus. The difficulty in analysing the persona is compounded by the fact that the man's identity in real life is known and that we know enough about him to realize that he was all but transparent. Felix Rex (de Coninck?) of Ghent carried letters for Erasmus on his travels through western and central Europe (1528–32). He was muscular and a tippler, but also educated and in possession of a faith that veered from Erasmian to Lutheran and even radical evangelical. Eventually he became librarian to Albrecht of Brandenburg, a convert to Lutheranism and the first duke of Prussia.[154] With a few strokes Erasmus managed to endow his Polyphemus with many of Rex's characteristics:

POLYPHEMUS   Usually I confess to God, but to you I admit I'm not yet a perfect follower of the gospel, just an ordinary chap. My kind have four gospels. Four things above all we gospellers seek: full bellies; plenty of work for the organs below the belly; a livelihood from somewhere or other; finally, freedom to do as we like. If we get these, we shout in our cups [with Horace and Ovid], *Io triumphe, Io, Paean*! The gospel flourishes! Christ reigns!
CANNIUS   That's an Epicurean life, surely not an evangelical one.
POLYPHEMUS   I don't deny it, but you know Christ is omnipotent and can turn us into other men in the twinkling of an eye.
CANNIUS   Into swine, too, which I think is more likely than into good men.
POLYPHEMUS   I wish there were no worse creatures in the world than swine.[155]

What is difficult to interpret is Polyphemus' fourth and final commandment: *ut liceat quod lubet agere*. At the time Erasmus often complained in similar terms about the arbitrary licence of both Protestant spirituality and Protestant ethics, and this sentiment clearly colours his portrait of Rex. But while Cannius can censure Rex's 'Epicurean life,' Erasmus himself, as we know, thought highly of Epicurean ethics. Also, there is more to Polyphemus' Epicureanism than just tippling and wenching. His fourth commandment is the exact equivalent of the only rule that Rabelais would later give to the 'monks' and 'nuns' of his abbaye de Theleme: 'FAY

CE QUE VOULDRAS.'[156] For Rabelais, as for Erasmus himself, the religious dimension of freedom was indispensable.

For good reasons Erasmus resisted the temptation to denounce his opponents as 'Epicureans.'[157] They often did this to him, and it caused him profound distress. In 1526 the Louvain theologian Josse Clichtove proclaimed Erasmus an Epicurean for ascribing the pleasures of sex to human nature rather than to fallen man.[158] Erasmus answered at length. Three years later when the Spanish Franciscan Luis de Carvajal likened him to Lucian and Epicurus, it seemed to Erasmus as if the Spanish friar had taken a leaf out of Luther's book,[159] although in another emotionally charged moment he claimed that unlike Luther no Catholic critic had sunken so low as to call him an atheist, an Epicurus, a Democritus.[160] By the middle of the sixteenth century, in Counter-Reformation Italy Epicurean subversion of all religion and even Epicurean gratification of various appetites became a standard charge against Erasmus.[161]

Typically, Luther had called him not only an Epicurean, but an *Italicus Epicureus*.[162] It was indeed the brutal attacks that Luther had unleashed in his *De servo arbitrio* that aggrieved Erasmus to no end. To give just one example of Luther's language: 'You utterly reek of Lucian and your breath has the foul, drunken odour of Epicurus.'[163] Luther's table talk shows how freely the smear of Epicurean unbelief (picked up in Italy) flowed from his lips, and his famous impromptu epitaph for Erasmus provided a worthy climax: 'he lived and died an Epicurus, without a minister, without a consolation; he has gone to hell.'[164] Erasmus' reaction was compulsive. In the *Hyperaspistes*, his reply to Luther, he repeated 'Lucian, Epicurus' and the other names he had been called almost *ad nauseam*,[165] and he also complained about them in letters to Luther himself, to Luther's ruler, the Elector John of Saxony, and to Johannes Fabri, future bishop of Vienna: 'that with Lucian I do not believe that there is a God, and with Epicurus I believe that God does not bother with the cares of man.'[166] Erasmus assiduously took up his complaint again in 1534 with his *Purgatio* against Luther.[167]

What upset Erasmus so profoundly was, I think, that Luther tended to equate Epicureanism with atheism when he called Erasmus an Epicurus. There was one other reproach that had always disturbed him in equal measure, and that was being called a heretic. Both were worse than attempts on his life; they threatened his claim to life everlasting, for Erasmus did believe in divine retribution. Since both reproaches were aimed at the same target, they also called for analogous replies. Erasmus often tried to demonstrate that views that were termed heretical by his critics were not incompatible with the essential tenets of Christianity; now he resolved to show that Epicurus was congenial with Christ. This, however, meant returning to the argument of *De contemptu mundi* – and returning to its fallacy.

The final colloquy of the last edition printed in Erasmus' lifetime (March 1533), and newly written at that time, is entitled *Epicureus*.[168] It is a dialogue between 'Hedonius' – *nomen est omen* – and 'Spudaeus,' who initially says he favours the Stoics but never defends any of their positions, while Hedonius dominates the conversation in Socratic fashion. His discourse develops with the stately flow of a morality sermon.

The principal argument is that of *De contemptu mundi*. It is made early on and then repeated many times: 'there are no people more Epicurean than godly Christians,' for 'nothing is more wretched than a bad conscience,'[169] and by analogy a good conscience is the highest good and source of true felicity. Consciousness of wrongdoing 'destroys the amity between God and man.' To restore the state of grace, a process of cleansing is proposed in language steeped in traditional terminology:

> Those who have washed away their stains by the lye of tears and the soap of repentance or the fire of charity are not only unharmed by sins but the sins often pave the way to a greater good.[170]

The true Epicurus and even Cicero, whose *De finibus* lies during their conversation in Spudaeus' lap, are further ignored when Hedonius defines God as the supreme good.[171] As usual, Epicurean moral teachings fare better. Nature, which to Hedonius is God's creation, is our mother, not our stepmother; she provides the godly man with his simple needs. If thus on occasion we are reminded of the Epicurean sentiment of the *Moria*, more typically Hedonius seems bent on opposing Mistress Folly. With regard to the pleasures of the marriage bed, he proposes to take the union between Christ and the church for a model.[172] Pleasures to him are either godly or insanely wrong; there is no room for foolish amusements and harmless follies. 'A natural fool differs from a brute beast only in bodily appearance; but the brutes nature produces are less wretched than those stupefied by monstrous lusts.'[173] The common crowd regularly hunts for the wrong kind of pleasures.[174] The resulting pangs of conscience and fear of death can be avoided in only two ways, by either 'madness or unbelief.' Therefore, so does it follow from Erasmus' context, sane people cannot avoid them but have to face them. Even a wretched old sinner has to do so. '"While there's life there's hope." I urge him to take refuge in God's mercy.'[175] When Luther read the *Epicureus* he pounced upon 'madness or unbelief' as means for avoiding the fear of death and ignored the context. Thus Luther could arrive at the satisfying conclusion that Erasmus was indeed an atheist Epicurean. Moreover, Luther unfairly ignored the other key term in this passage: 'hope.' A better reading of the *Epicureus* might be that Erasmus dwelt so often on the pangs of conscience because he saw them as a bridge between the Catholic sacrament of penance and the gratuitous hope of the Protestants. And that, at least, would be a point on which the aged author of the *Epicureus* has gone well beyond the argument of the youthful *De contemptu mundi*.

CONCLUSION

Erasmus was not an Epicurean. He never doubted the immortality of the human soul nor the existence of a provident, caring God. He had no use for the notion of an everlasting, infinite universe, and he showed no interest in atomism. Some aspects, though, of the Epicurean system were germane to his ways of thinking and living. Not only that he loved gardens; he was clearly sympathetic with Lucretius' approach to nature and likewise with Epicurus' modest lifestyle and basic definition of pleasure as absence of pain. Like the Epicureans he believed in freedom of the will; he also shunned public office and abhorred martial heroism and war in general. All along his life he was confronted with varying amounts of explicit information about Epicureanism – a good deal of it misleading. Moreover, in his incessant readings he may without realizing have crossed bridges that led back towards Epicurean tenets. For example, N.W. DeWitt has gathered evidence for some echoes of Epicurean thought in the Bible, for instance in Ecclesiastes and especially in Paul's First Letter to the Thessalonians.[176] Epicurean fellowships were likely present in the cities along Paul's missionary itinerary and, given the compatibility of Epicurean and Christian ethics, followers of Epicurus who longed for faith in the hereafter and an assurance of redemption may well have been converted to Christ. DeWitt sees Epicureanism and Christianity as the two earliest movements motivated by a mandate for missionary work among the lower and middle classes.[177] If this is so, the resulting rivalry would easily account for the hostility to Epicurus that Christianity inherited from Judaism. The basically defensive tradition thus initiated was bound to influence the young Erasmus. In his favourite Greek father, Origen, he would frequently find a harsh, well-informed polemic against Epicurus. Augustine, whom he rarely failed to consult, was equally knowledgeable and mostly negative. Lactantius zeroed in on the Epicureans in all his writings, one of which Erasmus actually edited.[178] To the African father the Epicurean system was the target most worthy of his polemics. He often cited Lucretius and, in general, had much to say about the Epicureans, some of it accurate. The Christian tradition thus formed, generally critical but grudgingly recognizant of Epicurus' moral probity, was handed down to the Middle Ages. Peter Abelard (1079–1142) was a notable exception to the prevailing denigration. In his *Dialogus* Abelard emphasized that the pleasure that Epicurus extolled flowed from peace of mind rather than gratification of the flesh. Abelard's spokesman for philosophy even equates this pleasure with the beatitude that Christ calls the kingdom of heaven.[179] With *De contemptu mundi* the young Erasmus made himself an exponent of this Christian tradition. In ignoring all of Epicurus' thought except his ethics, he bravely avoided the traditional abuse but also deprived himself of any chance of doing justice to Epicurus. Two decades later, with the *Moriae encomium*, Erasmus exhibited quite a different approach to Epicureanism. Italian humanists of the fifteenth century had revived interest in Epicurus and his followers. Finding in Lucretius and Diogenes Laertius a wealth of more authentic information, they were less eager to condemn the system, and some showed outright sympathy. Erasmus' place can probably be found between that modest fifteenth-century revaluation and the more robust Epicurean revival of the seventeenth century. At least in the *Moria* he adopted Valla's antagonistic juxtaposition between Epicureans and Stoics and with his pillorying of the latter he put himself at odds with his own considerable sympathies for Stoic thinkers and the philosophical trend that was going to dominate the rest of his century. Finally, in the seventeenth century we can find some echoes, at least, of Erasmus' changing view on Epicureanism, especially in France, and these will be examined in chapter 7.

SIX

Doctoring the Truth: Cardano's Erasmian Physic for the *Libertins*

ERASMUS LEARNS TO HUSBAND THE TRUTH

In line with some initial knowledge of Greek sceptics such as Pyrrho and Carneades,[1] probably gained from such works as Cicero's *Academica* and *De finibus*, Erasmus soon appreciated the merit of doubt. He also learned to treat veracity as a virtue that required cautious handling. A Pyrrhonist, however, he was not. Doubt had its limits. The central tenets of the Christian religion and ethics always were to him an a priori truth. The primary and indispensable source of truth was the Gospel, reporting the actions and words of Jesus and his apostles. Satan, by contrast, was the father of lying. He had invented it, so to speak, when he coaxed Eve to eat the apple, telling her: 'You will be like God.'[2] Sin was born and truth was lost – *omnis homo mendax*, sang the Psalmist and repeated Paul (Psalm 116 [115]:11, Rom. 3:4) – but the Gospel teachings opened a way of return, past sinning and lying, to the wholeness of Eden. Erasmus' *philosophia Christi* was, he said, 'nothing else but the renewal of nature, as it had been created, that is, good (*instauratio bene conditae naturae*).'[3] In fact, God's truth was never lost completely. Some portion of it had come down to the pagan sages of the ancient world, to be reclaimed by the humanists of Erasmus' own age. The classics, at their best, offered a perfect complement to the truth of scripture, not only by teaching virtue, but also by professing the immortality of the human soul and everlasting rewards for a life of virtue.

Simple and absolute as truth was in itself, it definitely ceased to be so when it became entangled with human language. *Res* and *verba*, the portrayal of the former through the latter, and the problems encountered in the process, were basic to the practice and theory of rhetoric, both classic and humanist. To take for example Cicero, whom Erasmus had read and pondered and edited in all phases of his life: no humanist would be unaware of the chasm between Cicero's writing and his actions, ever since Petrarch had lamented it when finally setting sight on Cicero's private letters.[4] Erasmus also knew about this tarnish of the great Roman's reputation from Plutarch's comparison between Cicero and Demosthenes, and in his *Lingua* he echoed Augustine's verdict that Cicero's speech deserved admiration, but not so his character.[5] Erasmus' criticism was muted, however. He found it more important to stress that no Christian could fail to be uplifted by reading Cicero's moral dialogues. In praising Cicero, Erasmus too was carried away by the lure of *verba* when he exclaimed: 'what profound reflections on the true felicity of man, which clearly show that he practiced what he preached.'[6]

Veering from the truth became a problem that touched Erasmus personally early on in his writing career. Rhetorical praise had a way of turning into flattery and even adulation. Girolamo Cardano would later categorically pronounce that in contact with those who wielded power deception was indispensable.[7] Erasmus did not theorize, but when addressing crowned and mitred heads, his hyperbolic praise was not immune from deliberate falsehood and betrayal of his most cherished ideals. A case in point is the *Panegyricus* for his own ruler, Duke Philip the Handsome of Burgundy (1504). While supervising the printing of his oration, he was uncomfortably aware of the problem. He tried to relieve his conscience, and perhaps meet future criticism, with a letter dated 'at the printing house.' In it he argued on the one hand that he had never intended to flatter and had, in fact, written truthfully, and on the other hand that when crediting the prince with some qualities dear to his own heart, he was merely urging him to embrace them. The latter defence, while it clashed with the former, was valid. Philip is repeatedly reminded that his overriding obligation is to his subjects, and some pages in the oration read like another one of Erasmus' antiwar manifestos. One point he made is pregnant with significance for his subsequent thoughts and their resonance throughout the period here covered. 'And did not,' he asked, 'the apostle Paul himself often use this device of correcting while praising (a sort of holy adulation)?'[8]

Not always, however, did Paul coat his corrections with praise. In an incident described to the Christians of Galatia (Galatians 2:11–14) he uttered a blunt censure, and the person censured was none other than Peter, the foremost among Christ's disciples and now Paul's fellow apostle. At Antioch, so Paul explained, he had reproached Peter 'to his face.' By observing the Mosaic dietary laws, Peter had caused confusion among the recent converts from gentility. The thought of a public falling-out between the two leading apostles gave pause to the patristic commentators. Augustine, leading the way to a generally accepted interpretation, decided that Peter was indeed at fault and that he had accepted Paul's reprimand in silence.[9] The Greek fathers, however, starting with Origen, had understood the incident quite differently. Among the Latins, Jerome adopted and reinforced the Greek position, thus causing a protracted controversy between himself and Augustine. Jerome argued that Paul had charged Peter with ὑπόκρισις (or *simulatio,* according to the Vulgate), and that that term was the key to the correct understanding. Peter's observance was not sincere; it was simulated, designed to put the Jewish Christians at ease. Paul knew and condoned this; therefore his public reprimand was equally simulated, designed to reassure his own flock of gentile Christians.[10] To Augustine the thought of such deliberate deception in the Gospel was intolerable. It shook the very foundations of the Christian faith. That was the issue Erasmus had to face in his notes on Galatians for the first edition of his New Testament (1516). The position he took was curious. He first showed that Jerome had supported his understanding by mistranslating a term from the Greek. Κατὰ πρόσωπον could mean either 'in public' or 'to his face,' but not, as Jerome had wanted 'on the surface, i.e., not from the heart.'[11] Having thus deprived Jerome of a crucial prop for his simulation theory, Erasmus went on, nonetheless, to summarize it. He did not say that he agreed, but he clearly showed more regard for Jerome than for Augustine, whose case he did not bother to present. He merely mentioned that Augustine rejected Jerome's view and that this had led to their famous dispute about lying.

What favourably impressed Erasmus in Jerome's argumentation – we shall soon see it borne out by his later statements – was the number of other incidents of holy deception that Jerome had found in scripture. Christ himself was no exception: 'our Lord, who had neither sin nor the flesh of sin, took upon himself the pretence of sinful flesh (*simulationem peccatricis carnis*).'[12] Another set of notes to the 1516 New Testament can supplement the ones on Galatians and clarify how under Jerome's guidance Erasmus came to form an appreciation of Paul as a holy deceiver. These notes refer to Paul's speech on the Areopagus (Acts 17:22–31), a topic that would keep Erasmus under its spell until the last years of his life and elicit comments from him that were still recalled in the seventeenth century.[13] The gist of his understanding of Paul's speech is already recognizable in 1516. Paul addresses the men of Athens by calling them, according to the Vulgate, *superstitiosos*. For the time being Erasmus retains the unfavourable meaning of that term, but emphasizes that the Greek should be translated as *superstitiosores*, 'somewhat superstitious.' Paul, he explains, was eager to make the term less offensive to his Athenian audience. This is the Paul, Erasmus adds, who wishes to become 'all things to all men that he might save all,' quoting 1 Corinthians 9:22, a verse that can be found uncounted times in Erasmus' work.[14] Likewise, Erasmus goes on, when Paul refers to the Athenian deities he avoids the unflattering term 'εἴδωλα, idols,' and instead uses 'σεβάσματα, objects of veneration.' Finally, Erasmus quotes Jerome's testimony that Paul 'with holy cunning (*pia quadam vafricie*)' even took the inscription he had read on the altar and adjusted it to his purpose. It had read: 'to the gods of Asia, Europe, and Africa, to the unknown and foreign gods.' Paul said: 'to an unknown God.'

In the 1518/19 edition Erasmus adds that those who wanted to convert pagans or rulers corrupted through their lack of proper education should use the same civility. 'With a good deal of cover-up (*multa dissimulantes*) they should lead them little by little to a better cast of mind. And perhaps good men should not be reproached when they acted in this sense in the courts of our kings.'[15] A fuller exposition of Paul's Areopagus sermon is found in Erasmus' *Ratio verae theologiae* (1518), a widely read piece, written and published in preparation for the new edition of the New Testament. The sermon stands as an example of Paul's *vafrities*. In the preceding section Erasmus reflects at length on the *varietas* of Christ himself, who in the gospels constantly varies his approach, as best it suits his holy purpose.[16] 'Proteus,' 'chameleon,' the provocative terms that Erasmus here uses to characterize Christ and Paul, would later be picked up by Luther and other critics to label Erasmus himself.

Between the 1516 and the 1518/19 editions of the New Testament, Luther appeared on the scene. The ensuing storm would eventually blow the issue of dissimulation all over the continent[17] and, as far as Erasmus was concerned, a long way beyond his personal sphere of flattery. We must briefly return to Paul's reprimand of Peter. Early in 1518 Erasmus was put on alert that his treatment of the dispute could cause him trouble. A letter from Johann Eck, professor of theology at Ingolstadt, took him to task for his general neglect of Augustine as well as his readiness to find mistakes in the Gospel texts. Quoting from one of Augustine's letters to Jerome over the Antioch incident, Eck added: 'If the authority of Holy Scripture at this point is shaky, can any other passage be free from suspicion of error?'[18] In his commentary on Galatians, published in the following year, Martin Luther also stated that Erasmus had been beguiled by Jerome and had short-changed Augustine.[19] Two months after he had written to Erasmus, Doctor Eck faced Luther in the Leipzig Disputation. In one sweep Luther derived from the incident at Antioch a challenge to the entire concept of papal supremacy. If Peter himself had flunked, so Luther argued, why should his successors, the popes, be infallible?[20] Again a few months later, in October 1518, the second edition of Erasmus' *Annotationes* to the New Testament came off the press. Eck and Luther may well have had an impact, for in comparison with the first edition, the notes on Galatians 2:11–14 appear here sevenfold expanded, enriched by much learned and relevant detail.[21] The substance of Erasmus' approach, however, has not changed. He is still torn between admiration for his beloved Origen and Jerome and grudging acceptance of Augustine's harsh critique of them.

From his initial admiration and unqualified support for Luther Erasmus soon moved to a precarious balancing act, which he maintained until the time of their controversy over free will. For the time being, he defended Luther's integrity and, especially, his right to expose what he too believed were disastrous shortcomings in the doctrines of the church and in every rank of its servants. The trouble was Luther's language, his lack of moderation and concern for the weaker or slower brethren – that is to say, the concern that Jerome had attributed to both Paul and Peter. Erasmus watched in dismay how the battle between the reformers and their Catholic opponents was heating up. *Exsurge Domine*, the papal bull condemning Luther, dated from June 1520, the imperial edict declaring him an outlaw from May 1521. Meanwhile, in October 1520 Luther published his *De captivitate Babylonica*, a crushing attack on Rome's system of sacraments, the cornerstone of Catholic dogma. Just in that period, from summer 1520 to summer 1521, one notices in Erasmus' letters an accumulation of statements that bring Paul's pious manipulation of the truth to mind, all insisting on concealment of the truth in appropriate circumstances.[22] Used justly, silence will not stamp out the truth. 'The truth must win. And the unspoken judgments (*tacita iudicia*) of men of good will acquire an authority which will retain their force even among posterity.'[23] The letters in question were addressed even-handedly to both assailants and defenders of the old faith. The finest, perhaps, went to a young German, Justus Jonas, for whom Erasmus felt warm affection and whose opting for Luther caused him sorrow. This is in part how he tried to dissuade Jonas:

> Furthermore when a prudent steward will husband the truth (*quum prudentis oeconomi sit dispensare veritatem*) – bring it out, I mean, when the business requires it and bring it out so much as is requisite and bring out for every man what is appropriate for him – Luther in this torrent of pamphlets has poured it all out at once ... and often a sort of immoderate energy, in my opinion at least, has carried him beyond the bounds of justice.
>
> That spirit of Christ in the Gospels has a wisdom (*prudentiam*) of its own, and its own courtesy and meekness. That is how Christ attuned himself to the feelings of the Jews. He says one thing to the multitude, who are somewhat thick-witted, and another to his disciples; and even so he has to bear with them for a long time while he gradually brings them to understand the celestial philosophy. With this in mind, he bids his followers preach first repentance and the impending kingdom of God, and keep silence about Christ [the Son of God].
>
> Thus does Paul become all things to all men, that he might gain them all for Christ, training his disciples to teach with all gentleness, without estranging any man by harshness of behaviour and language ... With what courtesy he preaches Christ to the Athenians.[24]

Erasmus' view on dissimulation did not escape censure in his own lifetime. The critics included Luther's belligerent supporter, Ulrich von Hutten, and his friends as well as Luther himself,[25] but also Noël Béda, Erasmus' nemesis among the Parish theologians and Alberto Pio, prince of Carpi, a client of the Medici popes.[26] Erasmus defended himself vigorously. In his *Spongia* ('Sponge applied to Hutten's spatterings'), he tried to clear himself with arguments we already know, such as:

> When Christ first committed the apostles to preaching the Gospel, he forbade them to disclose that he was the Christ. If the Truth personified commanded for a time to keep silent about that truth on whose knowledge and avowal depends salvation, what then is new when I have said somewhere that a truth should be suppressed?[27]

In his controversy with Alberto Pio he endeavoured to draw a line between explicit lying and simulation – a line that in common language was often blurred. He admitted that he had not always distinguished the terms clearly, nor had Jerome and Augustine. Perhaps he remembered his note on Acts 5:3, where he had written, on account of Ananias and Sapphira, that simulation was no different from lying.[28] It was true that he had said of Abraham, Judith, and other saintly persons mentioned in scripture that they used a lie (*mendacio uti*), but Pio intolerably twisted his words to mean they were habitual liars (*mendaciosi*).[29]

Among the next generation of critics one might mention a religious exile from Italy, Celio Secondo Curione, whose enthusiastic response to another aspect of Erasmus' thought we have encountered in an earlier chapter.[30] On his way to a chair at the University of Basel he obtained some financial support from the Erasmus endowment fund. But before moving to Basel, while living in Lausanne, within the orbit of Calvin, he had drawn a curious and unloving caricature of Erasmus trying to be all things to all men. In his *Pasquillus ecstaticus* (1544) two space travellers encounter in the heaven of Mercury a group of tormented souls. One is that of Erasmus. He hangs on a rope, suspended between two poles. Attached to his feet is a purse heavy with coin. On his head he has two big horns and tightened between them a kerchief functioning like a sail. With each gust of wind that hits this sail poor Erasmus is turned topsy-turvy. When the wind stops, the heavy purse pulls him back into an upright position.[31] Luca d'Ascia explains Curione's rancour: 'In Erasmus Curione condemns the justification of simulation. He reacts against the image of a *Paulus vafer.*'[32]

Curione's caricature must be seen in the context of the singular reputation Erasmus enjoyed in Italy before his works were globally condemned by the Roman Index of 1559. In the view of Italian Protestants, obliged to observe various degrees of clandestinity, Erasmus became the prototype of opposition to the papal church, the *luterano* par excellence, a surrogate for Luther himself, who could no longer be mentioned, being an excommunicated heretic. Clandestinity meant dissimulation and often entailed a participation in Catholic rites that amounted to simulation. This was the practice that was branded as Nicodemism by Calvin and bitterly attacked by exiles like Curione, who just recently had borne heavy sacrifices in order to live out their religious convictions in Protestant countries. While Curione thus vilified Erasmus' lack of unilateralism, other Italians were inspired by it. In her study of Inquisition records Silvana Seidel Menchi frequently noted expressions of doubt in the answers of the accused. Such expressions could mean feigned doubt (a tactical device to conceal one's true convictions), or genuine uncertainty (resulting in a request for instruction), or systematic doubt, leading to scepticism.[33] The author emphasizes how difficult it is to apply these categories to an actual statement (and one cannot help sympathizing with a committed inquisitor, who had to do just that if he was to pass fair judgment). Curione's indignation confirms indirectly the findings of Seidel Menchi. Erasmus' thoughts about truth and simulation could greatly comfort the Italian crypto-Protestants. As for Curione himself, we have seen already that eventually he came to think differently of the Italian Nicodemites, while in all probability he himself carefully concealed a growing adherence to radical beliefs.

CARDANO PRESCRIBES ERASMIAN PHYSIC TO THE FRENCH *LIBERTINS*

Jacob Burckhardt's characterization of Girolamo Cardano (1501–76), based on his famous autobiography, cannot be bested:

> Cardano is a physician who feels his own pulse, and describes his own physical, moral, and intellectual nature,

together with all the conditions under which it had developed, and this, to the best of his ability, honestly and sincerely ... He desires to spare neither himself nor others, and begins the narrative of his career with the statement that his mother tried, and failed, to procure abortion. It is worth remark that he attributes to the stars which presided over his birth only the events of his life and his intellectual gifts, but not his moral qualities ... Cardano admits that he cheated at play, that he was vindictive, incapable of all compunction, purposely cruel in his speech. He confesses it without impudence and without feigned contrition, without even wishing to make himself an object of interest, but with the same simple and sincere love of fact which guided him in his scientific researches. And, what is to us the most repulsive of all, the old man, after the most shocking experiences and with his confidence in his fellow-men gone, finds himself after all tolerably happy and comfortable. He has still left him a grandson, immense learning, the fame of his works, money, rank and credit, powerful friends, the knowledge of many secrets, and, best of all, belief in God. After this, he counts the teeth in his head, and finds that he has fifteen.[34]

That Cardano had not lost his faith in God did nothing to reassure the Italian inquisitors. In the winter of 1570/71 he was imprisoned and tried for heresy in Bologna. He had to abjure and move to Rome, but there he had influential protectors and could calmly live out his days. What precisely he was charged with in Bologna is a mystery. In the autobiography he said next to nothing about the trial. Mario Bracali has pointed to the existence of philo-Protestant circles in most of the north Italian cities where Cardano spent periods of his life. Thus it is possible that he was then in touch with, and influenced by, exponents of the Italian Reformation; for instance, Cardano studied at Pavia a few years before Celio Secondo Curione came to teach there. Later on, when Curione was a religious exile in Basel, they maintained friendly contacts.[35] A more likely hypothesis concerns Cardano's treatises on the immortality of the soul, where, reminiscent of Paduan Averroism, the case against immortality may seem more convincingly argued than eventually rejected.[36]

Cardano's vast body of writings exhibits a formidable amount of information derived from voracious reading, but also a wealth of personal experience and original thinking. He covers medicine, all imaginable sciences, including astrology, mechanics, magic (but not alchemy), also politics and, what is relevant here, a good deal of moral philosophy. He must have been a fast writer, unworried about organization at large, although in detail he likes to number his points. His formulations are often careless and sometimes cryptic. Modern readers also have to cope with countless typographical errors and omissions in the standard edition of his collected writings (Lyon 1663). Cardano's familiarity with Erasmus' work is obvious. Erasmus among the moderns and Galen among the ancients furnish the precedents that justify his own publishing of a catalogue raisonné of his writings.[37] He may not have referred to Erasmus as often as to Galen and other classical authors, but Erasmus' life and work still figure prominently in the steady flow of examples that come to Cardano's mind. Erasmus is named among the notables that show how poor orphans can attain greatness, although they never had a private tutor, also among those suffering from podagra and those who do not care for music, and so on. Like others, he paid a heavy price for his learning: *quot et quantas persecutiones Erasmus passus est!*[38] Other references are more discerning and sometimes peculiar, also critical. Erasmus' style, brilliant as it was, was felicitous rather than governed by rules and varied according to the many subjects he covered. As a writer of letters, however, he failed to understand that correspondence is no place for learned argumentation. He actually laid down rules for epistolography, but then did not follow them.[39] Another critical observation is directed to the *Colloquia*. Erasmus is too intent, says Cardano, on mixing sacred and profane topics. In the (five) accounts of conversations in the course of a meal the participants express themselves freely to the point of impudence.[40] The *Moriae encomium (Laus stultitiae)* fares no better. *Stultitia* is *stultitia*; one can find positive things to say about her, but Erasmus goes too far when he makes her outright desirable. Perhaps Cardano thought that in comparison with his own paradoxical essays, his *Encomium Neronis* and his scathing *De Socratis studio*, Erasmus' Mistress Folly was too lighthearted.[41]

In his birth horoscope of Erasmus, Cardano found that the stars helped him overcome the handicap of being a German, not a Roman, a barbarian, not an Italian. He was ordained, but preferred the mastery of many languages and an ample knowledge of Holy Scripture to becoming a prelate. Venus bestowed on him the gift of expressing himself so gracefully and arguing so dexterously as to even increase his wealth. 'Now not every one who has such a geniture will equal Erasmus, but as I have said elsewhere, it must necessarily come to pass that other such constellations, fortunate like that of Erasmus, will occur.'[42]

These and a number of other statements will attest Cardano's general familiarity with Erasmus' life and work, although references to his theological and spiritual writings are noticeably absent. But nothing of the above is of great relevance. To show that Erasmus was truly important to Cardano, we best turn to the latter's thoughts on deception. Deception is a property basic to the human condition. Varying the Renaissance commonplace about the uniqueness and dignity of man, Cardano puts it this way: unlike all other creatures, man is an *animal fallax*, a scheming, deceitful animal. Whatever can be conceived in the mind, man will figure it out and do it.[43] Despite man's ingenuity, Cardano's assessment of the human condition is somberly pessimistic. Eugenio Di Rienzo has placed Cardano in a grim tradition that reaches from Erasmus' adage *Homo homini lupus* and its ancient sources down to Francis Bacon and Thomas Hobbes.[44] By and large, the life of humans is misery and they try to make it bearable by means of delusion. To quote the proem of Cardano's *De consolatione*: 'It lies in the nature of all mortals that they believe to be more miserable, but wish to be seen as happier, than they actually are.' Kings make a show of their wealth, soldiers of their strength, and scholars of their trivia. 'People are, indeed, eager to be taken by others for something they are in no ways: therefore they spare no effort to hide their own and their relatives' vices and despicable actions and, while the fire thus smoulders, end up all the more tormented on account of their hollow reputation.'[45]

At the beginning of his *De sapientia* Cardano introduces divisions. *Divina sapientia* is owed to spontaneous inspiration. It cannot be learned, whereas *naturalis sapientia*, which aims for the good only, is acquired through dedicated study. *Humana sapientia* is manipulative and lets one act without an inner commitment. *Daemoniaca sapientia*, finally, practices deceit and aims for wicked goals. 'Divine and natural *sapientia* teach substance; human and demoniac teach pretense.'[46] Book III of *De sapientia* deals with the human kind, which comes close to the *prudentia* that Cardano examines in *Proxeneta seu de prudentia civili*. Both works offer his advice for success, or at least survival, in an unkind world, the archetypical prudent man being Ulysses. Later on Francis Bacon, in examining the conduct suited to public life, will describe a scale progressing from silence (*taciturnitas*) to dissimulation and, ultimately, simulation.[47] Cardano also knows that progression. Confronted with actual or potential hostility, one needs to conceal not only the facts but also one's intentions.[48] Silence is one way this can be done and thus a form of dissimulation. In other ways, Socrates, Cardano's *enfant terrible*, was a master of dissimulation. It is particularly suited to letter-writing, says Cardano, who perused Erasmus' collected letters and admits to practising himself what he recommends.[49] Since epistolography aims at persuasion, which to Cardano is yet another form of deception (*fallendi genus*), his acknowledgment of Erasmus' mastery of the art of rhetoric is, as Alfonso Ingegno points out, a correlate of his defence of dissimulation.[50] Finally, dissimulation is more civilized (*venustior*) than simulation, and the latter, while it is the most profitable and satisfying form of deception, is also the least harmless. It must not be used against guileless folk or even friends, due to the perversity of human nature, but is indispensable in the conduct of affairs. It differs from outright lying in that it can be freely used against all who treat us unfairly, while lying should be reserved for 'perverse' opponents. 'Particularly with those who hold power, simulation is necessary; this is why it is being constantly plied at court and with regard to governors and princes.'[51]

The link between Cardano's taste for dissimulation and Erasmus is made manifest in book III of *De sapientia*. The examples there given associate him uncomfortably with some illustrious companions.

> And if anyone ever managed to express together the told and the untold, this was Aristotle, for he was so sneaky in affirming the origin of the world, the rewards of the soul and the existence of gods and demons that he would assert these things blandly but offer no supporting arguments.

In that way Aristotle left himself wisely open to different interpretations. Luther acted in a similar fashion. From the outset he wanted to destroy the Church of Rome, but in his early teachings he was often deliberately casual, so as to raise suspicion without launching a frontal attack. Erasmus is next:

With that art do we see Erasmus praise the sacrament of penance, but the arguments he produced were strong on one side and weak on the other, and so he induced people not to embrace it. As with ships that thanks to the art of sailing can under the same wind move simultaneously in opposite directions, so he satisfied in one and the same book both Catholics and Lutherans. The technique I laud; the goal I blame, for in matters that pertain to the integrity of religion doubt is worse than falsehood.

Machiavelli is also mentioned in this context. If doubt were indeed worse than falsehood, even Machiavelli might cause less harm than Erasmus, for he uses deception to conceal a heresy:

Machiavelli said that whoever wanted to defend the faith without arms was bound to perish. So, as he elsewhere asserts, the unarmed Christ was condemned owing to the envy of the Jews. Who does not see from this that in his opinion, which, however, he did not dare to express, Christ perished due to human intervention and not because he offered himself up of his own will?

Of those writing about religion the most deceitful, however, was Mohamed. Erasmus, however, was also assigned another device of dissimulation that was not necessarily related to religion. Apparently he had learned it from Aristotle and Cicero: 'In his letters Erasmus says the things he does not want to say in such a way that we must assume the affirmation came from someone of the party opposed to him.'[52]

In yet another case Cardano found Erasmus' technique of ambiguity very much to his taste and actually copied it. The subject was witchcraft, and Cardano opened the passage by saying that Erasmus was usually sceptical (*minime superstitiosus*) and always ready to laugh about human gullibility. He then proceeded to quote, word for word, on two full folio pages, parts of two of Erasmus' letters that he had probably read in the collection reprinted in the *Opera omnia* (1538–41), one of an early date (1501), the other late (1533). The early letter offers a long account of a witchcraft investigation in a town near Orléans; the later one reports an incident near Freiburg. Erasmus does not question the existence of the demons or, indeed, the devil in person, who was

allegedly involved in these events along with the demons.
Erasmus simply avoids raising this issue. In the earlier event the
demonic intervention has no tangible consequences. Erasmus
treats the occurrence as a tremendous crime, due to human greed
and duly persecuted by the law. The later case is different.
Erasmus begins his account by stating that he cannot vouch for
the truth of all the gossip that is circulating. 'This, however, is
only too true: the town has burned to the ground, and the woman
confessed and was executed.' In the end he terms unconfirmed
but not incredible a speculation that the demon in question was
jilted by the woman and took his ferocious revenge. On the one
hand he concludes that 'this event is so recent and so consistently
reported that it cannot be an invention,' on the other hand he assigns the report to the category of *vulgi fabulae*. In this case ambiguity may well veil Erasmus' scepticism. Cardano does not
distance himself from Erasmus' ambiguity. Here and throughout
this chapter he is eager to offer carefully thought out reasons for
doubting the omnipresence of demons, but then his scepticism
also extends to the very doubts he has proffered.[53]

Cardano does not fail to show his appreciation for the sage of
Rotterdam,[54] but in keeping with his habit of viewing things
sceptically, his critical statements about Erasmus somehow seem
more interesting.[55] The very dissimulation that Erasmus practised so masterfully is to Cardano not a virtue but a necessary
evil. Erasmus, as we have seen, frequently pointed to Paul and
Christ himself as the holy models that would justify dissimulation. While this view is logically embedded in his conviction that
it was divine accommodation that caused the Gospel to withhold
and conceal some truths for the time being, the argument was not
free from self-interest. In Erasmus' laments about the tragic lack
of restraint that marked the Reformation, there is an element of
self-defence. He was no doubt conscious of his own inclination to
'husband the truth' and welcomed precedents that would excuse
it. Cardano rarely selects his examples from the Bible,[56] and that,
I think, not merely with an eye to the Inquisition. I did not find
that he ever referred to the dissimulation of Peter in Antioch and
Paul in Athens, or to Christ's silence before Pilate. When Erasmus
says *vafer Paulus*, Cardano says *vafer Aristoteles*.[57] Cardano – and
this is important for the reception of his work in seventeenth-
century France – looks for no ethical cloak to veil the stark fact
that deceit is deceit and lie is lie. Ruse must repay ruse, and

manipulation must repay manipulation, not with the intent of harming bystanders, but in self-defence, with the Machiavellian resolve to survive in a world sated with deceit and oppression. In Erasmus, Cardano says, he admires the technique of equivocation, but not necessarily the use to which Erasmus put it.[58] To Erasmus dissimulation is an approved means for advancing causes he believes in; to Cardano it is the dominant part of *sapientia humana*, a natural impulse and non-committal.[59] Erasmus' endeavour to create a moral support for deception must have seemed unnecessary and possibly dishonest to him.

As we prepare to look at Erasmus' presence among the *libertins* of seventeenth-century France, we should be aware of the larger and more visible presence there of Cardano. Although, as we shall see, some leading figures also turned directly to Erasmus' writings, a hefty dose of Erasmian physic was administered by the Italian doctor, and dissimulation was a large ingredient of that physic. The majority of Cardano's works were first published in Basel, with the support and collaboration of Italian religious exiles living in that city. From Basel Cardano's books easily found their way into France; witness the catalogues of French libraries. While some were soon being reprinted in Lyon and Paris, a fresh and intensive phase of editing and publishing set in towards the middle of the seventeenth century. The principal promoter of this Cardano renaissance was Gabriel Naudé. During his residence in Rome he had diligently collected unpublished Cardano manuscripts; subsequently he edited a number of them, including Cardano's autobiography (1643). He also stood behind the French translation of the unsettling *De prudentia* (first published in Lyon, 1623 and 1635).[60] Finally, Naudé seems to have conceived the plan for Cardano's collected works, an enterprise later realized by his friend Charles Spon in ten large folio volumes (1663), opening with Naudé's own biography of the author and a critical assessment of his work. While Naudé questioned Cardano's veracity, he defended him loyally against the savage attacks of Julius Caesar Scaliger. Like Erasmus, Cardano was to Naudé one of the great polymaths of all times. In his own writings he recalled, among other texts by Cardano, a provocative section on claims of divine inspiration as a means for grabbing political power.[61]

Interest in Cardano's work remained closely connected with the issues of dissimulation and simulation. Montaigne, on one occasion, sees in simulation the only alternative to self-deception.[62] Unlike Rabelais, who clearly used Cardano as a source, Montaigne does not borrow directly from him; however, in view of the material collected by Ian Maclean, it would seem improbable that Montaigne had completely overlooked Cardano, and possible that he had looked at him closely.[63] Scepticism apart, they certainly shared strong anti-Aristotelian and pro-Epicurean leanings. Pierre Charron also drew inspiration from Cardano. Like the latter, he considered dissimulation as a necessary tool for rulers and, with a glance at a page by Cardano, he wrote cynically about the evolution of religious beliefs, an idea that had already crossed Erasmus' mind.[64] Guy Patin, the physician, was, as his letters show, very much aware of Cardano, and François de La Mothe le Vayer saw in him a forerunner who had also treated the Christian religion as a fabrication designed to impress gullible souls.[65] Some adversarial reactions were as shrill as La Mothe's insinuations. Julius Caesar Scaliger (d. 1558) began the chain of critics thundering against the moral and intellectual defects and, especially the impiety, even atheism, of Cardano and, for that matter, Erasmus too. So also did later the priest François Garasse (d. 1631) and the Jesuit Théophile Raynaud (d. 1663), both of whom included Cardano in their denunciations of supposed *libertins* like Charron.[66] Pierre Bayle, finally, devoted to Cardano a careful biographical article in his widely read *Dictionnaire historique et critique*. Bayle relied heavily on Naudé, giving, for instance, ample space to his defence of Cardano against Scaliger. Cardano's ideas, said Bayle, were definitely peculiar, but his style was digressive and often obscure. Interesting is Bayle's take on Cardano's veracity: Naudé was right, he kept lying and made no bones about it, but then he 'only claimed to show what the malign influences of his star would have made of him, had he not corrected them.'[67] Make-believe was an exciting issue, and will remain one, as we now turn from Cardano's intervention to other channels of Erasmus' radical appeal.[68]

SEVEN

Epicureanism, Scepticism, and Libertinage in Early Modern France

The specific strand of Erasmus' thinking that touched the world of the *libertins* largely thanks to Cardano is by no means the only trace of an unsettling influence the sage from Rotterdam exercised in early modern France. Rabelais, the most fervent of his French followers, will be considered later in another context.[1] In view of his enthusiasm, one is bound to be curious about the reaction of the other outstanding light of French literature in the sixteenth century, Michel de Montaigne (1533–92). It is not difficult to claim Montaigne for a culture of radicalism. While there was, and is, much controversy about his adherence to, and even merger of, basically opposite ideologies – Catholic fideism on one hand, scepticism and Epicureanism on the other – his massive influence on the seventeenth-century *libertins* is undeniable. Did Erasmus contribute to Montaigne's shameless ease in airing his unconventional thoughts? That Montaigne, besides owning a copy of the Paraphrases of the Apostolic Letters, knew the *Moria*, the *Adagia*, and probably a good deal more of Erasmus' work is an assumption that underlies the approach of those who have written about Montaigne's debt to him. While acknowledged or otherwise provable influences are minimal, the affinity between them is, in Margaret Mann Phillips' words, *quelque chose de beaucoup plus profond*, a certain *resemblance de famille*.[2] In Montaigne's case as that of other authors to be covered in this chapter, I decided that I must overcome my reluctance to consider influences that defy solid documentation. I felt justified in doing so because the issue is significant and the writers to be examined here are closely interconnected, some admitting that they borrowed from Erasmus, while others do not.

In Montaigne's own case Margaret Mann Phillips speculates that, given the political and religious climate in which he lived, he may have had good reasons not to make a show of his admiration for Erasmus. In fact the only time Erasmus' name occurs in Montaigne's *Essais*, the author's continual self-examination touches upon the issue of truthfulness and finds that he speaks the truth, not as much as he would like to, but as much as he dares.[3] Montaigne thus raises the issue of dissimulation that will recur with regularity on the following pages. His only reference to Erasmus is spontaneous, but also random in the sense that other authors he admired might have provided an equally good example.

> If I had been able to see Erasmus in other days, it would have been hard for me not to take for adages and apophtegms everything he said to his valet and his hostess. We imagine much more appropriately an artisan on the toilet seat or on his wife than a great president, venerable by his demeanor and his ability. It seems to me that they do not stoop from their lofty thrones even to live.[4]

The general inclination to bias that Montaigne here notes is only one of his countless assessments of human weaknesses reminiscent of Erasmus' *Moria*. But what brings him fully into the orbit of Mistress Folly's speech is the idea that happy delusion, her very own gift, makes human weakness bearable, even enjoyable. Montaigne illustrates 'the great advantage in not being wise' with reminiscences of Erasmus' adage II x 81, *In nihil sapiendo iucundissima vita*. According to the adage, Thrasylaus and (quoting Horace) Lycas both despaired when they were cured of a lunatic delusion that had actually brought them enduring happiness.[5]

Our suspicion that Montaigne lent an ear to the enticing oratory of Mistress Folly gains momentum from his Epicurean penchant. Epicurus' teachings are cited in the *Essais* with remarkable frequency. Montaigne knew them primarily from Lucretius, one of his all-time favourites, but also from Diogenes Laertius. It is true that Seneca and the ancient Sceptics may have impressed him even more than Epicurus, yet Jean-Charles Darmon has credibly argued that it is indeed Montaigne who prepared the way for seventeenth-century French Epicureanism. To be sure, Montaigne does not exempt the Epicureans when he taxes all philosophical systems and schools with irrelevance, but at the same time he freely uses the Epicurean arguments to fault the systems of all other schools. Darmon sees him initiating a dialogue between scepticism and Epicureanism that will mark French thinking for an entire century, and even points to a link between Lucretius' presentation of Epicurus' tenet of the plurality of worlds and Montaigne's fideist trust in the infinite power of God.[6] Asks Montaigne:

> Why, in truth, all-powerful as he is, would he have restricted his powers to a certain measure? In whose favour would he have renounced his privilege? Your reason is never more plausible and on more solid ground than when it convinces you of the plurality of worlds.[7]

Next Montaigne proceeds to quote Lucretius. In so far as the notion of multiple worlds challenged the uniqueness of human beings, Montaigne here sets an important accent for the later *libertins*. But the link to divine omnipotence could also anticipate the Christian orientation of French Epicureanism in the seventeenth century. In fact, scholars have looked back from him to the *Epicureus*, Erasmus' pious last colloquy.[8] However that may be, Montaigne seems infinitely closer to the Epicureanism of Valla, which is also being adduced in this context, and especially the yet more insolent Epicureanism of the *Moria*. For Montaigne, as for Mistress Folly, Epicurean impulses do not lead to confinement in a system of philosophy but to a liberating way of life – a way of life in tune with nature.[9] *Voluptas* and *felicitas* are what Moria always promises her audience, while Montaigne, in an often-quoted passage early in the *Essais* (I 20), writes:

> All the opinions of the world agree on this that pleasure is our goal, though they choose different means to it ... Whatever they say, in virtue itself the ultimate goal we aim at is voluptousness (*volupté*).

So much for the Stoic wise man! In sharp opposition to the Aristotelian tenet, still powerful in his day, that truth can be tested and known, Montaigne follows the Epicureans – and *Moria* – in insisting that the senses can uncover truth, but the intellect cannot. Man 'cannot escape the fact that the senses are the sovereign masters of his knowledge; but they are uncertain and deceivable in all circumstances,'[10] and so in the end scepticism seems to prevail. Whether or not the senses afford intellectual satisfaction, whiffs of frank sensuality breeze throughout the *Essais*. Richard Popkin assesses Montaigne's importance for modern thought as 'probably second only to that of Erasmus.' He believes that Montaigne was 'probably mildly religious,' but insists that judging his sincerity is ultimately guesswork.[11] The ambiguity found in Erasmus' work recurs here in intensified form and so is passed on to the French intellectuals of the seventeenth century.

Montaigne's fideist scepticism was given new and broad exposure in the work of Pierre Charron (1541–1603), who was during the last years of Montaigne's life in constant contact with him and apparently became his son by adoption.[12] He certainly became heir to Montaigne's thinking; central ideas of the *Essais* as well as much detail are found again in Charron's *De la Sagesse trois livres*, published in 1601 and reprinted many times in the seventeenth century. Whereas Montaigne ingenuously rambles, Charron is soberly systematic. The term *sagesse* stands for the study of human nature, especially in terms of ethics; it is autonomous of religion, a point that particularly appealed to the *libertins*. But since profane study everywhere ends in doubt, *sagesse* will in the end force the mind to accept divine revelation and faith.

Opinions, again, differ sharply as to whether Charron's fideism can be taken at face value or whether his scepticism is pervasive and even amounts to covert atheism. As with Montaigne, recent writing seems to tilt towards sincerity. Christian Belin, a devoted advocate of the integrity of Charron's faith, sees him profoundly influenced by Augustine, Thomas Aquinas and, indeed, Erasmus. He has found in Charron's *Sagesse* convincing echoes of Erasmus' writings, but not necessarily evidence of his radical legacy. Charron offers a classification of Christian virtues reminiscent of Erasmus' rules (*canones*) of a truly Christian life in the *Enchiridion*. His concepts of education and pastoral rhetoric are influenced by Erasmus' *De pueris instituendis* and *Ecclesiastes*, respectively. Charron's humanistic view of Christ is reminiscent of the colloquy *Convivium religiosum*. In these regards, says Belin, Erasmus rather than Montaigne, the Erasmus of the *Enchiridion* and the *Paraclesis*, would seem to be Charron's *maître spirituel*.[13]

There is, however, one aspect of Charron's debt to Erasmus that holds out radical potential, and it is a significant aspect. Montaigne already had ridiculed the anthropocentric world vision projected by Genesis and the Renaissance philosophers alike. What reasons did humans have to feel so proud, so unique? In a long, unusually coherent section, Montaigne had argued that the animals were not inferior, indeed in many respects superior, to humans, with whom they shared the emotions, the intellect, and even the gift of religion. When talking of horses, Montaigne used the word 'soul (*ame*).'[14] Charron is slightly less direct; but he also seems to attribute to animals spiritual qualities along with their undoubted intelligence.[15] Both, moreover, did shockingly little to reassure their readers of the immortality of the human soul, and here, indeed, could be echoes of Cardano as well.[16] Montaigne constantly quotes Lucretius. It stands to reason that his stance, which Charron followed, was encouraged by the Epicurean concept of mortal soul atoms diffused in the body, which left the human animal little room for uniqueness. Charron not only followed in his master's footsteps, he also drew inspiration from Erasmus, who without surrendering an anthropocentric view of creation, yet found occasion to relegate humans to the status of other creatures. According to *De pueris instituendis* and *De recta pronuntiatione*, natural instinct gives brute animals an advantage over humans, who must learn to speak and to reason. Striving after wisdom is, according to Mistress Moria, what makes humans the unhappiest of all creatures. Other animals attain, like bees, great happiness unless, like horses, they choose to adopt man's emotions, such as a thirst for glory, and end up sharing his misfortunes.[17] In the *Enchiridion*, finally, Erasmus juxtaposes the physical superiority of animals to the divine quality of the human soul; hence man is *prodigiosum quoddam animal*. The term impressed Charron so much that he borrowed it.[18] Afterwards the *libertins* would continue to ridicule Genesis (actually more fiercely than Erasmus and Rabelais had done). If humans were deprived of their uniqueness and returned to their proper status among the other animals, why should not all of them have a mortal soul? Even a Descartes was horrified,[19] and the Jesuit François Garasse (1585–1631), famous for his rants against the 'atheists' of all times, including Cardano, knew where to place Charron. For Garasse he is the most recent link in the annals of impiety that start with Cain and lead to Judas, Democritus, Epicurus, Mohamed, Machiavelli, Erasmus, the Protestant reformers, and Rabelais.[20]

In the early seventeenth century Erasmus' lights continued to shine brightly over the guild of anti-conventional minds commonly known as *libertins érudits*. In France, as elsewhere, his works retained a more or less mandatory place in the personal libraries of self-respecting intellectuals.[21] Midway along the trail of radical ideas from Erasmus to the Enlightenment one finds the self-styled *Tétrade*, a foursome of like-minded friends, namely Pierre Gassendi, Gabriel Naudé, François La Mothe le Vayer, and Guy Patin. One of these four, Guy Patin (1602–72), demonstrated a level of admiration for the sage of Rotterdam striking enough to elicit a thoughtful study.[22] Dean of the Paris faculty of medicine, Patin has left a rich correspondence, freely flowing, wide ranging, in the best humanist tradition. In the exercise of his profession the good doctor was an unenlightened conservative, but he was committed to the traditional humanist values of tolerance and freedom of thought. Much space in his letters is reserved for news from the *république des lettres*, such as comments on recent publications that came to the attention of himself or his friends. Political news from home and abroad also receives attention, as does the chronicle of court and society, gossip for the most part, but not without stinging barbs directed at some powerful faction, especially Mazarin's. Patin's unfailing ire is reserved for the monks, the Jesuits, in particular.

An often quoted letter mentions plans for a weekend to be spent at Naudé's home in Gentilly in the company of Gassendi and Patin himself. There will be a *débauche*, but not of the ordinary kind, since Patin drinks little wine and the stomachs of his two friends do not tolerate any at all.

> And nevertheless it will be a *débauche*, but a philosophical one, and perhaps something more. For all three of us, being cured of superstition and freed from the evil of scruples, which is the tyrant of consciences, will perhaps go almost to the holy place ... [In a similar meeting with Naudé a year ago,] there were no other witnesses, and there should not have been any. We spoke freely about everything, without scandalizing a soul.[23]

What about this widely ranging conversation might have scandalized inopportune witnesses? Possible topics come to mind when we look at Patin's heros, the great men whose portraits decorated, he says, his study. Erasmus comes first; he is surrounded by other humanists and by Grotius, Rabelais, Montaigne, Charron, and Naudé, but also by Saint François de Sales (Gassendi's portrait was added after that letter had been written). This tribute is certainly sincere, but Patin also wants it to be a little provocative. He calls his selection odd and asks, tongue in cheek: *Que dites-vous de cet assemblage?*[24] The same touch of irony appears when Patin remarks, amid much praise, that his fellow-*libertin* La Mothe le Vayer smells like a billy goat ('metaphorically of course,') and, at age seventy-eight, is marrying a forty-year-old 'Sibyl.' Reporting the death of his friend Grotius, Patin adds: 'some say he was a Socinian.' But he also showed interest for Grotius' theological writings – a fact that is not reflected in his letters.[25]

In the light of such ambiguities, what then did Patin write about Erasmus, and what did he think? As he pens his letters he often spares a thought for *le bon Érasme*; indeed, he is idolizing him a little. After Augustine and Thomas Aquinas, Erasmus is Christianity's *plus bel esprit*. Patin recommends that his correspondents read his works, specifically the Adages, the *Institutio principis christiani*, the *Moria*, the *Lingua,* above all the Colloquies and the letters, but also the New Testament Paraphrases.[26] Actually, the letters hold a special fascination for Patin. In his library he has the *Opus epistolarum* and also the *Opera omnia* and some other books of Erasmus.[27] He concerns himself with certain aspects of Erasmus' life, claiming, for instance, that he never was a monk.[28] Patin likes to attribute uncomplicated bons mots to his hero, some of which are not likely to have flown from Erasmus' pen.[29] At no time, however, do the good doctor's letters reveal a serious concern with the deeper thoughts of Erasmus, whether spiritual or philosophical, and in this case I see no reason to think that there is a great deal that we are not told. For Patin, Erasmus is above all the free spirit who hated the monks and scourged abuses in church and society. Patin thus stands for a radical simplification of Erasmus' legacy that helps prepare the way for his role in the Enlightenment.

Patin, in his easy way with Erasmian terms, once called his friend Pierre Gassendi (1592–1655) a 'Silenus Alcibiadi.'[30] Among the libertine *Tétrade* Gassendi is the intellectual heavyweight. His reappraisal of Epicurus and Greek atomism helped to launch modern science. In fine Pyrrhonist fashion, he demoted Aristotle and rejected Descartes' desperate attempts to save the notion of human knowledge as reliable source of truth – a feat that reverberates throughout modern philosophy.[31] Gassendi was a *libertin* and very *érudit* indeed, but he also was a priest and dignitary of

the church. In his case too, opinions on his sincerity have differed
diametrically. The Epicureanism that he established as a leading
intellectual trend of his time was a Christian Epicureanism, and
since he counted Erasmus along with Lucretius, Charron, and
Montaigne among his masters,[32] it is not fanciful to assume that
he knew the colloquy *Epicureus*, perhaps even realized the fundamental flaw in Erasmus' argument.[33] His own Christian Epicureanism is certainly different from that of Erasmus, who had only
endeavoured to prove the compatibility of Epicurus and Christ in
terms of ethics, wisely avoiding even mention of Epicurean atomism and theology. By contrast, Gassendi boldly forged ahead.
Since Epicurus had used the concept of prolepsis to prove the existence of the gods,[34] Gassendi saw fit to argue that Epicurean
prolepsis was consistent with the knowledge of the true God – a
knowledge initially revealed to the first humans and then gradually spreading with the intellectual progress of mankind. He did
not embrace, but might have encouraged, the radically *libertin* argument that the concept of God is nothing but an evolving human invention.[35] Quite possibly, he was aware of Erasmus'
notions of evolving religion and providential accommodation. By
contrast, Erasmus was clearly no help when Gassendi proceeded
to reconcile Epicurean atomism with the Christian view of creation, arguing that the world created by God was indeed a world
composed of atoms, although not eternal, as Epicurus had claimed.
Prudently Gassendi argued that in view of the narrow limits of
our knowledge, humility should prevent us from assuming that
Epicurus' atomic theory necessarily militated against the creation
and the immortality of the soul, as taught to us by scripture and
the doctrine of the church.[36]

The Epicurean-*libertin* company in which Gassendi placed
Erasmus is one that Erasmus himself would have found uncomfortable. What, we may wonder, would he have done with the
testimony of Gassendi's friend, François de La Mothe le Vayer
(1583-1672), a protégé of Mazarin and once a candidate for tutoring the young Louis XIV? At some point in his *Dialogue sur la divinité*, La Mothe turns to Erasmus. He cites a number of historical
examples that can shake the trust in providence: evil-doers who
prospered and pious persons who perished. This, says La Mothe,
will encourage those who abuse religion by acknowledging the
gods in the fashion of Epicurus, who claimed that they were indifferent to what befalls humans. Erasmus, on the other hand,

insisted that 'nobody deserves better to be called an Epicurean than Christ,' alluding to Epicurus' name, which in Greek means 'helper.'[37] La Mothe did not say whether he thought that Erasmus' version of Epicurus' religion was any better than the authentic one. He certainly was in a cynical mood when he wrote these lines. For those who tried to reconcile Epicurus with Christ, as Erasmus had done, La Mothe found an unexpected ally in Saint Justin Martyr, who is made to argue that even atheists relying on *raison naturelle* were good Christians since Christ, the logos, *was* the *raison naturelle*. The wise king Solomon is praised for worshiping the gods of his many pagan concubines. Constantine the Great's wise rule netted him divinization on the part of the heathens and sainthood on the part of the Christians. Next came Girolamo Cardano; according to La Mothe, he had boldly concluded that one should value the false religions along with the true one.

La Mothe rarely identifies his sources, so we cannot say whether he was here indebted to an Erasmian vision that presented the gates of paradise flung open widely.[38] According to his friend Naudé, Erasmus had helped pave the way to the muddled notion that each man could be saved in his own religion.[39] The *libertins* certainly took the growing tolerance for the various religions of the world to a new level. In La Mothe's case, it may be particularly difficult to find threads of sincere Christianity in the fabric of his scepticism. Also, Erasmus' hesitant advocacy of dissimulation pales in comparison to the practices adopted and recommended by La Mothe and his fellow *libertins érudits*. True to his maxim that *bene vixit qui bene latuit* (well lived he that hid well), La Mothe called the topics he discussed with his learned friends 'smuggled goods (*marchandises de contrebande*),' obviously unfit for public display.[40]

Gabriel Naudé (1600–53) was another loyal admirer of Erasmus, whom he duly mentioned in many places of his *Advis pour dresser une bibliothèque* (1627) and his *Bibliographia politica* (1633). Librarian to Cardinal Mazarin, Naudé was a humanist of universal learning, but the issue of dissimulation is also pertinent to much of his work. He was not only Mazarin's protégé, but also a close friend of the fervently anti-Mazarinian Guy Patin. In Naudé's dialogue *Le Mascurat* (1649), a partisan of Mazarin appears to win out over his opponent, who is, however, given the opportunity of marshalling all the pertinent accusations against the cardinal.[41] Naudé shows himself to be a master of the subtle art of enticing readers to reach conclusions opposite to what is actually said. Such an implied conclusion is the viciousness inherent in political power. In his political writings Naudé makes no secret of his substantial debt to Machiavelli and to Cardano, whom he had launched in France.[42] Another conclusion is that the religions of the world are created by political powers for their own ends and therefore, like the political powers themselves, are subject to change and even obliteration. That Christianity should be an exception is not exactly made plausible.[43] Patin imputed to his late friend Naudé a religious indifference resulting from his long stay in Rome at the papal court.[44]

To end this chapter, it is appropriate to glance ahead to Pierre Bayle (1647–1706) and Jean Le Clerc (1657–1736). The article on Erasmus in Bayle's *Dictionnaire historique et critique* (1697) remains a pioneering achievement. Looking backward, it has been termed 'the most remarkable piece written so far about Erasmus.' Looking forward, Bayle is credited with making Erasmus 'the church father of the Enlightenment.'[45] As for Le Clerc's edition of *Desiderii Erasmi Roterodami opera omnia* (1703–6), there is general agreement that it opened a new era both of accessibility of Erasmus' work as a whole and of its scholarly investigation. Even today it is indispensable for Erasmus research. Radical interpretations of Erasmus do not end with the seventeenth century, and both Bayle and Le Clerc helped in some ways to keep them alive, but the window they opened permitted new light to be shed on all aspects of Erasmus' work, not only the radical ones. We are reaching here the final years of the time frame that was set for this study, and so we may use their work, succinctly, as a vantage point from which to look back to the way we have come in this chapter.

Pierre Bayle takes the sceptical segment of French thought in the seventeenth century as well as the debate about its nature to a final level of intensity.[46] The problem is whether this 'super-sceptic,' who questioned just about everything that came his way, from Abraham's moral conduct to Newton's gravitation, still embraced Christian fideism as the final alternative, the stop to all questioning as, for instance, Gassendi had done, or whether he was a crypto-atheist, blazing a way to the irreligious component of the Enlightenment. Did he not shock his contemporaries when he said that a religion tainted with superstition and corruption was worse than no religion at all? Yet even though denounced by the Calvinist orthodoxy, he rightly belongs to the Huguenot

Refuge, having experienced in his own family the savagery of Louis XIV's persecution of his co-religionists. Thus he could not but empathize with Erasmus' predicament of being torn apart between the Scylla and Charybdis of Catholic and Protestant intransigence. Bayle's Erasmus badly wanted the church reformed, but amid the unfurling tempest failed to see that the Protestant camp was indeed achieving this. He had not enough trust in God's providence.[47] Even as Bayle formed the concept of his *Dictionnaire*, Erasmus figured prominently in it. The sample article devoted to him in Bayle's *Projet et fragmens d'un Dictionnaire critique* (1692) may actually be longer than the corresponding treatment in the fully executed work.[48] But although his intensive study of Erasmus' writings must have nurtured Bayle's scepticism, his biography is definitely not an exercise in radicalism. Its landmark status notwithstanding, it may disappoint today's readers. It certainly is a far cry from Erasmus' own brilliant pen-portraits of his friends More, Colet, and Vitrier. It does not capture a personality. The *Projet* discusses, without much order, a number of biographical issues, uncovering much that was improbable or even patently false in the usually cited information. Bayle diligently researched his topics in a multitude of authors; indeed, it may come as a surprise how many writers before and in his time had dealt with Erasmus. Guy Patin is one that is frequently mentioned. But despite this comprehensive search for information, even the definitive article offers no coherent account of Erasmus' life, nor a comprehensive assessment of his character, while devoting exhaustive discussions to such issues as the date of Erasmus' birth, the status of his parents, and his spat with Julius Caesar Scaliger. Bayle is perhaps most 'Erasmian' in his ambiguous remarks about the words an author, specifically Erasmus in his *Colloquia*, puts into the mouth of his characters. *Les loix du Dialogue* absolve the author from responsibility for what a character is made to say in accordance with the part he or she is given, but it is still the author who has chosen to present characters whose discourse may be edifying or, indeed, heretical.[49]

If Bayle thus brought to culmination a trend that since Montaigne had mingled contradictory sceptic and fideist positions in almost inscrutable ways, Le Clerc steered free of such conundrums. For him reason was not at odds with the faith of a Christian. Scripture answered to reason in all aspects that mattered; scepticism was a blind alley. As Mansfield pointed out, here lies, differences of character apart, the principal reason for the growing alienation between Bayle, the dissident Calvinist and sceptic, and Le Clerc, the Remonstrant and proto-*philosophe*.[50] More confidently than Bayle, Le Clerc announces the eighteenth-century understanding of Erasmus as a harbinger of the Enlightenment. He does so in the prefaces to several volumes of his great and beautiful edition of Erasmus' *Opera omnia* as well as in his *Abregé de la vie d'Erasme tiré de ses lettres*, published in volumes 5 and 6 of his *Bibliothèque choisie*. Le Clerc understands the values of the letters as a biographical source. They permit one to see an Erasmus 'without make-up, *sine fuco*,' who will eventually throw his usual caution to the winds.[51] Le Clerc also understands how much the *Adagia* and the *Colloquia* have contributed to Erasmus' continued relevance, but he is not ready to give up the seventeenth-century obsession with Erasmus' writing on religion. To paraphrase Le Clerc, we flay the great man; we blame his timidity and dissimulation. Depending on whether he criticizes Catholics or Protestants, he draws either praise or outrage. He is accused of standing back from either side when, in fact, he assisted both by trying to bring them to their senses.[52] He saw the importance of a cult with its mysteries, if ordinary people were truly to revere God and follow his commandments.[53] Sometimes Le Clerc still used Erasmus as he had been used in the past. In his polemic against Richard Simon he quoted Erasmus' New Testament *Annotationes*,[54] although like Simon and Spinoza, whom he also opposed, Le Clerc himself employed the new method of historical-critical exegesis that rendered the reliance on dogmatic proof-texts largely redundant. The *Paraphrases* are, according to Le Clerc, Erasmus' best-liked and least-criticized religious book; the *Annotationes*, on the other hand, bring us face to face with Erasmus' radical potential:

> I know there are highly learned men who would say that Erasmus was unduly eager to collect a variety of readings on places that refer to Christ's divinity and that he thus opened the path for those who deny it. In this way they wanted to make him suspect of crypto-Arianism. [But his Apologies prove that this is a denigration] ... And as to the variety of readings, if it is true what he says about the manuscript codices and patristic texts in which some places are read differently, we have no reason to get angry with him, as for us too it is not right to protect the truth with lies that it does not need at all.[55]

Le Clerc knew this problem first hand. Although his own theology cannot be termed radical, he set little store by the Trinity or, for that matter, providence, and consequently was himself accused of being a Socinian – the charge that throughout the seventeenth century had been associated most often with radical readings of Erasmus.

EIGHT

Radical Echoes of Erasmus in Seventeenth-Century England

THE GREAT TEW CIRCLE

In the seventeenth century England produced a stunning volume of radical writing, especially during the period of Civil War and Commonwealth in the middle of that century, when the official procedure for licensing books had largely ceased to function. Meanwhile Erasmus' books continued to be widely available and read. In 1628 the young John Milton found in Cambridge the *Moriae encomium* in everyone's hands.[1] If my sampling holds true, however, an acknowledged or otherwise evident presence of Erasmus in radical books and pamphlets is rare, which does not, of course, preclude that he was read and consulted. Catholic-bashing was then a favourite pastime for countless English writers, radical or not, and given Erasmus' ambivalent position, it is understandable that neither the Protestant phalanx nor the defenders of Rome were eager to mention him.

Erasmus' presence is manifest, however, on the estate of Great Tew near Oxford, where Lucius Cary, Lord Falkland (1610–43), played host to a circle of learned friends. In the political turmoil of the 1630s Great Tew was a haven of critical but ultimately irenic endeavour. Bruce Mansfield compared its atmosphere to that of Plato's *Symposium* or Erasmus' colloquy *Convivium religiosum*.[2] Falkland tragically reflects the tensions of the time in his own person. Amid inner torment, the young irenicist joined the king's army and died on the battlefield of Newbury. The outstanding member of the Tew circle was William Chillingworth (1602–44), like Falkland a royalist and equally short lived. For some years he had been a Catholic, and his stay with the Jesuits of Douai may have contributed to his familiarity with patristic literature and his passion for altercation. The latter he subsequently turned against Rome in his principal work, *The Religion of the Protestants*, which was largely written at Great Tew. Another member of Falkland's circle was the learned John Hales (1584–1656), a master of Eton, who attended the Synod of Dordrecht in 1618 and, as a result, 'bade John Calvin good night.'[3] Great Tew housed an exceptional library, and in view of Falkland's admiration for Erasmus, we can expect that the latter's work was well represented.[4] Erasmus is singled out as 'a person much esteemed by my lord, your father' in a dedicatory letter addressed to Henry, Falkland's son, prefaced to a posthumous publication. Erasmus, in turn, would certainly have approved of the sort of companions that Falkland chose in preference to 'hawking and hunting gentlemen ... [men] such as neither cloy nor weary any with whom they converse.'[5]

The writings of the Tew circle reflect a harmonious blend of Christian humanism and the new scepticism wafting across the Channel from France and Holland. Several of its members had in their formative years come under the influence of Sextus Empiricus. Among the charges levelled against the Tew men was not only Pyrrhonism, however, but more ominously, if rather unfairly, Socinianism.[6] Thus it came that, humanism apart, Erasmus' influence motivated them also in more provocative ways, and this is why their principal concerns deserve our attention.[7]

Bold points in the tradition of Christian humanism were taken up at Tew. Falkland confronted the claim that belief in the church's infallibility was necessary to salvation with the example of such as had said that even pagans could be saved, to wit, Erasmus (and Justin Martyr, Clement of Alexandria, and Vives). Falkland also condemned the killing of alleged heretics; this was an atrocity never practised, he argued, in early Christianity.[8] Chillingworth rejected the death penalty outright, especially as a punishment for theft, as 'sir Thomas More did' (in the first book of *Utopia*).[9] Hales, a fine Grecian and well versed in the church fathers, wrote *A Tract concerning Schisme and Schismaticks*, composed originally for the benefit of Chillingworth. Apart from providing rational definitions, Hales demonstrated undisputable links between ambition, superstition, and dogmatization on the one hand and freedom of conscience and religious toleration on the other. 'Why may I not go, if occasion requires, to an Arian Church...?,' he asked, echoing Erasmus, perhaps knowingly so.¹⁰ Chillingworth, moreover, came close to Erasmus' letter to Volz, prefaced to the *Enchiridion*, and *Moria* when in one of his sermons he drew on Matthew 23 for the warning example of the Pharisees, their folly, their hypocrisy, their contempt for simple folk: 'there were many poor souls whom the Pharisees kept out of heaven for company.'¹¹ Falkland trod the same path when he quoted Erasmus writing: 'Religion has come down to Sophistry and a Myriad of Articles.'¹²

The circle's sceptical orientation comes into focus in the way it disposed of the central claim of its Catholic opponents that their church was infallible in its teaching of doctrine. The Tew men's premise was that all claims to infallible truth were unsound, and they looked to ecclesiastical history for evidence. Chillingworth noted, as Erasmus had done so often, that dogmas were usually valid for a limited time only and therefore could not be proven with the consensus of authoritative voices from that period. Nor was there really a consensus: fathers, scholastic doctors, and monastic orders, all tended to disagree with each other. To quote Falkland: 'Erasmus tells us, that he who is a heretick among the Dominicans, is orthodox to the Scotists.'¹³ Chillingworth concluded that ultimately no dogma could overrule the freedom of thought.

> I should have represented to him [Bellarmine] Erasmus's complaint against the protestants, whose departing from the Roman church occasioned the determining and exacting the belief of many points as necessary, wherein, before Luther, men enjoyed the liberties of their judgments and tongues and pens ... And from hence I should have collected ... that divers men, who held external communion with that church, which now holds these [points] as matters of faith, conceived themselves no ways bound to do so, but at liberty to hold as they saw reason.¹⁴

Erasmus' attitude to the Catholic practice of oral confession was sceptical, even cynical, to Chillingworth.

> Erasmus tells us of himself, that though he did certainly know, and could prove, that auricular confession ... were not of Divine institution; yet would not say so, because he conceived confession a great restraint from sin, and very profitable for the times he lived in; and therefore thought it

expedient, that men should rather by error hold that necessary and commanded, which was only profitable and advised, than by believing, though truly, the non-necessity of it.[15]

Falkland made the same point in a debate about the Creed of the Apostles. Echoing Erasmus (and the Socinians, for that matter), the Tew men believed that it covered all that was necessary for salvation, but this was not to say, as the Catholics did, that it had been instituted by the apostles themselves. Falkland could see how such a belief, unfounded though it was, could take hold. The creed could indeed be taken to express the faith of the apostles; however, attributing to them the words commonly used in the liturgy was acting like a physician who exaggerated the gravity of a patient's condition to make him swallow a bitter medicine.

> Some of great authority (moved by a good meaning) might thus deceive others; these, thus deceived, might deceive others, till, being generally spread, other good men, being loath to oppose them for the same reason, for which others desir'd to spread them (as we saw Erasmus, who beleeved your confession, not to have been instituted by the Apostles, yet would not reprehend them that said so, thinking it an error, that would increase Piety), they be at last taken to have been commanded by the Apostles, without contradiction.[16]

Apart from attributing to Erasmus this kind of sceptical and charitable opportunism, the Tew circle was sympathetically aware of the precarious hold the Church of Rome had had on him. Chillingworth gleefully quoted to his Catholic opponents a sentence from one of Erasmus' letters. There was no lack, Erasmus had said, of great theologians willing to admit 'that there was nothing in Luther that could not be defended by good and allowed authors.' Chillingworth had actually found that statement in the Catholic *Index expurgatorius* which, he said, often publicized what it was meant to suppress: 'The Divine Providence blessedly abusing for the ready manifestation of the truth this engine intended by you for the subversion and suppression of it.'[17] Falkland knew well that for a long time Erasmus had been the victim of 'the Bigotts of both parties,'[18] although only the worst of the Catholics would decry him as 'a more pestilent Heretick then Luther.' Rejected by his own side, he had been left to the Protestants as a precious gift.[19]

A century later, John Jortin, one of Erasmus' early biographers, looked back to his hero and the Tew circle. He mused that if Erasmus, Chillingworth, Hales, John Locke, and also some other luminaries less inclined to scepticism had been contemporaries, they all, despite their differences on points of theology, could have agreed on the same confession of faith (no doubt along the lines of the Apostolic Creed).[20]

SOCINIANS AND QUAKERS

Without embracing specifically Socinian doctrines, the Tew circle was no doubt acquainted with Socinian literature. Hales, as we have seen, would have been at ease in an Arminian church. With the ascent of Parliament and the fall of the monarchy, a number of Socinian books began to be published in England. Commentaries on Hebrews and Galatians by Johannes Crell (and Jonasz Szlichtyng) were published in 1646 and 1650, respectively, in a free translation by Thomas Lushington. In 1651 a Latin version of the Racovian Catechism appeared, and an English translation followed a year later. Equally important were three texts translated by John Bidle (1615–62): the *Dissertatio de pace et concordia ecclesiae* and a life of Fausto Sozzini by Samuel Przypkowski, and the *Brevis disquisitio* by Joachim Stegmann senior, all published in 1653. Another 'classic,' Johannes Crell's *De uno Deo et Patre*, anonymously translated, followed in 1665. Numerous other Socinian books, imported from the Continent, showed up in many English libraries.[21] In 1647 Bidle, the major figure of English Antitrinitarianism, began to publish his own writings. If he drew inspiration directly from Erasmus, he does not say so. This presents quite a contrast to his fellow-sufferer, Paul Best (1590?–1651). Both were for a time in 1647 the Parliament's prisoners in the Gatehouse at Westminster[22] when Best broke into print with his only, it seems, publication, a pamphlet entitled *Mysteries discovered*. It is a plea for his release from jail and the restoration of a modest rent that was his livelihood, but above all it is a frank testimony to his Unitarian conviction. He had previously spent some years on the Continent, fought under Gustavus Adolphus at Lützen, and visited Poland and also Transylvania, still home of a vigorous Unitarian church. In his pamphlet he presents 'the mystery of God,' the almighty Creator, in its opposition to the Trinitarian 'mystery of iniquity' of 2 Thessalonians 2:7.[23] With rare audacity he advances the Socinian understanding of Christ, and then calls on none other than Erasmus to confirm it. The Son is not equal to the 'indivisible' God Father, nor is he co-eternal with him.

> The inauguration or anointing of our blessed Saviour was his baptisme ... which is therefore termed the beginning, viz. of his Gospel, John 1:1 and 1 John 1:1, and that new creation, 2 Cor. 5:17, so that Christ is to us both God and his Word ... not that the word is Christ, or Christ life everlasting, but in a figurative sence after a Scripture manner and meaning, according to the character of that beloved Apostle, as Erasmus observeth in his argument to his Epistles.[24]

Among many other Bible verses, Best refers to John 14:1 and 1 Thessalonians 3:11 to pin down the distinction between God and Christ, and then adds: 'it being the observation of the learned Erasmus, that where God is put absolutely the father is understood, as John 8:54.'[25] The two references to Erasmus are unparalleled throughout the short tract. Best's reliance on him calls his standing among the Transylvanians to mind. Also reminiscent of Transylvanian precedents is Best's treatment of the long history of the false Trinitarian doctrine down to the 'third Reformation' that will not be complete until apocalyptic times.[26]

Especially as an annotator of the New Testament, Erasmus was again consulted by the leading Socinian sympathizer of the next generation. Stephen Nye (1648?–1718) was for forty years until his death the rector of a small rural parish and always considered himself a member of the Church of England in good standing. His orthodoxy, however, is more than doubtful in view of *A Brief History of the Unitarians also Called Socinians*, which he published anonymously in 1687. Nye does offer some unbiased information on the history of that movement which he himself calls a heresy, but only in passing. His book is really a collection of arguments, and especially Bible passages, that had helped the Unitarians (that is, Arians and Socinians) to show the correctness of their cause. His own Unitarian position, according to John McLachlan, would eventually amount to Sabellianism in that he came to see the Father, the Son, and the Holy Spirit as modes of the one God.[27] In typically latitudinarian manner, he promoted a proposal (attributed to his friend Thomas Firmin) to form 'fraternities' within the Church of England for the purpose of raising simple folks to the heights of

Unitarianism.[28] As for his *Brief History*, McLachlan notes that, although unlicensed, it seems to have circulated freely and suggests that the advisors of the Catholic King James II made no attempt to suppress it because it would demonstrate the subversive potential of Protestantism.[29] Despite the title of his *Brief History*, Nye did not equate Unitarianism with Socininanism. Indeed, he distanced himself from the Socinians in that he did understand the beginning of the Gospel of John as referring to God's creation of the universe, effected through the Word that later became incarnated in Christ, rather than the 'new creation,' brought about with the birth of Christ.[30] Moreover, he clearly sided with those Socinians in Transylvania who refrained from praying to Christ, as did their Polish co-religionists, on the authority of Fausto. He also kept his distance from some English Socinians in that he rejected Bidle's anthropomorphism and his understanding of the Holy Spirit as a person.[31]

Early in his *Brief History* Nye launches an elaborate claim concerning Erasmus' patronage of the Antitrinitarian cause. The official anathema notwithstanding,

> not a few of the most learned and celebrated Writers of the Church, whether Catholick or Reformed, have certainly been either Arians or Socinians, or great Favourers of them; though they have used much Caution ... [First and foremost among these] D. Erasmus, the restorer of Learning, has given occasion both to his Friends and Enemies to think him an Arian.[32]

For evidence Nye quotes Erasmus' annotations on Philippians 2:6 and Ephesians 5:5 ('the word God being used absolutely doth in the Apostolick Writings always signifie the Father'),[33] and scholia in Erasmus' edition of the letters of Jerome stating that the Arians, while heretics, surpassed the orthodox in learning and writing. Thus, Nye concludes, 'Tis believed, Erasmus did not make himself a party to that which he esteemed the ignorant and dull side of the Question.' In a letter to Pirckheimer, 'he speaks as openly as the times would permit a wise Man to speak: I (saith Erasmus) could be of the Arian perswasion, if the Church approved it.'[34] Nye then turns to his next Socinian sympathizers, Grotius, 'Socinian all over,' and the Jesuit Petau. He obviously refused to take Erasmus' countless assurances of Catholic orthodoxy at face value. Apart from impressive scholarship, he seems to have found in Erasmus an alternation of bold assertions and prudent denials that he set out to expose and, in his own writing, to replace by a prudent show of seeming neutrality.

Other specific references to Erasmus in his *Brief History* are to the notes on John 1:15 and 3:13 (pp. 88, 90f.), Acts 2:20 (pp 113f.), Romans 9:5 (pp. 117f.), and 1 John 5:7–9 (pp. 151–3). Many of Nye's Erasmian proof-tests had been used before by Antitrinitarian writers, but it seems obvious that in addition to more recent Bibles, Erasmus' New Testament was in easy reach when Nye wrote his *Brief History*.

An anonymous letter printed as a post face of Nye's *Brief History* was presumably written by Henry Hedowrth and addressed to Thomas Firmin (1632–97). It refers repeatedly to Chillingworth. Together with Chillingworth and the author of that letter, its recipient can represent the environment in which Erasmus' legacy found its niche. Firmin not only saw to it that Nye's *Brief History* was published; his house and library in London's Lombard Street stood always open to unconventional visitors, among them John Locke.[35] Unlike their French counterparts, these English sceptics and latitudinarians with a propensity to Unitarianism do not challenge the modern reader to make a stark choice of opposing assessments. There is no question here of either pious fideism or radical dissimulation and religious scepticism bordering on atheism. Not that caution would have been unnecessary; bellicose avowals of Socinianism could land men like Best and Bidle in prison. But among many English intellectuals a confident expectation obtained that reason would prevail and that, within certain limits set by the authorities, one could speak one's mind on touchy issues, especially if one joined in the national passion for locking horns with the rams of Rome. Here Erasmus, dismissed by the Catholic controversialists, was welcomed with open arms.

By contrast, I could not discover much interest for Erasmus among the English proponents of more extreme views and convictions. These would include political radicals from Thomas Hobbes on the highbrow end to Gerard Winstanley on the popular end. On the side of religious radicalism, among the Quakers neither Samuel Fisher nor Anne Conway had occasion to mention him, although both were among the rare beneficiaries of superior education. William Penn (1644–1718), however, in his substantial body of writings, referred to Erasmus a number of times. In support of the Quakers' absolute refusal to swear an oath he quoted at length an English translation of Erasmus' paraphrases of Matthew 5:33–7 and James 5:12.[36] Was he also aware, one wonders, of the relevant annotations in Erasmus' New Testament, where the injunction against oath-taking is qualified?[37] On other occasions he consulted Erasmus' New Testament along with more recent translations of the Bible, and he was familiar with the Paraphrases, which were widely disseminated in England. In *A Discourse of the General Rule of Faith and Practice* (1673), he quoted a passage from the paraphrase on 2 Peter 1:19–21, which he liked so much that he repeated it on two more occasions.[38] He also dealt with this paraphrase and the corresponding part in the Annotations in one of his controversies. The refusal to address any individual in the polite second person plural, insisting on 'thou' in the place of 'you,' goes to the heart of traditional Quakerism. In his important *No Cross, no Crown* (1668), Penn found weighty support for this practice in a section of Erasmus' *De conscribendis epistolis*. Erasmus, 'a learned man and an exact critick in speech,' had plainly shown the absurdity of the flattering use of the plural.[39] Finally, the potential that Erasmus could have for Penn's radical conviction is fully shown by a single line he quoted from *De sarcienda ecclesiae concordia*: 'We grant to be Justified by Faith, that is, Hearts to be Purged.' Overall, Penn will hardly contradict the conclusion that Erasmus' appeal in seventeenth-century England was more demonstrably to rationalists and sceptics rather than evangelical radicals.

JOHN LOCKE AND ISAAC NEWTON

The pre-eminence of John Locke (1632–1704) and Isaac Newton (1642–1727) on the one hand, and on the other the fact that Erasmus was a somewhat remote star on their celestial globe – both these factors render an extensive treatment here unnecessary. Locke and Newton represent a new frame of mind at a time when the voracious appetite for anti-Catholic polemic had been sated and the ideals of Christian humanism had grown dim. Yet there are Erasmian ties here that need to be examined briefly. As was mentioned,[40] Locke often visited the house of Thomas Firmin. He shared the Unitarian and latitudinarian views of that remarkable London mercer and his friends. Jortin later saw a trail of rational religion that ran from Erasmus to Locke via the Great Tew circle,[41] but the strongest Erasmian bond was Locke's friendship with his younger contemporary, Jean Le Clerc. During his exile in Holland (1683–9), Locke was one of the foremost contributors to Le Clerc's journal, the *Bibliothèque universelle et historique*. Among the books Locke reviewed for the *Bibliothèque* was a study of Erasmus by the Jansenist priest Jean Richard. In the course of challenging Richard's alignment of Erasmus with the persecuted Jansenists, Locke turned him into a crypto-Protestant.[42] After Locke's return to England, Le Clerc exchanged dozens of letters with him. Le Clerc was looking for English patrons to whom he might dedicate some of the labours of his ever-industrious pen. After consultation with Locke, he approached Thomas Herbert, Count Pembroke, to whom Locke himself had dedicated his *Essay concerning Human Understanding*. Le Clerc's letter to Pembroke was an animated defense of Erasmus (and Hugo Grotius), which Locke no doubt could endorse.[43] Erasmus' influence has been demonstrated in Locke's educational writings,[44] but may be harder to show in his political masterpieces. However, Erasmus comes unquestionably into play when Locke presents his religious views often in defiance of traditional orthodoxy. Like his friend Le Clerc, he was denounced as a Socinian. In his defense he took an Erasmian stance and wrote sarcastically:

> My Bible is faulty again, for I do not remember that I ever read in it either of these propositions, in these precise words, 'there are three persons in one nature, or, there are two natures in one person.'[45]

In keeping with his non-sectarian and eclectic approach, Locke had nothing to say about the Trinity and Christ's atonement, but unlike the Socinians he affirmed his pre-existence. Like his friend Le Clerc, and unlike other deists, he did not completely subordinate revelation to reason. He argued that the miracles of Christ and his disciples deserved credence, although most others did not. Again like the Socinians, he had no regard for original sin and predestination; he also shared their thinking about divine retribution.[46]

Religious toleration, a crucial cause for Locke, had by then become enveloped in a framework of political studies that no longer set much store by Erasmus, but a debt to him can indeed be found in Locke's *Paraphrase and Notes* on some major Pauline epistles. Written in retirement, it was in the course of publication when he died in 1704. Locke never mentioned Erasmus but, as an excellent critical edition demonstrates, there is good reason to assume that he perused not only the New Testament Annotations, accessible to him in the collection *Critici sacri*, of which he owned a copy, but also Erasmus' Paraphrases, of which he did not own a copy.[47] In a number of verses the *Paraphrase and Notes* show agreement with Erasmus' interpretation, while in others Locke was likely aware of Erasmus' disagreement with the critics that he himself followed.[48] This is how Locke paraphrased 1 Corinthians 8:6: 'there is but one God the father and author of all things to whom alone we address all our worship and service.' This rendering is quite distinctive and corresponds closely to Erasmus' paraphrase, only that Locke's minute changes, not borne out by either the Greek text or Erasmus, accentuate that prayer and worship are due exclusively to the Father.[49] Locke, moreover, follows in the footsteps of many earlier Antitrinitarians inspired by Erasmus' notes when he fails to find a reference to original sin in Romans 5:12 and support for Christ's eternal divinity in Romans 9:5.[50] Also in their paraphrase of Romans 8:30 both Locke and Erasmus differed sharply from the Calvinist, predestinarian understanding of that verse.[51] Like so many before him, the English philosopher thus drew on Erasmus for his unconventional religious convictions.

In 1690 Locke sent his friend Le Clerc a lengthy disquisition entitled *An historical account of two notable corruptions of Scripture, in a letter to a Friend*. As we shall see later, the author proves himself to be an uncompromising Antitrinitarian. He is not named; he was Locke's good friend Isaac Newton. The discoverer of gravity had an enduring interest in theological questions. He devoted to them many hours of painstaking study and, on occasion, untrammelled speculation. He thus filled many pages, all of which remained unpublished until after his death. He excerpted Lord Falkland's *Discourse on Infallibility* and, like Locke, belonged to the circle around Thomas Firmin.[52] Newton's religion, in line with that of his friends, was centred upon scripture – scripture that, its divine inspiration notwithstanding, needed to be subjected to rational scrutiny. He was at pains to find natural, historical, or mechanical explanations for biblical accounts, but his rational approach still left some space for revelation. He had a soft spot for biblical prophecy and believed, like for instance Daniel De Breen, that Christ would be ruling the Millennium from above, unseen by humans. Newton owned a rich collection of books on the early history of the church – the field to which the majority of his unpublished manuscripts is devoted. The history of the early church was inextricably linked to the development of Christian dogma, and Newton's interest in the latter likely inspired his attention to the former. As might be expected of a member of Firmin's circle, Newton's library and that of Locke, to which Newton no doubt had access when in London, were generously supplied with the classics of Socinianism as well as authors like Aconcio and Castellio.[53] In his theological manuscripts he cited repeatedly Christophorus Sandius, author of the *Bibliotheca antitrinitariorum*, a bio-bibliographical dictionary of Antitrinitarianism, and historian of its beginnings. In old age Newton was once visited by Samuel Crell, descendant of a noted family of Polish Socinians in exile. They talked about one of the visitor's works, which was then being printed, and on parting Newton handed Crell a gift of two guineas.[54]

Newton held Socinian positions on the Trinity and predestination. While not denying Christ's pre-existence, he refused to acknowledge the Son as co-eternal and equal to the Father. About the atonement he was ambiguous. He did accept divine retribution, but was silent about its extent. Concerning the invocation of Christ he wrote: 'Prayers are most prevalent when directed to the Father in the name of the Son' (which, according to Erasmus, had been the practice of the apostles).[55]

Among Newton's theological writings one stands out, and that is the previously mentioned *Historical account*. The second part contains a critical exposition of 1 Timothy 3:16, replete with references to various editions of the New Testament and patristic commentary. Like a long line of Antitrinitarian interpreters before him, Newton rejected the reading that Christ was 'God manifest in the flesh,' arguing that it was a deliberate manipulation of the Greek text dating from the sixth century. Erasmus is not mentioned here, but this was a stone that he had got rolling, although himself he was not prepared to go further than expressing pointedly his doubt about the alleged proof of Christ's divinity.[56] The first part of Newton's disquisition offers a painstaking dissection of the *Comma Johanneum* (1 John 5:7–8), and here it is that his debt to Erasmus comes to light. Although he consulted scores of other commentators beginning with the Greek and Latin fathers, Erasmus remains his principal guide throughout the long argument and the initial source of his most important proof-texts.[57]

Newton's treatment is exhaustively detailed, one could say, scientific, and admirably demonstrates his reliance on scripture as the unique source of religious certainty. For while he claims no more than the falsity of the *Comma*, it is obvious that for him this means the collapse of the entire Trinitarian doctrine. Newton attached exceptional importance to the *Historical account*. It was the only theological manuscript that he considered releasing to the printers. He gave it to Locke, suggesting that the part on the *Comma* should be considered first. Locke sent the whole to Le Clerc, who agreed, somewhat unenthusiastically, to translate and publish it, anonymously of course. But Le Clerc also faulted the author for not having consulted Richard Simon's *Histoire ciritique du Nouveau Testament*. Newton dutifully made up for this omission; but in the end it was he who requested that the revised text not be published, although Le Clerc tried to allay his fear that the author might be identifiable.[58]

While Newton's reliance on Erasmus in the disquisition on the *Comma* is unparalleled, the latter was only the core of a comprehensive argument that the Gospel knew no Trinity of common substance. In two follow-up letters to Locke Newton presented a substantial survey of places in which, he argued, scripture had been corrupted and pressed into serving against the Arians. In the codices to which Erasmus had had access, a number of Newton's 'corruptions' did apparently not show up; so he is mentioned here only once. But many of Newton's proof-texts are well anchored in Socinian exegesis. Here Erasmus' pioneering role is obvious, and Newton's direct consultation of his work likely.[59]

JOHN MILTON

Given the evident status of *Paradise Lost* among the classics of early modern Europe, it was tempting to allot John Milton (1608–74) some space in our next chapter, which deals with Erasmian echoes in early modern literature. There can be no doubt about Milton's admiration for Erasmus; he called him, on account of his learning, 'the wonder of his age.'[60] Especially literary works like the *Moriae encomium* and the *Colloquia* were standard fare in the schools where Milton was educated, St. Paul's, London, and Cambridge. Erasmus' influence on him has been termed 'all-inclusive.'[61] Yet within the framework of this study, Milton's place is here and not among the luminaries of literature discussed in the next chapter. To find a demonstrable influence of Erasmus, we have to turn to Milton's prose work, his critical writing on theology, also on ecclesiology and its implications for English society. His elaborate rejection of the orthodox doctrine of the Trinity can now be seen as the culmination of the radical trends discussed in this chapter, although in the seventeenth century it was not permitted to become public knowledge.

In view of the attention Milton the critic paid to Erasmus, Milton the epic poet cannot of course have been unaware of him. At least some of Milton's radical theology was bound to infiltrate the process of poetic invention. But Adam and Eve, the protagonists of *Paradise Lost*, owe no visible inspiration to Erasmus' *Moriae encomium*, and this, as we shall see, sets them apart from More's Utopians, Rabelais' jolly giants, and Cervantes' errant knight. The carefully laid-out Garden of Eden, in which Adam and Eve toil with the requisite gardening tools,[62] bears no resemblance to the mythical Golden Age evoked by Mistress Folly, nor is it a blueprint for a Utopian future. Moria's playful attitude to sexuality may perhaps resonate with the primordial couple in their initial, not-yet-mortal state.[63] With the Fall, however, when they turn fully human, their amorous passions become sinful and revolting, although somewhat redeemed by the chastity of faithful marriage. Eve is a veritable antipode of Mistress Folly, submissive, unoriginal, and incapable of transformation. While Moria pokes fun at noble and bourgeois characters alike, '*Paradise Lost* presents the first couple as a proto-modern bourgeois couple; labour is divided between them; she prepares the meals, he talks to angels.'[64] Their folly leads to mad intoxication and the Fall; in the *Moriae encomium* folly ultimately leads to grace.

In Milton's prose work Erasmus' 'all-inclusive' influence may be traced to adages, rhetorical concepts, and educational ideas; it may show in their mutual commitment to toleration and pacifism, their loathing of superstition, also in the preference for free will that was passed on to Milton through the medium of Dutch Arminianism. There was, however, a much more controversial issue that had Milton turn to Erasmus explicitly and intensely. Against the background of his own bitter experience, he published between 1643 and 1645 several pamphlets on divorce.[65] These led to furious denunciations of heterodoxy, much as Erasmus' statements on the same issue had done. In view of the misery caused to many estranged couples, Erasmus had wished to see a more liberal practice that would allow a number of grounds for divorce other than merely adultery by the wife, as apparently sanctioned by the Bible. He argued that the relevant scripture texts on divorce and remarriage (especially Deuteronomy 24:1–4, Matthew 19:3–9, and 1 Corinthians 7:39) were open to widely different interpretations and that, as a result, the tradition of the Roman Church revealed a maze of contradictions. He also called for *aequitas naturalis* to blunt the rigour of the law, a term taken up by Milton and, before him, Hugo Grotius, to develop a concept of equity based on natural law.[66] On the basis of Erasmus' arguments Milton reached the radical conclusion that the Canon Law entirely lacked divine sanction and had no standing in England. Hence his advocacy of divorce went much further than the English crown, the Parliament, and the Anglican church were prepared to go. It was, as he noted, precisely the situation prevailing in England that had first caused Erasmus his scruples about the divorce laws; 'Erasmus professes he begun heer among us the same subject [i.e., treating divorce], especially out of compassion, for the need he saw this Nation had of some charitable redresse heerin.'[67] There were other grounds for charging Milton with heterodoxy. In view of the Old Testament patriarchs he found that polygamy could not be faulted, but here he was hardly prompted by Erasmus. More significantly, he believed that soul and body died together, and together will be resurrected on Judgment Day, a view that was held by many Reformation radicals, especially the Socinians, and encouraged, at least, by views Erasmus had expressed.[68]

As we know today, these aberrations from orthodoxy pale in comparison with Milton's critical 'heresy'(as it would have been judged then), his Antitrinitarianism. In view of the fate of Bidle, Best, and other persecuted Antitrinitarians, it is not surprising that the great work he devoted to this matter remained a closely guarded manuscript. It filled an ample volume that, he said, was 'his dearest and best possession';[69] presumably he continued to revise it until his death. Not until 1823–5 was it rediscovered and swiftly published in the Latin original as well as an English translation with the title *A Treatise of Christian Doctrine*. Milton develops his position with the utmost care and an independence that has no equal among the other English Antitrinitarians. He rarely names his sources, heretical ones never, but Maurice Kelley, the annotator of the critical edition, refers to a considerable number of parallels between Milton's text and those of Socinian authors, both continental and English. Analogies to the Racovian Catechism, in particular, would seem to be too numerous to be merely accidental. In fact, in 1650 the London printer William Dugard obtained a licence to print the catechism, after Milton, in his capacity as a Latin secretary to the Council of State, had examined it.[70] Milton was not, however, a Socinian. Unlike the Socinians he held the Arian view of the Son as generated before the Creation and God's agent in the latter, but not equal to the Father, not co-eternal and not co-substantial. He also criticized the Socinians for rejecting Christ's atonement.[71] Like Bidle and his followers, but contrary to the Poles, he maintained that the Holy Spirit was a person (although 'spirit' in scripture often had a less concrete meaning).[72] The Creation, in which Christ participated as the Father's agent, was not, as generally assumed, a *creatio ex nihilo*, but shaped of matter previously created by God.[73]

Among Milton's many sources of inspiration, Erasmus was just one. Kelley has pointed out a number of parallels, and more could no doubt be found. In some cases they would agree, in others they would not. As mentioned elsewhere, Erasmus had lent great weight to the fact that the Greek text uses the definite article, 'the God,' when referring to the Father, but not so when referring to the Son, and afterwards most Antitrinitarians had eagerly taken up Erasmus' point. Milton did not. He pointedly omitted the argument when discussing John 1:1, and on one occasion disdainfully referred to conclusions 'to be lured out from among articles and particles by some sort of verbal bird-catcher.'[74] For clear evidence of Erasmus' 'all-inclusive' influence on Milton, one should turn to the crucial chapter 'Of the Son of God' (I 5). Kelley points out that all patristic references in that chapter come from Erasmus, a clear indication of the diligence with which Milton sought his guidance.[75] Amid many pages replete with citations from scripture where Erasmus often proved helpful,[76] Milton sets out to deliver his knock-out punch to those who will not see 'that the Father alone is a self-existent God.' Here 'only two passages are relevant,' he claims. The first is John 10:30: 'I and the Father are one.' Whether or not this could be taken to refer to one essence had been the subject of a long-drawn-out debate, and Erasmus' paraphrase may well have been its cradle.[77] In his *Apologia* against the Spanish monks he boldly moved to the attack, claiming that the paraphrase was one of the many proofs of his Trinitarian orthodoxy. The terms he used, such as *pariter potentes – idem volentes*, indeed did not agree with the Arians' insistence on Christ's inferiority to the Father, but nor did they favour the concept of consubstantiality, and Erasmus himself suggested soon afterwards that the Arians had had no grounds to fear John's words.[78] Milton reinforces this understanding by citing other proof-texts that denied the Son's equality with the Father, but he does not here mention Erasmus. Milton's second key passage, the *Comma Johanneum* (1 John 5:7–8) is even more standard fare in the Trinitarian controversy, and here he expressly mentions Erasmus' comments and invites the reader to check them out (as Fausto Sozzini had also done). Like Erasmus he points out that even if the verse about the three heavenly witnesses and their unity was admitted, in view of the three earthly witnesses also said to be 'one,' unity could never have meant 'one essence.'[79]

Milton's pervasive scrutiny of Erasmus' New Testament is not unlike the careful attention paid to it by Locke and Newton. What is different, however, apart from the unique factor of undetermined echoes in *Paradise Lost*, is the militancy displayed in the *Christian Doctrine*, less subtle and ironical perhaps but, in turn, more passionate than Erasmus' style in the *Moria* and his controversies, and certainly without Newton's scholarly restraint. One example will suffice:

> But it is amazing what nauseating subtlety, not to say trickery, some people have employed in their attempts to evade the plain meaning of these scriptural texts. They have left no stone unturned; they have followed every red herring they could find; they have tried everything. Indeed they have made it apparent that, instead of preaching the plain, straightforward truth of the gospel to poor and simple men, they are engaged in maintaining an extremely absurd paradox with the maximum of obstinacy and argumentativeness. To save this paradox from utter collapse they have availed themselves of the specious assistance of certain strange terms and sophistries borrowed from the stupidity of the schools.[80]

Milton hoped that his *Christian Doctrine* would reach the widest possible public, although, of course, only after his death. He addressed the Epistle 'To All the Churches of Christ and to All in any part of the world who profess the Christian Faith.' The passage quoted above, now that we can read it in print, will warrant calling him a radical Erasmian.

NINE

The Taste of Erasmian Spice in Some Classics of Early Modern Literature

The focus of this chapter differs from that of the others. The writers that it will examine for the most part lived in different epochs and cultural environments. The bond that ties them together is literary achievement. Amid a great diversity of approaches, all have written works that can be counted among the classics of world literature. Such radical ideas as their authors may have derived from their acquaintance with Erasmus' writings were bound to reach incalculable numbers of readers. All of these works are readily available today, whereas their counterparts in other chapters languish in research libraries and on the desks of unfashionable scholars. To be sure, the work of outstanding minds can change the world without ever achieving a mass circulation, but great works of literature not only offer food for thought, they also dispense delight and enchantment. Erasmus would have been glad to be associated with writing of this stamp. While the Erasmian sources are as varied as the works to be discussed here, Erasmus' one and only contribution to the classics of world literature yields a commanding influence. The *Moriae encomium* sprayed sparks of radicalism among the finest writing of the early modern age.

THOMAS MORE'S *UTOPIA* (1516)

From its first appearance the *Moriae encomium* was tenaciously attacked, mostly from the point of view of conservative Catholicism. In Louvain and elsewhere Mistress Folly's satirical sallies against theologians and ecclesiastics in general as well as her equation of the Christian faith with folly were greeted with outrage.

What was never addressed, however, was her presentation of a humanity persistently in search of pleasure and felicity. None of the early critics mentioned Epicurus; none looked across to Valla's *De voluptate*. The most prominent of them, Maarten van Dorp, expressed his dismay at Christ's testimony and heavenly bliss being labelled 'foolishness (*stultitia*)' and the life to come 'lunacy (*dementia*).' These are indeed the terms used in the *Moria*, but Dorp was silent on that other term that ties the sacred and the foolish together: *felicitas*. Erasmus interjects it pointedly three times in his answer to Dorp; in the *Moria* he had used it many times more.[1] The quest for happiness is, after all, the thread that runs through Folly's speech. The only early reader to seize on this aspect, and to put down in writing that he did so, was Thomas More, the author of *Utopia*. While readers of *Utopia* will have no trouble in finding other parallels to the *Moriae encomium*,[2] they may be puzzled to discover that More says almost nothing about folly.[3] All the more striking is the fact that the theme of pleasure and the contest between Stoics and Epicureans are taken up with an intensity and a vigour reminiscent of Valla's *De voluptate*, and in a way that compellingly invites a comparison with the *Moria*.

There can be no doubt about the extent of More's familiarity with the *Moriae encomium*. It was written in his home, says Erasmus, with his friends partaking in the process.[4] It was specifically offered to More by its dedicatory letter and by the pun on his name in the title, and it was vigorously defended by him against Dorp's attack. That letter to Dorp was composed while More was working on *Utopia*, shortly after his purported talk, in a garden at Antwerp, with Raphael Hythloday, the narrator of the tale about the Nowhere-island.[5] *Utopia* can be read as a sequel to More's letter to Dorp. Its length alone proves that More took Dorp's arguments very seriously, but More must also have realized that by focusing on Mistress Folly's lampooning of scholastic theology, Dorp was far from fathoming the true philosophical depth of Erasmus' declamation. By picking up the theme of pleasure as man's destiny, More's *Utopia* was to set the record straight and do justice to his friend's work.

To be sure, *Utopia* was written to deal with questions then uppermost in More's mind: whether he should join the royal court and, if he did, what policies, ideal and practical, he should work for and what frustrations he must expect. That inquiry, however, would certainly benefit from investigating the respective values of pleasure as against virtue and duty in a citizen's calling – investigating, that is to say, the precepts of the Epicureans and the Stoics. Of all Greek philosophy the tenets of these two schools are the only ones that seem to elicit intensive debate among of the Utopians,[6] and in More's mental dialogue with Mistress Folly that very issue is resolutely given prominence over her other serious concerns.

More had, then, considerable knowledge of Epicurus and Lucretius, and he had read that the newly discovered American Indians were Epicureans of sorts.[7] It is not improbable that he also knew Valla's *De voluptate*.[8] It and Erasmus' *De contemptu mundi*, written long ago but not yet published, could have loomed in the background during the intermittent discussions between the two friends. The relevant section of *Utopia* is squarely based on the four key terms of the classical debate between Epicureans and Stoics, pleasure, virtue, nature, and reason; but like Valla and Erasmus, More adds to them a new perspective, the precepts of the Christian religion. In fact, More can be seen as trying to do what Mistress Folly wisely did not attempt, namely to reconcile the conflicting positions of Valla's interlocutors. As will be seen, More's gallant endeavour would lead to a measure of confusion and, in the end, should rather have discouraged others from trying to do the same thing.

In one regard the Epicurean leanings of the Utopians are blissfully uncontroversial. Guided by the wise provisions of their founder-king Utopus, they maintain a garden culture that has no equal in the cities of sixteenth-century Europe. To the Utopians it is a generous source of both produce and pleasure (*sive ad usum civium, sive ad voluptatem commodius*). Each house gives access to a large community garden full of 'vines, fruits, herbs, flowers.' In a life otherwise marked by strict uniformity the neighbourhood gardens provide an opportunity for experimentation and friendly rivalry from street to street.[9] Gardens apart, the Utopians have to weigh their propensity to pleasure against the precepts of their religion and their moral rules.

> They discuss virtue and pleasure (*voluptas*), but their principal and chief debate is in what thing or things, one or more, they are to hold that happiness (*felicitas*) consists ... They never debate about happiness without uniting certain principles taken from religion as well as from philosophy, which uses rational arguments.[10]

With their rational bent of mind, the Utopians never give a thought to the silly refinements of scholastic logic with which, says Hythloday, we torture our young men.[11] Also Stoic principles do not fare well with them. They judge it 'extreme madness,' Hythloday says twice, to 'pursue hard and painful virtue and not only to banish the sweetness of life but even voluntarily to suffer pain from which you expect no profit.'[12] In military matters, they have no taste for bravery and self-sacrifice. If this sounds uncannily like Valla or Mistress Folly, More is not willing to write off virtue so lightly. Although Hythloday suggests in one passage that the partisans of virtue are haters of pleasure,[13] the Utopians believe that the two are compatible. Hythloday's account of their ethics, which covers quite a number of pages,[14] can be summarized like this. God's purpose for humans is to live according to nature, and that is: to be guided by reason to a life of virtue, which is the unfailing source of happiness. However, behind this smooth concept there loom considerable difficulties. Hythloday finds that the Utopians 'lean more than they should to the school that espouses pleasure as the object by which to define either the whole or the chief part of human happiness.' In another place, however, he qualifies his assessment: 'they are somewhat too much inclined to this attitude of mind: that no kind of pleasure is forbidden, provided no harm comes of it.'[15] The proviso is crucial; it is ultimately based on their belief in the immortality of souls and accountability after death.

Now – to return to the Utopians' chief topic of debate – what is the source of happiness? Hythloday offers several answers. According to a contrary school (*adversa factio*, identified as Stoics in a marginal) it is uniquely virtue. But according to the dominant school of Epicurean-minded Utopians, virtue impels human nature to seek decent pleasure, which is the source of happiness.[16] If virtue, not nature, is the primary motor, we are beckoned back into Stoic territory. But not for long: on the next page nature is the moving force. Nature bids us to pursue a happy life by making pleasure the goal of all our actions. To follow that prescript of nature is what the Utopians define as virtue.[17] In a third passage Hythloday says that reason is the source of happiness. In the first place reason induces us to love God, who had made us capable of happiness, and secondly reason urges us to lead a life full of joy.[18] But is reason really so powerful? Just before that, Hythloday had said that reason needed the support of certain principles taken from religion and philosophy, or it would be too weak to investigate happiness. The Utopians also admit that pleasures that conform to nature are striven for by the senses as well as reason.[19]

Virtue, nature, reason – of the three it is clearly nature that receives the most attention in the Utopians' philosophy of pleasure. But again, on several counts the reader may get somewhat confused. Hythloday can speak, in terms reminiscent of Lucretius, Valla, and Mistress Folly, of Mother Nature, who sovereignly provides gentle but firm guidance to her children.[20] But, more typically perhaps, he sees humans as God's creatures entrusted to the leadings of nature. It is God's purpose for humankind that we should live in accord with nature (*secundum naturam*), and nature conditions us to make pleasure the goal of all our actions.[21] However, we can seek pleasure by means fair or foul. Only good and decent pleasures bring happiness; foul means net 'false pleasures (*voluptates falsae, adulterinae*)' that yield gratification contrary to nature (*praeter naturam dulcia*).[22] How can nature condition us to seek pleasures that are contrary to nature, and what, precisely, stirs us to seek such wicked pleasures? Hythloday prefers to move on to safer ground and explains in considerable detail what the Utopians consider to be false pleasures, namely ostentatious dressing, foolish honours, inherited nobility and wealth, gems, dicing, and hunting. Needless to say that such social evils have absolutely no place in Utopian society. Hythloday himself associates them with the courts of Europe, as did Erasmus in the *Moria*.

Hythloday then turns to the Utopians' idea of genuine pleasure. They distinguish pleasures of the mind (*animus*) and body. Mental pleasures matter the most; they consist primarily of virtuous conduct, a good conscience and, ultimately, heavenly delights.[23] Bodily pleasures range from sustenance and sex to the enjoyment of music and, most importantly, good health. Even the base pleasures of the senses are legitimate and deserve to be enjoyed, but only in moderation. The Utopians reinvented the Epicurean rule that sometimes a lesser pleasure must be forgone for the sake of securing a greater and that no pleasure is worth having at the price of causing pain that outweighs the pleasure. They add, however, that the rule is useless without the vital distinction between right and wrong.[24]

Man is a social creature. The Utopians, who practise community of goods, also want pleasures to be enjoyed in common. Affording pleasure to others by providing for their needs justifies self-indulgence. 'When nature bids you to be good to others,' so say the Utopians, 'she does not condemn you conversely to be cruel and merciless to yourself.'[25] One is reminded of Moria, who had asked: 'Can he who hates himself love anyone else?' On the other hand, quite a few Utopians, and highly admired ones at that, desire to toil for others without any thought of themselves. Some even 'entirely reject the pleasures of this life as harmful. They long only for their future life by means of night watches and sweat.'[26] Most Utopians find this behaviour unreasonable; but in the name of religious tolerance it is respected, even revered. This is as close as the Utopians ever come in joining Moria as she leaps from Epicurus' pigs to the folly of Christ. They give rather qualified approval to the merits of asceticism. It is madness, they think,

> to exhaust the body by fasts, to injure one's health, and to reject all other favors of nature, unless a man neglects these advantages in providing more zealously for the pleasure of other persons or of the public, in return for which sacrifice he expects a greater pleasure from God.[27]

Does Hythloday wish the Utopians were more resolutely committed to a strict spiritual discipline? Is this why he finds them too much inclined to think that no harmless pleasure is forbidden? In an enigmatic statement he says that in comparison with their proneness to pleasure-seeking,

> what is more astonishing is that they seek a defense for this soft doctrine from their religion, which is serious and strict, almost depressing (*tristis*) and hard.[28]

Seeing the Utopians' emphasis on virtue and altruism, and their low ranking of physical pleasures, it is not easy to agree with Hythloday that their moral doctrine is soft. And why should their religion be severe and depressing? As Hythloday describes their beliefs and worship, the salient qualities are cheerful confidence, reasonableness, tolerance, and aversion to proselytizing zeal. The 'not so very few' that actually practise asceticism in order to merit heavenly rewards do so in ways reminiscent of St Francis. They eschew learning and humbly toil in the service of their fellow men.[29]

Hythloday is wise not to mention Epicurus. Since he denied the immortality and accountability of the human soul, he would in the eyes of the Utopians have been unworthy of their citizenship and even subhuman.[30] In their philosophy of pleasure, religion is a key factor. Their notions of true and false pleasures and of the pursuit of happiness by means fair or foul culminate in their expectation of everlasting joys and pains after death. 'Finally – and religion easily brings this home to the mind which readily assents – God repays, in place of a brief and tiny pleasure, immense and never-ending gladness.'[31] In view of their aversion to asceticism, it is not quite clear what brief and tiny pleasures the Utopians are willing to forgo in the name of their religious beliefs. At any rate, they deem it 'extreme madness,' one recalls, to give up pleasures and suffer pain without a prospect of reward, and no reward can be richer than the joys hoped for in heaven. Here we are close to the view expressed by Erasmus in *De contemptu mundi*.

A final remark by Hythloday suggests once again that the Utopians have thought long and hard about virtue and pleasure. They believe, he says, that they have come as close to the truth on that matter as human reason can, so long as divine inspiration does not provide a holier insight.[32] Are we amiss to think that the author of *Utopia* himself has thought long and hard about virtue and pleasure, also about their respective places in his own daily life, and was awaiting further clarity from divine illumination?

Hythloday's endeavours at understanding the moral concepts of his islanders do not turn *Utopia* into a radical book. *Utopia*, though, is a radical book. It is radical in its scathing social criticism that equals, indeed surpasses, anything Erasmus wrote in the *Moriae ecomium* or elsewhere. Unlike Erasmus, Hythloday does not believe that the evils of European society can be tackled with remedial measures. The existing institutions are beyond reforming. They must be abolished and replaced by new and different ones. Private property, which is at the root of all corruption, must disappear; society must learn to share all goods evenly in complete fairness. More knows that this will not happen; his *Utopia* is a utopia. But, as J.H. Hexter emphasizes, he has the courage to imagine a model of society that is more radical than either Plato's *Republic* or the Gospel message.[33] In Plato's *Laws* communism is deemed to be the best system of society, but since it is beyond people's capacity, one has to settle for the second best, which is responsible private ownership.³⁴ Hythloday makes no such compromises. Plato's *Republic* had caught More's attention early on and apparently also been a topic of his conversations with Erasmus. In his portrait of More Erasmus recalls: 'As a youth he even worked on a dialogue in which he supported Plato's doctrine of communalism, extending it even to wives.'³⁵ Only the experiment with free love was one that More preferred not to transplant into Utopia.

Another source of inspiration for More was Amerigo Vespucci. More knew Vespucci's account of his first voyage, which, the Italian adventurer claimed, had taken him to America. He describes the natives' communal way of life. Private property is restricted to what a woman can carry around with her. Marriage does not exist, but children are apparently attributed to individual fathers.³⁶ Vespucci calls the lifestyle of his Americans 'Epicurean,' but does not say for what reasons. Perhaps he was thinking of the penchant for unbridled erotic pleasures that he attributes to them. To the Utopians, however, sexuality, while natural, is subject to definite restraints. The same must be said for Mistress Folly. Sexuality runs as an undercurrent through her light-hearted (but not lightweight) pummelling of the Stoics and her affection for the happy pigs of Epicurus' herd. As Hythloday describes it, the Utopians' investigation of pleasure and virtue, nature and reason is more serious and perhaps more profound. More launches a sober probe into the potential of Epicurean and Stoic impulses, Christianized and otherwise, and comes up with somewhat confusing results. He has opted for entering the garden of Epicurus by the narrow gate.

RABELAIS AND ERASMUS: A CONTEST OF SUBVERSION OR A PACT OF IRREVERENCE?

In 1532 François Rabelais, then approaching the age of fifty, had an opportunity to introduce himself to Erasmus and eagerly seized it. His letter which, as far as we know, was neither answered nor repeated, is now famous. 'Father' he calls Erasmus and even, Erasmus permitting, would call him also 'mother' – a mother who had nurtured him unseen, as it were, in her womb, without even knowing his name. 'You taught me,' he tells Erasmus, 'you nourished me with the chaste suck of your divine learning.'³⁷ In the same year Rabelais began to publish the chronicle of his jolly giants, Gargantua and Pantagruel. He was already well acquainted with Erasmus' work, and this acquaintance grew in breadth and depth in the course of his literary career. The prologue to *Gargantua* (1534) opens with memorable echoes to the adage *Sileni Alcibiadis* (III iii 1); indeed, adages constantly come to Rabelais' mind. M.A. Screech believes that amid all Erasmus' writings the Annotations to the New Testament have found the greatest resonance in Rabelais' work. As an example he cites *Gargantua*, chapter 10, where a reference to Matthew 17:2 is clearly inspired by Erasmus' note.[38] The true dimension of Erasmus' influence, however, is not revealed by such direct borrowings but by the congeniality of their views in many important matters, some of them quite audacious.

Rabelais never met Erasmus and, except for the famous letter, never mentions him. Rabelais' most prominent patrons, however – Cardinal Jean Du Bellay and, especially, his brother Guillaume Du Bellay, sieur de Langey – entertained important relations to Basel at the time of Erasmus' residence there, and while Rabelais studied and taught medicine at Montpellier, he was befriended by Bishop Guillaume Pellicier, admirer of Erasmus and protector of a circle of Montpellier students who likewise venerated Erasmus and, in some cases, fell foul of the Inquisition. In Paris Rabelais was acquainted with Erasmus' correspondents Etienne Dolet and Guillaum Budé.[39]

Rabelais' debt to Erasmus is undoubted, and so is the irregularity of his life as a member of Catholic monastic orders. But how radical his religious views really were turns out to be highly controversial. If he has a place in the history of Erasmus-based radicalism, that place must be ample. The chronicle of his giants was published in over a hundred editions in the sixteenth century and must thus have reached broad sections of the francophone public as well as many others who possessed a fairly advanced command of French. A curiously amplifying adaptation of *Gargantua*, the *Geschichtklitterung* of Johannes Fischart, appeared in 1575 in Basel and was often reprinted. An outstanding English translation of Rabelais' work, by Thomas Urquhart, appeared in the seventeenth century.[40]

In what is perhaps the most influential of all studies of Rabelais, Lucien Febvre, while fully conscious of the extent to which Rabelais is indebted to Erasmus, gives a startling assessment of their respective bents to daring:

Rabelais' acts of daring were all committed by Erasmus, only in much more accentuated form, less good-natured, less rustic, more cutting ... when one looks at passages in Rabelais and compares them to passages in Erasmus, one is struck by their timidity ... Nowhere does Rabelais indicate that he has seen how a clever man might use the daring interpretations, innuendos and sometimes clever evasions in Erasmus to plant a series of disquieting doubts in perceptive minds.[41]

Febvre's best argument in support of his claim perhaps is the treatment of Genesis. The first chapter of *Pantagruel* offers a genealogy of giants from antediluvian times down to King Gargantua and his son, Pantagruel, whose birth is described in the next chapter. The lineage survived the Flood thanks to the giant Hurtaly, who sat astride Noah's ark and directed it with his legs and feet, while being revictualled by the ark's grateful crew through the chimney. Thus Rabelais, together with the Hebrew sources that inspired him, pokes gentle fun at the biblical account of the Flood. But his little tale need in no way have left a lurching doubt in the mind of his contemporary readers as to whether the story of the Deluge, and Genesis as a whole, was fiction. Modern readers who might suspect Rabelais of such a subversive intent should consider how widely the tale of the Flood was still believed in the nineteenth century.[42] All the more stunning by comparison, as Febvre rightly emphasizes, is Erasmus' adage *Sileni Alcibiadis*, beloved by Rabelais and so many of their contemporaries, in which we are invited to reject the factuality of the events in the garden of Eden and much else in the Old Testament in order for the allegorical truth to shine forth more brightly: from the creation of Adam out of dirt and of Eve from Adam's side while he was sleeping to the stories of Loth and Samson, according to Erasmus' sweeping verdict, we find the sort of tales spun in Homer's craftshop: *ex Homeri officina profecta fabula*. And Homer to him is *pater omnium fabularum*. Again modern readers will realize, but sixteenth-century apparently did not, what an exceptional distance Erasmus has travelled on the road to the demythologization of ancient history, profane *and* sacred.[43] But unlike modern readers, Rabelais' contemporaries would need no learned commentary to savour his implicit mockery of the many princely families that also traced their ancestry back to Noah.[44] It is not only the Old Testament that invites Erasmus' critical scrutiny. The New Testament does even more so as he labours to expose incorrect translations and interpretations. We recall how conservative theologians took him constantly to task for his insistence that key dogmas of the church were unbiblical. Rabelais, by contrast, had little reason to fear his critics on this particular issue; however, there were others.

Another issue that supports Febvre's contention is the status and veneration of the Virgin Mary. Febvre is right in pointing out that Erasmus often (although by no means regularly) prefers to call her 'mother of Jesus' rather than 'mother of Christ' or even 'mother of God.'[45] Her perpetual virginity, Erasmus says, is not supported by the New Testament, but to reject and perhaps even to doubt it is unacceptable in view of the consensus that particular belief enjoyed among the earliest fathers.[46] In chapter six of *Gargantua* Rabelais describes the distinctly strange birth of the baby giant from his mother's left ear. Rabelais admits that the story defies credence; but it is recorded, he claims, in writing, and neither the Bible nor anything else suggests that it should be discarded. 'Est-ce contre nostre loy, nostre foy, contre raison, contre la Saincte Escripture?' The reader would be hard put not to compare Gargantua's unnatural nativity with the miraculous birth of Christ from a virgin mother. In an ironic jab in the first edition, later suppressed, Rabelais has the Sorbonne theologians define faith as believing the seemingly impossible (the old *credo quia absurdum*). If it were God's will, Rabelais concludes, all women would from now on give birth through the ear. It is attractive to think, with Screech, that Rabelais here takes his clue from Erasmus' note on Hebrews 11:1, that like Erasmus he contrasts the wrong scholastic understanding of 'faith in things that possess no appearance of likelihood' with the correct approach. 'Not,' says Erasmus, 'faith (*fides*) in things that we believe because they must be believed, but trust (*fiducia*) in things we hope for.'[47] Modern readers must weigh here their options: is Rabelais doing one or both of two things, preaching trust in God or poking fun by association at the miraculous birth of Jesus? Again many sixteenth-century readers might have enjoyed the story without such concerns.

When it comes to radical discourse about the Virgin Mary, Erasmus easily surpasses Rabelais. He bluntly points out that perpetual virginity requires her, even after Jesus' birth, never to have had intercourse with a man (and leaves it to the reader to wonder about the other children that Matthew attributes to her). He also had to defend himself for an impatient reaction to a canon's servant droning on about Mary's blessed womb (*viscera*, intestines).[48] A vigorously sarcastic scrutiny of Mariolatry can be found in Erasmus' colloquies *Naufragium* (The Shipwreck) and *Peregrinatio religionis ergo* (A Pilgrimage for the Sake of Religion). In the former the desperate sailors intone the *Salve Regina* and call on Mary with titles such as *Stella maris* – titles that are nowhere assigned to her in scripture (Erasmus' *ceterum censeo*). To the objection that the Virgin never undertook a voyage by sea, the narrator points to the origins of her cult in the pagan myth of the goddess Venus:

> Formerly Venus was protectress of sailors, because she was believed to have been born of the sea. Since she gave up guarding them, the Virgin Mother has succeeded this other who was not a virgin. [49]

Thus Mary's cult, like the tales of Genesis, should be approached with ancient mythology in mind. The other colloquy takes the reader to the shrine of Our Lady of Walsingham. It starts charmingly with a letter that Mary addresses to 'Glaucoplutus' ('owl-rich': Ul-rych Zwingli), complaining both about the silly requests with which she was beseeched in former days and the hard times on which she has fallen now that the Reformation has drastically curtailed the flow of pilgrims. At the climax of the colloquy the visitors are allowed to kiss a crystal phial with the Virgin's milk that is fifteen hundred years old and therefore 'hard: you'd say powdered chalk, tempered with white of egg.' In the same savage fashion St Bernard has his usual title of *doctor mellifluus* changed to *lactifluus* on account of the legend that records how he was once allowed to taste Mary's milk from the same breast that the Jesus baby had sucked. The visiting narrator also addresses to the phial representing Mary herself a half-way evangelical prayer, asking for 'the milk of gospel doctrine,' but also for 'dove-like simplicity,' and is rewarded by signs of approval: 'For the sacred milk appeared to leap up, and the Eucharistic elements gleamed somewhat more brightly.'[50]

The colloquy *Naufragium* was published in August 1523, and in the autumn of that year Erasmus had an opportunity to make amends to the Virgin. To please a pious friend, he wrote a short mass for the shrine of Our Lady of Loreto.[51] The *Peregrinatio* to Walsingham was newly added to the Colloquies edition of February 1526. Two years later Erasmus wrote his Reply to the Spanish monks, who had correctly sensed some ambiguity in a passage of his *Modus orandi*. This passage, he now claimed, stated clearly that the perpetual virginity of Mary 'belonged to the things that, in view of the traditional consensus of the fathers and the church, we hold must be believed no less as if they were stated in scripture.'[52] Rabelais, on the other hand, inserted in his *Quart Livre* of 1548/1552 (chaps. 19, 21) a scene closely resembling Erasmus' *Naufragium*. At the peak of the storm a passenger calls upon the Virgin, but the one to do so is the distraught, frantic Panurge, while the good king Pantagruel calmly invokes the help of God the Lord, piously adding 'but your holy will be done.' If this means that Rabelais too made amends with the Virgin, Erasmus certainly had done so more forthrightly, but then Erasmus had also affronted her more flagrantly.

So far we have looked at evidence in support of Febvre's contention. In a number of other cases inviting comparison, however, I don't see why Erasmus should be awarded the palm of irreverence. In the story of the little nun, for example, Rabelais does not seem to lag behind. He borrowed the tale from Erasmus' colloquy *Ichthyophagia* (the fish diet) with an unusual degree of directness. A nun has been made pregnant by a 'young man.' When her condition can no longer be concealed and she stands accused before her abbess, she explains that she was raped but could not scream for help because the attack happened in the dormitory, where the rule prescribes strict silence. Rabelais amplifies Erasmus' story a little and, in doing so, adds poignancy to it. The alleged rapist is a young lay brother (*briffault*), employed by the nuns to collect alms for them. When asked why she did not report the assault sooner, the nun explains that, afraid to remain in a state of mortal sin, she confessed to her attacker before he departed – as if he had been a priest – and had as her penance laid upon her to conceal what had happened.[53] If Rabelais thus pokes the embers of audacity in one way, he douses it in another. His context is innocuous in comparison with the frame that Erasmus gives the story. Erasmus has it told by a Dominican in a solemn homily on the Saviour's death 'to temper the sadness of his sermon.'

Here is another example of what seem to me matching degrees of boldness. The only rule that regulates the life of his anti-monks and anti-nuns in Rabelais' abbey of Theleme is *Fay ce que vouldras*.

As pointed out earlier, this corresponds exactly with the fourth and final rule in the gospel of the Epicurean Polyphemus in Erasmus' colloquy *Cyclops*: 'to be free to do as you like.'[54] Rabelais knew the *Colloquia* exceedingly well. Assuming that this particular passage left a mark in his memory, the rule of Theleme certainly does not suggest that he understood Erasmus' words merely as a pointer to dangerous Lutheran licence. For Rabelais, the line expresses a freedom that nature herself, he says, bestows on those well born and well educated – an inner freedom that leads them to embrace virtue and repulse vice. Febvre associates Rabelais' explanation with a passage in Erasmus' *Hyperaspistes secundus*, where those well born and well educated are said to be the least inclined to evil deeds – an inclination that was opposed to nature and usually due to a misdirected upbringing and a wicked will rather than nature.[55] Whether or not Rabelais here remembered Erasmus' analogous words – the contexts are actually quite different -- there is that striking affinity in their trust in the natural goodness of human nature.

Erasmus had never questioned the existence of everlasting retribution as a counterpoint to the everlasting bliss enjoyed in heaven, but he had repeatedly to defend his view that the fires of hell were metaphorical and the torments of the condemned souls mental rather than physical, which made them actually *more* painful.[56] Eventually, in 1533, he wound his way to an ambiguous formulation that would not entirely preclude the bodily suffering of the reject along with the more intense mental one.[57] While Rabelais' approach again is quite different, it is no less radical. Epistemon's mercifully short visit to hell, which he equates with the *Champs Elisées*, has been shorter than he would have wished, for the devils are *bons compaignons* and the damned, who exercise a bizarre occupation, include, apart from several popes, Epictetus. The Stoic philosopher par excellence presides over a banquet seasoned with dancing and plenty of white and red wine.[58] Elsewhere Rabelais, borrowing from Erasmus' *Apophthegmata*, finds generous space for a charming tale about a dumb little devil who is cheated of his spoils by a cunning labourer and his indelicate wife.[59] Rabelais' characters constantly refer to the devils in the course of their plentiful swearing but, as happens often in his discourse, there is a space beyond joking. When he blames *l'esprit maling* for King Picrochole's tumble into undertaking a senseless, bloody, and ultimately self-destructive war, Satan becomes a frightening reality. Screech finely points out that seduction by that same *esprit maling* seems to account for Panurge's decay. An ingenious prankster and trickster at first, he ends up as a despicable, selfish wimp with deadly fear in his heart and shit in his pants. Likewise, Erasmus perceives Reuchlin's opponent Pfefferkorn to be dominated by Satan. Both authors fully understand the naive nature of popular hell-and-devil lore, but neither of them doubts the existence of an evil power that can seduce human beings and prompt them to do base and vicious deeds.[60]

In pursuit of our quest here we must turn to some pages of Rabelais' tale where he would seem to be more daring than Erasmus, not less. Both are untiring and often abrasive in their critique of monastic orders and their members. If Rabelais' Frere Jean, a wild character by any standards, wins our grudging admiration, he does so for actions that are by no means exemplary of monastic ideals. In fact, none of Rabelais' characters seems to cherish them. Erasmus, however, despite savage and frequent criticisms, often expresses sincere respect for the ideals that gave birth to monasticism and the way they were realized before corruption set in. Towards the Franciscan Jean Vitrier and the Benedictine Paul Volz he expressed feelings of the warmest friendship. When Volz and also another close friend, the Augustinian canon Maarten Lips, got ensnared in doubts about their vocation and felt inclined to leave their monasteries, Erasmus, who had himself done just that, nonetheless counselled them to soldier on.[61] Forever concerned to keep matters in balance, he must have considered that for some, though perhaps not for many, the monastic way of life was right. There are no corresponding traits in Rabelais' work or, as far as we know, in his life either. His good friend and fellow Franciscan friar Pierre Amy left, like himself, his monastery but, unlike Rabelais, or for that matter Erasmus, did so in open defiance of his superiors.

Erasmus' advice to Volz and Lips is given in his letters to them. Perhaps it will be argued that epistolography, even if it is as versatile as Erasmus', cannot be compared to Rabelais' giant lore, which is saturated with satire and therefore subject to the stylistic rules of satire. We should not seek in Rabelais' work what has no logical place there. Against that I would maintain that both authors expected to be understood on more than one level. Rabelais exercised a deliberate choice; his critique of monasticism is single-minded and quite unlike Erasmus' balanced approach. In the famous letter to Volz prefaced to the 1518 re-edition of the

Enchiridion (Ep. 858), Erasmus used a single text to combine critique and praise. He lashed out at contemporary monks and friars, their rivalries and their endemic corruption. *Tyrannis* and *sanctimonia* are the key terms that he uses to brand their pharisaic shortcomings. Yet that same preface speaks with sincere admiration about the untainted beginnings of the monastic movement. By contrast, Rabelais' abbey of Theleme brings no balance but only paradox. It completely reverses, and consequently subverts, monastic values.

Analogous conclusions can be drawn from the two authors' references to popes and the papal office. Both had some firsthand experience of the Roman curia. While Erasmus wrote of the ruling Pope Leo X with extravagant flattery, Rabelais never did anything of the kind, although Pope Clement VII had reportedly dandled Rabelais' son Théodule on his lap,[62] and although, when he so wanted, Rabelais too knew how to flatter, as he demonstrated in the case of King Francis I. Erasmus had reasons for doing what he did. He was anxious to win papal approval for his New Testament and at least implicit release from his monastic vows, whereas Rabelais put up with his irregular position without visible discomfort. That difference, however, pales in view of both writers' audacious critiques of the papacy. Erasmus' satire of Pope Julius II in the *Julius exclusus* is so biting that he consistently preferred to disown the work. Rabelais is equally *osé*, and coarser into the bargain. He has Pantagruel and his party visit the island of the Papimanes, who are indeed maniacs. They worship the pope as their god and the Decretal, the official collection of papal decrees, as their gospel. If only they could meet the pope, they sigh. They would kiss his arse and also his testicles, for testicles he must have. 'When the world runs out of balls, it won't have a pope any more.' Rabelais here hints at the myth of Popess Joan, well known to his contemporaries. She still figured among the busts of all the popes in the cathedral of Siena, and she was taken seriously by Luther. Legend had it that after Joan all popes had their private parts inspected as part of their installation ceremonies, lest another deceitful woman soil the purity of the apostolic succession.[63] The poor Papimanes only possess the crudely painted picture of a pope, which they venerate as their most precious icon. When the visitors assert that they have seen the real pontiff, the admiring crowd reverently kisses their feet. The visitors eventually depart with an act of cruel deception; they promise to return to Rome and persuade the pope to visit the Papimanes in person. In this case too Rabelais is more radical; he never steps beyond the boundaries of satire and thus has no opportunity to follow Erasmus on his typical search for balance. In his *Moria* Erasmus paints a devastating picture, 'as things are today,' of 'these impious pontiffs who allow Christ to be forgotten.'[64] But once the *Moria* is published, he takes pride in pointing out to his critics that Leo X read Mistress Folly's speech and liked it.[65] Then again in a private letter he goes so far as to write: 'I perceive that the absolute rule of the *Roman high-priest* [in Greek] is the curse of Christianity'; and in published statements too he continues to bemoan papal 'tyranny.'[66] But he is also willing to work constructively for change. With Leo X's successor, Adrian VI, a fellow Dutchman ascends the papal throne. Erasmus had known him for many years and initially had rather disliked him. But in view of Adrian's earnest desire for reform Erasmus changes his mind and offers his cooperation.[67]

The same difference in approach prevails when we turn to the cult of the saints. The maritime storms in Erasmus' colloquy *Naufragium* and in Rabelais' *Quart Livre* are merely one of the countless occasions both authors have found to express comparable sarcasm about invoking the saints' help. The desperate supplicants do not hesitate to promise them return favours that they have no intention of delivering. The questionable value of prayers to the saints does not, of course, mean that prayers per se are unavailing. Rabelais' approach resembles that of Erasmus; both often use mirth and laughter to guide their readers to the religious values that they actually hold dear, but neither does so in the case of saints worship, although Erasmus is cautious. He states in the *Modus orandi* that praying to the saints is neither prohibited nor requested. His strong preference, as always, is for prayers addressed directly to God.[68] In his remarkable biography of Jerome he defies traditional legends to show the true personality of the saint chosen by him to be his model, to the point of having his own portraits fashioned after Jerome's.[69] Also, and perhaps less predictably, he often expresses his genuine affection for Saint Francis, the paragon of simplicity, humility, and love.[70] Once again we find Erasmus here on a path on which Rabelais did not follow him, and the parting of their ways is significant. Rabelais never sees the slightest need for placating the saints. Proud loyalty to his native region cannot, for instance, induce him to acknowledge Saint Martin, the premier saint of Touraine. Erasmus, by contrast, does Martin the singular honour of pronouncing him a true Silenus along with Diogenes, Epictetus, Christ, and John the Baptist.[71] Here we cannot simply explain Rabelais' stance by saying that a respectful mention of some great saints would have carried him beyond the scope of his satirical giants' tale. In the comprehensive program of humanist and evangelical education that Gargantua develops for his son not a single scholar-saint is recommended for study. Neither John Chrysostom nor Augustine nor Bernard is apparently deemed worthy to join the classics, the physicians, astronomers, even Talmudists and Cabbalists that can guide Pantagruel to secular and sacred enlightenment. Perhaps this was to be expected, seeing that the sainted fathers had had no place in Gargantua's own education. As to Rabelais himself, not a single father is mentioned in Jean Plattard's careful examination of his sources.[72] If we think of Erasmus' life-long commitment to reading, editing, and translating patristic texts, the difference could not be more glaring.

All Thelemites have their own chapels attached to their private quarters, but their spacious abbey lacks a central church where the community could have congregated to celebrate mass. Where they occur, Rabelais' rare references to masses are hardly edifying. Young Gargantua's daily routine includes 'twenty-six or thirty masses,' sandwiched between a giant breakfast and a miserly half hour of study. Obliged to attend on the island of the Papimanes *une [messe] basse et seiche*, Frere Jean vents his displeasure. He would have preferred a solemn Requiem mass with 'bread and wine' to appease his empty stomach.[73] By contrast, when Erasmus harshly criticizes the proliferation of silent masses and the lack of devotion of congregations attending mass, he really expresses his concern for the dignity of the liturgical ceremony. And while it is true that all ceremonies, including the mass, do not form part of the essential core of his Christian religion, Erasmus is far from sharing Rabelais' cavalier neglect. Likewise in the deathbed scene of Erasmus' colloquy *Funus* the last confession and administration of the sacrament of the dying is duly mentioned. Not so in the deathbed scene of Rabelais' Raminagrobis, who has taken good care to chase away a horde of monks and friars.[74] The absence of such references to sacramental ceremonies need not say much about Rabelais' religion, but neither can it enhance in his readers Catholic devotion, as Erasmus is set on doing in many places. Although the progress of the Reformation affected their discourse and perhaps even their outlook in successive works, both authors showed no inclination to join the reformers. They were not Protestant propagandists. They attacked and ridiculed Catholic institutions not because those institutions were Catholic, but because they malfunctioned. Moreover, they decried rigid dogmatism regardless of confession.

Blasphemy is another and more serious matter. Erasmus was often accused of it by Luther as well as his conservative Catholic critics; today these charges seem without substance. Erasmus' colloquy *Naufragium* makes sport of the saints and the Virgin along with their superstitious implorers, but there the fun ends. No one utters a blasphemy. Indeed, two passengers entrust their fate to the Almighty in exemplary evangelical fashion, exactly as does Pantagruel in Rabelais' tempest.[75] But now compare this to Panurge's pathetic behaviour in that same tempest. Amid litanies of meaningless babble, his fear of death causes him to equate his fate with that of the crucified Christ in agony, aping his sigh of thirst – *un peu de vinaigre*, wines Panurge – and his dying words: *Consumatum est* and *in manus* (Father, into thy hands I commit my spirit).[76] The Papimanes can also be deemed blasphemers when they use Jahweh's words to Moses, *Ego sum qui sum* (Exodus 3:14), to refer to the pope: *celluy qui est*, and when they long for him to come like the long-awaited Messiah.[77] The bread and wine that Frere Jean craves during the Papimane mass to fill his empty stomach may perhaps not be consecrated, but the Eucharistic clue is unavoidable and, of course, sacrilegious. But again we should take to heart Febvre's frequent warnings that Rabelais' contemporaries, the people for whom he wrote, thought and spoke differently from what we might assume. Did they even think of blasphemy when they read these passages? Rabelais' sworn enemies, a Calvin, a Guillaume Postel, and later a Father Garasse, certainly did, and they said so too. But the *libertins* and free-thinkers of seventeenth-century France and England by and large did not say that Rabelais was an unbeliever who denied the existence of God, and probably they did not think it either. Nonetheless, they called him a free spirit, an *impie*, and 'Master of Scoffing.' '*Gargantua* est le livre de chevet par excellence des libertins.'[78] What is clear is that Rabelais, long before serious scholars began to discuss whether or not he was an atheist in the modern sense, encouraged in some readers a sarcasm, even a cynicism towards religion that went way beyond Erasmus' irreverent stabs at superstition and corruption, proferred in support of true evangelism. On the other hand, Erasmus' New Testament scholarship continually encouraged criticism of the divine Trinity, the doctrine at the centre of Christian theology, and in this matter Rabelais kept silent. Who of the two, Erasmus or Rabelais, has shown more daring may be a moot question; each made his own choice of audacities. But neither of them meant to subvert religion (or, for that matter, morality and the political state). Both authors knew how entertaining and also challenging irreverence can be and served ample portions of it, but ultimately with the intention of improving things, not destroying them.

Both foes and friends of Rabelais in early modern Europe frequently called him an 'Epicurean.' Those who did so certainly did not think of Erasmus' advocacy of a Christian Epicureanism, nor of his dallying with Horace's light-hearted herd of Epicurus' piglets in the *Moria*. Those who called Rabelais a follower of Epicurus or of Lucretius and the 'French Lucian' mostly meant that he was a profligate, sometimes also that he was an unbeliever. Rabelais, of course, was neither, but though he knew Erasmus' *Moria* well, it is questionable whether the various types of folly that he described owe much to Mistress Folly's speech. Panurge's blind *philautie*, I think, does not.[79] To find an author who was more directly inspired by her, we now turn to Cervantes.

CERVANTES AND HIS RADICAL MUTATIONS OF *MORIA*'S CONCEPTS OF FOLLY

The reader of Erasmus' *Moriae encomium* comes face to face with a variety of fools. Mistress Folly is rather loose and gracefully inconsistent when it comes to nomenclature and classification. She describes various degrees of feeble-mindedness and also the type of the professional fool attached to the courts of princes. At greater length she examines other men absorbed in the unenlightened exercise of their profession, deluding themselves with a miserable kind of happiness.[80] What is relevant, however, to the following discussion are three kinds of folly that she distinguishes quite clearly.

1 Criminal fools, whose selfish actions bring harm to others or cause the perpetrator guilt and despair. This is an insanity sent from hell.[81]
2 Endearing fools, whose harmless follies – 'desirable, ... known to come from me,' says Moria – bring pleasure to themselves and to

others. This, we may assume, is the kind of happy folly that is most readily accessible to 'those who have no traffic at all with any kind of learning and follow Nature for their only guide.'[82]

3 The fools in Christ, whose happiness is meek acceptance of suffering and, in rare cases, the bliss of divine rapture.[83]

The second kind of folly, the one that is neither satanic nor divine, but profoundly human, could hardly be found in Rabelais, but in Cervantes its presence is striking.

Miguel de Cervantes' first substantial work, *La Galatea*, was published in 1585, shortly after an unprecedented number of Erasmus' works had appeared on the Index of the Spanish Inquisition.[84] This goes some way towards explaining why Erasmus' name never appears in Cervantes' work. True, he could have borrowed from Erasmus precise words and specific ideas without mentioning the source, as Rabelais did so often, and he too did that although, it seems, rarely. There is, however, general agreement on the vast influence that the central aspects of Erasmus' thought must have exercised on Cervantes, although opinions differ considerably as to which aspects and whether the influence was direct or intermediate. He may well have read some of Erasmus' books before he began himself to write, during his five-year stay in Italy where, to the frustration of inquisitors, quite a few of those books remained in circulation.[85] In Spain this was no longer the case, but earlier in the century an Erasmian movement had flourished on the peninsula. Without entering the debate about its nature and origins, it is safe to say that Cervantes was its most prominent heir.

The following discussion is based on the premise that Cervantes was familiar with the *Moriae encomium*. Many authors assume that he was, and Antonio Vilanova, in particular, has drawn attention to some sentences in the prologue to the first book of *Don Quijote* that are uncannily reminiscent of Mistress Folly's idiom.[86] Moreover, 'Fierabrás' balm,' a potent concoction containing oil and other ingredients that Don Quijote cooks in an empty oil flask, has been compared to Moria's account of pious ecstasy that let several saints drink 'oil by mistake for wine.' Also Don Quijote's dream in the cave of Montesinos calls to mind two of Moria's reminiscences from the classics: there are the prisoners in Plato's cave who can see nothing but the shadows of real things and laugh at the returned escapee who tries to enlighten them;

and there is Horace's Argive, who enjoys imagining plays in the empty theatre and, when cured of his illusion, bitterly complains about his loss. Likewise Don Quixote, emerging from the cave, deeply regrets the loss of his beautiful illusion.[87] If one looks beyond the *Moriae encomium* for stimuli that the author of *Don Quijote* might have derived from Erasmus' work, the Caballero del Verde Cabán's hospitality and ensuing conversations could be held against Erasmus' colloquies *Convivium religiosum* and *Convivium poeticum*, Don Quijote's deathbed scene against the colloquy *Funus*, and so on.[88] Despite Cervantes' loyal adherence to the tenets of Spain's Catholic reform, at the core of his religion is a simple, trusting faith in a benevolent God, very much after the heart of Erasmus.[89] Just because Cervantes feels safe in his loyalty to the Catholic church he can on occasion look at superstitious practices with an Erasmian smile.[90]

There is, however, a difference between Erasmus and Cervantes that must be addressed before we proceed any further. In so far as Cervantes was acquainted with Erasmus' writings, it makes sense to assume that he was primarily interested in literary works like the *Moriae encomium* and the *Colloquia*. All of these are by varying degrees didactic (though certainly less so than most of Erasmus' treatises that got translated into Spanish) – all were designed to impart to the reader serious instruction pleasantly wrapped into a literary plot. Also, the *Adagia* that may have catered for Cervantes' huge appetite for proverbs were for the most part a teaching tool. Whether *Don Quijote* was written with a similarly strong intention to convey a *Weltanschauung* is debatable. In my opinion, it has been argued convincingly that Cervantes is not greatly weighed down by a load of ideology, that above all he wants to entertain, to dish out stories, whether picaresque-satirical or romantic-pastoral, largely unencumbered by a concern for consistency and persuasion.[91] The chivalric romances are the ruin of his hero Don Quijote. Does Cervantes really believe they are such a danger to the mind of the reading public? Why should they be more so than the melodramatic tales of lovelorn shepherds and nobles with which he laces the adventures of Don Quijote? The chivalric romances themselves were a narrative engine rather than an expression of concerns. This view does not preclude the presence of much common sense wisdom and the occasional hint at true convictions. If this view of *Don Quijote* holds true, it would be a mistake to expect much by way of radical reactions to Erasmus in the field of ideology. If there are radical echoes, we must look for them elsewhere.

While Cervantes has no care for sorting out and specifying diverse forms of madness, manifestations of folly run through the fabric of *Don Quijote* like a red thread. As stated earlier, it is here taken for granted that Cervantes was familiar with the *Moriae encomium* when he created his own complement of fools. Fools of various stripes are everywhere in his story. There is the noble Cardenio who, like Ariosto's Orlando, has become deranged on account of a jilted love. Amid rebounds of his earlier sanity, he tumbles into acts of senseless violence.[92] There are the two madmen mentioned in the prologue of Part II, one maltreating dogs in a more bizarre fashion than the other. There are the two maniacs in the Seville madhouse who believe themselves to be Jupiter and Neptune, respectively. It seems that they need to be confined because they are dangerous to the public.[93] There is the bachelor Carrasco who plays knight-errant in order to beat Don Quijote at his own game. 'Who is the crazier,' he is asked, 'he who is so because he cannot help it, or he who turns crazy of his own free will?'[94] Above all there are the two protagonists, Don Quijote, the knight-errant of the *Triste Figura*, and his squire Sancho Panza, both in varying degrees given to persistent delusion. Throughout the near thousand pages of his book Cervantes never tires of carefully describing and defining their changing conditions, not from any desire to categorize varieties of madness and sanity, but because he understands that an analysis of their complex characters is crucial to the success of his work. Here, in fact, lies the novel approach by which he has carried any inspiration he may have received from Erasmus' Moria a giant step further. She is content to describe various types of folly rather than individuals possessed of them. When Erasmus later had to defend his satire he would always point out that he had refrained from personal attacks. Mistress Folly herself is alone to emerge from his pages as an individual – a fictional individual, of course, complex, ingenious, and disarmingly charming.

Don Quijote and Sancho Panza are not merely specimens of everyone's harmless follies; they are fully developed fictional individuals. The former's madness does not call for confinement in an asylum, although his friends are anxious to restrict his movements. Don Quijote turns out to be a man of high moral principles, well educated, well mannered, humane, reasonable, even wise. But for the most part his actions are dictated by the consistent delusion that he is destined to bring back a golden age of knight-errantry that, of course, never existed except in the literature of chivalric romance that he knows inside out. In rare moments he is compelled to accept the real state of things and admit that he has acted in a state of delusion,[95] but usually he can salvage his delusions by adding to them a new level. He simply assumes that his delusion is true but has been wickedly transformed by evil enchanters into what now appears to be reality. The supreme incident of Don Quijote's mistaking reality for a mean disfigurement of his delusion occurs when he finally sets eyes on the girl he has for so long assumed to be his beauteous and noble Lady Dulcinea. What he sees and hears is a coarse, foul-mouthed country wench, but that of course is an outrageous act of concealment, caused by a sorcerer's wand. With an intuitive understanding of human psychology Cervantes suggests that at times Don Quijote is not entirely unaware of his mad obsession because he has triggered it consciously. When he is splendidly welcomed to the duke's castle, 'it may be said that this was the first time that he really and wholly believed himself to be a true knight-errant and not a fanciful one.'[96]

With the same psychological finesse Cervantes understands that guilt and innocence are not absolute categories. On the whole Don Quijote's delusions do not cause harm to others but rather puzzlement and welcome amusement. Being such a true-to-life character, he has, however, his lapses. The sheep that he spears, mistaking them for enemy knights, die needlessly, and the bark he uses in his assault on a river-castle-alias-watermill is wrecked and has to be paid for.[97] Above all, most of the prisoners on their way to galley-slavery whom he helps to escape are criminals like Ginés de Pasamonte, a notorious robber,[98] and his wanton act of liberation will come to haunt Don Quijote in the course of subsequent adventures. With all that, however, he faithfully sticks to his principle that he will not 'willingly and knowingly offend anyone.' When he prescribes for himself a lover's penance, he proposes to imitate 'Amadis, whose madness did not prompt him to do any damage ... but who confined himself to tears and sighs.'[99]

If Don Quijote were not far too manly to cry, he might have done so with good cause on many occasions. Usually his preposterous adventures result in fun to the bystanders and hurt to himself. His grandiose self-regard could be inspired by Moria's sister Philautia.

It is innocent; but blissful it is only while his delusions fire him with energy and satisfaction. The outcome typically is that he is trampled, beaten, robbed of part of an ear and half of his teeth, although Cervantes will not leave him mauled so badly that he could not embark on the next adventure. With his visit to the castle of the duke and duchess[100] his innocent folly reaches a tragic intensity. Perhaps not until the age of the Baroque with its emphasis on tension and conflict could Moria's pleasurable type of folly be presented in such a radical configuration. As mentioned, Don Quijote is at the height of a happy delusion. He is surrounded by people who seem to believe in knight-errantry so fully that he too can set aside his lurking doubts and gracefully accept that his fame has earned him this place as guest of honour in a princely household. Everything, of course, is cunningly and sumptuously laid on by his hosts. Especially the duchess derives from Don Quijote's fantasies a pleasure that can verge on cruelty. Up to this point all his 'adventures' had been of his own making, fruits of his deluded mind. Now 'adventures' unfold all of their own before his astonished eyes; all he has to do is participate. His dragon-killing sally to the remote kingdom of Candaya is effected instantly thanks to the services of a wooden Pegasus. The bystanders play their roles so efficiently and the theatre machinery works so well that the blindfolded knight believes himself to be crossing various heavenly spheres while not moving an inch from the spot where he mounted his winged charger. Likewise Altisidora, a girl from the duchess' entourage, so credibly feigns infatuation with the wiry old knight and even her death of a broken heart that Don Quijote is completely duped.

Throughout Cervantes' novel, Don Quijote and his squire Sancho Panza are matched so as to present contrasting specimens of Moria's flexible model of harmless folly. To compare the two is certainly legitimate, although Cervantes has no thought for systematic typification; he is far too busy fashioning and shaping the unique characters of his two protagonists amid the steady flow of his digressional tales. While the knight-errant is forever courageous, even foolhardy, as when he insists that a hungry lion be turned loose on him,[101] his squire is fearful, apprehensive of threats to his body and his property. Only thanks to his unquestioning loyalty to his master can Sancho Panza be induced to share the former's adventures and the complement of blows with which they usually end. While Don Quijote is stoic (in the popular sense of the term), even masochistic in inflicting the odd penance upon himself, Sancho is an Epicurean (again in the popular sense of the word), always eager for tangible pleasures, such as replenishing his sizeable stomach or finding a comfortable resting place. At the novel's end a tragic climax is reached. The delusion of knight-errantry is shattered for good. The experience leaves Don Quijote on his deathbed, sound of mind but robbed of all vital energy, while Sancho Panza, past his sincere grief at the loss of his master, can look forward to a comfortable future amid his family and the village community.

Sancho Panza deserves a characterization of his own. He is illiterate, naif, simple, but far from dull-witted; indeed, he is endowed with wonderful common sense that often shines up in his inexhaustible store of proverbs. He is also resourceful; a petty theft now and then and the odd trick or lie are all excused by his natural bonhomie.[102] He knows that Dulcinea does not exist, but smartly tells his master that he has seen her and spoken to her. He even manipulates Don Quijote into kneeling adoringly at the feet of the peasant wench who, he believes, is the enchanted queen of his heart.[103] In minor matters Sancho will show some gullibility, but his supporting role in the knight-errant farce is calculated. Ever so badly does he want to believe that in the end he will be a governor in his master's fantasy kingdom. In view of Don Quijote's insistence that Dulcinea's supreme beauty must be believed without being seen,[104] the duchess tells Sancho, tongue in cheek, that 'there is no reason to doubt anything simply because we have not seen it with our own eyes,' that in failing to believe in the enchantment, he is himself the victim of an enchanter. Sancho is almost swayed, but not quite: 'the truth is that the one I saw was a peasant lass and that was what I took her to be and set her down for.'[105] Throughout the cruel 'adventures' put in scene by the ducal couple, his humble deference is pierced by snatches of healthy scepticism.[106] This scepticism becomes more pronounced over time; his conversation is increasingly marked by good, down-to-earth sense. Even Don Quijote takes note. 'Every day, Sancho,' he says 'you are becoming less stupid and more sensible.'[107] The duchess takes special delight in his droll as well as sensible pronouncements. In pursuit of the unending masquerade the duke does appoint Sancho Panza governor of an 'island.' When the duchess suggests he take his donkey along with him to his new post, he agrees, saying, 'I have seen more than one ass going up to a government.'[108] As a governor Sancho Panza displays his fine qualities to the full. He hands down Solomonic judgments and tackles corruption on all levels. After a week, when he is satisfied that his appointment is but cruel sham, he quits. On his way back to Don Quijote, Sancho offers the crowning demonstration of his, and his inventor's, sane Erasmian religion. He meets his former neighbour, the Moorish convert Ricote, who had been forced to flee the village when all Moriscos were banned from Spain. Now he has returned, well disguised among a group of German pilgrims, or rather beggars posing as pilgrims, hoping to recover the savings that he had hidden when he was forced to run. As Sancho promises not to betray his friend, the readers are left in no doubt as to what Cervantes thinks about the merciless intolerance of the Spanish crown.[109] The thing Sancho will not do for Ricote is accompany him as the latter had wished. He is not the fool in Christ who would welcome martyrdom. Not for him is, as he had said on another occasion,

> the kind of love I have heard the preacher say we ought to give our Lord, for Himself alone, without being moved by any hope of eternal glory or fear of Hell, but, for my part, I prefer to love and serve Him for what He can do for me.[110]

To sum up, Cervantes has devoted his masterpiece to that phenomenon of guileless folly that, as Mistress Moria discovered, is central to the human experience. The fool who causes 'no harm to his conscience' but 'all the more pleasure' to the others is centre stage to the *theatrum mundi*. Compared to him, Moria's other models, the criminal fool who gratifies himself at the expense of others and the religious fool who turns the other cheek and pines for the rare moment of ecstatic rapture, are not important to Cervantes and largely ignored in his great novel. The text just alluded to needs to be quoted more fully. It is the friends of Don Quijote, the intellectual and social elite of his village, of whom Cervantes says in a given moment:

> They did not care to take the trouble of disabusing Sancho of his errors, for it seemed to them, as they were doing no harm to his conscience, it was better to leave him his illusions and there would be all the more pleasure in listening to his nonsense.[111]

These same friends, however, try doggedly to disabuse Don Quijote of his illusions, which, if unchecked, they fear will leave him in the end with his conscience intact, but with a cracked mind in a body broken by many beatings. Cervantes need not turn to Erasmus or any other source to realize how complex the human psyche is; his own experience was teaching him that despite the saving grace of harmless follies, humans are never completely innocent. Even the pleasure we derive from watching the follies of others, if indeed it is pleasure and not annoyance, is not always innocent. Cervantes' rich and thoughtful orchestration of Moria's enticing tune has left a definite impact on world literature. But did he develop Erasmian impulses in a *radical* sense? He did, I think, by neglecting all but the truly original aspect of the *Moriae encomium*. His take on Erasmus' *theatrum mundi* is radical in that it goes to the roots of the human experience. He does not rest before he has fashioned his characters with the fullest measure of psychological credibility fiction can afford.

BEN JONSON AND SHAKESPEARE

Thomas Chaloner's English translation of the *Moriae encomium* (1549, reprints 1560, 1577) opened the gates for a flood of new appreciation of the work. Two all-important aspects of Moria's speech, foolery and the Epicurean quest for happiness, return in Elizabethan drama with a radical spin and an infinity of new twists – so much so that the scholars investigating these plays have regularly looked to Erasmus for clues. Two leading playwrights of the period deserve particular attention in this respect and a short discussion in this place; Shakespeare, of course, and Ben Jonson. Jonson (1572–1637), who had received a humanistic education at London's Westminster School, was well versed in the Greek and Latin classics. His familiarity with Erasmus' writings shows in the form of quotations and paraphrases scattered throughout his work. Writing usually for the stage, Jonson aimed to please a public that savoured stark drama and droll, often ribald language. A telling example of his pickings from Erasmus is found in his miscellaneous collection entitled *Timber, or Discourses* (1641):

> The Body has certain diseases, that are with lesse evill tolerated, then remov'd. As if to cure a leprosie, a man should bathe himself with the blood of a murthered Child: So in the Church, some errors may be dissimuled with lesse inconvenience, then can be discover'd.[112]

The passage that Jonson translates literally is found in *De libero arbitrio*, Erasmus' attack on Luther's theology. While Luther's scorn was provoked by the argument itself rather than the crudeness of the comparison (based on Pliny's *Naturalis historia*), Jonson may well have been enticed by the latter, but also by the context, Erasmus' often repeated argument that truthfulness is not always expedient. It is worth noting that Jonson, who for some time was an avowed Catholic, would know Erasmus' defence of free will against the German reformer.

None of Erasmus' works proved more inspirational to Jonson than the *Moriae encomium*. Erasmus' defence of Folly's speech in a long letter to Maarten van Dorp, usually printed together with the *Moriae encomium*, offered arguments that Jonson could relate to his own person and situation, manifestly so in 1605, when he was in prison because of an offensive play. In the argument that he borrowed, Erasmus emphasized that Moria had attacked no person by name, and then he quoted Jerome, who had said that a critique of faults in general could not constitute slander. Erasmus' argument appears first in a dignified letter Jonson sent to Robert Cecil, earl of Salisbury, and more fully again in *Timber, or Discourses*.[113] A related argument, that an author's characters must speak true to form and that therefore he should not be held responsible for everything they say, especially when the character is Folly in person, allows Jonson to borrow from Moria the noble aphorism *Oratio minime mendax animi speculum*, which he renders as: 'No glasse renders a mans forme, or likenesse, so true as his speech.'[114]

More Erasmian influences have been found throughout Jonson's work; the play *Volpone*, in particular, cast in wicked Venice, reminded some scholars of the *Moriae encomium*. One character, Mosca, delivers a lovely song on the omnipresence of folly that reads like a summary of Moria's endearing central argument.[115] The aims of the two works, of course, are different and call for different literary styles and devices. The multiple intrigues and upsidedowns of Jonson's plot are not required in Moria's oration. She is lucid, even rational, whereas Jonson's characters are so gullible that for us they seem to defy any expectation of credibility, but the conventions of the stage at his time were obviously different. Of Erasmus' various types of folly, not the endearing one but rather the worst prevails in *Volpone*: the folly of those whose greed and willingness to harm others reach criminal proportions. Moria zeroes in on those who hold power in the church and the state, but rarely matches the savage words and deeds produced on Jonson's stage.[116] While she exposes the guilt but does not sit in judgment, he is more radical. Harsh punishment is meted out at the play's end. Only three naive visitors from England get off lightly, because they did no harm (although they too had meant to do some, at least). Jonson's characters are linear; only Mosca, the trickster, and Volpone himself show some complexity. Volpone is a source of many good laughs, but at the same time he is relentless in his pursuit of all sorts of pleasures, taking advantage of his wealth, in fact increasing it, as others fall prey to his guile. In short, what Jonson brings to the London stage is a rougher, less light-hearted version of Moria's message.

In Ben Jonson's work some borrowings from Erasmus were found that are indisputable; in the plays of William Shakespeare (1564–1616) there are none such. Most Shakespeare scholars are nevertheless convinced of his familiarity with some of Erasmus' writings, above all Chaloner's translation of the *Moriae encomium*. Indeed, it has been suggested that in act II, scene ii, of *Hamlet* when Polonius accosts the Prince of Denmark and finds him reading, the book Hamlet reads is none other than the *Moriae encomium*.[117] If one is willing to assume that Folly's speech was recurrently on Shakespeare's mind when he wrote *King Henry IV*, *Hamlet*, *King Lear*, and some other plays, many specific words and phrases can be associated with that source of inspiration.[118] Mistress Folly proclaims the whole world to be a stage on which all must perform their parts, one actor often being assigned several parts. Tearing off the masks would spoil everything.[119] She is echoed by Jaques, a character in Shakespeare's *As You Like It* (II vii 138–41):

All the world's a stage,
And all the men and women merely players.
They have their exits and their entrances,
And one man in his time plays many parts.

Considering Shakespeare's powerful imagination, it might be enough that he had read the *Moriae encomium* once in his youth to engage him in a lifelong play of hide-and-seek with Erasmus' Mistress Folly. Whatever else may have intensified their encounter, the outcome is that Shakespeare takes Moria's already nuanced play around folly and wisdom to a dazzling range of extreme applications. To put it simply, there is a circular argument here that calls to mind the classic commonplace, reflected by Paul in Titus 1:12 and repeatedly recalled by Erasmus,[120] that the Cretans were always liars. 'A Cretan said,' goes the argument, '"all Cretans are liars."' If the assertion is correct, the asserter, himself a Cretan, does lie, and therefore the Cretans do not. But if they do not, the asserter does not either and truthfully says that they are liars, and so on. By application, Mistress Folly can be expected to say foolish things but we, her audience, are also fools, and what sounds foolish to a fool is likely the truth. But how can be true what Folly speaks true to her character? Shakespeare constantly plays upon that reversibility of true and false notions. In his *Twelfth Night*, V i 15–20, the Clown puts it like this:

> Marry, sir, [my friends] praise me, and make an ass of me. Now my foes tell me plainly I am an ass, so that by my foes, sir, I profit in the knowledge of myself, and by my friends I am abused, so that, conclusions to be as kisses, if your four negatives make your two affirmatives, why then, [I am] the worse for my friends and the better for my foes.

Shakespeare, however, advances the same radical step beyond Moria's foolery that we had noticed in Cervantes. Whereas she deals with humanity in anonymous examples and categories, Shakespeare puts individuals on the stage, many of them subject to change in mood and character, always unique, and in their uniqueness more complex than Erasmus' categories, though in some ways reminiscent of them. Jaques in *As You Like It* is a 'melancholy;' he is broody and ingenious. He has none of Moria's gaiety but shares with her an existential need of freedom and the conviction that only folly grants that freedom. This is the kind of folly that, Moria declares, is

> desirable above everything, and is known to come from me. It occurs whenever some happy mental aberration frees the soul from its anxious cares and at the same time restores it by the addition of manifold delights.[121]

In the great scene set in the wild wonderland of the Ardennes forest, Jaques proclaims:

> I am ambitious for a motley coat [as worn by fools and clowns] ...
> It is my only suit,
> Provided that you weed your better judgements
> Of all opinion that grows rank in them
> That I am wise. I must have liberty
> Withal, as large a charter as the wind,
> To blow on whom I please; for so fools have. (II vii 44–9)

The duke calls him a 'libertine' (II vii 65); he needs to be free of every convention. At the play's happy ending, when every injustice is righted and every love requited, Jaques remains a solitaire. He does not join his peers who return from their exile to the stately world of the court. Like Mistress Moria, he knows all about the *theatrum mundi*.

A fool's freedom, so treasured by Jaques, is also the privilege of the professional fools retained by princes. Moria states that most rulers cannot do without them, and Shakespeare's plays prove her right. Amid the court culture of flattery and lying, the fools, says Moria, 'can speak truth and even open insults and be heard with positive pleasure.'[122] That certainly is what the clown Feste in *Twelfth Night*, perhaps Skakespeare's finest exemplar of the sort, excels in doing, for instance, when he proves to countess Olivia that she is a fool (I v 33–62). Feste is also part of the plot that drives poor Malvolio, a foolish gentleman by any standards, to the edge of pathological insanity. The plotters do this simply by pretending that he is demented and treating him accordingly.

Pretense of folly and madness, matched against the real thing, is also a major theme in *Hamlet*. In the crucial scene construed around the play in the play,[123] Hamlet marks the moment when he switches from resolute lucidity to acting the fool. By arranging for the portentous masque about his father's murder to be staged, he knows that he is laying claim to the fool's licence. 'I must be idle' (i.e., mad), he says (III ii 83), and turns to talking nonsense to the king, insulting Polonius, the lord chamberlain, and embarrassing Ophelia. He continues to ridicule Polonius along with Guildenstern and Rosencrantz, before forcing the queen, his mother, to face the dreadful truth (III iv). She subsequently endeavours to excuse his murder of Polonius as an act of dementia. While Ophelia ends up truly deranged, Hamlet continues to pepper his discourse with insults and extravagant cynicisms – all of this so calculated that it must appear as madness and can be passed off as such by him who knows better, the guilty king. Amid the overwhelming complexities of Hamlet's role, his smart follies and pretended insanity are perhaps the aspect that is easiest to analyse. This is also the aspect that is relevant here, and we shall be well advised to leave it at that.

Amid the tight concatenation of ruthless and tragic events that mark the plot of *King Lear*, Moria's legacy of follies returns, raised to a yet higher power. Shakespeare finds unexpected and masterful ways to describe how under the impact of pain and grief the balance between lucidity and lunacy in Lear's mind is shifting decisively towards the latter. His decline begins with a display of folly, with blatantly unwise and unfair decisions for which Shakespeare does not offer a rationale. He does, however, bring back the court fool to expose them without mercy (I iv). But apart from revealing unwelcome truths, Lear's fool also ascends to a new height of folly. When others abandon and betray the old king, the fool chooses to follow his master on his path of tribulations. For the fool it is a way of the Cross, his own secular version of Moria's folly of the Cross. In recognition of this choice, he passes his coxcomb to Kent, an old, faithful vassal, who likewise elects to share his master's miseries in spite of the injustice he has suffered from Lear. 'Would that I had two coxcombs'(I iv 90) to give away, says the fool. Lear himself deserves to wear one as much as Kent. While Lear goes mad, Edgar, the sole knight of flawless perfection, spends the better part of the play in the protective disguise of a madman. In the end he is the only one left to inherit Lear's kingdom.

Neither in *Hamlet* nor in *Lear* does Shakespeare find any space for Moria's favourite specimen, the common, amiable, innocent fool. Hamlet and Lear, the tragic fools, bring us face to face with some frightening truths about the human condition, but play is play. When it is done we can return to ordinary life. At the end of her speech, Moria also returns from the exceptional to the ordinary. After glancing at the rare and momentary experience of ultimate felicity enjoyed in religious rapture, she levels again with her audience of common fools: 'And so I'll say goodbye. Clap your hands, live well, and drink, distinguished initiates of Folly.'[124] Shakespeare, stepping down from the world of Hamlet and Lear, invents Falstaff. Falstaff is unique. 'His vision of life,' in Walter Kaiser's words, 'is Stultitia's, ... pushed to its most outrageous conclusions.'[125] To decent folks he is a 'damned Epicurean rascal' (*Merry Wives of Windsor*, II ii 253). Although he has no taste for Epicurus' rule of moderation, he is an Epicurean not only in the vile sense intended here. He is it also in a much superior way, is indeed 'a plump, sleek porker from Epicurus' herd,' like the great Horace himself, loved and quoted by Moria. His life of pleasure is folly, carefully hedged with wisdom. In the same breath as Moria quotes Horace, she also remembers the popular saying: 'To play the fool in season is the height of wisdom.'[126] From time to time Falstaff can ascend to that height of wise folly. Like Shakespeare's Feste, he is a 'fellow ... wise enough to play the fool' (*Twelfth Night*, III i 53). Like all Shakespeare's fools, Falstaff is clever with words, and while that dexterity is usually a source of mirth to the public, his words can also reveal profound wisdom. Suffice it to recall his famous monologue on honour on the eve of the battle of Shrewsbury:

> Can honour set-to a leg? No: or an arm? No. ... Honour hath no skill in surgery, then? No. What is honour? A word. ... What is that 'honour'? Air ... Who hath it? He that died o' Wednesday ... But will it not live with the living? No ... Therefore I'll none of it ... (*1 Henry IV*, V i 127–39)

To be sure, Falstaff is a devotee of Moria's attendants, Hedone (Pleasure), Tryphe (Sensuality), Comus (Revelry), and above all her own sister Philautia (Self-love), but he also possesses a quality that the harmless common fools, Moria's special darlings, typically miss: self-awareness. While they are blissfully blind to their own follies, Falstaff acts consciously and measures the result critically. An accomplished liar, he is yet brutally honest with himself when he recruits his first levy for the king's army against the rebels. Most of his soldiers are jailbirds, despicable in valour and appearance. (The probable reason transpires from a second muster later on: who can afford it, bribes to be let off the roll.) Falstaff is duly ashamed, but glibly brushes off Prince Henry's criticism: 'food for powder, food for powder; they'll fill a pit as well as better.' And without a witness present, he is again brutally honest when this comes true: 'I have led my raggamuffins where they are peppered: there's not three of my hundred and fifty left alive' (*1 Henry IV*, IV ii 58f, V iii 35f. Cf. *2 Henry IV*, III ii). Falstaff is proud to have people laugh at his follies. 'I am not only witty in myself, but the cause that wit is in other men' (*2 Henry IV*, I ii 8f.).

Moria's fools cannot laugh at themselves; only she can, and Falstaff can do it even better than her. After the merry wives of Windsor had him thrown into the Thames, concealed in a basket full of filthy linen, he muses about the possible outcome of that adventure:

> And you may know by my size that I have a kind of alacrity in sinking. If the bottom were as deep as hell, I should down. I had been drowned but that the shore was shelvy and shallow: a death that I abhor; for the water swells a man; and what a thing should I have been when I had been swelled! I should have been a mountain of mummy. (III v 9–15)

Later, as Falstaff waits amid midnight magic in the Windsor forest for the hoped-for consummation of his adventure with Mrs Ford, having been persuaded to deck himself with a pair of huge horns, he is quite aware of his ridiculous position. He consoles himself with the thought of the diverse transformations that Jupiter endured in the course of his amorous encounters, for example, visiting Leda in the guise of a swan. 'O omnipotent love! How near the god drew to the complexion of a goose! ... For me, I am here a Windsor stag; and the fattest, I think, i' the forest (V v 6–11).'

Selfish and self-aware, Falstaff has none of the naivety of Moria's common fools; he also lacks their innocence. His fooling is by no means harmless. His crimes range from embezzlement based on a phony promise of marriage (*2 Henry IV*, II i) to break-and-enter entailing the use of violence (*Merry Wives* I i 93–98) and even to armed robbery (*1 Henry IV*, I ii). The English knight would rightly rank among Moria's criminal fools; at the very least he might be placed with the courtiers who, like Penelope's suitors, fritter away the substance of others.[127] But while Moria is unsparing with fools of this class, Shakespeare contrives to blunt the moral conscience of his public so that our sympathies normally rest with the fat malfeasant rather than his victims. What redeems Falstaff in our eyes is that, like Mistress Folly, he stands for nature and freedom in defiance of the stifling laws and norms of a stale society. 'The only law,' writes Walter Kaiser, 'that the fool can follow and remain a fool is the lawless law of nature.'[128] In his extensive analysis of Falstaff, Kaiser finds him to be the most exciting and the most enigmatic fool among Moria's numerous offspring.

Falstaff's gyration between the social strata of army, royal court, townsfolk sports, and outlaw jaunts is indeed enigmatic. In *1 Henry IV* Prince Harry, later King Henry V, opts to participate in Falstaff's banditry and his revelries, but he always knows that this is temporary adventure. In due course he will 'please again to be himself,' like the sun hidden by the clouds but eventually breaking free (*1 Henry IV*, I ii 173–95. Falstaff is the one who for a long time – too long – maintains the illusion that he can straddle the divide between the tavern of Eastcheap and the palace of Westminster. The knight agrees to be a captain and play at war. When his Harry becomes king, he fully expects to play a leading role at his court. The king's reaction is honest and brutal: 'I know thee not, old man: fall to thy prayers / ... I have long dream'd ... / But being awake, I do despise my dream' (*2 Henry IV*, V v 45–9). A hope for rewards is held out if Falstaff reforms himself, but at the play's end he is left with his lies and his debts. In an epilogue the author announces his intention to bring his immensely popular hero back in a play of King Henry V and have him there die of the sweat. This is not going to be. But meanwhile Falstaff is brought back, bulk, swagger, and all, in *The Merry Wives of Windsor*.

Here the glorious fool is eased into his proper station – moving not among army chiefs and royals, but as a lone and lowly noble hanging out with the merry townsfolk. The court is now worth to Falstaff no more than a fleeting, disillusioned thought,[129] and instead of wielding power in the king's entourage, his endeavour is now to seduce burghers' wives and to keep the creditors at bay. To be sure, the townsfolk do not deal tenderly with the old, fat fool. Three times he becomes the butt of increasingly devastating practical jokes. With *The Merry Wives* Shakespeare brings his radical redimensioning of Moria's world of fools to its logical conclusion. While the rest of the cast draws delight from Falstaff's folly, he himself pays dearly for his dumb delusions. For him there is no sublimation leading to the folly of the Cross. Instead he strays into the mock magic forest laid out by his tormentors, and is scared out of his wits. His healthy suspicion is bested by superstition. Of his former wisdom only some chastening self-awareness has been left, and that every time a blow has fallen. When he has been soundly trounced by the little elves, alias children of Windsor, he finally realizes that he has been 'made an ass.' 'Have I laid my brain in the sun and dried it, that it wants matter to prevent so gross o'erreaching as this?' (V v 130f.). He even admits to 'the guiltiness of my mind' (V v 118f.); in return he is invited to come along when all get together to celebrate the happy resolution of the play's multiple plots: 'let us every one go home, / And laugh this sport o'er by a country fire; / Sir John and all' (V v 217–19). It is tough love, but the good folks of Windsor do compensate the monstrous knight for the rejection he had suffered at the hands of his king.

Radical interpretations of some of Erasmus' points in the New Testament and his other religious writings carried appreciable weight in early modern Europe, but today their relevance has largely disappeared. By contrast, his influence on early modern literature, whether or not it led to radical ends, lives on in the glamour of classical works. While Franck, Castellio, and Fausto Sozzini, even Erasmus himself, no longer cause much stir beyond scholarly circles, Rabelais, Cervantes, and Shakespeare are read wherever western culture reaches. The dragon's teeth that Erasmus had sown have sprouted to be a field of giants.

Conclusion

Numerous authors of the sixteenth and seventeenth centuries read Erasmus and, we have seen it, were encouraged to form radical views by what they had read. We must now ask the intriguing, but difficult, question whether Erasmus had meant to be so read. Was it his intention to foster revolutionary, heterodox, subversive, in short radical views? Since in his lifetime he was persistently accused of dispensing poison, can he have ignored the radical potential that his writings might hold for future generations? Our question has been asked before. Cornelis Augustijn concluded that 'Erasmus was subjectively a conservative *par excellence*, and thus not very aware of the objectively revolutionary character of his life's achievement.' Silvana Seidel Menchi, who gives telling examples for a 'radicalization' of Erasmus' thought in the course of its transmission to others, also assumes that this development was not what he had intended and, especially in his latter years, was apt to cause him regrets, but that it was legitimate, 'l'expression de la métamorphose inévitable que subit la pensée, lorsequ'elle devient principe d'action et de transformation de la réalité.'[1] Both views are insightful and can be supported with selective evidence. On the other hand, a push for radical action might be exactly what Erasmus intended. Sometimes he was well aware of his daring; the *Julius exclusus* and the *Acta Academiae Lovaniensis* were so radical that he was never prepared to admit even a partial authorship. The intent clearly was to discredit and malign an unworthy pope and, in the second tract, a hated opponent, Aleandro. In Wittenberg both tracts were received as an incentive to action. Sometimes Erasmus' considerable powers of self-deception caused him to claim candidly that an incendiary statement was harmless. On occasion he expressed regret for things he had said earlier, and sometimes, not often, he admitted that he had been wrong.[2] He never tired of answering such criticisms as he was aware of; indeed, his superior intelligence allowed him often to anticipate criticism. Usually, not always, he would defend a bold statement rather than change it. His defences included qualifying what he had written before or pairing it with assurances of his personal orthodoxy. As he grew old, his prudence increased.

Intended or not? A most interesting test case is Erasmus' influence on the Anabaptist movement, the earliest major segment of the so-called Radical Reformation. I hope to show that he did not initially foresee and later did not quite realize, and therefore never intended, the impact of his words in Anabaptist circles. When he was preparing the first, 1516 edition of his New Testament, Erasmus was keenly aware of certain dogmas of the Church of Rome that could not be supported with scriptural evidence. We have seen examples of this awareness, and soon shall see more. One such dogma was, I believe, the sacramental baptism of infants, although it may not have been until 1527 that we find him stating clearly that little children were not as yet baptized at the time of the apostle Paul.[3] By 1533 he had changed his position. True, infant baptism was not mentioned in scriptures, but by the time of Augustine it was so well established that one could assume it had been practised at the time of the apostles. Paul baptized three families, among them presumably children.[4]

At issue here was not merely a point of history but also, and to Erasmus chiefly, a problem of religious ethics. The rite of baptism carried a profound symbolic meaning. How could the dignity of the rite be preserved, he wondered, if it was administered to ignorant babes? In the argument that prefaces his Paraphrase of Corinthians (1519) he found an occasion to state his concern. Paul's letters dealt with some hard-to-die traditions that the brethren in Corinth had to abandon on their way to embracing Christianity, 'but today we believe that it suffices to be sprinkled with a little water, and presto you become a perfect Christian.'[5] Later, when the Spanish monks attacked this provocative sentence, Erasmus answered quite sensibly that what he had criticized was not the sacramental character of baptism but, on the contrary, serving the sacrament regardless of whether its profound meaning was understood.[6]

The Spanish monks were not the only ones to find fault with Erasmus' view of baptism, for it was linked to a more comprehensive issue. His Catholic and Protestant critics regularly insisted that he was suspect of Pelagianism, and they often did so in view of his translation and understanding of Romans 5:12–14, traditionally seen as the scriptural anchor of the doctrine of original sin. Already in the first, 1516 edition of his New Testament his treatment of this passage in Romans had occasioned an attack by Edward Lee, and other Catholics followed suit right down to the Council of Trent and beyond. The issue also came up in Erasmus' controversy with Luther over free will.[7] In the end Erasmus was induced to extend his notes on Romans 5:12–14 to extreme length (more than six folio columns in LB). The passage invites complex explanations, and other approaches to it have been encountered on earlier pages; but what concerns us here can be expressed very simply. Erasmus argued that in these verses Paul was not talking about original sin, that is, the sin of Adam to be visited upon his entire offspring, but about actual sin. In his usual fashion Erasmus added that he did not insist on an interpretation that ruled out original sin and that he did not speak in favour of those who denied it completely. If, however, the interpretation of Paul's words that he preferred was correct, the apostle clearly had no business to baptize innocent babes (so as to offset the stain of original sin). As Erasmus put it, Paul did not here deal with infant baptism, nor had he any reason to do so, as it was not practised in his time.[8]

Anyone intent on exploring the Gospel idea of baptism was bound to turn to Christ's final mandate for his disciples to preach and baptize, and to Peter's discharge of that mandate on the day of Pentecost (Matthew 28:18–20; Mark 16:15–16; Acts 2:14–41). In rendering the three relevant passages Erasmus stuck closely to the Vulgate translation. Thus, according to Matthew, Christ instructed the apostles: 'Go therefore and teach all nations; baptize them in the name of the Father, the Son and the Holy Spirit; teach them to observe all that I have commanded you.'[9] In 1522 Erasmus published his Paraphrase on Matthew. Here he has Jesus sum up at some length the creedal instruction that he expects the apostles to give to the catechumens, first in order to ready them for baptism and then again after the rite was performed.[10] The Paraphrase on Acts followed two years later. In Erasmus' exposition Peter ends his address to the crowd by reminding them of a specific act in their past life that they needed to repent. When Pilate sat in judgment over Christ, did they not keep on shouting 'Crucify him'?[11] As a result of Peter's sermon, about three thousand souls got themselves ready to be baptized. Erasmus does not suggest that beyond Peter's powerful sermon any more catechizing was needed before the mass baptism, but then the venue was exceptional: the day was Pentecost and Peter's audience of Jews was understanding and sympathetic. Erasmus had no reason to speculate what preparation for baptism might mean in different circumstances. Baptizing infants is not mentioned anywhere in Acts; as Erasmus believed then, it was not practised at the time of the apostles. Also, before moving on in his paraphrase, he explained again Christ' words in Matthew to mean that instruction ought to be given both before baptism and following it.

The apostle Philip's encounter with the Ethiopian eunuch (Acts 8:27–39) offered Erasmus another opportunity to make his point. He amply expanded the text of Acts 8:35, so as to have Philip carefully catechize the Ethiopian before admitting him to the act of baptism.[12] Erasmus had voiced that concern for appropriate instruction even more explicitly two years earlier in his Paraphrase on Matthew. It opened with a prologue addressed to the reader that was much noted and soon became controversial. In the course of explaining his motives for undertaking the paraphrase, he castigated the church once again for its failure to minister meaningfully to ordinary people. He also suggested remedies, for instance a collection of model sermons that could be repeated by the rank and file of priests. He then went on:

> Moreover it would, I believe, serve this end greatly if the children who had been baptized, at the threshold of puberty would be ordered to attend such sermons as could explain to them sensibly what the pledge (*professio*) made at the time of their baptism really entails.

Thus instructed, these adolescents should be subjected to an exam. If they passed, they should be asked whether they were ready to commit to what the parents and godparents had pledged on their behalf at the time of baptism.

> If they answer 'yes,' that pledge should be renewed in public, before a congregation of peers, in a ceremony suitably

chaste, grave and magnificent, as it behooves that pledge which is holy beyond all others.

This last sentence shows how highly Erasmus thought of the sacramental character of the baptism that Christians traditionally received in their infancy. Nothing was further from his mind than rejecting infant baptism. In his prologue to the paraphrase he did, however, admit that his suggestion might mistakenly be understood as a repetition of baptism: *quod videatur iterari baptismus,* and this is what his Catholic critics, Noël Béda and the Spanish monks, chose to do.[13] They accused him of violating the sacramental doctrine of the church by frivolously *adding* a new form of baptism (not of rejecting the traditional one). In one of his answers to Béda Erasmus defended himself at length. What he had written, he said, was no more than a modest proposal, and it was up to individual bishops and priests whether they wished to implement it. No mandate from Rome was required, for all that was involved was adapting the Gospel precedent to a new situation. Christ had ordered that adult converts be instructed before and after their baptism. Now that mostly infants were baptized, it was important to ensure that instruction retained its proper place alongside the rite.[14]

While Erasmus thus answered some Catholic critics, interest in his views on baptism was also expressed, and quite poignantly, in another camp. Many authors of the sixteenth-century Radical Reformation, who can in one way or another be associated with Anabaptism, and specifically with the rejection of infant baptism, received some spiritual guidance from Erasmus' writings. A substantial body of scholarly literature documents the influence he exercised in these circles from the earliest Anabaptists in Zurich down to Menno Simons,[15] and the baptismal rite was bound to be an issue here. By 1522 debates on infant baptism, generated by objections to the rite, were occurring in various places. In Wittenberg the so-called Zwickau prophets were challenging Luther to give it up. From Halle or Allstedt Thomas Müntzer did likewise. More protests were voiced in Basel and in Strasbourg.[16] Also in 1522 Erasmus published his Paraphrase on Matthew and, moreover, received two visitors that would soon be involved in the debate about infant baptism, Huldrych Zwingli from Zurich and Balthasar Hubmaier from nearby Waldshut.[17] Whether and how these various manifestations and events were related need not concern us, except in the case of Erasmus' visitors.

In 1523 Hubmaier, who was in Zurich for the Second Zurich Disputation, talked with Zwingli about infant baptism.[18] After some hesitation Zwingli had made up his mind to maintain it and no doubt recognized that Erasmus' ideas could be used in its defence, but he could not persuade his opponents. In January 1525 the first believer's baptism took place in Zurich, based on the view that an earlier baptism received in infancy was invalid. Such an act, to orthodox churchmen, was a sacrilegious repetition, or ana-baptism. The following Easter Hubmaier himself received the believer's baptism, and in January 1525 he stated in a letter to Oecolampadius that in his own ministry he had replaced infant baptism with a simple presentation of the infant to the whole congregation, followed by a sermon on Matthew 19:13–15.[19] In May 1525 Zwingli published an extensive treatise, *Von dem touff. Vom widertouff. Unnd vom kinderetouff*, with the last section dealing with infant baptism.[20] Hubmaier responded; in July he published in Strasbourg a pamphlet, *Von dem Christenlichen Tauff der glaübigen*, which discussed among others the passages in Matthew, Mark, and Acts, finding there a sequence that ran like this: 'i. The Word, ii. Hearing, iii. Faith, iv. Baptism, v. Work.' He did not mention Erasmus, but clearly had taken up his interpretation in the Paraphrases.[21] Already in 1521 he had counselled that the nephew of a friend should pursue his education by studying the Paraphrases, of which the earliest ones were then in print, as well as Erasmus' *Ratio*.[22] Although Hubmaier's pamphlet was discreet in its opposition to Zwingli's arguments, the Zurich reformer believed that he must reply directly. *Uber Doctor Balthazars Touffbuechlin waahrhaffte, gründte antwurt* appeared in November.[23] The pamphlet also related to Zwingli's ongoing debate with the Zurich Anabaptists about Augustine's advocacy of infant baptism and the practice prevailing at his time. Hubmaier penned without delay an answer (published at Nikolsburg in the following year) challenging, for instance, Zwingli's poor effort to find support for infant baptism in scripture.[24] These points, selected at random, should make it evident that Erasmus, whether he wanted or not, had become a participant in a widespread debate.

In a further pamphlet that Hubmaier published at Nikolsburg in 1526, Erasmus is an explicit witness. The title is descriptive:

Der Uralten und gar neuen leerern Urteil, das man die jungen Kindlen nit tauffen solle. Hubmaier offers apt quotations from Jerome, Cyril, Theophylact, and less convincing ones from other fathers, to show that they insisted upon teaching ahead of baptism, but most effective among all the testimony he adduces are his citations taken from Erasmus' paraphrases. He refers to the paraphrase of Act 8:[35–8] and translates literally from those of Acts 2:41 and, especially, Matthew 28:20, which leads him to a questionable conclusion: 'Here Erasmus demonstrates openly that baptism was instituted by Christ for those instructed in the faith and not for young children.'[25] Abraham Friesen presents impressive evidence to show that instruction and belief as prerequisites of baptism remained the centrepiece of Anabaptist theology. He quotes the Hutterite Peter Walpot, who in 1577 referred explicitly to Erasmus' paraphrases, and we may assume that many others were also aware of them.[26] On the other hand, Erasmus' idea of baptismal renewal was, of course, irrelevant to the Anabaptists, who rejected infant baptism. It was taken up, however, or independently matched, among other reformers. Zwingli is assumed to have drawn inspiration from Erasmus' prologue to the Matthew paraphrase when he proposed as early as 1523 a confirmation rite (*Firmung*) that soon was observed regularly in Zurich, a first among the Protestant churches.[27] We have seen earlier that the relevant passage of Erasmus' prologue also netted a well-honed summary in Franck's *Chronica* of 1531. Baptism is also the topic of the fourth (and last) book of Servetus' *Christianismi restitutio* (1553). Amid his passionate denunciations of infant baptism, Servetus lays great stress on the teaching that must precede the act of baptism and has itself sacramental character. He refers to all the passages that Erasmus too had adduced, and his frequent use of the term *resipiscere* brings to mind Erasmus' translation, while his suggestion that the baptismal instruction could be repeated many times (*saepius*) is reminiscent of Franck's reading of Erasmus' prologue.[28]

Was Erasmus ever *aiming* to promote something as radical as the Anabaptists' believer baptism? By 1522 he may have heard of protests against infant baptism, but in his paraphrase on Matthew there is nothing to encourage such protests. He used the term 'Anabaptists' in the summer of 1523, and from there on heard and also wrote a good deal about them. What he heard, depending on the peaceful or militant manifestations associated with the heretical conviction, filled him with compassion or abhorrence,[29] but did not cause him to make changes in his paraphrases. The relevant texts in Matthew, Mark, and Acts were not obscure; he was clearly not the only one to pay careful attention to what was said there. In 1527 he ruled out the observance of infant baptism in the Apostolic church, only to change his view five years later. The reversal came in reaction to his Catholic critics, who, incidentally, did not call him an Anabaptist. That he was ever aware of Hubmaier's citations does seem less likely. While his impact on Anabaptist thought was no doubt considerable, I think one can exclude that he had a secret wish, even fleetingly, to encourage the replacement of infant baptism by believer's baptism.

It is equally hard to think that Erasmus might have knowingly offered the Anabaptists support for another one of their radical positions. The context was the swearing of oaths, an issue on which his notes and paraphrases had provoked criticism from quite a series of Catholic opponents. As usual, he had answered them. The Anabaptists believed that Christ forbade taking oaths of any sort, and they may well have drawn inspiration from Erasmus, since his Catholic critics tended to interpret his comments analogously. The refusal to take any oath figured in a widely known statement of Anabaptist doctrines, the Schleitheim articles of February 1527. Although Erasmus was never well informed about Anabaptist beliefs, the refusal of the oath was the kind of thing that he may have been aware of, even though we have no record that he ever mentioned it. Nor is he known to have said anything about the subject of another, and more important, article of the Schleitheim manifesto. It stated that the 'world,' with all its institutions, was Satan's domain and instructed believers to withdraw from it. Some Anabaptists would later set up segregated communities, isolated from the rest of society as far as was possible, in a desire to achieve perfect Christianity. In this, as in their refusal to swear, they may have felt encouraged by Erasmus, who in his initial notes on Matthew 5:33–7 had emphasized that Christ's categorical 'Do not swear at all' was intended only for perfect Christians. He repeated that interpretation when he answered the Spanish monks at the turn of 1528. We noted earlier that Sebastian Franck, who always perceived an unbridgeable gulf between the 'world' and spiritual Christianity, took a particular interest in Erasmus' statements about swearing.[30] If Erasmus' notion of the perfect, never-swearing

Christian had any influence on Anabaptists and other sects that embraced radical segregation, that influence was certainly not intended. Franck, who was widely read in radical circles, had also drawn attention to Erasmus' sceptical assessment of the fires of hell. Erasmus' comments would likely have horrified a simple Anabaptist, but they prepared the way for the radical Socinian conclusion that everlasting punishment simply meant non-existence after the Judgment. Again this could never have been Erasmus' intention. Hell to him remained a reality worthy of awe-struck contemplation, although it must never be a cause of despair.[31]

Intended or not? We must now consider some cases where Erasmus was neither unaware of, nor indifferent to, radical interpretations and even actions that flowed from his statements, and yet did nothing to prevent or at least mitigate that effect. His long note on 1 John 5:7–8 has been discussed at various places in this study.[32] In the first edition of the New Testament, 1516, he noted in a terse four lines that the reference to the three witnesses in heaven that were one was missing in the Greek codices. Therefore he would not translate it. In the second edition, 1519, he saw no reason as yet to say anything more. At that point he did not foresee in any way that here he was triggering two hundred years of controversy.[33] In the third edition of 1522, however, his note was expanded to fill in excess of an entire column in LB, and another column's worth of comment was added in the fourth edition of 1527.[34] These elaborations reflected a first wave of criticism, coming from the conservative Catholic camp (of which more will be said below). In a number of direct answers to the critics he parried polemic with polemic; in the expanded note on 1 John 5:7–8 he was therefore free to concentrate on factual argumentation. He presented the conflicting evidence of the various Greek and Latin Bible codices he had consulted and quoted a number of fathers who apparently had not known the *Comma*, or had read it in a diversity of ways. His own view clearly emerged: John had written no more than what he had translated in 1516: 'Therefore there are three that witness, the spirit, the water and the blood, and the three are one.' 'One' (in the Greek text εἰς τὸ ἕν, not simply ἕν) suggested mutual agreement, but it was later tempting to claim that unity of essence or nature was meant. That in turn spurred fourth-century interpolators to relegate the original three witnesses to the earth and add three witnesses in heaven, the Father, the Son, and the Holy Spirit.

Erasmus had promised, however, to restore the *Comma* in his Greek text and Latin translation, if just one Greek codex that had it would come to light.[35] And since one did appear in England, he did restore the *Comma*. Doing so by no means equalled a retraction. In the note he explained that he had done it in order to avoid being slandered and that he suspected that the Greek text in the English manuscript was translated back form the Latin. In 1527 he discussed some more codices and the Greek edition of Aldus, also that of the Alcalá scholars, which he had finally seen in the meantime. Above all, he enlarged on an argument he had used already in the 1522 addition. If the interpolators had hoped to defeat the Arian heretics by offering scriptural proof for the dogma of the triune godhead, they had deluded themselves. The reference was clearly to agreement in faith and testimony, and not to unity in essence, as was shown by *unum* (one) found in other Bible verses, where the latter interpretation would be absurd. And then he added that if the church were to use its authority to demand a different exposition, one ought to submit to the church, if and when it pronounced a clear rule. In the meantime, however, one was free to explore the truth in an unpolemical way, for God did not grant to all people the same insight: *Deus aliis alia patefacit.*[36]

Erasmus' omission of the *Comma* came under attack at once. The first assailants were Lee and Zúñiga; Erasmus answered the former in 1520, the latter in 1521. At that time the mysterious appearance of the English manuscript indicated that the attacks that appeared in print represented a groundswell of conservative Catholic opposition. In 1527 the Spanish monks in conference at Valladolid included the *Comma* among their objections, and Erasmus answered them without delay. He referred them to all he had written before about the conundrum in John's letter and pointed out that in his paraphrase of it (published in December 1520), he had chosen to stick to the Vulgate. Then he asserted once again:

> What is being questioned here is not whether the Father, the Son and the Holy Spirit have a single essence, for on this I totally agree with those who have chipped away at my argument, but what is tested is which of the two readings

represents the apostolic truth: ours, which is now in common use, or that of the Greeks.[37]

We have seen a number of times how Erasmus pointed out in his Annotations that a specific dogma, despite its authoritative character, was not anchored in scripture, but here he made the point with a radical emphasis. Only one version of the text can lay claim to a truth warranted by the apostles, and it is not the Vulgate with its *Comma*.

The theologians of Wittenberg, Zurich, and Geneva followed Erasmus' lead and eliminated the *Comma* from their Bibles. Today it can be taken for granted that Erasmus' judgment was correct. The fact that the magisterial Protestant churches accepted Erasmus' treatment of 1 John 5:7–8 without delay can exemplify a point we had made in the introduction. Here a radical move soon ceased to be radical when it found broad acceptance. This, however, is less than half of the *Comma* story. While the Catholics continued to accuse Erasmus of favouring Arianism, or even wishing to restore it, he received a first indication that he could expect as much from the Protestant camp, the accord on the *Comma* notwithstanding, when he read Luther's *De servo arbitrio* in February 1526.[38] By the summer of 1530 he was aware of similar charges coming from Strasbourg;[39] the most brutal ones, however, stood in a letter from Luther to Nikolaus of Amsdorf of 11 March 1534, that was published without delay. Erasmus felt obliged to answer, in April, with a *Purgatio adversus epistolam Lutheri*.[40] By that time the Antitrinitarianism of the early modern age had come to life. The *Comma* remained a regular issue in Antitrinitarian theology, as was evident in our survey of some of its major exponents. To this could be added the testimony of simple folks interrogated by inquisitors and of pamphlets without intellectual ambitions.[41] Most of this development occurred in the century and a half after Erasmus' death, but he cannot have been unaware of the scandal that marked the beginning of modern Antitrinitarianism. It is assumed with good reason that a book Erasmus referred to in a letter of 1532 was none other than Servetus' *De Trinitatis erroribus*. If this is accepted, considering his hypersensitivity to the use of his name in suspect publications, he would hardly have been uninformed of the fact that Servetus had named him once and precisely in connection with the *Comma*.[42]

Erasmus revised his note on 1 John 5:7–8 a last time for the 1535 edition. He made two minor additions intended to round up his argument, but otherwise did not change anything. Indeed, what could he have changed, short of tampering with the philological scholarship on which his case rested? In the *Apologia ad monachos hispanos* he had gone out of his way to list eighty places in his work that could prove his orthodoxy with regard to the Trinity. One cannot help thinking that the more he affirmed his own faith in the doctrine, the more he realized that he was undermining that of others. But he had no choice. When he translated and paraphrased the Gospel verses on baptism, he was comfortably in agreement with the Vulgate. The ceremony to revitalize, not repeat, baptism that he outlined was no more than a proposal for individual bishops to take or to leave. With the *Comma Johanneum* things were entirely different. As he emphasized, here one had to choose either truth or untruth. Erasmus was confident that personally he could remain orthodox and still choose the truth, but *Deus aliis alia patefacit*.

The Spanish monks also criticized two of Erasmus' annotations because they cast doubt on the established doctrine that the sacramental celebration of the Eucharist was authenticated by the combined witness of Matthew 26:26–8, Mark 14:23–4, Luke 22:17–20, and 1 Corinthians 11:23–5. It was alleged that during the last supper Jesus himself had consecrated the bread and the wine when he said: 'this is my body ... this is my blood' and offered both to the disciples. This set the holy precedent for the priest's consecrating the host and the wine before he shared them with his congregation. The statements criticized by the Spaniards were in the notes on 1 Corinthians and Mark.[43] In the former Erasmus pointed out that the Greek text had 'receive, eat this my body' while the Vulgate read 'receive, eat, this *is* my body.' Thus according to the Greek, Paul's rendering of Christ's words seemed to refer to bread and wine already consecrated, rather than to Christ's consecrating them. Analogously the words in Mark, literally taken, suggested that the disciples had been offered the cup and drank from it *before* Christ proclaimed: 'this is my blood.' When Erasmus made these remarks, and also pointed out an incongruity in the text of Luke, he by no means wanted to question that Christ's words instituted and validated the Eucharistic celebration. The point was, as he said in the note on 1 Corinthians:

> In all things one must submit to the judgment of the Church; this statement, however, seems to refer to the

offering of the already consecrated body. In matters of this sort, which cannot be taught securely from the testimony of scripture but rather depend on human conjecture, I do think it is advisable not to make such strong assertions ... And perhaps it would be safer when the eminent clerics refrained from making bold pronouncements on everything that cannot be taught [from scripture]; after all they are human and can err.

When Erasmus revised his Annotations for the 1522 edition, he realized that his comment on Mark was apt to cause him trouble. He therefore added that Mark could have reported the events representing consecration and communion in reverse order, using *protohysteron*, a device of classical rhetoric. Erasmus did not say that this was plausible, and should not have thought so either, given the low opinion he had of the evangelists' skill with words. In the 1527 edition he changed the just-quoted statement from Corinthians, shortly before it was to be singled out for censure by the Spanish monks. He dropped the barb about self-righteous clerics and instead concentrated on the central issue. How could scripture set an all-important precedent when there was no clear evidence that Christ had consecrated, using those words? Prudently he added that the church's decrees were valid anyhow and that Paul had said that faith was all the more meritorious when reason could not support it.

In his answer to the Spanish monks Erasmus, far from making excuses, defended himself with a vengeance. With regard to Mark, even orthodox theologians expressed different opinions on the consecration formula; Thomas Aquinas as well as Gabriel Biel had affirmed that. The Canon Law *Decretum* quoted only one obscure source that proclaimed it a heresy to challenge the rite's conformity with Christ's example. As to the comment on Corinthians, Erasmus' defense was elaborate, although by then he had changed his text. He told the Spaniards that the 'eminent clerics' he had targeted were individual theologians, not ecumenical councils passing decrees, and further that, 'subject to the authority of the church,' he must insist on his right to doubt in matters that were not yet evident to him. Not that he personally found the church's consecration formula problematic, but there were aspects that he wished to see clarified beyond dispute. 'About the substance of the Eucharist we have now learned how to deal with those [who oppose its presence], but not so about the form of words.' The practice of the early church should be the precedent to follow, but what precisely was it? Erasmus summarized the points that seemed clear. The priest alone performed 'the mystery of consecration,' then also called 'benediction,' but apart from that the whole congregation must participate. The faithful must be induced to contemplate the mystery in their hearts, not simply to watch the ceremony with their eyes. *Sursum corda* and *gratias agamus* were words of profound meaning. What Erasmus here writes touches upon the essence of his view of the Eucharistic sacrament, as he had expressed it already in the *Enchiridion* and in other places. The liturgical performance was deficient in dignity and value unless the congregation participated spiritually to the full. As late as 1533, in *De ecclesiae concordia*, he insisted again on this point: 'The participation of the people is of particular importance after the priest has said "*sursum corda*" and "*gratias agamus*." Then, while the priest falls silent, every one present talks to God.'[44]

At the turn of 1528, when Erasmus answered the Spanish monks, the Eucharistic practice was a burning issue close to home in Basel, where he resided, and reluctantly he had become involved when the city council asked for his advice. This is not the place to discuss the various opinions of Luther, Karlstadt, Zwingli, and Oecolampadius in the debate over substance and symbol. Erasmus knew that he had influenced the Swiss reformers[45] who declared that Christ's body and blood were merely symbols of the bread and wine actually consumed. In the *Enchiridion* he had chosen the stark formulation that 'Christ despised ... the eating of his own flesh and the drinking of his own blood if they were not eaten and drunk spiritually as well.' For him personally, as he told the Spanish monks, the question of substance was settled; he remained committed to the Catholic doctrine of transubstantiation. And so he chose to make a stand over the conundrum of Christ's words rather than the yet more crucial issue of substance, which presented him with a huge personal dilemma.[46] Clearly, the position of the Swiss appealed to him. It was rational and valued the active faith of the individual communicant. What held him back, however, was again his respect for what he deemed to be many centuries of Catholic consensus.[47] He knew he sat on a small island amid the raging sea of controversy. Especially in view of the Protestant emphasis on *sola Scriptura*, Christ's words and actions were of crucial importance, and what Erasmus had said, and continued to say, about the uncertainty of that precedent and the paramount importance of the congregation's spirituality left the way open to radical solutions. It was with sadness that he witnessed these in Basel. The mass was ceasing to be celebrated. All that remained was the preaching of a sermon, the singing of German hymns by women and children, 'and at some point bread is handed out as symbol of the Lord's body.'[48] But budge he would not. In the pertinent annotations he had stated the facts. He could not help it if what he had written encouraged radical action, or at least what to Erasmus himself most certainly was radical action. Not only Catholics reacted to Erasmus' position. Calvin later noticed his emphasis on inconsistencies in the Gospel accounts and protested.[49] Beza declared that Erasmus had completely failed to understand the patristic concept of consecration.[50] Sebastian Franck's noted interest in Erasmus' comments on Mark 14[51] points to yet more radical approaches. In the end, bodies like the Quakers and the Salvation Army would simply do away with the Eucharistic celebration.

Erasmus' misgivings about the plenary powers of the papacy found expression throughout his writings, and therefore were noted at all times.[52] One of his annotations will provide us with a useful example because, as so often in this study, the sequence of revised editions offers some indication of either the constancy of his mind through two crucial decades or his willingness to make changes. According to Matthew 16:18, Jesus proclaimed in front of his disciples: 'you are Peter; you are the rock on which I will build my church.' It was an easy step to maintain that this statement empowered not only Peter himself but also the Roman popes who claimed to be his successors. Erasmus' approach was different. The bulk of his note dates from the 1519 edition; there he explains that the rock was not Peter himself so much as the profession of faith that Peter had pronounced in the preceding verses. It was that profession of faith that set a standard every Christian needed to follow. When Cyprian affirmed that the rock was Peter, it could be understood in the sense that Peter was not a person, but a type, representative, as Origen had said, of all Christians. Augustine had gone further and argued that the rock was Christ himself, not Peter, and that was mostly Luther's position too.[53] In 1527 Erasmus added that this could seem extreme, but in so far as Augustine did not want 'to place the foundations of the church upon a man,' he was not so far away from his, Erasmus' own, position.⁵⁴

By the time Erasmus revised his note for the 1527 edition he had already answered Zúñiga, who declared that it 'smacked of Lutheran ungodliness.' Soon afterwards the Spanish monks also condemned his note (and corresponding words in the paraphrase).⁵⁵ Erasmus stood his ground. The only concession he made in 1527 was to invite the readers to choose for themselves, but he continued to marvel at those who brought the Roman pontiffs into the equation. A year later he assured the Spanish monks in his answer that he most loyally accepted the papal primacy, provided it was used 'for building, not destroying, the house of God.' He also reaffirmed his scepticism: did Christ confer that primacy to Peter? Was it ever transferred to the bishop of Rome through the consensus of his peers? Was it acknowledged in the earliest church? Balthasar Hubmaier, who in 1525 had close ties to the great German Peasant Rebellion, echoed Erasmus' explanation of the rock: 'On the confession of its own faith is the Christian church built.'⁵⁶ We have seen earlier how Sebastian Franck produced a sweeping summary of Erasmus' comments; their radical potential is also demonstrated in Calvin's reaction. Calvin referred to Augustine and, especially, Cyprian in much the same was as Erasmus, but did not mention the latter. Nor did he mention Origen, whom the Genevans disliked at least as much as they disliked Erasmus. Clearly, Calvin had no taste for Origen's and Erasmus' conclusion that the rock represented the faithful at large. Christ's words were addressed to his disciples only, and thus it was upon the apostles collectively that the church was to be built.⁵⁷ Is it amiss to think Calvin reserved the same role for the *Compagnie des pasteurs* of the church of Geneva?

Erasmus never conceded the point on which he differed so drastically from the Spanish monks and Calvin: the rock on which Christ was building his church were the faithful collectively. His interpretation of Matthew 16:18 agreed with his concept of consensus – the consensus that was vital in the life of the church and important in politics as well. He may not have read Hubmaier's and Franck's terse summaries of his note, but he cannot have ignored that his own words were apt to encourage rebellion. In 1525, while being safely sheltered by the walls of Basel, he watched how the Peasant Rebellion erupted a short distance from the city and began to spread to other regions of Germany and Austria. The peasants claimed that their demands were motivated by the Gospel, and when Erasmus in 1526 launched his first *Hyperaspistes* against Luther, he quite properly assessed the Saxon reformer with a share of responsibility for provoking both the rebellion and its merciless suppression.[58] Erasmus had defended the right of Bohemia's Utraquist congregations to choose their own priests – the right that then became a prominent demand of the peasant rebels.[59] The practice, he said, had once been common, but had been abandoned when it caused 'tumults among the mob.[60] 'Tumults' were indeed what he then experienced, yet he stuck to his own egalitarian interpretation of that crucial verse in Matthew (and to his frequent denunciations of the predominantly immoral conduct of the secular and ecclesiastic elites). And he wanted his harsh words to be noted. His comments on the *Comma Johanneum* and the Eucharistic consecration were based on an accurate reading of the Greek text. Here he could not yield. Here and in similar cases, as a philologist, he could not depart from the clear meaning of the words in the Gospel, although his church might do so. But in Matthew 16:18 it was not the Greek text that was at issue, it was the interpretation. While he acknowledged that other expositions were possible, he stuck to his own, although he must have been aware of its subversive potential.

Perhaps we can say in conclusion that when Erasmus' words invited radical interpretations and reactions, this outcome was not always intended, and when it was intended, he may sometimes have come to ignore his original intent. But sometimes radical interpretations would indeed reach down to the roots of his thinking and bare convictions that were as radical as radical readers made them to be.

Notes

In citing works in the notes, I identify those that occur most frequently by the following short titles or abbreviations:

Allen	*Opus epistolarum Des. Erasmi Roterodami.* Ed. P.S. Allen, H.M. Allen, and H.W Garrod. Oxford 1905–58.
ASD	*Opera omnia Desiderii Erasmi Roterodami.* Amsterdam 1969–.
BFP	*Bibliotheca Fratrum Polonorum.* Irenopoli post annum 1656. [Amsterdam 1668]. *The Works of Fausto Sozzini,* found in vols. 1 and 2, have now been reprinted: *Fausti Socini Senensis opera omnia in duo tomos distincta.* Ed. Emanuela Scribani. Siena 2004.
Cardano, *Le opere*	Girolamo Cardano. *Le opere, le fonti, la vita.* Ed. Marialuisa Baldi et al. Milan 1999.
CEBR	*Contemporaries of Erasmus: A Biographical Register of the Renaissance and Reformation.* Ed. P.G. Bietenholz and T.B. Deutscher. Toronto 1985–7.
Colloquia Turonensia	*Colloquia Erasmiana Turonensia.* Ed. Jean-Claude Margolin. Paris–Toronto 1972.
CWE	*Collected Works of Erasmus.* Toronto 1974–.
DBI	*Dizionario biografico degli Italiani.* Ed. A.M. Ghisalberti et al. Rome 1960–.
De falsa	*De falsa et vera unius Dei Patris, Filii et Spiritus Sancti cognitione libri duo, (Albae Iuliae) 1568.* Introduction by A. Pirnát. Utrecht 1988.
Erasmi opuscula	*Erasmi opuscula. A supplement to the Opera omnia.* Ed. W.K. Ferguson. The Hague 1933.
Erasmo, Venezia	*Erasmo, Venezia e la cultura padana nel '500.* Ed. A. Olivieri. Rovigo 1955.

Eresia e Riforma	*Eresia e Riforma nell'Italia del Cinquecento. Miscellanea I* (Biblioteca del 'Corpus Reformatorum Italicorum'). Florence–Chicago 1974.
Formazione storica della alterità	*La formazione storica della alterità. Studi di storia della tolleranza nell'età moderna offerti a Antonio Rotondò.* Ed. Luisa Simonutti et al. Florence 2001.
LB	*Desiderii Erasmi Roterodami opera omnia.* Ed. J. Le Clerc. Leiden 1703–6; repr. 1961–2.
Scrinium Erasmianum	*Scrinium Erasmianum.* Ed. J. Coppens. Leiden 1969.
TRE	*Theologische Realenzyklopädie.* Ed. G. Krause et al. Berlin 1977–.
WA	*D. Martin Luthers Werke. Kritische Gesamtausgabe.* Weimar, 1883–.

Without specifically referring to them, I have persistently used Anne Reeve's three volumes of *Erasmus' Annotations to the New Testament*, London 1986 and Leiden 1973, 1990, which mark all the variants between editions published during Erasmus' life.

INTRODUCTION

1 Israel, *Radical Enlightenment*, 1. Historians have a fairly clear notion of politics and politicians labelled 'radical' in the nineteenth century and also of the 'Radical Reformation,' a term that became indispensable in the second half of the twentieth century. Within the context of the sixteenth-century Reformation the term 'radical' for a while occasioned intensive debate between Marxist and non-Marxist historians, but since the unification of Germany much of this debate has become obsolete.
2 *A Glossary of Later Latin to 600 A.D.*, ed. A. Souter (Oxford 1949), s.v.
3 Seidel Menchi, *Erasmo in Italia*, 16–18. Cf. Léon-E. Halkin, 'Erasmianism as a religious outlook was ... a movement heralding Catholic Reform' and 'the Second Vatican Council – an Erasmian Council, if ever there was such a thing' (Halkin, *Erasmus: A Critical Biography*, trans. J. Tonkin (Oxford 1993), 290, 295.
4 Bruce Mansfield, *Interpretations of Erasmus, c. 1750–1920: Man of His Own* (Toronto 1992), 373–5.
5 Gilly, 'Erasmo, la Reforma radical'.
6 Miguel A. Granada, *El umbral de la modernidad. Estudios sobre filosofía, religión y ciencia entre Petrarca y Descartes* (Barcelona 2000), 261–87, ch. 6: 'De Erasmo a Bruno: Caza, sacrificio y metamorfosis en la divinidad.'

Granada convincingly associates the last section of Bruno's *Spaccio de la bestia trionfante* (3.3; cf. also *Epistola esplicatoria*) with reminiscences from Erasmus' *Moriae encomium*: the satire of hunters publicly performing slaughter like a sacred ritual, but in truth degenerating to the bestiality of their prey (ASD IV-3 104, 120; CWE 27.102, 112), and the true Sileni as opposed to the inverted Sileni. Christ, who in Erasmus' adage (III iii 1, ASD II-5 164, CWE 34.264) is the paradigm of a true Silenus, to the radical pantheist Bruno becomes an inverted Silenus. The *Spaccio* was specifically mentioned in the final summation of Bruno's 'heresies.' Reading the *Spaccio*, one is constantly reminded of Erasmus' texts. I used a Rome 1888 edition. There is an English translation of this bizarre work with a helpful introduction and notes by Arthur D. Imerti, Rutgers University Press, 1964.

7 Like Erasmus, Bruno advocates religious toleration, protests against war, and criticizes the traditional schools of 'pedant' philosophy and theology. He moves well beyond Erasmus in his satirical jabs against the Trinity, the two natures of Christ, the virgin birth, and the veneration of saints. He is also blunter than Erasmus in his critique of the Jews, the German nation, and the Lutherans. His flippant use of biblical references would have left Erasmus uneasy, and the equation of divine providence with fate and the rejection of Christianity together with all established religions would have horrified Eramus. Bruno's enthusiasm for the ancient Egyptians and a pantheistic cult of nature he attributed to them, as well as his cosmology, lay completely outside the sphere of Erasmus. Finally, Erasmus would never have wanted to die as a witness for the truth of radical ideas. See Miguel A. Granada, *Giordano Bruno. Universo infinito, unión con Dios, perfeción del hombre* (Barcelona 2002), especially 153–7, 344f.; Frances A. Yates, *Giordano Bruno and the Hermetic Tradition* (London 1964), especially 164–9, 252–7, 355–7; *Giordano Bruno: Philosopher of the Renaissance*, ed. H. Gatti (Ashgate 2002), 151f. and passim.

8 Allen, IV, Epp. 1001.73–9, 1039.36–8, 147–50. CWE 7.34f., 121, 124. P.G. Bietenholz, '"Haushalten mit der Wahrheit." Erasmus im Dilemma der Kompromissbereitschaft,' *Basler Zeitschrift für Geschichte und Altertumskunde* 86 (1986): 9–26, here 21–4.

CHAPTER ONE

1 Franck, *Chronica*, II 201v–202r: 'ein geistliche unsichtbare versamlung, die wir glauben und nit sehen, frei im geist und glauben vom H[eiligen] geyst durchs wort regiert.'
2 Franck, *Chronica*, ibid.
3 Franck, *Chronica*, II 138v.
4 *Apologia ad monachos hispanos*,' LB IX 1066 (objections 38–40): 'videtur tribuere authoritatem sacerdotalem universo populo.' Cf. Allen,

VII, Epp. 1879, 1967; VIII, Ep. 2095 introductions. A second edition (Basel 1529) is enriched by an appendix of corrections to be applied to several of Erasmus' works. Franck did not make any use of this appendix. That Franck's source is the *Apologia ad monachos hispanos* was discovered by Rudolf Kommoss, *Franck und Erasmus*, 28, 32.

5 Franck, *Chronica*, II 142v. LB IX 1166 F, cf. 251 C, 361 E–F, 1179 B–C.
6 LB VI 88 E, so in the 1519 edition. In the 1527 edition Erasmus added that in his *Retractationes* Augustine had questioned his own interpretation, but had left it to readers to choose for themselves.
7 Franck, *Chronica*, II 142v. LB VI 415f., 418. Franck also picks up the monks' objection 95, an attack on papal indulgences, derived from Erasmus' *Enchiridion*.
8 Franck, *Chronica*, II 141v. Erasmus, LB IX 1082 C–D (objections 71–2). Paraphrase on John 4:21 and a letter 'Pio lectori,' attached to the Gospel of John since the second edition of the Paraphrases: LB VII 528 F, 649f. Independently Franck (*Chronica*, II 141v, 142r) referred to the paraphrases of Roman 3, esp. 27–8 and Galatians 2:16: LB VII 787, 950.
9 Rummel, *Erasmus' Annotations*, 167–9. Cf. below, 199–201.
10 Franck, *Chronica*, II 141v. Erasmus, LB IX 1084–7. Cf. Notes on Matt. 1:23, 12:46–8, Luke 1:26–9, 2:23: LB VI 9f., 69f., 223f., 234f., and VII 289.
11 Franck, *Chronica*, II 141v, see, e.g., *Modus orandi Deum*, ASD V-1, 172. CWE 70.224f. Franck also referred to the *Colloquia* (as the monks had done) and additionally to the *Enchiridion* and *Moriae encomium*.
12 Franck, *Chronica*, II 141v. Erasmus, LB IX 1080f. (objection and response 66). Franck (142r) also compiles material from objections 92 and 96 in order to attack the Catholic fast, the cult of saints, and pilgrimages.
13 Franck, *Chronica*, II 140r–v. LB IX 1062–4, cf. V 155 D.
14 Franck, *Chronica*, II 140v. The monks (objection 35, LB IX 1064) referred to Erasmus' note on Mark 14:24 (LB VI 205). Franck also picked up from Erasmus' response 35 references to Thomas Aquinas and Gabriel Biel and added a new reference to John Fisher's retort to Luther's *Babylonian Captivity*, claiming, on questionable grounds, that Fisher agreed with Erasmus' point. See John Fisher, *Opera* (Würzburg 1597; repr. 1967), 206–10. A line in Franck's inimitable language seems to refer to the Eucharist carried around in processions or publicly elevated during mass in a lavishly decorated monstrance – a custom branded by Erasmus as superstition: 'Das heyligthum zeygen und braechtlich auffwerffen verspottet er als Aposteitzlerey und aberglauben, exemplo Hieronimi in Annot. Math. 23.[5]' (*Chronica*, II 142v).
15 Franck, *Chronica*, II 140v. LB IX 1066.
16 Franck, *Chronica*, II 140v. LB IX 1068–70 (objections 41–4). Notes on Matt. 19:3 and 1 Cor. 7:39, LB VI 97f., 692–703.
17 Franck, *Chronica*, II 142r. LB IX 1089 (objection 93).

18 Franck, *Chronica*, II 140v–141r. LB IX 1070–5 (objections 45–53). Notes on Matt. 2:6, 27:8; Mark 1:2; Acts 1:1, 10:38; Rom. 8:3; 1 Cor. 4:3; 2 Cor. 2:13: LB VI 12–14, 140f., 152 F, 433f., 476–8, 600 C, 673f., 758 C. In their objections 45 and 46 the monks allowed that Erasmus had also said individual mistakes would not impair the authority of the Gospel. Franck chose to ignore this.
19 Franck, *Chronica*, II 140v–141r. Note on Acts 10:38: LB VI 476 E.
20 Franck, *Chronica*, II 138v–139r, 141r–142r. LB IX 1032, 1077–80, 1083f. (objections 56–63, responses 60, 74). Notes on Matt. 1:23, Luke 4.8: LB VI 9f., 246 F.
21 Franck, *Chronica*, II 141r–v. LB 1078f.
22 Franck, *Chronica*, II 141r. LB IX 1076f. (objection and response 55).
23 Franck, *Chronica*, II 142v, quoting Erasmus without guidance from the Spanish monks: LB VI 125C–E (note on Matt. 24:23, as in the 1522 ed.): 'Audimus monachos passim clamantes: "ecce Christus hic est" ... Vult ille communis esse omnium, qui sol est mundi. Non dignatur circumscribi loco, non includi titulis humanis aut cultu ceremoniisve.' Franck paraphrases: 'Allenthalb ist Christus ... er will yederman gemein sein, der da ist die Sonn der welt, will sich nicht lassen mit einer statt umbzeünen oder einschliessen.'
24 Franck, *Chronica*, II 142r: Erasmus says, 'es sey eben der leib under oder in dem Sacrament des altars wesenlich nach der substantz, der am creütz ist gehangen, aber nitt ein solcher, nempe idem corpus, sed not tale quod in cruce, sunder ein geystlich glorificierter leib.' Franck translates from Erasmus' dedicatory preface to his edition of *Algeri opera* (Freiburg 1530), Allen, VIII, Ep. 2284.69–71. Cf. LB IX 1064f. and Augustijn, *Erasmus*, 150f.
25 Franck, *Chronica*, II 142v. LB VI 36f. On this issue see below, 55f.
26 Franck, *Chronica*, II 142r. LB IX 1054–60 Franck refers to the *Enchiridion*, the dedicatory preface of the New Testament to Leo X (Allen, II, Ep. 384), and a long note on Matt. 11:[30] (LB VI 63–5).
27 Franck, *Chronica*, II 142v. LB VI 416 E. Erasmus explained that by 'Pharisees' he meant priests who incited the princes to wage war, or even did so themselves.
28 Franck, *Chronica*, II 140r. LB IX 1060 A (objection 23); cf. VII sign. **3v.
29 Franck, *Chronica*, II 140r, 203r–204v. Erasmus, LB IX 1054B–1060A (objection and response 22), esp. 1054E–57E. In part the same sections were also quoted by Sebastian Castellio in *De haereticis an sint persequendi* (1554) and by Mino Celsi in *In haereticis coercendis quatenus progredi liceat* (1577). Franck translated independently of Gerard Geldenhouwer, who had earlier published several tracts in Strasbourg that also featured parts of Erasmus' response 22. See Cornelis Augustijn, 'Gerard Geldenhouwer und die religiöse Toleranz,' *Archiv für Reformationsgeschichte* 69 (1978): 132–56.

30 Franck, *Chronica*, II 142v. LB IX 1078 (objection 59). Notes on Matt. 5:37 and 1 Cor. 15:31: LB VI 31f., 737f.
31 Franck, *Chronica*, II 140r. Erasmus, LB IX 1060–2 (objection and response 28. LB VII sign. **3v. Franck's last point corresponds with objection 25 and is taken from Erasmus' Argument prefixed to 1 Cor.: LB VII 855f.
32 Franck, *Chronica*, II 142r: die alten nit seind kůn gwesen etwas zů diffinieren, ec. Welcher art, seind, ob die kinder zů tauffen seind, ob man jn die Eucharistiam geben soll, sunder dise stück mit auffgezogner aussœrterung geerwirdiget.' LB IX 1041C (response 5).
33 Franck, *Chronica*, II 138v. LB VI 1080, IX 1033. The monks here stated that they were following the 'latest' edition. As in objection 45, they meant the 1522 edition. Much the same point is made in objection 3, based on *Modus orandi*.
34 LB IX 1033–47. Annotations on Mark 1:2 (objection 13), Rom. 9:5 (objections 7, 12), Phil. 2:6 and Col. 2:9 (objection 8), Tit. 2:13 (objection 9), Heb. 1:8 (objection 10), 1 John 5:20 (objection 11). LB VI 151–3 (the criticized part was suppressed in the 1535 ed.), 610–12, 867f., 888f., 971, 984, 1083f.
35 Franck, *Chronica*, II 138v–140r, 141r–v, 142v using objections 1–3, 5–11, responses 3, 12f., 18–20, 60: Erasmus, LB IX 1029–53, 1078F–1079A. Franck's rendering of part of response 60 is puzzling. Erasmus suggested that in the Apostolic and Athanasian Creeds to 'the Holy Ghost who proceeds from the Father' the Latins had added *Filioque* (from the Father and the Son). Erasmus concluded: 'Atque in his non dubito quin liceat Ecclesiae mutare quaedam; an idem liceat in Sacris Voluminibus, praesertim quod mutet aut etiam in diversum vertat sententiam, non est meum definire.' Franck (141r–v) referred only to the creeds, not to scripture, and continued: 'Aber in disen dingen zweifel ich nicht, das nit der kirchen gebuer, und in dem fall macht hab etwas zů endern.' *Nit* may or may not be a mistake: in any case, Franck fails to render Erasmus' point.
36 Franck, *Chronica*, II 141v. LB IX 1081f. (objections 68–9.). *Hyperaspistes I*: CWE 76.132; LB X 1264B; cf. also IX 699f. (*Supputatio* against Noël Béda).
37 Williams, *Radical Reformation*, 63–70. Roland Crahay, 'De l'humanisme réformiste à la réforme radicale,' *Revue de l'Université de Bruxelles* n.s. 19 (1969): 295–325, here 303f. Walker, *Decline of Hell*, 73–86. See also below, 202f.
38 Franck, *Chronica*, II 142r. LB IX 1091 (objection 99). CWE 66.113, LB V 56.
39 Walker, *Decline of Hell*, 124–7, 192–5, and passim.
40 Franck, *Chronica*, II 142r. Erasmus, LB IX 1090f (objection and response 97). CWE 66.93, 98. LB V 44 F, 47 C–D).
41 Franck, *Chronica*, II 142r. LB IX 1087f. (objection and response 90), CWE 27.235. ASD IV–1 166. LB VI 636.
42 Franck, *Chronica*, I 271v–277r.

43 Franck, *Chronica*, II 142v. LB VI 857 C–D.
44 Franck, *Chronica*, II 142v: 'strickt er den Christen ab alle gegenwőr ...; will doch den Fürsten jr recht nit genummen haben.' Erasmus, LB VI 317–21, 415f.
45 Erasmus, LB IX 1083f., cf. VI 585 B, 591C (as in the 1527 edition). All that Franck reported of the Spanish objections and Erasmus' responses was: 'In Annotat. Rom. v. sagt Erasmus, Hieronymus biege etwa die schrifft wider Jovinianum streittende, und Augustinus thue diss offt' (*Chronica*, II 141v.). The central issue, Pelagianism, is omitted.
46 Erasmus, LB IX 1075, 1082, 1091 (objections 54, 70, 98). Franck, *Chronica*, II 142r.
47 Franck, *Chronica*, II 141v.
48 'Welchs etlich Münch, die on Gottes nammen [a pun for *in Gottes Namen*] Ketzermeister und Inquisitores heretice pravitatis sollen sein, dahin bedeüten, untt rechen ihm allhie auff, er verleügne, radbrech, marter, oder bieg alle autoritet unnd schrifft, so von der Gotheit Christi bezeügen, so Erasmus diss nit handelt, noch sein fürnemmen an disem ort ist, ob Christus Gott oder nit Got sei, den er anderswa wol lxxx. mal, welche loca er selbs alle an den Bischoff Hispalensem, Alphonsum Mauricum anzeücht, bezeügt, sunder was der Griechisch und ursprünglich text vermőg, und wie faule argument etwan etlich in so trefflichen sachen füren, und nichts aussrichten, dann das sy den ketzern zům gespőtt vnd gelåchter werden, und sy nit damit gewinnen, sunder in jrer ketzerey vil verstockter machen. Derhalb will Erasmus vil damit auffmuntern, zů dem brunnen und notwőr jagen,und den brunnen des rechten texts anzeygen, was er in grund und seiner urspringlichen zungen vermőg, was zů oder darvon thon sey... das legen jm nachmals vil übel auss, als hab er vom glauben geschriben, diss oder das adseriert (Franck, *Chronica*, II 139r).
49 Franck, *Chronica*, II 142r–v (based on Erasmus' responses 13 and 75, LB IX 1047 E–F, 1084 C): 'We believe in Mary's eternal virginity although it is not expressed in Holy Scripture. Likewise we believe in several sacraments not expressed there either, but come down to us from our ancestors or established. For with some things it is *not* enough to believe them although we cannot indicate a cause for doing so. We read nowhere that the apostles, when they preached to the crowd, announced or expressed Christ's divine nature. The [other] three evangelists nowhere call him God; alone John does so in scant places. Peter and Paul, in Athens, call him a man.' The 'not' in 'Dann in etlich ding ist nit gnůg das mans glaubt' seems to pervert the meaning. One can only speculate whether this 'not' would lead some of Franck's readers to attribute an unwarranted scepticism to Erasmus.
50 Allen, IX, Ep. 2587.18–27. Dejung, 'Sebastian Franck,' 39–119, here 44.
51 For some details see below, chap. 3.

52 Perhaps there had been a preceding exchange of letters between Franck and Erasmus. On 6 March 1531 Erasmus answered a missing letter, perhaps from Franck, that among other things had expressed disappointment about Erasmus' staying at Catholic Freiburg. See Ep. 2441 (Allen, IX, 153–6).
53 Allen, IX, Ep. 2615.372–80. Dejung, 'Sebastian Franck,' 42–5.
54 The first and second editions were published by Hans Vanier, Ulm, 1534 and 1542; see the bibliography in Dejung, 'Sebastian Franck,' 70–93. Franck's translation is correct and complete, if sometimes awkward. His additions, while perhaps uncalled for, do not add new radical touches.

The Epicurean factor in *Moria*, which is examined below in chap. 5, did not visibly affect Franck, but one should not ignore that two other works with a similar Epicurean panache also attracted and delighted him: Thomas More's *Utopia* and, especially, Gianozzo Manetti's *De dignitate et excellentia hominis*. For the latter see P.G. Bietenholz, 'Riflessi dell'umanesimo italiano nell'opera de Sebastian Franck,' in *Rapporti e scambi tra umanesimo italiano ed umanesimo europeo*, ed. Luisa Rotondi Secchi Tarugi (Milan 2001), 121–34, esp. 125–7.
55 Dejung, 'Sebastian Franck,' 73.
56 B. Becker, 'Nederlandsche vertalingen van Sebastian Franck's geschriften,' *Nederlands archief voor Kerkgeschiedenis* n.s. 21 (1928): 149–60; G. Von Gemert, 'Die niederländischen Texte Sebastian Francks,' in *Editionsdesiderate zur frühen Neuzeit*, ed. H.-G. Roloff (Amsterdam 1997), 2:669–85.

CHAPTER TWO

1 LB IX 1015–94 (first published in 1528). The extensive use that Sebastian Franck made of the *Apologia* was discussed above in chap. 1.
2 Erasmus' distinct preference was for the simple and concise Apostolic Creed, which, he believed, deserved its name, although the redaction dated from the time of the Council of Nicaea; see *Ratio verae theologiae*, LB V 92 D. For his distinction between teachings explicitly stated in scripture that must not be questioned and others not so stated that may still be revered, although even ecumenical councils should tread cautiously when sanctioning such traditions, see, e.g., the *Apologia* against the Spanish monks, LB IX 1038, 1065 (responses 3 and 36).
3 For the debate with Colet, see *De taedio et pavore Christi*, LB V 1265–94; CWE 70.1–67; for the controversy with Lefèvre, see CWE 5 Ep. 597.
4 A convenient summary of New Testament annotations that were of interest to Antitrinitarian apologists is found in *De falsa et vera Unius Dei Patris ... cognitione* (1568; see below, 42–6). Nearly half of the ones there listed are identified already in Lee's *Annotationes in annotationes Erasmi* and Erasmus' *Responsio ad annotationes Lei* (ASD IX-4 73–335;

CWE 72.67–419), to wit John 1:1, 8:25; Rom. 1:4, 9:5; Phil. 2:6; Col. 1:15, 2:9; 1 Tim. 1:6, 1:17, 3:16; Tit. 2:13, 3:4; Heb. 1:3; 1 John 5:7–9. See Coogan, *Erasmus, Lee,* and Cecilia Asso, *La teologia e la grammatica. La controversia fra Erasmo ed Edward Lee* (Florence 1993).
5 LB VI 1080 C–D, 1081 D–E.
6 Gilly, *Spanien,* 277–98 and passim, here 284. Gilly, 'Erasmo, la Reforma radical,' 312–30.
7 Gauss, 'Der junge Michael Servet,' 424f.
8 Sebastian Franck did so at just this time; the Antitrinitarians of Transylvania would do so later. See below, 43.
9 First occurrence: Michael Servetus, *De Trinitatis erroribus libri septem,* [Haguenau] 1531, repr. 1965, 23v (on 1 John 5:7, cf. below ...). Second occurrence: M[ichael] S[ervetus] V[illanovanus] (so signed in the colophon), *Christianismi restitutio,* [Vienne] 1553, repr. 1965, 695: Servetus rejects Erasmus' correct interpretation of Irenaeus 3:21. Other examples of Servetus' dependence on Erasmus' translations and annotations: *De Trinitatis erroribus,* 3v–4r (Matt. 16:20, LB VI 89f.), 4v (John 1:30 and Acts 17:31, LB VI 345, 502),14v (Heb. 2:7, LB VI 985), 34v (1 Tim. 2:5, LB VI 932). *Christianismi restitutio,* 77 (John 8:58, LB VI 379f.), 525 (Matt. 28:19, LB VI 148).
10 Gilly, 'Erasmo, la Reforma radical,' 326: 'Servet estudió después con gran detenimiento tanto las apologías cuanto las anotaciones, paráfrasis y ediciones patrísticas de Erasmo, sirviéndose continuamente de ellas en sus dos primeros escritos.' Detailed research will be needed to show whether or not this statement is too genereous. E.M. Wilbur in his critical translation of Servetus, *Two Treatises,* identifies in some cases Sante Pagnini or the Vulgate as Servetus' source.
11 Servetus, *De Trinitatis erroribus,* 17v–20r. LB VI 867f., cf. VII 996, IX 1043, 1045. Gilly, *Spanien,* 289f., and 'Erasmo, la Reforma radical,' 327f.
12 Gilly, *Spanien.,* 290f., and 'Erasmo, la Reforma radical,' 228–230. LB VI 371f. Servetus, *De Trinitatis erroribus,* 65v. *Two Treatises,* 101f.
13 Bainton, *Hunted Heretic,* 44–8.
14 Servetus, *Christianismi restitutio,* 703: 'Ille est proprie Messias, proprie Christus, proprie unctus, proprie Rex, proprie Sacerdos, Propheta, Salvator.' See below, 42.
15 Servetus, *Christianismi restitutio,* 272: 'Ipse Christus qui sanctificat, et nos qui sanctificamur, ex eodem plasmate participiamus et ex eodem Deo sumus: ideo nos fratres ibidem [Heb. 2:11–17] vocat.' Elisabeth Feist Hirsch, 'Michael Servetus and the Neoplatonic Tradition: God, Christ and Man,' *Bibliothèque d'Humanisme et Renaissance* 42 (1980): 561–75.
16 Gilly, *Spanien,* 278f.
17 LB VI 1079B–1081F. Servetus, *De Trinitatis erroribus,* 22v–27v. *Two Treatises,* 35–8. *Christianismi restitutio,* 22f.
18 Allen, VIII, Ep. 2615:335–7.

19 See below, chap. 4. For Servetus' influence, see Castellio, *De arte dubitandi*, 89, n. 19. Especially important is the contact with the exiled law professor Matteo Gribaldi, a committed Antitrinitarian, who had come to Basel after witnessing Servetus' trial in Geneva; see Guggisberg, *Castellio*, 81f., 109f. In 1563, ten years after Servetus' death, the last work of Bernardino Ochino, *Dialogi XXX*, was published in Basel, translated into Latin by none other than Castellio. It contained a dialogue on the Trinity, indebted to Lelio and Fausto Sozzin; see Rotondò, *Studi e ricerche*, 99f.
20 Bainton, *Hunted Heretic*, 176. Gauss tentatively suggests another motive for Servetus' visit. In '*Der junge Michael Servet*,' 459, she draws attention to Calvin's initial neglect of the Trinitarian theology.
21 Servetus, *Two Treatises*, xxix.
22 *Catechesis Racoviensis*, ed. G.I. Oederus (Frankfurt–Leipzig 1739), preliminary plate facing a portrait of Fausto Sozzini, 'haeresiarcha.' The roots give way to a solid trunk, labelled 'Faustus Socinus, Laelii consanguineus.' At the top of the tree figure Daniel Zwicker and Daniel De Breen.
23 Aldo Stella, *Anabattismo e antitrinitarismo in Italia nel XVI secolo. Nuove ricerche storiche* (Padua 1969), 28f, 78–81; Aldo Stella, 'Influssi erasmiani sui riformatori radicali,' in *Erasmo, Venezia*, 87–104.
24 Lelio Sozzini, *Opere*, 25–8.
25 Lelio Sozzini, *Opere*, 31f.
26 Lelio Sozzini, *Opere*, 53f., 184, 187. LB VI 89.
27 It included a firm denunciation of the Anabaptists and Servetus: 'Catabapatistarum errores omnes fugio, Serveti dogmata, Arianismum totum execror horreoque.' Lelio Sozzini, *Opere*, 96.
28 For good reason Bullinger did not remind the Italian of the explanation he too had given ten years earlier that the truth ought to be taught 'pro ratione loci, temporis ac personarum commode et prudenter.' Erasmus could have said as much. On dissimulation, see below, chap. 6.
29 Lelio Sozzini, *Opere*, 103–28; written towards the end of his life and not printed until 1568. Cf. Valerio Marchetti, 'Dall'esegesi erasmiana all'ermeneutica sociniana,' in *Erasmo, Venezia*, 225–40.
30 Rotondò in Lelio Sozzini, *Opere*, 104, 363. Antonio Rotondò, *Calvin and the Italian Anti-Trinitarians*, trans. J. Tedeschi and A. Tedeschi (Saint Louis, MI, 1968), 5–10.
31 Lelio Sozzini, *Opere*, 111f. The other interpreters have gone astray: '1. quod unum Deum esse Christum cum Patre somniarunt illique coeternum et coequalem; quare etiam creatorem cum illo unum esse commenti sunt; 2. quod creationis vocem non intelligerent de recreatione seu renovatione, reconciliatione et recapitulatione restaurationeque recipi.'
32 It needs to be borne in mind that Lelio may have found points first made by Erasmus in the Bibles of Pagnini, Castellio, and Beza, and in

commentaries to various parts of the New Testament by Oecolampadius, Melanchthon, Calvin, and others.
33 Lelio Sozzini, *Opere*, 113f., 123. LB VI 840–2, 1077f.
34 Lelio Sozzini, *Opere*, 125f., e.g.: 'verbum illud Dei factum est, inquam, caro, id est vilis, pauper, miser, maledictum, vermis et non homo, quasi omni potentia destitutus esset, mortis se obiecit crucis.' Lelio concluded that here, as elsewhere, the Gospel always referred to the human Christ and had no room for another, eternal Christ with all the hallmarks of divinity ('qui fuit in forma Dei vel dives vel verbum deus vel vita luxque'). Erasmus' paraphrase, by contrast, is based on the assumption of an eternal Christ: LB VI 777f., VII 929.
35 Lelio Sozzini, *Opere*, 104n. LB VI 375f.
36 Erasmus, *Enarratio in Psalmum secundum*, LB V 206 B. Lelio Sozzini, *Opere*, 111, cf. 98. Williams, *Radical Reformation*, 1143f. Cf. also above, 37.
37 Lismanini's letter to a Polish baron is preserved in Stanisław Lubieniecki's *Historia reformationis polonicae*, 1585 (repr. with introduction by H. Barycz, Warsaw 1971), 118–26, here p. 122: 'Erasmus scribit in Apologia ad Jacobum Sturmium, quia Pater principium est filii, juxta hoc major est Pater velut causa et principium. Quapropter et Dominus dixit, Pater meus major me est, eo quod Pater est. Patris autem vox quid alium significat, quam causam et principium ejus, qui ex ipso genitus est? Haec Erasmus.' This does not sound like Erasmus' diction; nor did he address an apology to Sturm. Erasmus' *Apologia ad Jacobum Stunicam* at least raises the issue: LB IX 316f., 396 E. Lismanini seems to be alluding to John 1:1–2 and 14:28. For 'the seeds of Erasmus,' see Lubieniecki, 18, and for Lismanini's contacts with Sozzini, see Lelio Sozzini, *Opere*, 270f. and passim.
38 Alba Iulia (1568, repr. with introduction by A. Pirnát, Utrecht 1988); henceforward quoted as *De falsa*).
39 *De falsa*, 91–8. List of annotations with a bearing on the Trinitarian controversy: Matt. 13:33, 24:36 (Mark 13:32) / John chap. 1 / John 5:27, 8:25–7, 8:57, 10:30, 10:35, 17:3 / Rom. 1:4, 1:7, 9:5, 11:36 / 2 Cor. 13:14 / Eph. 1:17, 5:5 / Phil. 2:6, 3:3 / Col. 1:15, 2:9 / 2 Thess. 2:16 / 1 Tim. 1:1 (Tit. 2:13) / 1 Tim. 1:17, 3:16, 6:15 / Tit. 2:11, 3:4 / Heb. 1:3, 2:7, 2:10 / 1 John 5:7. See also, above, n. 4.
40 *De falsa*, 47. See below, 153 n. 54.
41 All three were dedicatory epistles for major new publications, the paraphrase of John and the edition of Hilary, both dated 5 January 1523 (Epp. 1333 and 1334), and the edition of Irenaeus, dated 27 August 1526 (Ep. 1738).
42 See below, p. 56f. Allen V, Ep. 1333.369f. Cf. also Erasmus' note on Luke 1:2, attempting to place Luke in a chronological order of witnesses: LB VI 218, ASD VI-5 442.

43 CWE 9.250; Allen, V, Ep. 1334.145–7.
44 CWE 9.243; Allen, V, Ep. 1333.377–83.
45 CWE 9.250; Allen, V, Ep. 1334.151f.
46 Or 'the most monstrous, *omnium portentuosissimus*,' since he reduced 'all Christianity to phantastic language and complicated myths.'
47 CWE 12.296f; Allen, VI, Ep. 1738.121–4,140–2. Erasmus' source was Irenaeus.
48 *De falsa*, 75, 186–93.
49 *De falsa*, 40: 'Is in concilio sub Gregorio Nono coacto palam Quaternitatis Longobardum convicit, et libellum de eadem egregium nobis re liquit, quem Papa tum primum prohibuit.' The reference appears to be to the Lateran Council of 1215. Gregory IX reigned from 1227 to 1241.
50 *De falsa*, 41, where he is called Ioannes Beliardus. He is identified by Fausto Sozzini, BFP I 328a. The reference is to his *De S. Trinitate libri tres* (Paris 1569).
51 *De falsa*, 123.
52 István Monok, 'The Distribution of Works by Erasmus in the Carpatian Basin during the Sixteenth and the Seventeenth Centuries: Summary of Statistical Spread,' in *Republic of Letters. Humanism, Humanities: Selected Papers of the Workshop Held at the Collegium Budapest in Cooperation with NIAS* (Budapest 2005), 35–43.
53 Johann Sommer, *Refutatio scripti Petri Caroli* (printed in 1582) in *Opera omnia*, ed. Anton F.W. Sommer (Vienna 1996–9), II 221. LB VI 936. Antal Pirnát, 'Der antitirinitarische Humanist Johann Sommer und seine Tätigkeit in Klausenburg,' in *Renaissance und Humanismus in Mittel- und Osteuropa*, ed. J. Irmscher (Berlin 1962), 49–60. Guggisberg, *Castellio*, 278f., cf. 265f.
54 Sommer, *Opera omnia*, II 91–101 (*Refutatio scripti Petri Caroli*), IV 159–63 (*Theses de Deo trino*, also in Lubieniecki's *Historia*, 235). Especially II 94: 'Quam fuerit persuasum vulgo Novi testamenti libros a Platonicis non dissentire docet vox illa celebrata Aurelij philosophi Platonici; qui lecto Ioannis Euangelii non dubitavit pronuntiare: Dispereram, nisi barbarus ille (nempe quia Iudaeus erat et rudi sermone sua scripserat) breviter complexus est quaecunque de divina ratione, principio et dispositione ... Plato et Heraclitus tradiderunt [sic] (Postellus, De orbis concord. Cap. 3).' II 96f.: 'Ac initium quidem habuisse Apostolorum ad huc tempore istam perversam philosophandi rationem facile potest colligi, si Pauli et Ioannis verba de Antichristo, de sapientia humana et inani philospohia, item de difficultate scriptorum Pauli testimonium diligentius consideretur, ubi non Paulo ipsi impingitur ministrata erroris occasio, sed lectoribus qui peregrinas opiniones ad scripta illius afferebant, ac ad eas omnia quae legissent referebant.' Antal Pirnát, *Die Ideologie der Siebenbürger Antitrinitarier in den 1570er Jahren*, trans. E. Roth (Budapest 1961), 17–53.

55 Sommer, *Opera omnia*, II 42f. (preface to *Refutatio scripti Petri Caroli*). Sommer did not claim Erasmus for the Antitrinitarian succession.
56 Sebastianus Castellio, *Dialogi IIII de praedestinatione, de electione, de libero arbitrio, de fide* ..., Aresdorffij, per Theophil. Philadelph. [Basel, Pietro Perna] 1578. Faustos' preface, signed 'Felix Turpio,' refers to four champions of free will in the recent past: Bibliander, Melanchthon, who had switched his support from Luther back to Erasmus, and Castellio, but the first 'magnus ille Des. Erasmus Roterodamus fuit, qui Martino Luthero apertissime hac in re obstitit et ... adeo omnes Lutheri copias et machinas, quibus veritatem oppugnare instituerat, fregit atque suvbertit, ut vix ad eas penitus delendas ac dissolvendas aliquid requiri praeterea posse videatur.' See below, chap. 4.
57 Here are some additional cases where Erasmus is specifically indicated as a source: BFP I 152 b (Col. 1:20), 449 b (1 Cor. 13:8), 546 b (Acts 15:18), 572 a (Acts 17:31), 582 b (Heb. 9:28 and 1 Pet. 2:24), 618 a (Rom. 5:7), 646f. (Rom. 7:24), 725 a (1 Cor. 12:13), II 39f. (1 Cor. 9:21), 214 b (Rom 4:22), 399 b (Eph. 1:10), 418 (1 Tim. 3:16). Without naming Erasmus, his translations are used in BFP II 5 a (Gal. 5:6), 134 b (Gal. 3:19), 138 b (Col. 1:19–22), 432 b (Heb. 2:10).
58 BFP I 239–43, II 585–7. LB VI 1079–82, IX 275–84.
59 E.g., *Enarratio in Psalmum 33*, LB V 402 C (referring to Gal. 4:19): 'Semen est verbum Dei cui, si accesserit fides, gignit novam creaturam,' and repeated references to Paul's conviction that faith in Christ produces a *nova creatura*, LB V 1176 C, IX 1248 A (2 Cor. 5:17, Gal. 6:15). Cf. Augustijn, *Erasmus*, 141. Neither in his Annotations nor in his Paraphrase of John does Erasmus elaborate on *mundus per ipsum factus est* in John 1:10. Like Lelio, Fausto emphasizes the significance of 2 Cor. 5:17, but unlike his uncle, also refers to Gal. 6:15: BFP I 80 b, II 137 b. See also below, p. 54 on Rom. 6:6.
60 Domański, '*Explicatio primi capitis Evangelii Ioannis*,' 99–102. BFP I 80 b, 82b–83a. LB VI 338 E, VII 502 F.
61 LB VI 335–7. BFP I 75–85, II 594 a.
62 LB II 53f. BFP I 79 b. Some, but by no means all, footnotes in BFP seem to be generated by the editors rather than Fausto. In this case, the reference might as well have been to Erasmus' notes on John 1: 1–3. See also BFP II 591, and moreover I 641, where Fausto favours the interpretation that 'the Word' and not 'God' is the subject, a point that Erasmus apparently deemed too obvious to mention.
63 BFP II 647, referring to Erasmus' *Apologia de 'In principio erat sermo*,' LB IX 111f.
64 Cf. above, p. 36.
65 Regarding the next verse (John 1:15), however, Fausto applauded Beza and others, who (following Erasmus) explained that Jesus' 'coming before' John the Baptist did not express a pre-existence in

time but a higher authority. BFP I 83f., 145 b, 635 b, 799 b. LB VI 339–42. Gilly, *Spanien*, 280.

66 BFP I 77 b, 83 b, also 329 a.; cf. above, pp. 44–6 Among Lelio's papers inherited by Fausto there was probably a letter from the Zurich minister Johannes Wolf to Lelio that examined Platonic origins of the Trinitarian concept; see Lelio Sozzini, *Opere*, 248–59, esp. 253f.; cf. 372, 394.

67 BFP I 328 a, 345 b, 375 a. LB VI 405f., VII 625.

68 BFP II 377f., 581f. LB VI 610f.; cf. LB IX 1002f., 1043–5 (both indicated in a footnote of BFP II 377).

69 LB VI 379E. Servetus, *De Trinitatis erroribus*, 67v., 69v. Lelio Sozzini, *Opere*, 107. BFP II 379 b: 'Quemadmodum igitur Christus alias monuit Judaeos, ut ambularent, dum lucem haberent, et saepius illis non obscure minatus est, futurum, ut gentibus daretur regnum Dei, ipsi vero eo privarentur, sic hoc loco non sine tacitis minis monet eos, ut, antequam gentibus fidei ostium aperiatur, agnoscant se esse Christum.' Also BFP II 504f. One wonders whether some seventeenth-century readers of Fausto may have interpreted this in an apocalyptic sense.

70 2 Kings 2:1, 11; 2 Cor. 12:2. BFP I 146, 283 b, 674f., 813, II 610. LB VI 352: Erasmus argued that by saying that *filius hominis*, the human Christ, was in heaven and descended from there, a veiled hint at his divine nature was given, just as (in 1 Cor 2:8) the 'Lord of glory crucified' implied the two natures simultaneously held. Cf. Williams, *Radical Reformation*, 1165–9.

71 BFP I 575f., 613 a, II 145 a, 234 a. LB VI 576 C.

72 BFP II 418f, 600 a. LB IX 406f.

73 BFP I 556 b. LB VI 1046, VII 1088.

74 BFP I 148f., 541 b, II 221–7 (where Erasmus and Beza are named in a footnote), 362 b. LB VI 584–92, VII 793.

75 BFP I 100f. LB, VI 594.

76 BFP I 395f., II 581. Actually, Erasmus saw in this verse a direct affirmation of Christ's two natures, unusual amid the many veiled ones to be found in the New Testament: LB VI 417, VII 645, IX 1025 C.

77 BFP II 539 a. LB IX 1034 C–D. The texts are quoted in my article 'Fausto Sozzini and the New Testament Scholarship of Erasmus,' in *Faustus Socinus and His Heritage*, ed. L. Szczucki (Cracow 2005), 11–28, here 21. Cf. also LB VI 1080 C; BFP II 645.

78 BFP I 99–106. For Erasmus' more enlightened approach, see LB VI 597 D, 599f., VII 799f., although a reference in the *Ratio verae theologiae* is closer to Fausto's understanding: LB V 86 D.

79 Domański, 'Explicatio ... primi capitis Evangelii Ioannis,' 83–98.

80 Erasmus, *Ratio verae theologiae*, LB V 131 B.

81 *Ratio verae theologiae* in Erasmus, *Ausgewählte Schiften*, ed. W. Welzig (Darmstadt 1967–80), III 418 (portion of the text not in LB): 'Quod si quis sibi permittit in his [allegoriis] ludere nonnunquam, huic plus

erit veniae in exhortando, in consolando, in reprehendendo quam in asserenda veritate.' Cf. Augustijn, *Erasmus*, 99.
82 Zbigniew Ogonowski, 'Le rationalisme dans la doctrine socinienne,' *Movimenti ereticali in Italia e Polonia* (Florence 1974), 141–57, esp. 151–3.
83 BFP I 45–8. LB VI 36f. (n. 26), 276 D–E, VII 37, 380.
84 BFP I 62b–63a. LB VI 892–94; cf. sign. *6v. For details see my article 'Fausto Sozzini and the New Testament Scholarship of Erasmus,' 24f.
85 BFP I 1–2.
86 See above, 44.
87 *Ratio vera theologiae*, LB V 119 B: 'Christus aliquoties fallit suos ad tempus allegoriarum enigmatibus, quo post altius inhaereat, quod volebat intelligi.' In the *Ecclesiastes* Erasmus described a progression by degrees in this process: LB V 1093f.
88 BFP I 329: 'Quod animadvertens magnus ille Erasmus Roterodamus de Scripturae figuratis loquendi modis agens, sic divine scriptum reliquit: "Haud scio, quo consilio visum est aeternae Sapientiae adumbratis simulachris et insinuare se piis mentibus, et prophanis, ut ita dicam, imponere."' Fausto dropped Erasmus' first word and thus caused it to be more searching (and also syntactically incorrect). Erasmus wrote: 'Sic, haud scio quo consilio, visum est aeternae sapientiae': LB V 119 C.
89 BFP I 280. Williams, *Radical Reformation*, 1162f.
90 *Catechismus ecclesiarum Polonicarum unum Deum Patrem confitentium*, Starnopolis [Amsterdam] 1680. *The Racovian Catechism*, ed. and trans. Thomas Rees (London 1818; repr. 1962).
91 Bruce Mansfield, *Phoenix of His Age*, chap. 7.
92 *Martini Ruari nec non ... aliorumque virorum doctorum ... epistolarum selectarum centuriae*, Amsterdam 1677–81, 44, 67, 95, 97, 99, 101, 105, etc.
93 [Daniel Zwicker], *Revelatio catholicismi veri*, n.p. [shortly after 1652], 62: 'Diese Wendung und Abrede Petavii kompt mir fast so vor als die Köhler-rede Erasmi, welcher, da er in seinen *Annotationibus* über den Ort in Röm. 9.5 ihn genugsam erwiesen und gesagt hat, dass er nicht kräftig genug were, die Arianer zu überweisen, da spricht er endlich doch: "so die Kirche lehren würdt, dass dieser ort nicht anders sölle ausgelegt werden als von der Gottheit des Sohnes, so muss man der Kirche gehorchen." Wiewohl Erasmus auch bald wieder hinzusetzt – welches auch auf Petavii verordnung allhie kann gesagt werden: "Aber dieses hat keine krafft, die Ketzer zu überweisen oder dieselben, welche nichts denn nur die Schrift annehmen und hören."' Cf. LB VI 611 E–F, CWE, 56.249–51, cf. 32. The 'Köhler-rede' about deference to the teaching of the church was added in the last edition of the *Annotationes*, 1535. Zwicker also adduced Erasmus' note on Rom. 9:5 in his *Novi Foederis Josias*, 16.
94 Zwicker's *Henoticum Christianorum* (Amsterdam 1662) is a summary of Mino Celsi's *In haereticis coercendis quatenus progredi liceat*, a long

treatise in which Erasmus was extensively quoted. In his *Ecclesia antiqua inermis* [c. 1666], 45, Zwicker writes: 'Hoc tantum addo, functionem magistratus bellicam vel ab Erasmo in Annotat. Luc. 3:[14] et 22:[36] ... dici non esse puritatis evangelicae, neque hoc jus ex evangelicis praeceptis (aut fidei analogiam) peti posse.'

95 The tragic turning point for Zwicker came at the time of Constantine and the Council of Nicaea. To describe the dire consequences of clerical greed and secular interference, Zwicker found it useful to quote from Erasmus' famous letter to Paul Volz, published as a preface to the 1518 edition of the *Enchiridion*; see Zwicker's *Novi Foederis Josias*, 40, and Allen, III, Ep. 858.510–13. For Zwicker's study of the ante-Nicene fathers, see Bietenholz, *Zwicker*, 61–9, 107–13; Martin Muslow, 'The Trinity as Heresy: Socinian Counter-Histories of Simon Magus, Orpheus, and Cerinthus,' in *Histories of Heresy in Early Modern Europe: For, Against, and Beyond Persecution and Toleration*, ed. John Christian Larsen (New York 2002), 161–9, here 163–6.

96 Bietenholz, *Zwicker*, 221, 232.

97 Bietenholz, *Zwicker*, 220f. One notes the absence of all Castellio Bibles.

98 Bietenholz, *Zwicker*, 40f.

99 [Daniel Zwicker], *Irenicum Irenicorum*, [Amsterdam] 1658, 91–104. After giving a first rendering of Luke 12:15, Zwicker adds: 'rectius ad verbum et paulo clarius: Vulgata et Erasmus,' and he quotes these.

100 Zwicker, *Novi Foederis Josias*, 15f.

101 Zwicker, *Novi Foederis Josias*, 15. Regarding Acts 20:8, however, Erasmus is not among the editors preferring 'church of the Lord' to 'church of God.'

102 See above, chap. 1.

103 Zwicker, *Novi Foederis Josias*, 6: In support of Erasmus' argument that Jesus' own resurrection was intended, and not the resurrection of the saints at the time of his death, Zwicker adduces an analogy with Acts 13:33 and concludes: 'ex resurrectione mortuorum ... eum tandem etiam nominans Jesum Christum.' Cf. Fausto Sozzini in BFP I 572.

104 LB VI 554–8, esp. 555 D: 'eundem esse filium Dei, id quod semper fuerat ... Caro declaravit hominem, virtus et Spiritus sanctificationis declarat Filium Dei ac Deum.'

105 E.g., Erasmus, *Apologia ad Jacobum Stunicam*, LB IX 309–11.

106 Zwicker, *Novi Foederis Josias*, 16: Referring to the Son, 'qui nobis directe hunc verum Deum Patrem ostenderit, et qui ipsemet quoque semper in Scriptura a vero Deo distinguitur ... [Scriptura] tantum de Filio loqui caeperit, ipsum tandem solum, et non Patrem, verum Deum esse declarans. Quis hoc credat, credereve possit?' Cf. *De falsa*, 98.

107 See above, 53f.
108 Zwicker, *Het II. deel van de revelatie des duyvel-diensts onder de Christenen* (1675), 10. Bietenholz, *Zwicker,* 178f. Erasmus, LB VI 589 B–C.
109 Andrew C. Fix, *Prophecy and Reason: The Dutch Collegiants in the Early Enlightenment* (Princeton 1991).
110 See Trapman, 'Brenius et le Socinianisme,' 219–31. Kolakowski, *Chrétiens sans Église,* 199–206. *Biografisch lexicon voor de geschiedenis van het Nederlandse protestantisme,* Kampen 1978– , IV 55f. (article by J. Trapman). Fix, *Prophecy and Reason,* op. cit. note 109, 67–72.
111 Daniel De Breen, *Compendium theologiae Erasmicae* (Rotterdam 1677). Two years later two Dutch translations were published independently of each other. A German translation appeared in 1794. J. Trapman, 'Erasmus Seen by a Dutch Collegiant: Daniel De Breen (1594–1664) and His Posthumous *Compendium theologiae Erasmicae,*' *Nederlands archief voor kerkgeschiednis* 73, no. 2 (1993): 156–77.
112 In one of the Dutch translations an attempt is made to identify De Breen's own work. For an – incomplete, to be sure – identification of texts taken from Erasmus, and often from his New Testament Annotations and Paraphrases, see P.G. Bietenholz, 'Erasmus en het zeventiende-eeuwse antitrinitarianisme; Het geval Daniel Zwicker en Daniel de Breen,' *Doopsgezinde Bijdragen* n.s. 30 (2004): 101–24, here 120f.
113 De Breen, *Compendium,* 197f. Allen, Ep. 1202: 285f.
114 De Breen, *Compendium,* 198: 'Si veritas ipsa jussit eam veritatem ad tempus sileri, citra cujus cognitionem ac professionem nulli contigit salus, quid novi, si dixero alicubi supprimendam veritatem?' Also 213f., 220f.
115 De Breen, *Compendium,* 236f. Allen, III, Ep. 916: 364–88. CWE 6.248f.
116 The *Annotationes,* with some of De Breen's other writings appended, were published in the year of his death, 1664, in Amsterdam by his nephew Frans Kuyper. The same collection, with some new introductory matter, reappeared in 1666, also in Amsterdam.
117 De Breen, *Annotationes,* New Testament, II 93b. Erasmus, LB VII 1064.
118 Trapman, 'Brenius et le Socinianisme,' 226–8.
119 De Breen, *Annotationes,* New Testament, I 79a: 'Joannes novae creationis ac restitutionis omnium opus, quod per Christum ultimis temporibus fieri debebat, descripturus.'
120 De Breen, *Annotationes,* New Testament, II 69b. Erasmus, LB VI 867f., specifically 868 C. Cf. Fausto Sozzini in BFP II 583–5. De Breen also offers succinct interpretations in tune with Socinian doctrine on John 1:10, 15, 3:13, 8:58, Rom. 1:3–4, 9:5, Philip. 3:3, Col. 1:15–17.
121 De Breen, *Annotationes,* New Testament, II 7b–8a. Erasmus, LB VII 793f.
122 De Breen, *Annotationes,* New Testament, I 91b, 100b, II 12b, 69b (John 8:58, 17:3–5, Rom. 9:5, Phil. 2:7.
123 De Breen, *Annotationes,* I 103b: 'Non est in his verbis exclamatio ad Patrem, ut nonnulli censent, sed ad Christum ipsum sermo dirigitur ...

Thomas ... agnoscit eum pro domino et Deo suo Messia Judaeis promisso.' Erasmus, LB VI 417 D. Cf. above, 54.
124 De Breen pronounces analogously on the Proconsul Sergius Paulus of Act. 13:12.
125 LB V 1064 E–1067 A. De Breen, *Annotationes*, New Testament, I 120b-121a.

CHAPTER THREE

1 *Adagia*, III vii 1. ASD II-6 395–424. CWE 35.178–214. Other relevant texts are: the adage I iii 1, *Aut regem aut fatuum nasci oportere* (One ought to be born a king or a fool), a plea for wise, well-educated rulers, immune against the common follies and the temptations of power, and Erasmus' long pacifist note on Luke 22:36 ('let him ... sell his mantle and buy a sword.' LB VI 317–21, CWE 31.227–36), rejecting any literal understanding of the verse.
2 Franck, *Chronica*, I 142r–62r, here 160r.
3 See the editors' notes to this adage in ASD II-6 395–7.
4 The cranes, however, escape the eagle's rage thanks to their superior intelligence. Franck, *Chronica*, I 158v. ASD II-6 408. CWE 35.193f. Franck also refers to the adage I iii 1 (see above, n. 1). A passage there is equally typical of Erasmus' conviction: 'Do we not see fine cities, created by the people, overthrown by the princes? Or a state enriched by the toil of its citizens, and looted by the princes' greed? Plebeian lawyers make good laws, princes violate them; the people seek for peace, the princes stir up war' (CWE 31.235).
5 See above, 30 n. 54. Patrick Hayden-Roy, *The Inner Word and the Outer World: A Biography of Sebastian Franck* (New York 1994), 196f.
6 *Das Kriegbuechlin des frides* ... (with a lengthy summary and the year of publication on the title page; the names of the author and the publisher are not given) (Augsburg, H. Steiner, 1539). Second ed.: *Krieg Buechlin des friedes* ... (again without Franck's name) (Frankfurt am Main: Cyriacus Jacob zum Bock, 1550; anastatic repr., Hildesheim 1975). Thanks to the reprint the second edition is relatively accessible; therefore it is quoted here. There is a not always adequate adaptation in modern German: Wollgast, *Zur Friedensidee*. The bibliography of Quast's *Francks 'Kriegbüchlin'* (pp. 185–202) indicates the intensity of research devoted to the *Krieg Büchlin*. See also Sigrid Looss, 'Sebastian Francks Auffassungen zu Frieden und Krieg im historischen Kontext,' in *Sebastian Franck (1499–1542)*, *Wolfenbüttler Forschungen*, vol. 56 (Wiesbaden 1993), 119–30.
7 Franck, *Krieg Büchlin*, 215r: 'Das das vielfaltig kriegen unnd rumoren eyn gewiss zeychen sey des Jüngsten tags und anderen zůkunfft des Herrn, das das gerichte uber die welt und erlösung der gerechten nit ferre sey.' For a recent discussion of various

approaches to Franck's eschatology, see Quast, *Francks 'Kriegbüchlin,'* 139–41.

8 Franck, *Krieg Büchlin*, 3r. Franck's chapter 6 includes a summary of recent wars derived from Johann Eberlin von Günzburg's treatise *Mich wundert dass kein gelt mehr im land ist*.
9 Quast, *Francks 'Kriegbüchlin,'* 76–8, 146–83.
10 Franck, *Krieg Büchlin*, 128r–130v, 149v–151r. Wollgast, *Zur Friedensidee*, 176–9, 198f. Quast, *Francks 'Kriegbüchlin,'* 60–6. In part Franck's critique is also directed to Bucer.
11 See below, chap. 4. Celsi, *In haereticis coërcendis*, 112–15, 121f.
12 Allen, III, Ep. 858.78–83, 103–16, 236–9, 378–82.
13 Kommoss, *Franck und Erasmus*, 85–92. Franck also refers to the following pleas for peace and tolerance: Erasmus' Ep. 288, to Antoon van Bergen (*Krieg Büchlin*, 67r–68r); the chapter on warfare in the *Enchiridon militis christiani* (*Krieg Büchlin*, 151r, 156r); two substantial notes to the New Testament (*Krieg Büchlin*, 143r–144r, 149r–v) – Luke 22:36, 'Let him sell his cloak and buy a sword,' and John 20:21, 'Peace be with you' (LB VI 317–21, 415–16); also Erasmus' paraphrases of the parable of the tares (Matt. 13:24–30) and Paul's dictum, 'the weapons we wield are not merely human' (2 Cor. 10:3–6): LB VII 79–81, 933A–C in *Krieg Büchlin*, 147r–v, 156r–v. Franck's interpretation of the parable of the tares is remarkably radical in that it seems to rule out the death penalty not only for heretics but also for criminals: 'das man nicht mit gewaldt im glauben handtlen soll, darumb niemandt kriegen, toedten oder vertreiben , ya auch die uebelthaeter nitt toedten.' This is not what Erasmus said. See also *Krieg Büchlin*, 175v. A survey and partial translation of all Erasmus' major texts related to peace and war is found in *Guerre et paix dans la pensée d'Érasme*, ed. and trans. Jean-Claude Margolin (Paris 1973). See also Rummel, *Annotations*, 163–7.
14 Adagia IV i 1: ASD II-7 11–44. CWE 35.399–440.
15 ASD II-7 12; cf. CWE 35.400f.
16 ASD II-7 15–22; the quotation is on p. 22; cf. CWE 35.403–12.
17 ASD II-7 22–6. CWE 35.412–16.
18 ASD II-7 28. Among the Aristotelian tenets that contradict the teachings of Christ and thus contribute to the advent of strife Erasmus emphasizes private property; according to Aristotle, '*non posse florere rempublicam in qua sint omnia communia.*' CWE 35.419.
19 ASD II-7 26–32. CWE 35.419–23.
20 ASD II-7 32–8. CWE 35.423–31. Some parts of the text were added in the 1526 edition.
21 Matt. 5:38–42. Luke 6:27–31.
22 CWE 35.426. ASD II-7 34.
23 ASD II-7 34: 'sed apud recentiores, Christi vigore iam relanguescente.'
24 ASD II-7 34; cf. CWE 35.428
25 ASD II-7 38; cf. CWE 35.429–31.

264   Notes to pages 76–80

26 ASD II-7 38–40. CWE 35.431–5.
27 ASD II-7 41–4. CWE 35.435–40.
28 CWE 35.438. ASD II-7 42. Thomas More's *Utopia* was published in 1516, the year after this text had appeared in the 1515 *Adagia*. Cf. *Querela pacis*, CWE 27.312: 'But if war is unavoidable, it should be conducted in such a way that the full force of its calamities must fall on the heads of those who gave cause for it.'
29 For instance, in a way rather disrespectful of the House of Habsburg, Erasmus referred to aspirations to regain territories that in 1477 had been lost to France or French allies. He spoke of efforts to 'tear France apart' or 'make Germans out of the French,' or make Flanders German. ASD IV-2 91. CWE 27.315.
30 See below, chap. 5. *Dulce bellum inexpertis* also offers a minor parallel in the form of a speech by Nature personified: ASD II-7 18. CWE 35.406f.
31 The rudimentary structure can be indicated like this (giving the initial page in ASD IV-2 / CWE 27): Concord is the basic principle of nature; only humans have abandoned it (61 / 293); throughout his life Christ taught nothing but peace and, in theory at least, his church took up his teaching (68 / 299); the fallacy of reasons justifying war presented by Christian princes and preachers (78 / 305); advice for those who are genuinely tired of war (86 / 310); deterrents with regard to starting wars (92 / 316); concluding appeal for peace (98 / 320). In general see Brachin, 'Vox clamantis,' and Otto Herding's introduction to his edition of the *Querela pacis*, ASD IV-2 3–56.
32 ASD IV-2 62–4. CWE 27.293–6.
33 CWE 27.301. ASD IV-2 72: 'Vide, quaeso, quam insignem concordiam exigat in suis Christus: non dixit, ut sint unanimes, sed ut sint unum, neque id quocumque modo, sed sicuti nos, inquit, unum sumus, qui perfectissima et ineffabili ratione sumus idem, et illud obiter indicans hac una via servandos esse mortales, si mutuam inter sese pacem aluerint.'
34 ASD IV-2 76f. CWE 27.303f.
35 ASD IV-2 66–8, 90f. CWE 27.296–9, 314f.
36 ASD IV-2 78, 81f., 86. CWE 27.305, 307f., 311.
37 ASD IV-2 82–4. CWE 27.307–9.
38 In Italy the ruthless lord of Rimini, Sigismondo Malatesta, was widely rumoured to have invited the Turks to invade the peninsula, and in 1503 Venice concluded a peace with them. ASD IV-2 78, 84, 96. CWE 27.305, 310, 319.
39 ASD IV-2 90 CWE 27.314.
40 ASD IV-2 92–4. CWE 27.316–18.
41 CWE 27.307, 313–15. ASD IV-2 80, 88–91. In the same breath, however, Erasmus speaks of the 'foolish populace' that is easily misguided by influential people seeking their own profit. Cf. Brachin, 'Vox clamantis,' 261.

42 CWE 27.321. ASD IV-2 98. It might be recalled, however, that Erasmus had earlier said that nations were prone to be infused with an unhealthy level of patriotism; see above, 78.
43 ASD IV-2 86, 99: 'hactenus nihil actum foederibus, nihil promotum affinitatibus, nihil vi, nihil ulciscendo.' CWE 27.310f., 321; cf. also *Institutio principis christiani*, CWE 27. 284f., where many of the points here made are anticipated.
44 ASD IV-2 82f. CWE 27.307, 309.
45 CWE 27.315. ASD IV-2 92.
46 CWE 27.306. ASD IV-2 80.
47 CWE 27.321. ASD IV-2 98. R.J. Knecht, *Francis I* (Cambridge 1982), 67f.
48 ASD IV-2 99. CWE 27.321.
49 *Querela*, ASD IV-2 63–7, 72. CWE 27.294–8, 301. *Dulce bellum*, ASD II-7 14f. CWE 35.402f.
50 *Krieg Büchlin*, 34v–35r, 38v–39v.
51 *Krieg Büchlin*, 27r.
52 *Krieg Büchlin*, 29v.
53 *Krieg Büchlin* 35v–39v, 73v.
54 *Krieg Büchlin*, 39v–41v, 43r–v, 70v–72v. Franck, without Erasmus' guidance, refers here to Lucretius and to the Italian humanist Gianozzo Manetti, whose *De dignitate et excellentia hominis* had recently been published in Basel; see P.G. Bietenholz, 'Riflessi dell'umanesimo italiano nell'opera di Sebastian Franck,' in *Rapporti e scambi tra umanesimo italiano ed umanesimo europeo*, ed. L. Rotondi Secchi Tarugi (Milan 2001), 121–34, here 125–7.
55 Franck, like Erasmus, steers clear of original sin; Satan's seed in us, not Adam's seed, causes our ruin.
56 *Krieg Büchlin*, 36v, 44r.
57 *Krieg Büchlin*, 74v–75r. It is true that in one place Franck's presentation renders Erasmus' argument more logical. He copies Erasmus' reference to devotional cannibalism occurring when certain ancient peoples piously killed their incapacitated elders. In Erasmus' account this detail had been given awkwardly ahead of the inception of homicide. Franck inserts it after Cain's fratricide, where it makes better sense: *Dulce bellum*, ASD II-7 19f. CWE 35.408f.
58 *Krieg Büchlin*, 74v, 104v–105r. Agrippa, *De incertitudine*, beginning of chap. 80.
59 ASD VII-2 28. CWE 35.419.
60 ASD IV-2 70–2, 75, 78; II-7 32, cf. 26. CWE 27.299f., 303, 305; 35.423f.; cf. 416.
61 *Krieg Büchlin*, 91v: 'Es mussten auch nach art des alten Testaments und nach gelegenheit der zeit und ursach in Israel krieg sein, die wahren Krieg der Christen mit jren feinden zů figuriern und fürbilden.' Also *Krieg Büchlin*, 48v–49v, 57v, 90v–91v, and arguments taken from Agrippa, 107r–v, 112r–113v.

62 See above, 72.
63 *Krieg Büchlin*, 7r: 'Dann ist ein Christlicher krieg, so ist er doch sonderlichen im Newen Testament unnd disen letsten zeyten so seltzam als die storcken im winnter.'
64 *Krieg Büchlin*, 112v; cf. 91r–92v; *Querela*, ASD IV-2 75. CWE 27.303. *Dulce bellum*, ASD VII-2 32. CWE 35.425.
65 Franck, *Krieg Büchlin*, 40r.
66 LB VI 242 D.
67 *Dulce bellum*, ASD II-7 28f., 32–4. CWE 35.419f., 425f. (mostly additions of 1526). *Institutio*, ASD IV-1.214–16. CWE 27.283–5. *Querela*, ASD IV-2 94. CWE 27.317. Allen, Ep. 288. See also José A. Fernández, 'Erasmus on the Just War,' *Journal of the History of Ideas* 34 (1973): 209–26.
68 *Dulce bellum*, ASD II-7 15f., 42. CWE 35.404, 437f. Allen, VII, Ep. 1819, 151–3.
69 *Krieg Büchlin*, 93v, 145v. ASD II-7 34. CWE 35.426f.; cf. Allen, I, Ep. 288, 105–7: 'Quod si qua iura bellum admittunt, ea crassa sunt et Christum iam degenerantem sapiunt ac mundanis opibus oneratum.'
70 Vives published between 1526 and 1529 several writings on peace and war, among them a *De Europae dissidiis et bello Turcico* (Antwerp 1526). Although Erasmus is never mentioned in these works, many parallels could suggest an influence, but clearly not in a radical direction. See Brachin, 'Vox clamantis,' 254, 257, 260.
71 *Dulce bellum*, ASD II-7 36. CWE 35.428. *Querela*, ASD IV-2 88. CWE 27.312.
72 KB, f. 3v: 'Dargegen beut ich hiermit an nach der mass der gaben Gotes und meines glaublins mein dienst allen kinndern des friedens und des liechts; die wöllen als glieder meines leibs mit mir leidenn das ungnedic gelück der warheyt und erstatten den fål Christi an meinem leib für seinen leib. Die andern kriegen jmmerzů hin; sie werden mir nichts abkriegen, noch von meines schreibens wegen jhr kriegen lassen, weil jhr Kriegssgott, der Satan, ohn underlass in jhnen ... nicht kann dann liegen, triegen, kriegen, darzů Schrifft biegenn.'
73 CWE 9, Ep. 1341A 686–8 (Allen, I, p. 19).
74 *Vox clamantis in deserto*: the title of Brachin's analysis is appropriate.
75 See above, 82.
76 Franck, *Krieg Büchlin*, 215r.
77 Franck, *Krieg Büchlin*, 219v : 'das jm [i.e., Antichrist] Gott den gar aussmachen wirdt,' 220r, 222r..
78 *Krieg Büchlin*, 223r–v.
79 German translations of the *Querela* and the *Institutio* by Leo Jud were published in Zurich in 1521. There were two German renderings of *Dulce bellum*, one by Ulrich Varnbüler, published in Basel in 1519, and the other by Georgius Spalatinus. Already in 1514 Spalatinus had published a German translation of the 'Letter to Antoon van Bergen'

(Ep. 288), the title of which is cited by Franck. This was reprinted in Augsburg, 1521, when Spalatinus' translation of *Dulce bellum* was published. Franck offers a paraphrase from Spalatinus' preface (*Krieg Büchlin*, 33r, 67r). In addition to Erasmus' pieces there was Josse Clichtove's *De bello et pace opusculum*, Paris 1523, which Franck apparently did not use. Among Franck's sources there were also writings on specific issues related to war and peace, especially by Martin Luther and Johann Eberlin von Günzburg. On this literature see the biliography in Quast, *Francks 'Kriegbüchlin,'* 185–8; Brachin, 'Vox clamantis,' 253–5; Heinz Holeczek, *Erasmus Deutsch* (Stuttgart 1983), 103, 106, 111, and passim; James Hutton, 'Erasmus and France: The Propaganda for Peace,' *Studies in the Renaissance* 8 (1961): 103–27. See also above, n. 70.
80 See above, 72.
81 Cf. Erasmus, *Institutio*: A sweeping legal prohibition 'would be ... justifiable in the case of wars, even if some of them might be just – although with the world in its present state, I am not sure that any of that kind could be found, that is, wars not caused by ambition, anger, arrogance, lust or greed.' CWE 27.284. ASD IV-1 215f.
82 Erasmus did, however, take up and of course reject the argument that an individual soldier could lawfully be paid to fight and kill, just as a butcher was paid to slaughter beef: ASD I-3 156, II-7 33f.
83 Franck, *Krieg Büchlin*, 229r–v., and see, e.g., Erasmus' colloquy *Militis et Carthusiani*, 1523: 'Soldier: "It's lawful to kill an enemy." Carthusian: "Maybe it is if he attacks your country. Then it does seem righteous to fight for wife and children, parents and friends, hearth and home, and for the civil peace. But what has this to do with your mercenary soldiering?"' CWE 39.333. ASD I-3 317.
84 Franck, *Krieg Büchlin*, 63v.
85 Erasmus, *Querela pacis*, CWE 27.314: 'If mutual love does not bind them [the Christians] together, a common enemy will surely unite them after a fashion, and there will be some sort of common purpose, even if true harmony is lacking ... And there is often some personal grievance between princes which forces the whole world to take up arms, though any grounds for starting a war ought to be a fully public concern, if anything is.'

CHAPTER FOUR

1 *Concerning Heretics*, an English translation, with introduction and additional texts by R.H. Bainton, was published in 1935.
2 Guggisberg, *Castellio*, 80–150. Joseph Lecler, *Histoire de la Tolérance au siècle de la Réforme* (Paris 1955) (in English: *Toleration and the Reformation*, trans. T.L. Weslow [London 1960]. Ferdinand Buisson, *Sébastien Castellion, sa vie et son oeuvre, 1515–1563* (Paris 1892; repr.

1964). Roland H. Bainton et al., *Castellioniana. Quatre études sur Sébastien Castellion et l'idée de la tolérance* (Leiden 1951). Eugénie Droz, *Chemins de l'hérésie, textes et documents* (Geneva 1971), II 325-432.

3 See above, chap. 1. In his *Krieg Büchlin* Franck made a remark that amounted to a categorical rejection of the death penalty: above, 253 n. 13.

4 'Nor was the parable addressed to the multitude, nor to princes, but to a select group of disciples to whom it was given to know the mystery of the kingdom.' After the passage quoted by Castellio Erasmus added: 'The parable, moreover, applies more particularly to the early days, when the Church was subject to pagan rulers': Castellio, *Concerning Heretics*, 173, 175; *De haereticis*, 79.

5 Castellio, *De haereticis*, 109f.; *Concerning Heretics*, 204f. Erasmus, LB VII 80 D–81 A.

6 Castellio, *De haereticis*, 74–88; *Concerning Heretics*, 169–83.

7 Castellio, *De haereticis*, 115f.; *Concerning Heretics*, 209.

8 Castellio, *De haereticis*, 75; *Concerning Heretics*, 170. Theodore Beza, *De haereticis a civili magistratu puniendis libellus* (Geneva 1554), 145f. Celsi, *In haereticis*, 89f.

9 Castellio, *De haereticis*, 74–81; *Concerning Heretics*, 169–75. In addition to the parable of the tares, Erasmus was influential when some other New Testament verses became normative in the toleration debate, e.g., Acts 5:1–11, 1 Cor. 5:11–13, 2 Cor. 2:5–8, 1 Tim. 1:19–20, 2 Tim. 2:24–6, Tit. 3:10–11.

10 Castellio, *Concerning Heretics*, 171; *De haereticis*, 76. *Consilium* in *Erasmi opuscula*, 338–61.

11 Castellio, *Concerning Heretics*, 172, 174, cf. 205; *De haereticis*, 77, 80, cf. 110. Celsi, *In haereticis*, 161f.

12 R.H. Bainton, 'Erasmus and the Persecuted,' in *Scrinium Erasmianum*, II 197–202, cf. 600f. Allen, I, Ep. 130; VIII, Ep. 2149. For the harsh statements of a later date, see, e.g., Allen, X, Ep. 2853; XI, Ep. 2965; also, somewhat more sympathetically, *De concordia*, ASD V-3 311f. See also below, 233f.

13 Castellio, *Concerning Heretics*, 218; *De haereticis*, 127f.

14 Castellio, *Concerning Heretics*, 213; *De haereticis*, 119.

15 Castellio, *Concerning Heretics*, 126, 129; *De haereticis*, 12, 18f.

16 Castellio, *Concerning Heretics*, 225f.; *De haereticis*, 138.

17 Castellio, *De haereticis*, 139–46; *Concerning Heretics*, 226–32.

18 Castellio, *Concerning Heretics*, 243–5; *De haereticis*, 160, 162.

19 Castellio, *Concerning Heretics*, 134 (with a correction), 219; *De haereticis*, 28, 128.

20 Castellio, *Concerning Heretics*, 248; *De haereticis*, 166.

21 Martin Steinmann, *Johannes Oporinus. Ein Basler Buchdrucker um die Mitte des 16. Jahrhunderts* (Basel 1966), passim. Michaela Valente, *Johann Wier. Agli albori della critica razionale dell'occulto e del demoniaco*

nell'Europa del Cinquecento (Florence 2003), 79–83, 129–32 on the various editions, 217–47 on the influence of Erasmus. Wier often quotes Cardano, another unorthodox physician whose works were published in Basel.

22 *Witches, Devils, and Doctors in the Renaissance: Johann Weyer, De praestigiis daemonum,* ed. G. Mora et al., trans. J. Shea (Binghamton, NY, 1991), 529–35. Erasmus, LB IX 1054 B–1057 E. Several pamphlets in Latin and German, based on the Inquisition section of the reply to the Spanish monks, were published in Strasbourg 1529–30: Heinz Holeczek, *Erasmus Deutsch* (Stuttgart 1983), I 213f., 301.

23 Allen, I, Epp. 143, 149 (cf. Ep. 130); VII, Ep. 2037; X, Epp. 2846, 2880. *Moria,* ASD IV-3 185f.

24 Celsi, *In haereticis coercendis,* 158–64 and passim.

25 On Georg Mayer, a follower of Caspar Schwenckfeld and pastor of Leeder in Bavaria, see my forthcoming essay "In the Footsteps of Erasmus: Georg Mayer and His Pleas for Religious Toleration," to be published in *Restauri storiografici. Studi in memoria R.H. Popkin* (Florence). *Von der heiligen Christlichen Kirchen* indicates Basel and 1596 as place and date of publication. Chapter 12, in particular, applies the term 'heretic' to those – many popes, among others – who wish to promote themselves by inventing novel and unbiblical teachings. Erring in good conscience, by contrast, is not a heresy, for freedom of faith is indispensable in Mayer's only true church, which is invisible. *Von der heiligen Christlichen Kirchen* can be attributed to the printer Konrad Waldkirch, son-in-law and successor of Pietro Perna, who had published Celsi's book. There is good reason to think that Waldkirch also printed (this time only indicating the year, 1595) Mayer's *Iudicium von der Freyheit des Glaubens ... dass weder den Vorstehern der Kirchen, noch den Fürsten unnd andern weltlichen Oberkeiten gebure und zustehe, die Ketzer ... zutodten, zuverfolgen, noch mit dem weltlichen Schwerdt zustraffen oder zu vertreiben.* This is a rich collection of testimonies in support of toleration culled from the works of Luther, Augustine, Erasmus, and many others. The text shows no dependence on either Castellio or Celsi. Waldkirch could also be responsible for the reprint of a further treatise by Mayer that had been printed several times before, starting in 1558: *Christlich Bedenken von dem alten Geschrey, dass man niemands leiden noch gedulten sol, der nicht in allem, ohne alle Widerrede Bâptisch oder Lutherisch ist* (n.pl. 1600). See Gilly, 'Erasmo, la Reforma radical,' 293–5; *VD-16. Verzeichnis der im deutschen Sprachbereich erschienenen Drucke des XVI. Jahrhunderts* (Stuttgart 1983), M 1690–1705.

26 Castellio, *De haereticis,* 118; *Concerning Heretics,* 211. Cf. Kutter, *Curione,* 109–18, 285. See also Albano Biondi's biography of Curione in DBI 31.443–9.

27 See below, 147f.

28 Erasmus' influence has been noted in writings dating back to Curione's years in Italy; see Kutter, *Curione*, 17–19, 283. Silvana Seidel Menchi, 'Sulla fortuna di Erasmo in Italia,' *Revue Suisse d'Histoire* 24 (1974): 537–634, here 605–7.
29 Seidel Menchi, *Erasmo in Italia*, 155–9, 164. Allen, V, Ep. 1474 introd.
30 LB V 578 D; also 557, 564, 580. CWE 70.118; also 77f., 89f., 121f.
31 LB V 558, 560, 571, 584–6. CWE 70.8, 81f., 102f., 130–5.
32 LB V 571f. CWE 70.104f. Allen, V, Epp. 1456, 1464.
33 Kutter, *Curione*, 198f. The first edition of *De amplitudine beati regni Dei dialogi sive libri duo*, published in 1554 without indication of the place, in the small town of Poschiavo, is very rare. A second, accurate, edition appeared in Gouda in 1614, and a third one in Frankfurt, 1617. The following references are to the more easily available Gouda edition.
34 Curione, *De amplitudine*, 131.
35 Marsilio Andreasi, *De amplitudine misericordiae Dei absolutissimi oratio*, 1550.
36 Curione, *De amplitudine*, 18: 'Non is qui manifesto Christianus sit, Christianus est, nec ea quae palam fit, carnis lotio est, sed qui in occulto Christianus fuerit, Christianus est, et baptismus cordis baptismus est qui spiritu constat, non externo opere ... Quod si externis symbolis atque elementis ea inesset vis atque divinitas, ut quoscunque attingerent, eos ad beatam vitam consignarent, iam Hymenaeus et Philetus et Alexander ... et Ananias una cum uxore Sapphira ... atque alii similes multi, qui quidem et aqua initiati simulque damnati sunt, beati omnino in coelesti regno essent.' Erasmus, *Concio*, cit. Lb V 568 C: 'Nullum [exemplum] exstat severius quam Ananiae et Sapphirae ad Petri correptionem subito collabentium, et tamen incertum an horum animae corporis interitu servatae sint.' CWE 70.98.
37 Albano Biondi in DBI 31.446f.
38 Curione, *De amplitudine*, 125–61, passim. See my 'Millenarismo ed Età dell'Oro nell'opera di Celio Secondo Curione,' in *Millenarismo ed Età dell'Oro nel Rinascimento*, ed. Luisa Secchi Tarugi (Florence 2003), 51–64.
39 Arno Seifert, 'Reformation und Chiliasmus: Die Rolle des Martin Cellarius Borrhaus,' *Archiv für Reformationsgeschichte* 67 (1986): 226–63.
40 Kutter, *Curione*, 201–12. Bietenholz, 'Millenarismo,' op. cit. note 38, 62.
41 Uwe Plath, *Calvin und Basel in den Jahren 1552–1556* (Zurich 1974), 47f., 80f., and passim; Gilly, *Spanien und der Basler Buchdruck*, 292–4 and passim; Lelio Sozzini, *Opere*, 160f., 260, and passim.
42 Kutter, *Curione*, 279.
43 Compare, for instance, Sebastianus Castellio, *De l'impunité des hérétiques. De haereticis non puniendis* (French and Latin versions of a formerly unpublished text), ed. B. Becker and M. Valkoff (Geneva 1971), 52, and Erasmus, *Moria*, ASD IV-3 146–8. For another similarity (the self-indulgent abdication of sober judgment), see *Moria*, ASD IV-3 92–4, and Castellio, *De arte dubitandi*, 82 (I 33). Liebing, 'Schriftauslegung,' 40f.

44 Erasmus, *De libero arbitrio*, LB IX 1248f. CWE 76.88f.
45 Eph. 2:8: 'For by grace you have been saved through faith; and this is not your own doing, it is the gift of God.' Castellio, *De arte dubitandi*, 96 (II 6). Erasmus, LB VII 976 F. For faith depending on the will, see *De arte dubitandi*, 89f. (II 3).
46 Liebing, 'Schriftauslegung,' 39.
47 Sebastian Castellio, *Defensio suarum translationum Bibliorum, et maxime Novi Foederis* ... (Basel 1562). Liebing, 'Schriftauslegung,' 40f.
48 Cf. their translations of 1 Cor. 12:10 and 1 Pet. 2:24.
49 Erasmus, e.g., *Ratio*, LB V 124 E–125 C. Castellio, *De arte dubitandi*, 175f. On the enigmatic passages in scripture, see also Castellio, *De haereticis*, 122f., 127f., and *Concerning Heretics*, 215, 218.
50 Liebing, 'Schriftauslegung,' 100f., 107–13.
51 Sebastian Castellio, *Dialogi IIII. De Praedestinatione, De electione, De Libero Arbitrio, De fidei* (Aresdorffij 1578). *De arte dubitandi* first appeared in print in 1937.
52 Guggisberg, *Castellio*, 251–4. Popkin, *History of Scepticim*, 11–14.
53 Castellio, *De arte dubitandi*, 62–7, here 64 (I 24f.).
54 Castellio, *De arte dubitandi*, 84 (II 1). Liebing, 'Schriftauslegung,' 74f.
55 See, e.g., Erasmus' introduction to *De libero arbitrio*, LB IX 1218, CWE 76.14f. For Castellio, see Liebing, 'Schriftaulegung,' 69.
56 Castellio, *De arte dubitandi*, 85–9 (II 2).
57 Guggisberg, *Castellio*, 274–7, in his last chapter (263–304), summarizing the author's extended research into Castellio's *Nachleben*.
58 Montaigne, *Essais*, I 35. Hans Rudolf Guggisberg, *Sebastian Castellio im Urteil seiner Nachwelt vom Späthumanismus bis zur Aufklärung* (Basel 1956), 42f., 69–72.

CHAPTER FIVE

1 Ferguson and Hershbell, 'Epicureanism in the Roman Empire,' 2257–327.
2 DeWitt, *Epicurus and His Philosophy*, 10.
3 ASD, I-1 35 (Ep. 1110). CWE 23.16.
4 CWE 23.39. ASD I-1 64f.
5 Plato, *Laws*, 8.845B. Augustine, *Confessiones*, 2.4.9–6.12. Another garden of the literary variety is found in Erasmus' colloquy *Apotheosis Capnionis*, written and published in the summer of 1522. We find ourselves 'standing by a little bridge leading to by far the most delightful of meadows. The verdure of grass and foliage, greener than emerald, so pleased the eye, clusters of flowers smiled with so unbelievable a variety of colours; everything was so fragrant.' Capnion, or Johannes Reuchlin, newly deceased, has just crossed the little bridge and is welcomed to this Garden of Eden by Saint Jerome. CWE 39.248. ASD I-3 269. Cf. P.G. Bietenholz, 'Erasmus

und die letzten Lebensjahre Reuchlins,' *Historische Zeitschrift* 240 (1985), 45–66.
6 The classic pronouncement on this particular aspect of 'the discovery of the world and of man' was made by Jacob Burckhardt (*Civilization*, 178–84). In the section entitled 'The Discovery of the Beauty of the Landscape' Pope Pius II deservedly figures as a key witness. On Italian Renaissance gardens, especially the Medicean ones, and their influence on other countries, see Luigi Zangheri, *Storia del giardino e del paesaggio. Il verde nella cultura occidentale* (Florence 2003).
7 Dante, *La Divina Commedia*, Purgatorio, c. 28. Bocaccio, *Decameròn*, 1.1.
8 CWE 39.182. ASD I-3 239. Erasmus' scene may be compared to the function of the garden of Epicurus in another philosophical symposium; see Valla, *On Pleasure*, 230–3.
9 CWE 39.176, 178, 189. ASD I-3 233, 235, 248.
10 Pliny, *Historia naturalis*, 19.19.50f.
11 Craig R. Thompson in CWE 39.172 . Paul Roth, 'Die Wohnstätten des Erasmus in Basel,' *Gedenkschrift zum 400. Todestag des Erasmus von Rotterdam* (Basel 1936), 270–81.
12 Allen, VI, Ep. 1756; VIII, Epp. 2141, 2147. CWE 12.366f.
13 Allen, VIII, Ep. 2156, to Johannes Brisgoicus.
14 Allen, V, Ep. 1365.82–5. CWE 10.21–3.
15 See below, 117.
16 For Erasmus' knowledge of Seneca's letters, see Epp. 56, 137; for his edition of *Senecae lucubrationes* (Basel, J. Froben, 1515), see Ep. 325.
17 Seneca, *Ad Lucilium epistulae morales*, ed. and trans. Richard M. Gummere (Loeb 1967–71), I, Ep. 21:10: 'Go to his Garden and read the motto carved there: "Stranger, here you will do well to tarry; here our highest good is pleasure." The caretaker of that abode, a kindly host, will be ready for you; he will welcome you with barley-meal and serve you water ... This garden does not whet your appetite; it quenches it. This is the pleasure in which I have grown old.'
18 Epicureanism has occasionally been treated in the flood of publications on Erasmus. See B.J.H.M. Timmermans, 'Valla et Erasme, défenseurs d'Epicure,' *Neophilologus* 23 (1938) 414–19; Marie Delcourt and Marcelle Derwa, 'Trois aspects humanistes de l'Épicurisme chrétien' in *Colloquium Erasmianum*, Mons 1968, 119–33; Bultot, 'Érasme, Épicure.' Walter H. Gordon, *Humanist Play and Belief: The Seriocomic Art of Desiderius Erasmus* (Toronto 1990), 121–30. Panizza, Valla's *De voluptate*.
19 CWE 66.134. ASD V-1 39.
20 CWE 66.165. ASD V-1 74.
21 CWE 66.165f. ASD V-1 74.
22 CWE 66.171. ASD V-1 80. These 'jardins monastiques' (as one scholar has touted them) bear a remarkable likeness to a description of the Elysian fields that Erasmus would later translate from Plutarch; Bultot, 'Érasme, Épicure,' 220f.

23 CWE 66.166f. ASD V-1 75f.
24 J.G. Blühdorn, 'Gewissen, philosophisch' in TRE, 13.192–213, here 198–202. John R. Porter, *Studies in Euripides'* Orestes (Leiden 1994), 307–11. In *De rerum natura* 3.1012–23, Lucretius speaks of the fear of punishment for our misdeeds and expresses horror at a sense of guilt that may cause us not to see that death is the final limit of such punishment. Thus, he concludes, 'the life of fools becomes hell on earth.'
25 I am not arguing that the final Chapter XII of *De contemptu mundi*, which alone warns of rash and ill-considered monastic vows, is an addition composed at the time of publication. However, Ep. 1196, written at the time of the publication of *De contemptu mundi*, shows that despite his growing misgivings over Luther, Erasmus continued to maintain all he had said in Chapter XII.
26 CWE 1, Index, s.v. 'Seneca' and 'Cicero.' In what has been preserved of Erasmus' writings of this period, I can find no references to Cicero's *De natura deorum*, but of course he may have read it anyhow.
27 See below, n. 107.
28 Augustine, *Confessiones* 6.16.26: 'Et disputabam cum amicis meis Alypio et Nebridio de finibus bonorum et malorum Epicurum accepturum fuisse palmam in animo meo, nisi ego credidissem post mortem restare animae vitam et tractus meritorum, quod Epicurus credere noluit.' For Erasmus' acquaintance with Jerome and Lactantius, see CWE 1, Index.
29 In CWE 1.222 Erasmus' mention (Ep. 113 of 1499) of the Scythian philosopher Anacharsis, one of the traditional seven sages, is footnoted with a reference to Diogenes Laertius, but Anacharsis is mentioned in Seneca's letters and many other places. The seven sages were proverbial, as was the Cynic Diogenes' search for 'a man,' mentioned by Erasmus in the *Antibarbari* and footnoted in CWE 23.41 with another reference to Diogenes Laertius. While I am not aware of references to Diogenes Laertius in the *Adagiorum collectanea* of 1500, I could be proven wrong when ASD publishes a critical edition of that work.
30 Epp. 23, 39, 45, 173.
31 Garin, *La cultura filosofica*, 72–92. Jones, *The Epicurean Tradition*, 142–53. *The Humanism of Leonardo Bruni: Selected Texts*, trans. Gordon Griffiths, James Hankins, and David Thompson (Binghamton 1987), 257f., 261f., 270f. and passim. For a letter by Filelfo that approximates Epicurean pleasure and Christian felicity, see ASD I-3 721n. It seems that Erasmus never referred to Cosma Raimondi, the most eager follower of Epicurus among the Quattrocento humanists.
32 CWE 23.75, 93. ASD I-1 97, 113. Likewise in the *Enchiridion militis christiani*, composed between 1499 and 1503, Erasmus mentioned only once 'Milesians, Sybarites, profligates, Epicureans, in a word, all the devisers of pleasures' that will seem 'nauseous' in comparison

with Christ: CWE 66.89. LB 5.42 C. The same view is expressed in one of only two references to Epicurus in Erasmus' preserved letters prior to the Italian journey, Allen, I. Ep. 157; cf. Ep. 20.
33 Robert Gaguin and John Colet had both corresponded with Ficino. William Grocyn and Thomas Linacre had, like Colet, studied in Florence; in London all three befriended and motivated young Thomas More, who by 1505 had translated *The Life of John Picus Erle of Mirandula*.
34 Jill Kraye, in *The Cambridge History of Renaissance Philosophy*, 377.
35 E.g., Augustin Renaudet, *Érasme et l'Italie*, 33: 'On ne peut donc exagérer l'influence qu'exercèrent sur le développement intellectuel, moral, religieux d'Érasme ces quelques mois passés en Angleterre, au cours desquels, à Oxford, il avait découvert, avec le premier humanisme anglais, une Italie qu'en Hollande et à Paris il n'avait pas pu qu'entrevoir.' For Screech (*Ecstasy and the Praise of Folly*, xx–xxi), the influence 'almost impossible to overstate' comes from 'Origen, Basil, Ambrose, Augustine ... This platonising evangelism is very different in emphasis from the magical mysticism of Ficino, or of Pico della Mirandola or even of John Colet.' Nonetheless, Erasmus 'was influenced by the Platonism he came across in Italy: It was probably there that he first saw how powerful a contribution Plato had made to the doctrines of ecstasy with his teachings in the *Phaedrus*.'
36 There is a short tribute to Pico in Ep. 16 and an early reference to Ficino's friend and fellow-Platonist Cristoforo Landino in Adage I i 9, CWE 31.58.
37 R. Bracht Branham, 'Utopian Laughter: Lucian and Thomas More,' *Moreana* 86 (July 1985) 23–43, esp. 26.
38 ASD I-1 450–69, esp. 464. Among the ribald caper of *Convivium sive Lapidae* (ASD I-1 604–17) Erasmus may have found some useful leads. From *Double Indictment* and *Hermotimus or Concerning the Sects*, which he did not translate, he might have retained some of Lucian's disdain of the Stoics.
39 Kaiser, *Praisers of Folly*, 78.
40 Epp. 200–16.
41 Allen, I, Ep. 302. CWE 2.215.
42 A.H.T. Levi in the introduction to *Praise of Folly*, trans. Betty Radice (n.p. 1993), xliv–xlv.
43 Renaudet, *Érasme et l'Italie*, 49, 57, also referring to Benvenuto of Imola who, in his commentary to Dante's *Commedia*, 'compte plus de cent mille épicuriens venus d'illustres familles.' For a positive assessment of Erasmus' Italian experience see also Jean-Claude Margolin, 'Les fêtes venitiennes d' Érasme, la cueillette des fruits mûrs, la préparation des moissons nouvelles,' in *Erasmo, Venezia*, 17–26.
44 Cantimori, *Eretici italiani*, 24ff. For a good example of that development, see Matteo Duni, *Tra religione e magia. Storia del prete modenese Guglielmo Campana (1460?–1541)* (Florence 1999).

45 Allen, III, Ep. 916.276–81. CWE 6.246.
46 Allen, VII, Ep. 1989. Renaudet, *Érasme et l'Italie*, 76, 78.
47 Allen, IX, Ep. 2465.1–39.
48 CWE, 8.368 n. 22. Allen, XI, Ep. 3032.185–232.
49 Renaudet, *Érasme et l'Italie*, 83: 'La date de l'arrivée d'Érasme à Venice est capitale dans l'histoire de ses contacts intellectuels avec l'Italie, de son évolution intellectuelle et de sa production scientifique, de sa création littéraire. La date est capitale sans doute dans l'histoire de l'esprit humain.'
50 CWE 33.14 (Adag. II i 1: *Festina lente*).This section was added in the 1526 edition. Aldus also published a revised edition of Erasmus' translations from Euripides, and it is fair to assume that in turn Erasmus was involved in the work on the important Aldine first editions of the letters of Pliny the Younger and the Greek Plutarch that were then being printed, perhaps also in the monumental Plato that appeared in 1513. In the just quoted addition of 1526 Erasmus goes on to list a number of Greek authors that he had been able to peruse in manuscript while he was in Venice preparing the Aldus *Adagia*. 'Among them were Plato's works in Greek, Plutarch's *Lives* and also his *Moralia* which began to be printed when my work was nearly finished.'
51 ASD II-8 253f. Erasmus' copy of a reprint of Traversaris's translation (Basel, V. Curio, 1524) is now in Cracow; see Maria Cytowska, 'L'influence d'Érasme en Pologne au 16e siècle,' in *Renaissance und Humanismus in Mittel- und Osteuropa*, ed. J. Irmscher (Berlin 1962), II 192–6.
52 Garin, *La cultura filosofica*, 72f.
53 Since Erasmus knew about Poggio even before he went to Italy, the following may be noted: Jill Kraye writes in *The Cambridge History of Renaissance Philosophy*, 380, that 'Poggio Bracciolini jokingly invited a friend to a pleasure garden jointly presided over by the Epicurus who lived on bread and water and the Epicurus who thought happiness derived from titillation of the senses.'
54 Adages I ii 38, iv 38 (CWE 31.179, 348). The passage quoted in *De pueris* (CWE 26.341. ASD I-2 72f.) is one of which Erasmus was very fond. Other references to it are in Allen, II, Ep. 337.104–6 and in ASD I-3 742.
55 Adage II iii 49 (CWE 33.161). Later, in the colloquy *Gerontologia* (CWE 39.452. ASD I-3 379), Erasmus put that saying into the mouth of a speaker who bears many traits of his perfect Christian Epicurean. He is pitted against the hedonistic type of Epicurean who, however, is also a survivor. See below, 135.
56 See, e.g., *Adagia. Sei saggi politici in forma di proverbi*, ed. and trans. Silvana Seidel Menchi (Turin 1980). In her substantial introduction (p. xiii) the editor states: 'senza l'Italia, e soprattutto senza Venezia, le *Adagiorum Chiliades* non sarebbero nate, o almeno non sarebbero

diventate quel "lavoro d'Ercole," che varerà la fama europea del suo autore.'
57 ASD I-4 187–351 (*Paraphrasis seu potius epitome in Elegantiarum libros Laurentii Vallae*); cf. Epp. 20, 23.
58 Epp. 67, 68.
59 Ep. 182.
60 Lorenzo Valla, *Opera omnia* (Turin, 1962), I 357–61, 428.
61 Erasmus, *De libero arbitrio*, LB IX 1218 E–F, 1231 A. CWE 76.15f., 48. *Hyperaspistes I*, LB X 1276 D, 1315 A–C. CWE 76.162, 250–2.
62 Valla, *On Pleasure / De voluptate*. The verbal refinements resulting from Valla's revisions need not detain us here. Divergent versions of the text were printed in Louvain in 1483, Cologne in 1509, Paris in 1512, and Basel in 1519, but only the latter two seem to have attained significant circulation.
63 P.S. Allen, *The Age of Erasmus* (Oxford 1914), 28. R.J. Schoeck, 'Erasmus and Valla: The Dynamics of a Relationship,' in *Erasmus of Rotterdam Society Yearbook Twelve* (1992), 45–63, here 47.
64 In Motta and Venice Girolamo Aleandro had earlier been the tutor of Grimani's nephew, Marino Grimani. When visiting Rome, Erasmus also would be offered a position in Grimani's household that might well have included some tutoring of the nephew. See Lorenzo Valla, *De vero falsoque bono: Critical edition*, ed. Maristella de Panizza Lorch (Bari 1970), xviii–xx; Allen, IX, Ep. 2465.35–43.
65 Allen, IX, Ep. 2443.285f.
66 Allen, IV, Ep. 1195.53f. CWE 8.171. Cf. Adages II i 34. Renaudet, *Érasme et l'Italie*, 84, 87.
67 Allen, I, Ep. 256.77–87. CWE 2.219f.
68 Philippe Renouard, *Imprimeurs et libraires parisiens du xvi siècle* (Paris 1964–   ) II, nos. 183, 201. CEBR I 79–81, III 71f. Bade wrote a dedicatory preface for *De voluptate*, dated 11 March 1512 and addressed to Guillaume Petit, the king's confessor, who five years later promoted the idea of a royal appointment for Erasmus in Paris.
69 ASD IV-3 42.
70 Panizza (in 'Valla's *De voluptate*,' 2, 12f.) takes Erasmus' acquaintance with Valla's treatise for granted, although she can offer internal evidence only.
71 Originally Leonardo Bruni, Antonio Beccadelli Panormitanus, and Nicxolò Niccoli were chosen to speak for Stoicism, Epicureanism, and Christianity, respectively. In later redactions they were replaced with Catone Sacco, Maffeo Vegio, and Antonio da Rho.
72 Valla, *On Pleasure*, 84, 128.
73 Riccardo Fubini, *Umanesimo e secularizzazione da Petrarca a Valla* (Rome 1990), 366. Interpretations of Valla's *De voluptate* vary a great deal; Fubini's seems to me particularly perceptive.
74 Valla, *On Pleasure*, 50f.

75 Valla, *On Pleasure*, 300f., 314f.
76 Valla, *On Pleasure*, 216f.: 'Quod si Elysii campi sunt, nostri certe futuri putandi sunt, qui vitam deorum beatorumque similem egimus. Et, o nimiam vim veritatis! Non invenerunt sapientissimi viri aliud bonum sive apud inferos sive apud superos quam voluptatem ... ex quo patet sicut premia nulla sunt defunctorum ita nec supplicia esse.' Typically, Hieatt and Lorch translate *inferi* and *superi* with 'hell' and 'heaven.'
77 Burckhardt, *The Civilization of the Renaissance*, 311.
78 Valla, *On Pleasure*, 258f. The Christian also warns of 'the Epicurean arguments that debauchery, adultery, profligacy, and almost every kind of disgraceful action cannot be condemned and must be numbered among the goods' (*On Pleasure*, 268f.).
79 Valla, *On Pleasure*, 220f., also 158f.
80 Valla, *On Pleasure*, 264f.
81 Valla, *On Pleasure*, 50–3.
82 Valla, *On Pleasure*, 116f., 122–31, 144–9; cf. 96–9, on the allurements of various parts of the female body.
83 Valla, *On Pleasure*, 292–7.
84 Valla, *On Pleasure*, 140f.
85 Valla, *On Pleasure*, 58f.
86 Valla, *On Pleasure*, 66–9, 78f. and passim. Hanna Barbara Gerl, *Rhetorik als Philosophie. Lorenzo Valla* (Munich 1974) 123.
87 Valla, *On Pleasure*, 58f., 62f., 66–9.
88 Valla, *On Pleasure*, 82–5, also 70–3, 90–9 and passim.
89 Valla, *On Pleasure*, 80f., 140f.
90 Valla, *On Pleasure*, 154f.
91 Valla, *On Pleasure*, 128f.
92 Valla, *On Pleasure*, 68f.
93 Valla, *On Pleasure*, 58f. The Stoic continues: 'Nempe ut appareat virgilianos sive magis epicureos agricolas non esse e numero stultorum atque errantium excipiendos.'
94 Valla, *On Pleasure*, 78–81, 212–15.
95 Valla, *On Pleasure*, 76f., 264f.
96 Allen, I, Ep. 222.1–11; II, Ep. 337.126–32. CWE 2.161, 3.116.
97 CWE 27.90. ASD IV-3 80.
98 Valla, *On Pleasure*, 58f.,110f., 164f.
99 CWE 2.91. ASD IV-3 81f. Cf. Valla, *On Pleasure*, 264f. According to the speaker for Christianity, the Stoics are 'guilty of dishonesty, living a different life from the one they professed – praisers of the virtues and lovers of pleasures.' The same point is made in Lucian's *Double Indictment*, 21, and in his *Convivium sive Lapithae*, 36: ASD I-1 614; cf above n. 38.
100 CWE 27.95, 97. ASD IV-3 89f., 92.
101 ASD IV-3 104. CWE 27.103. Valla, *On Pleasure*, 140–3.
102 CWE 27.105. ASD IV-3 106–8. Valla, *On Pleasure*, 142–5.

103 Valla, *On Pleasure*, 76: 'vestram legem ..., qui sapiens non sit eundem stultum, eundem improbum, eundem exulem, hostem, fugitivum, id est omnes huiusmodi esse, quippe adhuc nemo sapiens fuit.' Erasmus, ASD IV-3 180: 'Huic astipulatur quod ipse Christus evangelio negat quenquam appellandum bonum, nisi deum unum. Porro si stultus est quisquis sapiens non est et quisquis bonus idem sapiens (auctoribus Stoicis), nimirum mortales omneis stulticia complectatur necessum est.'
104 Valla, *On Pleasure*, 273, 338.
105 CWE 27.96f., 110f., 127, 133f. ASD IV-3 92, 116, 146–8, 164–6.
106 CWE 27.148. ASD IV-3 186f.
107 CWE 27.90, 92f., 142. ASD IV-1 80, 84, 178. Horace, *Epistles*, 1.4.15–16: 'Me pinguem et nitidum bene curata vises, / cum ridere voles, Epicuri de grege porcum.' Horace, it seems, is the author that most often came to Erasmus' mind as he wrote *Moria*. He also mentions repeatedly Democritus, a forerunner of Epicurus in Greek atomism, but he uses the 'laughing philosopher' as a stereotype without philosophical significance. Valla (*On Pleasure*, 72f.), by contrast, is more elaborate.
108 Lucretius, 2.1–24, 3.35–93, 995–1010 (on the perversions and their ultimate cause, the fear of death). *Lucretius*, ed. Cyril Bailey (Oxford 1947), I 60–4 (Prolegomena). Jones, *The Epicurean Tradition*, 46–8.
109 CWE 27.108f. ASD IV-3 112f.
110 CWE 27.99: 'What remarkable foresight of Nature it was, to level out all these variations and make all alike!' ASD IV-3 96.
111 ASD IV-3 88, 110, 112. CWE 27.95, 107–9. Lucretius, 5.821–36, 1362.
112 Allen, I, 19. CWE 9.320f.
113 DeWitt, *Epicurus and His Philosophy*, 23, 127–35.
114 Cf. above, n. 111. Epicurus actually distinguished three types of desire in the universal quest for pleasure. Some are natural and necessary, others natural but not necessary, and others yet neither natural nor necessary and therefore vain and causing imbalances. But the basic division is a twofold one between essential pleasures and superfluous ones. Epicurus, *The Extant Remains*, ed. and trans. C. Bailey (Oxford 1926), 86f., 100–3 (Letter to Menoeceus on Principal Doctrines). Diogenes Laertius, 10.127f. DeWitt, *Epicurus and His Philosophy*, 66. Jones, *The Epicurean Tradition*, 46f.
115 CWE 27.91. ASD IV-3 82.
116 CWE 27.97. ASD IV-1 92, from Horace, *Satires*, 1.3.44f., but Horace's point is mutual forbearance.
117 CWE 27.97 (cf. adage I ii 62), 103. ASD IV-3 94, 106.
118 CWE 27.98. ASD IV-3 96. Traditionally *philautia* was defined in entirely negative terms. Erasmus himself so described it in the adage I iii 92 (CWE 31.311). Luther too, opposing a statement by Johannes Duns Scotus, insisted in his 1532 Lectures on Galatians that love of

self was wicked and would not lead towards the love of God: Luther, WA 40.460–2; cf. Screech, *Rabelais*, 243.
119 Valla, *On Pleasure*, 138f.
120 ASD IV-3 94. CWE 27.98. Cf. Seneca, *Epistulae morales*, 1.6.7. Lactantius (*Institutiones* 3.17) accuses Epicurus of holding 'that a wise man does all things for his own sake' and 'there is no one who loves another but for his own sake.'
121 CWE 27.121. ASD IV-3 134.
122 According to a long note by Gerardus Listrius, or perhaps Erasmus himself, that first appears in a new edition of *Moria* (Basel 1515), these *ultrices picturae* are dramatic 'paintings on linen' of excommunicated persons on display at Rome: ASD IV-3 174f.
123 CWE 27.139.
124 CWE 27.84, 139. ASD IV-3 68, 174f. Ep. 222.
125 CWE 27.130. ASD IV-3 158. Cf. above, 124.
126 For Moria's last reference to the Stoics, see above, n. 107.
127 For a careful comparison between this last section of *Moria* and the discourse of Valla's spokesman for Christianity in the last book of *De voluptate*, see Panizza, 'Valla's *De voluptate*,' 18–25.
128 CWE 27.144, 148f. ASD IV-3 182, 188f.
129 CWE 27.150f. ASD IV-3 190.
130 CWE 27.148, 150. ASD IV-3 188, 190.
131 CWE 27.150. Years later when Erasmus was questioned by Joris van Halewijn, who was translating the *Moria* into French, he explained this passage: 'What we apprehend with our senses does not really exist, for it is not perpetual, nor does it always take the same form. Those things alone really exist which are apprehended by the contemplation of the mind': CWE 7.317 (Ep. 1115).
132 CWE 27.151. ASD IV-3 191.
133 Moria continues: 'Then when they come to, they say they don't know where they have been, in the body or outside it, awake or asleep ... All they know is that they were happiest when they were out of their senses in this way, and they lament their return to reason, for all they want is to be mad for ever with this kind of madness.' CWE 27.152f. ASD IV-3 192–4.
134 CWE 27.148–52. ASD IV-3 188, 190f., 194. For the Listrius commentary see above, n. 122.
135 Paul Oskar Kristeller, 'Erasmus from an Italian Perspective,' *Renaissance Quarterly* 23 (1970), 1–14, esp. 11ff.
136 CWE 27.114, 148. ASD IV-3 124, 188. See also *De contemptu mundi*, CWE 66.167, 170. ASD V-1 76, 79.
137 Screech, *Ecstasy and the Praise of Folly*, 191, 198. See, for instance, the colloquy *Apotheosis Capnionis* (1522). In the hour of Reuchlin's death a saintly Franciscan sees in his sleep how Jerome welcomes the venerable Hebrew scholar to the Garden of Eden (see above, n. 5). The

Franciscan states that 'he couldn't begin to describe even a vision of the real vision (*somnium rei*); he said only this, that he was ready to die a thousand times if he were allowed to enjoy that sight (*spectaculum*) again for one fleeting instant' (CWE 39.248–50. ASD I-3. 269–71).
138 Allen, X, Ep. 2700.35–53.
139 Epp. 999, 1211.
140 Valla, *On Pleasure*, 262f. Cf. Panizza, 'Valla's *De voluptate*,' 20.
141 Matt. 5:1–11. Future pleasure in paradise, though this may not have been Jesus' meaning, was certainly the common understanding.
142 Two English adaptations of the 'Ship of Fools' were published in 1509, the year Erasmus wrote in London the *Moria*: Germain Marc'hadour, *L'Univers de Thomas More* (Paris 1963), 167.
143 See below, 189–96.
144 See, e.g., Allen, III, Ep. 704.4–16; CWE 5.185.
145 Epp. 152, 1013, 1390.
146 Plutarch was a professed Stoic. Erasmus' translations contain one of his many vicious attacks on Epicurus: LB IV 51 D–E.
147 Allen, I, Epp. 180.48–50, 193.53. CWE 2, 81, 116f.
148 CWE 25.32, 88, 134, 150, 156f. ASD I-2 243, 337, 408, 434, 443. 'Surely virtue is its own great reward,' writes Erasmus in the *Institutio principis christiani*' (CWE 27.213. ASD IV-1 144) See also Roland H. Bainton, *Erasmus of Christendom* (n.p. 1972), 142f.
149 ASD V-2 38.
150 ASD I-3 46, 50, 202.
151 Epp. 957–9.
152 LB V 142 B: 'Nihil in vita homini suave esse posse, nisi adsit animus nullius mali sibi conscius, unde ceu e fonte scatet vera voluptas, fatetur et Epicurus ... Si sunt quae propius pertinent ad Christianismum, his antiquatis illa sequamur.' In 1519 Jan Šlechta surveyed for Erasmus the various religious beliefs in Bohemia and claimed that there were also 'Epicureans, who deny the immortality of the soul.' In his answer Erasmus expressed surprise at the survival of these 'foolish doctrines of Epicurus': Allen, IV, Epp. 1021.95–9, 1039.46–8. CWE 7.91, 122. See also the Paraphrase on Acts, LB VII 735f.; CWE 50.107f.
153 CWE 39.448–67, here 454. ASD I-3 381. See also the discussion of *Gerontologia* by Brenda Dunn-Lardeau in her article 'Érasme, pédagogue du bonheur, dans les *Colloques*,' *Renaissance and Reformation* 30, no. 1 (2006/7), 103–18. This is a special issue, entitled 'Le bonheur selon Érasme,' edited by Brenda Dunn-Lardeau.
154 Franz Bierlaire, *La familia d'Érasme* (Paris 1968), 78–81; also CEBR 3.150f.
155 CWE 40.863–76, here 869. ASD I-3 608f.
156 Rabelais, *Gargantua*, chap. 57.
157 The exceptions I found are harmless. In the *Epistola contra pseudevangelicos*, ASD IX-1 292, Erasmus states that some Protestants indulge in

drinking to the point 'ut coeperint esse Epicurei.' In a letter of 1533 Erasmus writes that Aleandro 'nunc Venetiae plane viuit Epicureum, non sine dignitate tamen': Allen, X, Ep. 2876.11f. Two decades earlier Aleandro himself had written Erasmus that he much preferred 'your friend Lucian' to the arrogant Stoics; see above, 120.
158 Erasmus' answer is *Dilutio eorum quae Iodocus Clithoveus scripsit adversus declamationem Des. Erasmi Roterodami suasoriam matrimonii*, ed. E.V. Telle (Paris 1968), 28f., 82, 86. CWE 83.129f., 133. Rummel, *Erasmus and His Catholic Critics*, I 73–9.
159 *Responsio ad cujusdam febricitantis libellum*, LB X 1678 E.
160 *Purgatio adversus Lutheri epistolam*, ASD IX-1 476.
161 Seidel Menchi, *Erasmo in Italia*, 230.
162 Luther, WA, *Tischreden*, V, no. 5535.
163 Luther, WA, 18.609.21–2, with a note listing analogous pronouncements.
164 Luther, WA, *Tischreden*, IV, no. 3963; also I, nos. 352, 432, 466, and III, no. 3795.
165 CWE 76.105, 123–5, 137, 155, 207, 214, 237, 295f.; cf. 77.707. LB X 1253 C, 1260 C–E, 1266 B–C, 1273 F, 1295 E, 1299 A, 1309 A, 1334 F, 1336 B, 1517 A. Jones, *The Epicurean Tradition*, 163–5.
166 Allen, VI, Epp. 1670.30f., 1688, 1690.20f.
167 *Purgatio adversus epistolam Lutheri*, ASD IX-1 460, 466, 473, 476, 478, 480, 482. See also Johann Koler's letter of 22 May 1534, Allen, X, Ep. 2936.59–64.
168 CWE 40,1070–94. ASD I-3 720–33.
169 ASD I-3 721: 'Nihil est miserius quam animus sibi male conscius.' The formulation, which Erasmus had used already in the *Paraclesis* (see above, n. 152), is here attributed to Plautus (*Mostellaria*, 544f.), but Plautus' statement conveys irritation and by no means contrition.
170 CWE 40.1075f. ASD I-3 721f. Kaiser, in *Praisers of Folly*, 191f., shows the relevance of this passage for Rabelais' *Tiers Livre*.
171 CWE 40, 1077. ASD I-3 723.
172 CWE 40.1084f. ASD I-3 730f. By contrast see *Moria*, CWE 27.95. ASD IV-3 90.
173 CWE 40.1078. ASD I-3 724.
174 CWE 40.1078f., 1087. ASD IV-3 724f., 732f.
175 CWE 40.1087; for Luther's reaction see C.R. Thompson's note on pp. 1093f.
176 DeWitt finds an Epicurean echo in 1 Thess. 5:13: 'You must live at peace among yourselves,' but suggests that Paul might likewise think of the Epicurean missionaries when he warns the Thessalonians of a false message 'of peace and security' (1 Thess. 5:3). DeWitt, *Epicurus and His Philosophy*, 85, 189 (also 182, 230, 319, on Ecclesiastes). For more detail see N.W. DeWitt, *St. Paul and Epicurus* (Minneapolis 1954). See also Ferguson and Hershbell, 'Epicureanism in the Roman Empire,' 2275–7.

177 DeWitt, *Epicurus and His Philosophy,* 26–32.
178 During his sojourn in Louvain, 1516–19, Erasmus obtained a manuscript of *De opificio Dei* and began to annotate the work. He later published it as an appendix to his *Vidua christiana*: Allen, VIII, Ep. 2103, introd.
179 Peter Abelard, *A Dialogue of a Philosopher with a Jew and a Christian,* trans. Pierre J. Payer (Toronto 1979), 89, 94, 97. Kraye in *The Cambridge History of Philosophy,* 375f., 383. Cf. Jones, *The Epicurean Tradition,* chap. 5, 'Medieval Interlude.'

CHAPTER SIX

1 Erasmus, *De copia*, ASD I-6, 132, *Antibarbari*, ASD I-1, 49, 70, 79. On his return from Italy Erasmus had Mistress Folly pay the sceptic philosophers of the Academy this compliment: 'For human affairs are so complex and obscure that nothing can be known of them for certain, as has been rightly stated by my Academicians, the least assuming of the philosophers': CWE 27.118; ASD IV-3, 130.
2 Gen. 3:5. LB VI 377f. (note on John 8:44).
3 Erasmus, *Paraclesis*, LB V 141 F.
4 Francesco Petrarca, *Epistolae familiares,* 24.3–4: *Le Familiari,* ed. V. Rossi et al. (Florence 1933–42), IV 225–34.
5 ASD IV-1 A 50. CWE 29.283. Augustine, *Confessiones,* 3.4.7.
6 Allen V, Ep. 1390; CWE 10.97.
7 See below, 152.
8 'Quid quod ipse Paulus Apostolus non raro hoc artificio quasi pia quadam utitur adulatione, laudans ut emendet?': Allen, I, Ep. 180. 57f. CWE 2.81. The *Panegyricus* is in ASD IV-1 1–93, CWE 27.9–75.
9 Augustine, Epp. 28, 40, 82. Also his *Epistolae ad Galatas expositio* in *Corpus scriptorum ecclesiasticorum latinorum* (Vienna 1866–), vol. 84. Biondi, 'La giustificazione della simulazione,' 12–26; P.G. Bietenholz, 'The Patristic Controversy about Galatians 2.11–14 and the Reaction of Erasmus of Rotterdam', *Shingaku-kenkyu* (School of Theology, Kwansei-Gakuin University) 50 (2003): 171–83, also for what follows here.
10 Jerome, *Commentarii in epistolam ad Galatas* in *Patrologiae ... series latina,* ed. J.P. Migne, (Paris 1844–1902), 26.307–438.
11 LB VI 807 D.
12 Jerome, *Commentarii in Galatas,* PL 26.340.
13 See above, 66.
14 Here and elsewhere Erasmus follows the Vulgate translation: 'save all,' although in his own translation he put, in accordance with the Greek, 'save some,' a change now generally accepted.
15 LB VI 501 E-F, cf. 502 F.
16 LB V.92–9. The argument begins: 'Neque vero confundit hanc harmoniam Christi varietas ... Nunc divinae naturae profert indicia ... Nunc

divinitatem dissimulans, hominem agit.' Cf. Allen, III, Ep. 916:364–70; CWE 6.248f.
17 On this topic see Zagorin, *Ways of Lying*.
18 CWE 5.289f. Allen, III, Ep. 769.43–5. Eck had no sympathy for the sceptical trend in Occamist theology, nor had apparently Erasmus, although the Occamists, especially Robert Holcot, expressed views on divine deceit and lying that might have been of interest to him; see Gordon Leff, *Medieval Thought from St Augustine to Ockham* (n.p. 1958), 291f.
19 Luther, WA 2.484, cf. 40.i.195.
20 *Resolutio super propositione XIII de potestate papae*, Luther, WA 2.235, 286f., 293f., 302, 305. Cornelis Augustijn, 'Erasmus von Rotterdam im Galaterbriefkommentar Luthers von 1519,' *Lutherjahrbuch* 49 (1982): 115–32.
21 LB VI 807–10. Later, in 1527, Erasmus published his Latin translation of John Chrysostom's commentary of Galatians that for the most part agreed with Origen's and Jerome's approach: LB VIII 288 D–290 E.
22 The letters in question were all published together in Erasmus' collection *Epistolae ad diversos*, 1521. P.G. Bietenholz, 'Haushalten mit der Wahrheit. Erasmus im Dilemma der Kompromissbereitschft,' *Basler Zeitschrift für Geschichte und Altertumskunde* 86, no. 2 (1986): 9–26, here 15–17.
23 Allen, IV, Ep. 1155. CWE 8.79.
24 Allen, IV, Ep. 1202. CWE 8.203f.
25 The pieces of the controversy with Hutten and his supporters are conveniently assembled in Ulrich von Hutten, *Opera*, ed. E. Böcking (Leipzig 1859–61), II.180–392 and discussed in Biondi, 'La giustificazione della simulazione,' 23–33.
26 Biondi, 'La giustificazione della simulazione,' 33f.
27 ASD IX-1 184; cf. also 136, 165f., 178f.
28 LB VI 454 E–F: 'Nam mentitur non solum, qui falsum dicit, verum etiam qui simulat.' Pio did not bring up the fatal sin of Ananias and Sapphira, nor did in this place Erasmus. In his paraphrase on Acts 5:1–11 he pointed out that this was a unique occurrence in the practice of the apostles. Ananias and Sapphira had lied to the Holy Spirit, and the Holy Spirit, not Peter, had put them to death (LB VII 684f.). Whether they were also damned, he said in another place, was not certain (see above, 104).
29 LB IX 1194–6.
30 See above, 102–6.
31 Biondi, 'La giustificazione della simulazione,' 34–8. Kutter, *Curione*, 97–109. Curione's pasquil, which also contained a reprint of a piece by Hutten, proved very popular and was translated into Italian, German, French, and English.
32 Luca d'Ascia, 'Curione Erasmista o Antierasmista' in *Erasmo, Venezia*, 209–23, here 219.
33 Seidel Menchi, *Erasmo in Italia*, esp. chap. 8. See also Biondi, La giustificazione della simulazione, 37–57.

34 Burckhardt, *The Civilization of the Renaissance in Italy*, 204.
35 Kutter, *Curione*, 227.
36 Mario Bracali, 'Per una storia dei rapporti tra filosofia e riforma. Appunti e ricerche su Cardano,' in *Cardano, Le opere*, 81–104, here 82–90; Eugenio Di Rienzo, 'La religione di Cardano. Libertinismo e eresia nell'Italia della Controriforma,' *Archivio di Storia della Cultura* 6, no. 1 (1993): 35–60, here 37f.; Ugo Baldini, 'Cardano negli archivi dell'Inquisizione e dell'Indice. Note su una ricerca,' *Rivista di Storia della Filosofia* 53 (1998): 761–6; Zagorin, *Ways of Lying*, 305. In general see also *Girolamo Cardano: Philosoph, Naturforscher, Arzt*, ed. E. Kessler (Wiesbaden 1994), where, among others, Di Rienzo's article is reprinted.
37 There are three versions; the latter two extend the list of precedents by adding the names of Cicero, Jerome, and Augustine. Cardano, *Opera*, I 55a, 61a, cf. 96a.
38 Cardano, *Opera*, I 527a, 633b, II 48b, 109b, 117a, 272a.
39 Cardano, *Opera*, I 147b, 518b. Cardano himself did not publish his letters.
40 Cardano, *Theonoston seu de tranquillitate, Opera*, II 378a.
41 Cardano, *De utilitate, Opera*, II 11a, cf. I 217b. In *De Socratis studio* an ironical exclamation: 'Haec igitur Socratica sanctitas!' could be a retort to Erasmus' famous 'Sancte Socrates, ora pro nobis.' *Opera*, I 157a.
42 Cardano, *Opera*, V 465b. On Cardano's astrology see Anthony Grafton, *Cardano's Astrology: The World and Works of a Renaissance Astrologer* (Cambridge, MA, 1999), e.g., 184: 'The old art of geniture could be stretched [by Cardano] to produce results, in the realm of introspective writing, that challenged comparison with those of Montaigne's new art of essay.'
43 Cardano, *De subtilitate, Opera*, III 551a: 'ut quicquid mente excogitari posset, id omne opifex maior ipsa cogitatione praestaret, essetque animal fallax. Nam belluae fallaces esse non poterant ob stultitiam, superi vero ob probitatem.'
44 Di Rienzo, *L'Aquila e lo Scarabeo*, 11, 145. François Tricaud, '"Homo homini Deus," "Homo homini lupus": Recherche des sources des deux formules de Hobbes,' in *Hobbes-Forschungen*, ed. R. Kosellech and R. Schnur (Berlin 1969), 61–70. Neither Di Rienzo nor Tricaud mentions a further link in that tradition: the *libertin* Guy Patin, who borrowed directly from Erasmus; see below, 288 n. 29. Erasmus, LB II 53–5; CWE 31.112–15.
45 Cardano, *Opera*, I 588; also *De prudentia*, I 361f., for the corruption of human nature.
46 Cardano, *De sapientia, Opera*, I 495a.
47 Francis Bacon, *Sermones fideles*, chap. 6: 'De dissimulatione et simulatione.' Cf. Zagorin, *Ways of Lying*, 256, 271–4.
48 Cardano, *De prudentia, Opera*, I 374b; cf. *De sapientia*, I 532.
49 Cardano, *De prudentia, Opera*, I 395b; cf. *De utilitate*, II 168f.

50 Cardano, *De prudentia, Opera,* I 395b, 399a; cf. *De sapientia,* I 544. Alfonso Ingegno, 'Cardano tra *De sapientia* e *De immortalitate animorum*. Ipotesi per una periodizzazione' in *Cardano, Le opere,* 61–79, here 66–8.
51 Cardano, *De prudentia, Opera,* I 394f.
52 This and the preceding quotations: Cardano, *De sapientia, Opera,* I 534f.
53 Cardano, *De subtilitate, Opera,* II 657–9. Allen, I, Ep. 143:68–185; X, Ep. 2846:124–52. CWE 2.5–9. Cardano's excerpt of Erasmus' first letter was soon copied again; see above, 43.
54 See, e.g., *Opera,* I 200a, 518b, 547b, 598a. See also above, 150.
55 See, e.g., *Opera,* I 135a (cf. 80a), 558f. Although Erasmus is not mentioned, one senses his presence behind some other views Cardano expresses. He pointedly sides with Machiavelli against Erasmus, when he berates the stupidity of those who think it is better for a prince to be loved than to be feared. In the same context he differs from Erasmus when he deplores the tolerance of more than one religion in a state; this is the cause of the troubles in Germany (*Opera,* I 539a).
56 Cardano chooses Paul to exemplify an exception from the rule that one should refrain from self-denigration and self-pity. He quotes 2 Cor. 11:23–6 and points out that Paul's account of his travails here is a means of instruction (*Opera,* I 547f.). Among the many forms of *sapientia humana* that Cardano distinguishes, there is one 'very close to, and practically undistinguishable' from the benevolent *sapientia naturalis.* 'Estque admirabilis, cum verbis cavillatoriis illud deludimus, hoc Servator ter usus est.' In all three cases the Saviour answers evasively, raising the debate to a higher, more universal level of morality: Matt. 21:23–7, 22:15–22; John 8:3–7 (*Opera,* I 561). In another passage Cardano, reminiscent of Erasmus' emphasis on accommodation, quotes Christ's words in John 10:30 and 12:45 as examples of 'occulti sermones et anticipes'(*De sapientia, Opera,* I 534b).
57 Cardano, *De sapientia, Opera,* I 548a.
58 See above, 153.
59 Cardano, *De sapientia, Opera,* I 495a: 'Quae autem ad permutandam opinionem hominum dirigitur, nihil habens proprium circa quod versetur, ad humanam sapientiam referri debet ... Ambigua et incerta humanae sunt sapientiae praemia ... Divina enim et naturalis sapientia esse docet, humana et daemoniaca, ut videatur.'
60 *La Science du Monde ou la Sagesse de Cardan,* trans. A. Choppin (Paris 1640). Di Rienzo, *L'Aquila e lo Scarabeo,* 228f.
61 Di Rienzo, *L'Aquila e lo Scarabeo,* 224f. Cardano, *De sapientia, Opera,* I 550b.
62 Montaigne, *Essais,* II.12: 'Les uns font accroire au monde qu'ils croyent ce qu'ils ne croyent pas; les autres, en plus grand nombre, se le font accroire à eulx mesmes.'
63 Ian Maclean, 'Montaigne, Cardano: The Reading of Subtlety/The Subtlety of Reading,' *French Studies* 37 (1983): 143–56. M.A. Screech,

'Girolamo Cardano's *De Sapientia* and the *Tiers Livre de Pantagruel*,' *Bibliothèque d'Humanisme et Renaissance* 25 (1963): 97–110.
64 Di Rienzo, *L'Aquila e lo Scarabeo*, 137–43, 198f., 211f. Cardano, *De sapientia, Opera*, I 536a; *De subtilitate, Opera*, III 551f. Charron, *De la Sagesse*, 445–9 and passim.
65 Di Rienzo, *L'Aquila e lo Scarabeo*, 227–32. Patin, *Lettres choisies*, V 165 (*Nouveau recueil*), on Cardano's geniture of Erasmus.
66 Di Rienzo, *L'Aquila e lo Scarabeo*, 142–4, 196–200, 214–16; Mansfield, *Phoenix of His Age*, 4, 57–9, 159–61. For Scaliger's success in France see Maclean, 'Montaigne, Cardano,' op. cit. note 63, 144. Cardano's replies to Scaliger are in his *Opera*, III 673–713.
67 According to Bayle, Cardano's 'ame fut frappé à un coin tout particulier ... Naudé prétend que Cardan étoit tel qu'il se représente: mais j'aimerois mieux dire qu'il a prétendu seulement montrer ce que les malignes influences de son étoile l'eussent rendu, s'il ne les eût corrigées.'
68 Bracali ('Per una storia ... Appunti su Cardano,' in *Cardano, Le opere*, 97) also draws attention to striking parallels with Erasmus' and Cardano's choice of words in the *Zodiacus vitae* of the Lutheran heretic Marcello Palingenio, a work regularly reprinted in Basel and very widely read in seventeenth-century France: 'Nam dissimulare tacendo/maxima plerumque est prudentia: vivere nescit,/ut bene vulgus ait, qui nescit dissimulare./Nonnunquam, mihi crede, nocet defendere verum,/temporis atque loci proinde est servanda hominumque/conditio semper, ne quid te laedere possit' (IV 683–8).

CHAPTER SEVEN

1 See below, 196–208.
2 Margaret Mann Phillips, 'Érasme et Montaigne,' in *Colloquia Turonensia*, I 479–501, here 480. In general, see Gisèle Mathieu-Castellani, *Montaigne ou la vérité du mensonge* (Geneva 2000), e.g., 107; Friedrich, *Montaigne*; and Popkin, *History of Scepticism*, 44–57.
3 Montaigne, *Essais*, III 2: 'Ie dis vray, non pas tout mon saoul, mais autant que j'ose dire.'
4 Montaigne, *The Complete Essays*, trans. D.M. Frame, 615 (III 2).
5 Montaigne, *Essais*, II 12; in Frame's translation, 366.
6 Darmon, *Philosophie épicurienne*, 12–17.
7 Montaigne, *Essais*, II 12; in Frame's translation, 390.
8 Donald Stone, 'Montaigne and Epicurus: A Lesson in Originality,' *Mélanges sur la littérature de la Renaissance à la mémoire de V.-L. Saulnier* (Geneva 1984), 465–71, here 469f.; Friedrich, *Montaigne*, 66–70.
9 Friedrich, *Montaigne*, 316, 322f.
10 Montaigne, *Essais*, II 12; in Frame's translation, 443–7. Darmon, *Philosophie épicurienne*, 16–19. Friedrich, *Montaigne*, 169–71.

11 Popkin, *History of Scepticism*, 56.
12 Popkin, *History of Scepticism*, 57–61. We only know of one book that Montaigne, while alive, gave to Charron. This was Bernardino Ochino's *Catechismo*, in which he refrained from dealing with the Trinity since to do so was, he said, troublesome and not conducive to salvation. Another member of that same radical circle, Sebastianus Castellio, is remembered in *Essais*, I 35. See above, 108.
13 Belin, *L'œuvre de Charron*, 9, 27, 53, 103, 155, 170, 263. For a contrasting view of Charron, see Gregory, *Genèse*, 3, 25f., 138f.
14 Montaigne, *Essais*, II 12; in Frame's translation, 330–58, especially 343, 354f., 357f.
15 Pierre Charron, *De la Sagesse*, ed. B. Negroni (Paris 1986), 207–19 (I chap. 34): 'Seconde consideration de l'homme, qui est par comparaison de luy avec tous les animaux.'
16 According to his critic, Julius Caesar Scaliger, Cardano (at the beginning of book 11 of *De Subtilitate*) followed Epicurus and Lucretius in positing the spontaneous generation of matter, Pythagoras in attributing a soul to animals, and Alexander of Aphrodisias in denying the immortality of individual humans: Di Rienzo, *L'Aquila e lo Scarabeo*, 197.
17 ASD I-2 28, 36–9; I-4 14; IV-3 112; LB V 15 A–B. CWE 26.300f., 309–11, 368f.; 27.108; 66.44f.
18 Belin, *L'œuvre de Charron*, 65, 153. LB V 11 E. CWE 66.41.
19 Gregory, *Genèse*, 45–7, 103.
20 Alan Charles Kors, *Atheism in France, 1650–1729* (Princeton 1990), 29f., 243; Mansfield, *Phoenix of His Age*, 57–9; Popkin, *History of Scepticism*, 100f.
21 Henri-Jean Martin, *Livre, pouvoirs et société à Paris au XVIIe siècle* (Geneva 1969), I 507 (chart of various authors represented in private libraries). Gabriel Naudé in his plan for a model library termed it inexcusable to ignore Erasmus; see below, 165.
22 Margolin, 'Guy Patin, lecteur d'Érasme,' in *Colloquia Turonensia*, I 323–58. See also Mansfield, *Phoenix of His Age*, 155f.
23 There is no critical edition of Patin's letters. I had access to, and am citing, an edition in five volumes (The Hague 1707, Rotterdam 1725); here I 34–6 (27 August 1648). The translation here quoted is in Popkin, *History of Scepticism*, 81.
24 Patin, *Lettres choisies*, I 142f. (2 December 1650). The others portrayed are Julius Caesar and Joseph Scaliger, Isaac Casaubon, Marc-Antoine Muret, Daniel Heinsius, Claude Saumaise, Jean Fernel, Jacques-Auguste de Thou, [bishop] Du Bellay, and Justus Lipsius. A few months later, Patin mentions in another letter (I 166f., 21 April 1651), over the mantlepiece (in the same room?), around a fine crucifix, the portraits of himself, his wife, his parents, Erasmus, and Joseph Scaliger. Throughout his letters the names of Erasmus and Scaliger often appear in conjunction. See also Jean Claude Margolin, *Érasme, précepteur de l'Europe* (Paris 1955), 264; Martin, *Livre, pouvoirs et société* (op. cit. note 21), I 482.

25 Patin, *Lettres choisies*, I 21f. (24 October 1645), III 32 (30 December 1664). Patin, *Lettres du temps de la Fronde*, 120 (13 July 1649). Margolin, 'Guy Patin, lecteur d'Érasme,' 333.
26 Patin, *Lettres choisies*, I 167 (21 April 1651). Margolin, Guy Patin, lecteur d'Érasme, 326, 335f., 341f.
27 Margolin, 'Guy Patin, lecteur d'Érasme,' 324–30.
28 Patin, *Lettres choisies*, II 323 (10 September 1662).
29 Patin, *Lettres choisies*, I 396 (19 September 1659); III 183 (21 September 1666); 313 (7 July 1669); II 103 (20 August 1660) offers an intriguing and more substantial example: 'ainsi les loups se mangent l'un l'autre; Erasme donc, tout bon homme qu'il étoit, s'est trompé lorsqu'il a dit: "*homo homini Deus, et lupus lupinam* [sic; *lupinum*?] *non est,*" mais en récompense il a dit vrai quand il a écrit: "*homo homini lupus.*"' Cf. above, 151.
30 Patin, *Lettres du temps de la Fronde*, 37 (8 January 1649).
31 Popkin, *History of Scepticism*, 91–8 and passim.
32 See Gascendi's letter to Henri Dufaur du Pibrac of 8 April 1621 in his *Opera omnia* (Lyon 1658), VI 2. After high praise for the Pyrrhonist Charron: 'si praesertim assederint illi, quorum ipse opera profecit, Montanus, Lipsius, Seneca, Plutarchus, M. Tullius. Hos sane et paucos alios ipsi comites adhibeo – paucos inquam, nam tales authores appareant mihi admodum rari in tam vasto gurgite. His ubi nonnunquam substituo Lucretium, Horatium, Iuvenalem, ubi Lucianum aut Erasmum. Deum immortalem, quam merae me chimerae delectant!' Cf. Murr, 'Gassendi's Scepticism as a Religious Attitude,' 22.
33 See above, 138f. Gassendi had praise for André Arnaud's attempt to rehabilitate Epicurus, which essentially follows the line of Erasmus' colloquy. See Tenenti, *Credenze*, 289f., 297.
34 A prolepsis to Epicurus is a notion that is immediately evident as a result of an often-repeated perception by the senses. It thus becomes the basis for rational judgments. See Cicero, *De natura deorum*, 1.43.
35 Darmon, *Philosophie épicurienne*, 160–4, 172–5. On Gassendi's view of Epicurus' religion see also Tenenti, *Credenze*, 300–5.
36 Gregory, *Genèse*, 177–81; Murr, 'Gassendi's Scepticism' 27f.; Lynn Sumida Joy, *Gassendi the Atomist: Advocate of History in an Age of Science* (Cambridge 1987), 179–81.
37 François de La Mothe le Vayer, *Deux Dialogues faits à l'imitation des anciens (sur la divinité et sur l'opiniatreté)*, ed. E. Tisserand (Paris 1922), 115: 'Érasme disait, il y a peu, que *nemo magis promeretur nomen Epicuri quam Christus*, sur l'allusion de son nom Ἐπικούριος, auxiliator'; also 121. Tenenti, *Credenze*, 297–9.
38 See above, 103.
39 *Lettres de Gabriel Naudé à Jacques Dupuy (1632–1652)*, ed. Ph. Wolfe (Edmonton 1982), 68.
40 Cavaillé, *Dis/simulations*, 141, 178.

41 Sophie Gouverneur, 'Le *Mascurat*: Un exemple d'écriture libertine,' in *Libertinage et philosophie au XVIIe siècle. 2: La Mothe-le-Vayer et Naudé* (Saint-Étienne 1997), 131–45.
42 Cavaillé, *Dis/simulations*, 199, 228, 246, and passim; Di Rienzo, *L'Aquila e lo Scarabeo*, 195–258.
43 Di Rienzo, *L'Aquila e lo Scarabeo*, 237 and passim.
44 Patin, *Lettres choisies*, III 393–6 (6 August 1670).
45 Mansfield, *Phoenix of His Age*, 236, 247, and the entire chap. 8 for what follows.
46 Elisabeth Labrousse, *Pierre Bayle* (The Hague 1963–4), I 269–71; Popkin, *Scepticism*, 295–302; Israel, *Radical Enlightenment*, 332f.
47 Bayle, *Projet et fragmens d'un Dictionaire critique* (Rotterdam 1692, repr. Geneva 1970), 259f.
48 Bayle, *Projet*, 225–79. For the finalized article see, e.g., the second English edition: *The Dictionary Historical and Critical* (London 1734–8), 800–15.
49 Bayle, *Projet*, 251f. Cf. Mansfield, *Phoenix of His Age*, 245f.
50 Mansfield, *Phoenix of His Age*, 257.
51 LB III, preface: 'Erat enim haec indoles Erasmi, ut diu celare non posset quod sentiebat, praesertim amicis et interdum quoque inimicis, si paullo commotior esset. Interdum quidem paullo cautius loqui videtur, sed mox ad ingenium redit, ita ut facile intelligas, quid revera senserit.'
52 LB IX, preface: 'Vituperamus, carpimus, erroris, dissimulationis aut timiditatis doctissimum virum arguimus; nec eo secius nostrum esse volumus. Cum scribit in eos, quos Judaismum revocare voluisse ait, tum alii aperte sibi hominem favere dictitant. Cum vero invehitur in eos, qui secessionem fecerunt, clamitant continuo adversarii suum esse. Utrique faventi plaudunt, dissentienti indignantur. An igitur, inquies, neutris partibus addictus fuit? Imo vero utrisque, dum et hos et illos ad mitiora et aequiora iudicia consiliaque revocare nititur.'
53 LB I, preface (4).
54 [Pierre Bayle], *Sentimens de quelques theologiens de Hollande sur l'Histoire critique du Vieux Testament composée par le P. Richard Simon de l'Oratoire* (Amsterdam 1685), e.g., 262, 267f., 271. Also Le Clerc, *Epistolario*, I 242, 252f., 255; cf. IV 413f.
55 LB VI, preface.

CHAPTER EIGHT

1 'Et cuique jam in manibus est ingeniosissimum illud *Moriae encomium*, non infimi scriptoris opus,' Milton, *Proclusiones*, VI; English trans. in *Complete Prose Works*, I 273f.
2 Mansfield, *Phoenix of His Age*, 149.
3 McLachlan, *Socinianism*, 70, 64–87 passim.
4 Trevor-Roper, *Catholics, Anglicans and Puritans*, 168f. , and further on the Great Tew Circle, 166–230.

5 Thomas Triplet's dedicatory letter in Falkland, *Discourse on Infallibility.*
6 Popkin, *History of Scepticism*, 65f. McLachlan, *Socinianism*, 67–76. For examples of Chillingworth's sceptical rejection of the certainty of faith professed by his opponents, see Chillingworth, *Works*, I 114f., II 318–21. Also, significant is the endorsement of Giacopo Aconcio (II 38). Aconcio had at the time of Elizabeth I been a military engineer, as was Chillingworth during the Civil War. See also Triplet's dedicatory letter, mentioned above.
7 Trevor-Roper (*Catholics, Anglicans and Puritans*, 189–92) emphasized the Tew men's debt to Erasmus and his "libertine' continuators,' among them Castellio, Aconcio, Ochino, and Fausto Sozzini himself. He sees Erasmus as the father of 'Socinianism' in the wider sense of sceptical rationalism, but also in the narrow sense, and states, somewhat inclusively I think, that he was 'cited by all the Great Tew writers.'
8 Falkland, *Discourse on Infallibility*, 14f., 24f.
9 Chillingworth, *Works*, I 240, III 435–8.
10 [John Hales], *A Tract concerning Schisme and Schismaticks wherein Is briefly discovered the Original Causes of all Schisme* (London 1642), 10: seeing 'that men of different opinions in Christian Religion, may not hold communion in *sacris*, and both go to one Church, why may I not go, if occasion requires, to an Arian Church, so there be no Arianism expressed in their Liturgy ... but contained only such things, as in which all Christians do agree?' Cf. James Hinsdale Elson, *John Hales of Eton* (New York 1948), 62, 116, and passim. A statement in a letter from Erasmus to Pirckheimer (19 october 1527) seems to have been well known in England; John Nye translated it later in his *Brief history*, 31. Wrote Erasmus: 'Quantum apud alios valeat autoritas Ecclesiae nescio: certe apud me tantum valet ut cum Arianis et Pelagianis sentire possim, si probasset Ecclesia quod illi docuerunt' (Allen, VI, Ep. 1893, 62–5).
11 Chillingworth, *Works*, III 47; Allen, III, Ep. 858, 266–9, 495–8; ASD IV-3 186f.
12 Falkland, *Discourse on Infallibility*, 111, addressing a Catholic opponent: 'I could next tell you of Erasmus his saying: "res deducta est ad Sophisticas contentiones, et Articulorum Miriades proruperunt. Religion is come down to Sophistry, and a Myriad of Articles are broken out," but [will not do so,] knowing that his words will not find so much respect (because he himself finds lesse favour) as those of others more allowed among you.'
13 Falkland, *Discourse on Infallibility*, 108–13. See also Chillingworth, *Works*, II 257f.
14 Chillingworth, *Works*, III 397f.
15 Chillingworth, *Works*, III 408; cf. 453 (on Beatus Rhenanus). For sources see LB V 170 and IX 1062–4.
16 Falkland, *Discourse on Infallibility*, 64.

17 Chillingworth, *Works*, II 240: 'one ingenuous confession of that great Erasmus ... "Non desunt magni theologi qui non verentur affirmare, nihil esse in Luthero quin per probatos authores defendi possit"' (Erasmus to Godschalk Rosemondt, 18 October 1520, Allen, IV, Ep. 1153.98–100). In *Works*, II 201, 210, Chillingworth placed Erasmus among other Catholic translators of the Bible. On Jerome's controversial acceptance of the Epistle to the Hebrews into the canon, cf. *Works*, I 218, II 345 with LB VI 1023f.
18 Falkland, *Discourse on Infallibility*, 187f.: 'Erasmus who, though himself no Martyr, yet one who may passe for a Confessor, having suffered, and long by the Bigotts of both Parties, and a dear Friend both to Fisher and his Colleague in Martyrdome, Sir Thomas More ... makes yet a longer confession: "Non obscurum est quot opiniones invectae sunt in orbem per homines, ad suum Quaestum callidos, conflictorum Mircaculorum praesidio."'
19 Falkland, *Discourse on Infallibility*, 161: 'so much that Erasmus is now generallie disavowed as no Catholicke, and given to us (whom wee accept as a great present), that Bellarmine will allow him to be but halfe a Christian and Cardinall Perron ... gives a censure upon him, which would better have become the pen of a Latomus, a Bedda, a Stunica, or an Egmondanus, then so learned and judicious a Prelate.' Falkland was obviously well acquainted with Erasmus' controversies.
20 John Jortin, *Remarks on Ecclesiastical History* (London 1846), II 420, as quoted by Mansfield, *Phoenix of His Age*, 278.
21 McLachlan, *Socinianism*, 92, 111–48, 193–5, 293.
22 McLachlan, *Socinianism*, 159f.
23 Best, *Mysteries*, 2.
24 Best, *Mysteries*, 4f.; cf. also 8, on the 'new creation' of John 1:3. Best refers to the short argument in Greek, placed in front of 1 John in Erasmus' New Testament (LB VI 1069f.), which he assumed to be by Erasmus himself.
25 Best, *Mysteries*, 4. Among his many proof-texts, Best lists John 8:58 as interpreted by the Socinians and initially Erasmus, while his Socinian understanding of Acts 20:28 and 1 John 5:7–8 runs counter to that of Erasmus.
26 Best, *Mysteries*, 15: 'I perceive how the Western Sun declineth to its period and setting. And as for that third Reformation which succeeded the Calvinian upon the Turkish Territories more remote from the Romish tyranny, especially, about Anno 1560, in Transilvania, Lithuania, Livonia and Poland, wee cannot expect [it] to be compleat before the revolution to the East, (where it first began). Revel. 7.9, 9.14, 16.12.'
27 McLachlan, *Socinianism*, 322.
28 [Stephen Nye], *An Account of Mr. Firmin's Religion and the Present State of the Unitarian Controversy* (London 1698), 50. In the same work, 8f.,

the English Unitarians are said to be followers of 'particularly and chiefly H. Grotius, who, it must be granted, was Socinian all over. And D. Erasmus, who, tho' he lived considerably before Socinus, commonly interprets that way.'
29 McLachlan, *Socinianism*, 321.
30 Nye, *Brief History*, 84–7, 141.
31 Nye, *Brief History*, 33, 108–14 (agreeing with Erasmus' interpretation of Acts 20:28), 159f. McLachlan, *Socinianism*, 296.
32 Nye, *Brief History*, 30f., also for what follows.
33 Nye ignores Erasmus' balancing act: LB VI. 851 E: 'Sic Patrem videtur appellare Deum, quasi Christus non esset Deus. Verum id alias admonuimus, Patrem ex consuetudine sermonis apostolici significari, quoties Deum absolute nominarit, quum ex plurimis locis palam sit et Christum illis vocari Deum.'
34 See above, n. 10.
35 McLachlan, *Socinianism*, 294–8, 313f., 325f.
36 William Penn, *A Treatise on Oaths*, in *Select Works*, II 104–6. LB VII 33 A–D, 1193 B–D
37 LB VI 31 E (on Matt. 5:37): 'Alioqui in causa fidei, aut pietatis, etiam Christus et Apostoli jurant.' Cf. below, 234f. Passing references to readings in Erasmus' New Testament: Penn, *Select Works*, II 11f. (2 Cor. 13:15; Gal. 6:16; Phil. 3:16), III 304f; see also Penn, *A Collection of Works*, II 325 (2 Cor. 2:17); 435 (John 1:9); 583 (John 1:4, 9); 588 (2 Cor. 2:10); 913 (1 John 2:27, etc.); also II 424 (Deut.).
38 Penn, *Select Works*, II 14: 'Erasmus tells us, "What man sets forth by man's device, may be received by man's wit: but the thing that is set forth by the inspiration of the Holy Ghost, requireth an interpreter inspired with the like spirit; and without the inspiration of it, the secrets of God cannot be known."' LB VII 1104 C–D. CWE 44.115; cf. LB VI 1061 E–F. Also Penn, *Collection of Works*, II 328, 347, 426. Neither Erasmus nor Castellio, however, is among the many witnesses cited in *The Great Case of Liberty of Conscience* (1670).
39 Penn, *Select Works*, I 426. ASD I-2 265–76. CWE 25.45–50.
40 See above, 178.
41 See above, 175.
42 Mansfield, *Phoenix of His Age*, 164f., 250.
43 Le Clerc, *Epistolario*, II 181: 'On les a accusé tous deux d'être pour l'indifference des Religions et même d'Atheïsme, parce qu'ils n'ont pas donné aveuglément dans les sentiments de la multitude ... Erasme avait écrit avec quelque moderation des Ariens et Grotius des Sociniens. Il n'en fallu pas davantage pour attirer à l'un le nom odieux d'Arien et à l'autre celui d'Antitrinitaire.' Also II 93f. 176f. (Epp. 202, 242, 244).
44 R. Fornaca, 'L'influenza di Erasmo sul pensiero educativo di John Locke,' *Saggiatore* 5 (1955): 407–32; 6 (1956): 39–71.

45 John Locke, *Second Reply to the Bishop of Worcester*, in *The Works* (London 1823, repr. 1963), IV 343. See McLachlan, *Socinianism*, 323–31. For Le Clerc's position, see *Epistolario*, II 160f. (Ep. 237).
46 Israel, *Radical Enlightenment*, 15, 462, 464–71, 478. Kim Ian Parker, *The Biblical Politics of John Locke* (Waterloo 2004), 42f.
47 Locke, *Paraphrase*, I 15, 87.
48 Locke, *Paraphrase*: according to the index, s.v. 'Erasmus,' parallels to Erasmus' notes can be found in Gal. 3:5, 5:20, 6:16; 1 Cor. 7:31; 2 Cor. 3:18, 7:11; Rom. 1:4, 2:8–9, 18, 3:25, 8:10–11, 9:5. Locke differs from Erasmus in Gal. 1:7, 16, 2:6, 3:20, 4:12, 19; 2 Cor. 1:6, 2:1, 5:19, 13:1; Rom. 1:5, 8:23; Eph. 4:9–10.
49 Locke, *Paraphrase*, I 206. LB, VII 885. Earlier, Servetus and Fausto Sozzini had used Erasmus' annotation (LB VI 704 D) to argue against Christ's eternal divinity.
50 Locke, *Paraphrase*, II 523, 564, 793f. In paraphrasing Rom. 3:25, Locke followed the patristic tradition indicated in Erasmus' note (LB VI 576) and, as a result, was denounced as a Socinian. In 2 Cor. 5:19 Locke, unlike Erasmus, avoided finding evidence for Christ's incarnation: *Paraphrase*, I 287, 470, II 508, 777f. LB VII 787, 925.
51 Locke, *Paraphrase*, II 558f., 790–2. LB VI 606, VII 804.
52 Newton, *Theological Manuscripts*, 127. H.J. McLachlan, *Socinianism*, 330f.
53 John Harrison, *The Library of Sir Isaac Newton* (Cambridge 1978). McLachlan, *Socinianism*, 326f. Newton, *Theological Manuscripts*, 12–14.
54 Newton, *Theological Manuscripts*, 15f.
55 Newton, *Theological Manuscripts*, 56; see also 15, 28f., 31, 54–7. Cf. Erasmus, *Modus orandi Deum*, ASD V-1 145f.
56 Newton, *Correspondence*, III 83–129 (Ep. 358), here 109–22. Cf LB V 936 and above, 46.
57 Cf. the following (**a** is Newton, *Correspondence*, III; **b** is LB VI): **a** 85, **b** 1079 D (Augustine); **a** 86, 91, **b** 1079 C, 1080 B; cf. LB IX 276 C–D (Beda); **a** 88f., **b** 1079 E–F; cf. LB IX 275f. (Jerome); **a** 94, **b** 1080 D–E (three ancient codices); **a** 109, **b** IX 1029–33 (*Comma Johanneum*).
58 Newton, *Correspondence*, III 82 (Ep. 357). Le Clerc, *Epistolario*, II 50–2, 58f., 66–72 (Epp. 187, 191, 195, 196). Newton, *Theological Manuscripts*, 5f. Stephen D. Snobelen, 'Socinianism and Newtonianism: The Case of William Whiston,' in *Faustus Socinus and His heritage*, ed. Lech Szczucki (Cracow 2005), 373–413, esp. 407f.
59 Newton, *Correspondence*, III 129–41 (Ep. 359): Phil. 3:3; 1 John 5:20; Matt. 19:17, 24:36; Eph. 3:9, 14; 1 John 4:3; Rev 1:11 (referring to Erasmus); Rom. 9:5; (Ep. 360) Phil. 2:6.
60 Milton, *Complete Prose Works*, II 709.
61 *A Milton Encyclopedia*, ed. W.B. Hunter Jr et al. (Lewisburg, PA, 1978–80), III 65–68: article on Erasmus by Rosemary Masek.
62 Milton, *Paradise Lost* 4.437–9, 8.319–20, 9.391.

63 Milton, *Paradise Lost*, 4.492–504, 736–75, 8.480–559, 9.1008–45, 1073–78.
64 Milton, *Paradise Lost*, ed. St. Orgel and J. Goldberg (Oxford 2004), xxix.
65 Milton, *Complete Prose Works*, II 145–58: Ernest Sirluck's introduction to the divorce pamphlets. Mansfield, *Phoenix of His Age*, 151.
66 LB VI 692–703, here 695 F. Milton, *Complete Prose Works*, II 329f.; cf. 237, 272, 350. Milton also consulted the *Responsio ad Phimostomum de divortio*, LB IX 955–65; CWE 83. 149–77.
67 Milton, *Complete Prose Works*, II 478. LB VI 702 E.
68 Milton, *Complete Prose Works*, VI 91–9: Maurice Kelley's introduction to the *Christian Doctrine*. Erasmus was ambiguous about polygamy, at least in the case of Henry VIII's 'great matter'; see *De vidua christiana*, LB V 734 B; CWE 66.201; and Allen, VII, Ep. 2040.41f. For the debate on thnetopsychism see also Chillingworth, *Works*, III 301, 427, 430, and, in general, Alistair Hamilton, 'A "Sinister Conceit": The Teaching of Psychopannychism from the Reformation to the Enlightenment,' in *Formazione storica della alterità*, III 1107–27.
69 Milton, *Complete Prose Works*, VI 121 (vol. VI contains exclusively the critical edition of the *Christian Doctrine*, translated by John Carey).
70 Milton, *Complete Prose Works*, VI 62–73. McLachlan, *Socinianism*, 187–9.
71 Milton, *Complete Prose Works*, VI 47–73, 272f., 444.
72 Milton, *Complete Prose Works*, VI 281–98.
73 Milton, *Complete Prose Works*, VI 87–90, 309: 'For not even God's virtue and efficiency could have produced bodies out of nothing (as it is vulgarly believed he did) unless there had been some bodily force in his own substance.'
74 Milton, *Complete Prose Works*, VI 245f. Cf. 238f., 249.
75 Milton, *Complete Prose Works*, VI 72.
76 Milton specifically refers to Erasmus when examining Rom. 9:5 (VI 242) and 1 Tim. 3:16 (VI 244). Without naming Erasmus, Milton may also have consulted his notes on the following: Matt. 1:23 (VI 241, LB VI 10); John 14:16 (VI 216, LB VI 397f.); Phil. 2:6 (VI 274f., 278, LB VI 867f.); Tit. 2:13 (VI 245, LB VI 971f.); Heb. 1:2–3 (VI 211f., LB VI 983f.).
77 Milton, *Complete Prose Works*, VI 218–22.
78 LB VII 585, IX 1025f., 1031 B–C. CWE 46.137.
79 Cf. below, 235f.
80 Milton, *Complete Prose Works*, VI 218.

CHAPTER NINE

1 Allen, II, Epp. 304.28–30; 337.449–70, 524–8. ASD IV-3, 188–94 (the term here is *insania* rather than *dementia*).
2 To name a few shared topics: both criticize the logic of the scholastics, the titles of nobility, hunting, dicing, the craftiness of lawyers.

They also insist on the uncertainty of the sciences, especially astrology.
3 All we hear is that the pleasure-loving Utopians take good care of fools and delight in watching them. More, *The Yale Edition*, IV, *Utopia*, ed. and trans. Edward Surtz and J.H. Hexter, 192f. All subsequent references will be to this edition of *Utopia*.
4 Allen, II, Ep. 337.126–34.
5 *The Correspondence of Sir Thomas More*, ed. Elizabeth F. Rogers (Princeton 1947), Ep. 15. Hexter, *The Vision of Politics*, 66f., 146–9. Since Dorp in his attack does not deal with the quest for pleasure, More does not either in his letter answering Dorp's arguments.
6 The Utopians have mastered Greek in no time, and on his visit to their island Hythloday brings them a library of works by Plato, Aristotle, Plutarch, Lucian, and others. Epicurus is never mentioned by name, although Hythloday learns of two opposing schools (*factiones*), one holding virtue for the supreme good, the other pleasure. To the former tenet a marginal adds: *hoc iuxta Stoicos*. The Utopians would certainly seem capable of developing analogous philosophies unassisted. See *Utopia*, 162f., cf. 158f., 180–3.
7 Epicurus is mentioned and lines from Lucretius are borrowed in More's *Epigrammata*, completed at about the same time as *Utopia*; see *The Yale Edition*, III/2, 20f., 142f., 168f, 354.
8 Surtz, *The Praise of Pleasure*, 23–35; chap. 4, 'The Fortunes of Epicurus in Utopia,' appears to be written on the assumption that More knew Valla's book.
9 *Utopia*, 120f. Baker-Smith, *More's Utopia*, 160.
10 *Utopia*, 160f. (the Yale translation modified).
11 *Utopia*, 158.
12 *Utopia*, 162f., 178f.
13 *Utopia*, 162: 'Neque enim quisquam unquam fuit tam tristis ac rigidus assecla virtutis et osor voluptatis.'
14 *Utopia*, 160–79.
15 *Utopia*, 144f., 160f.
16 *Utopia*, 162f.: 'Nunc vero non in omni voluptate felicitatem , sed in bona atque honesta sitam putant. Ad eam enim velut ad summum bonum naturam nostram ab ipsa virtute pertrahi, cui sola adversa factio felicitatem tribuit. Nempe virtutem definiunt secundum naturam vivere, ad id siquidem a deo institutos esse nos.'
17 *Utopia*, 164f.: 'Vitam ergo iucundam, inquiunt, id est voluptatem tanquam operationum omnium finem, ipsa nobis natura praescribit, ex cuius praescripto vivere virtutem defininiunt.'
18 *Utopia*, 162f.: 'Rationem porro mortales primum omnium in amorem ac venerationem divinae maiestatis incendere, cui debemus et quod sumus et quod compotes esse felicitatis possumus, secundum id

commonet atque excitat nos, ut vitam quam licet minime anxiam ac maxime laetam ducamus.'
19 *Utopia*, 166: 'Nam ut quicquid natura iucundum est ... non sensus modo, sed recta quoque ratio persequitur.'
20 *Utopia*, 176: 'gratique agnoscunt naturae parentis indulgentiam, quae foetus suos ad id quod necessitatis causa tam faciundum erat, etiam blandissima suavitate pelliceat.' Cf. also 164f.
21 *Utopia*, 162f., 164f., 166f.
22 *Utopia*, 166.
23 *Utopia*, 172f., 174f.
24 *Utopia*, 162f., 176f.
25 *Utopia*, 164f.
26 *Utopia*, 226f. (the Yale translation modified).
27 *Utopia*, 176–9.
28 *Utopia*, 160f. (the Yale translation modified).
29 *Utopia*, 216–37, esp. 224–7.
30 *Utopia*, 220f.
31 *Utopia*, 166f.
32 *Utopia*, 178f.
33 Hexter, *The Vision of Politics*, 88f., 120–37.
34 Plato, *Laws*, 739A–740A.
35 Allen, IV, Ep. 999. 2537. CWE 7.23.
36 I used the English rendering of *The First Voyage* by Vespucci in Robert M. Adams' edition and translation of *Utopia*, 2nd ed. (New York 1992), 104–7. For More's acquaintance with Vespucci and his awareness of the fictional character of that first voyage, see Baker-Smith, *More's Utopia*, 91f. See also *Utopia*, xxxi, cvi; and Surtz, *The Praise of Pleasure*, 23.
37 Allen, X, Ep. 2743.
38 LB VI 90f. See M.A. Screech's two lectures in *Colloquia Erasmiana Turonensia*, I 441–61, here 443f., 458.
39 See CEBR, s.v. François Rabelais, Jean Du Bellay, Petrus Decimarius, and Guillaume Pellicier. Rabelais still corresponded with Pellicier when the latter was the French ambassador in Venice and there too maintained contacts with dissidents, including Celio Secondo Curione, who subsequently fled Italy and lived in Basel. Pellicier himself was later charged with treason and heresy, but acquitted. See also Seidel Menchi, *Erasmo in Italia*, 267–9.
40 For Rabelais' popularity through the centuries, see Michael J. Heath, *Rabelais* (Tempe, AZ, 1996), 116–25. For Fischart, see Alfred Berchtold, *Bâle et l'Europe: Une histoire culturelle* (Lausanne 1990), II 687–91, 859.
41 Febvre, *The Problem of Unbelief*, 316, 326. Febvre's entire chapter 'Rabelais, Erasmus and the Philosophy of Christ' (307–33) gives evidence of Rabelais' debt to Erasmus and the affinity between their lives and, especially, their minds. See also Plattard, *L'Œuvre de Rabelais*, 191–3.

42 Febvre, *Unbelief*, 166–7, 317f. Screech, *Rabelais*, 45–7. Bietenholz, *Historia and Fabula*, 246, 370–2.
43 ASD I-3 151, II-5 168. Bietenholz, *Historia and Fabula*, 154–7. While the passage in *Sileni Alcibiadis* does not specifically refer to the Deluge, Erasmus was well aware of the corresponding Greek myth of Deucalion, and Lucian's having fun with that: LB I 755f.
44 Don Cameron Allen, *The Legend of Noah: Renaissance Rationalism in Art, Science and Letters* (Urbana, IL, 1949). Bietenholz, *Historia and Fabula*, 190–2, 197–201.
45 Febvre, *Unbelief*, 318.
46 Erasmus, *Modus orandi* and *Explanatio symboli*: ASD V-1 146f., 244–7. CWE 70.187f., 290–3.
47 Erasmus, LB VI 1112 F. Screech, *Rabelais* 134–7, also in *Colloquia Erasmiana Turonensia*, I 455–7.
48 Matt. 13:55. Also Allen, VI, Ep. 1679.93–103; VII, Ep. 1956; cf. Luke 1:42.
49 CWE 39. 355. ASD I-3 327.
50 CWE 39. 632f., 640. ASD I-3 478f., 482.
51 LB V 1327–36. Allen, V, Ep. 1391.
52 LB IX 1084 B: cf. ASD V-1 146f., CWE 70.187f. In the *Modus orandi* Erasmus takes on the Lutherans. In the case of the perpetual virginity of Mary they accepted the argument that something unscriptural must be believed, but rejected the same argument in the case of the adoration of the saints. But what if one rejected the argument in both cases? Erasmus did not say.
53 ASD I-3 524. CWE 40.706; cf. *Ecclesiastes*, LB V 861. Rabelais, *Tiers Livre*, chap. 19. Rabelais actually borrows the term *ichthuophagie* when mocking the friars in *Tiers Livre*, chap. 22.
54 See above, 138f.
55 Febvre, *Unbelief*, 315. Rabelais, *Gargantua*, chap. 57: 'FAY CE QUE VOULDRAS, parce que gens liberes, bien nez, bien instruictz, conversans en compaignies honnestes, ont par nature un instinct et aguillon, qui tousjours les poulse à faictz vertueux et retire de vice, lequel ilz nommoient honneur.' LB X 1454f: 'Fateor in quibusdam ingeniis bene natis ac educatis minus est pronitatis [ad malum]. Maxima proclivitatis pars est non ex natura, sed ex corrupta institutione, ex improbo convictu, ex assuetudine peccandi malitiaque voluntatis.' CWE 77.575.
56 LB IX 699f., 1081f.
57 Erasmus, *De praeparatione ad mortem*, ASD V-1 354: 'Hoc est Barathrum desperationis, et, ut Apocalypsis loquitur, "mors secunda." Cogitet quisque qualis sit illa vita, ubi summum malorum est immortalitas, ubi magna cruciatus pars est daeomnum et impiorum hominum societas, ubi ignis numquam exstinguendus, ad quem noster collatus mera glacies est; adde quod illic incendium est minima

dolorum portio, qui tamen tanti sunt, ut ab hominis intellectu comprehendi non possint, sicut nec piorum felicitas.' CWE 70.408.
58 Rabelais, *Pantagruel*, chap. 30.
59 Rabelais, *Quart Livre*, chaps. 45–7. LB IV 320 B.
60 Screech, *Rabelais*, 235, 243–5. Allen, III, Ep. 694.
61 Allen, III, Ep. 901; IV, Epp. 1070, 1075; V, Ep. 1529. Cf. also a related case of Johannes Oecolampadius. Erasmus used almost the same words to discourage his experiment with monasticism, Ep. 1102. In the colloquy *Apotheosis Capnionis* a saintly Franciscan, apparently Conrad Pellicanus, is worthy of receiving a heavenly vision: ASD I-3 269. CWE 39.250.
62 Allen, II, Epp. 335, 384, 466. Screech, *Rabelais*, 21.
63 Rabelais, *Quart Livre*, chaps. 48, 54; cf. *Tiers Livre*, chap. 12. Alain Boureau, *La papesse Jeanne* (Paris 1988), 39–41. Bietenholz, *Historia and Fabula*, 97–107.
64 CWE 27. 138f. ASD IV-3 172, 174.
65 Allen, III, Ep. 739.
66 Allen, III, Ep. 872 CWE 6.137–9 and note.
67 Allen, III, Epp. 608, 969; V, Ep. 1352.
68 ASD V-1 146. CWE 70.186f.
69 Compare Erasmus' portrait by Quentin Metsys (1517) with that of Jerome by Jan van Eyck (c. 1442). Peter G. Bietenholz, 'Erasmus von Rotterdam und der Kult des Heiligen Hieronymus,' in *Poesis et Pictura: Festschrift für Dieter Wuttke*, ed. S. Füssel and J. Knape (Baden-Baden 1989), 191–221.
70 See especially Allen, X, Ep. 2700. Tracy, *Erasmus of the Low Countries*, 136f. Bietenholz, *History and Biography*, 66–8.
71 *Adagia*, III iii 1, ASD II-5 162. Note also the presence of Epictetus, who had lorded it in Rabelais' luxury-resort hell: above p. 202.
72 Rabelais, *Gargantua*, chap. 23f.; *Pantagruel*, chap. 8. Plattard, *L'Œuvre de Rabelais*, 171–259.
73 Rabelais, *Gargantua*, chap. 21; *Quart Livre*, chap. 49.
74 ASD I-3 537–51. CWE 40.763–95. Rabelais, *Tiers Livre*, chap. 21. Oral confession is treated disrespectfully both in Erasmus' colloquy *Naufragium* and in Rabelais' *Quart Livre*, chaps. 19 and 49.
75 ASD I-3 325–32. CWE 39.351–67. Rabelais, *Quart Livre*, chaps. 19–22. Pantagruel is the first to realize that they are saved, like the fearless young mother in Erasmus' *Naufragium*, who is the first to reach safety.
76 Rabelais, *Quart Livre*, chaps. 18f., 21. Luke 23:46; John 19:28–30. *In manus* is also found in *Gargantua*, chap. 27, in a context that will hardly suggest blasphemy.
77 Rabelais, *Quart Livre*, chap. 49. The talk of the beggars in chap. 50 may not intend blasphemy, although Pantagruel thinks that it does.
78 Marcel de Grève, *L'interprétation de Rabelais au XVIe siècle* (*Études rabelaisiennes*, III) (Geneva 1961), passim; Grève, 'Rabelais et les libertins,'

139 and passim; Anne Lake Prescott, *Imagining Rabelais in Renaissance England* (New Haven 1998), 75–85 and passim.
79 According to Michael Screech, Rabelais' Pantagruel recognizes the court fool Triboullet and Judge Bridoye as true fools in Christ, while Panurge gradually slides into the kind of folly triggered by Satan. Walter Kaiser, however, points out how Panurge, even when wrapped up in his maddening dilemma over marriage, can still extol the care and kindness of Mother Nature in a manner worthy of Mistress Folly. To Kaiser, Pantagruel himself combines in his person the Epicurean fool and the fool in Christ of Erasmus' *Moriae encomium*. However that may be, these are apt demonstrations of the immense potential for evoking responses that radiated from Erasmus' masterpiece. Rabelais, *Tiers Livre*, chap. 15; Screech, *Rabelais*, 235, 243, 260–81; Kaiser, *Praisers*, 135, 159, 179–81, and passim.
80 ASD IV-3 112–18, 138–68. CWE 27:108–11, 122–35; cf. the preceding note.
81 CWE 27:111: 'sent from hell by the vengeful furies whenever they let loose their snakes and assail the hearts of men with lust for war, insatiable thirst for gold, the disgrace of forbidden love, parricide, incest, sacrilege, or some other sort of evil, or when they pursue the guilty, conscience-stricken soul with their avenging spirits and flaming brands of terror.'
82 CWE 27.108, 111. ASD IV-3 112, 118.
83 ASD IV-3 189–94. CWE 27.149–53.
84 *Index des livres interdits*, ed. J.M. de Bujanda, VI: *Index de l'Inquisition espagnole, 1583, 1584* (Sherbrooke 1993), 1063 and passim.
85 Seidel Menchi, *Erasmo in Italia*, 286–306 and passim.
86 Cervantes, *Don Quijote*, part I, prologue (1.11): 'It sometimes happens that a father has an ugly son with no redeeming grace whatever, yet love will draw a veil over the parental eyes which then behold only cleverness and beauty in place of defects, and in speaking to his friends he will make those defects out to be signs of comeliness and intellect.' Compare this with Moria's words quoted above, p. 129. See Antonio Vilanova, *Erasmo y Cervantes* (Barcelona 1989). Among the papers republished in this volume, see especially 'La *Moria* de Erasmo y el Prologo del *Quijote*,' 64–76. Since a Spanish translation of the *Moriae encomium* did not exist at the time, Vilanova suggests that Cervantes may have read it in an Italian translation. For Spanish editions and translations of works by Erasmus, see Marcel Bataillon, *Erasme et l'Espagne. Nouvelle édition* (Geneva 1991), II, 396–408.
87 Cervantes, *Don Quijote*, I, chap. 17; II, chap. 22 (1.124f.; 2.655). ASD IV-3 118, 190. CWE 27. 111, 150. The theme of a happy state of delusion rudely ended by the return to normalcy was first explored by Cervantes in *El licenciado Vidriera*.

88 For cautiously suggested echoes of Erasmus' *Lingua* (early on translated into Castilian) and *Adagia* in Cervantes' bold *Colloquio de los perros*, see Close, *Cervantes and the Comic Mind*, 32f., 48, 54.
89 We may assume that Don Quijote speaks for Cervantes when he often expresses himself as he does at the end of *Don Quijote*, I, chap. 7 (1.62): 'Leave everything to God, Sancho, and he will give you whatever is most fitting.'
90 Examples: in *Don Quijote*, I, chap. 8 (1.67): two Benedictine monks, having been exposed to Don Quijote's aggressive madness, depart, 'making more signs of the cross than the devil would be able to carry upon his back.' I, chap. 30 (1.263): Sancho refers to the imaginary 'lady Dulcinea, whom I love and reverence as I would a relic – not that I mean to say she is one.' II, chaps. 31f: the 'solemn-faced ecclesiastic' makes a laughing stock of himself. II, chap. 58 (2.883f.): St Martin is too smart to give his whole coat away.
91 In addition to the books of Anthony Close, *The Romantic Approach to 'Don Quijote'* (Cambridge 1978) and *Cervantes and the Comic Mind*, see August Rüegg, *Erasmisches im 'Don Quijote' des Cervantes* (Basel 1943) (Spanish trans. in *Anales Cervantinos* 4 [1954]: 1–40).
92 Cervantes, *Don Quijote*, I, chaps. 23f. (1.184–6).
93 Cervantes, *Don Quijote*, II, chap. 1 (2.514–17).
94 Cervantes, *Don Quijote*, II, chap. 15 (2.601).
95 Cervantes, *Don Quijote*, I, chaps. 17, 19; II, chap. 11 (1.126, 141f.; 2.576).
96 Cervantes, *Don Quijote*, II, chap. 31 (2.709).
97 Cervantes, *Don Quijote*, I, chap. 18; II, chap. 29 (1.134f.; 2.701–3).
98 Cervantes, *Don Quijote*, I, chap. 22.
99 Cervantes, *Don Quijote*, I, chaps. 25, 47 (1.199, 421).
100 Cervantes, *Don Quijote*, II, chaps. 30–57.
101 Cervantes, *Don Quijote*, II, chap. 17 (2.611–17).
102 Cervantes, *Don Quijote*, I, chaps. 19, 20, 21, 23 (1.142, 147f., 160f., 182).
103 Cervantes, *Don Quijote*, I, chaps. 30f.; II, chap. 10 (1.265–9, 2.566–73).
104 Cervantes, *Don Quijote*, I, chap. 4 (1.45). I cannot see any parallel here to Rabelais' gibe at the Sorbonists; see above, 199.
105 Cervantes, *Don Quijote*, II, chap. 33 (2.731f.).
106 Cervantes, *Don Quijote*, II, chaps. 41, 44, 58 (2.773, 790, 886).
107 Cervantes, *Don Quijote*, II, chaps. 11f. (2.580; cf. 577f.).
108 Cervantes, *Don Quijote*, II, chap. 33 (2.734).
109 Cervantes, *Don Quijote*, II, chap. 54.
110 Cervantes, *Don Quijote*, I, chap. 31 (1.270f.).
111 Cervantes, *Don Quijote*, I, chap. 26 (1.215).
112 *Ben Jonson*, VIII 596. Erasmus, LB IX 1217 D, cf. X 1279 E; CWE 76.12, cf. 170. *Luther's Works*, 33. 53.
113 *Ben Jonson*, VIII 633f. (*Timber*, 2306f., 2334–9). Allen, II, Ep. 337, esp. 167–75. Cf. Kaiser, *Praisers of Folly*, 30.

114 *Ben Jonson*, cit. VIII 625. ASD IV-3 74f. Allen, II, Ep. 337:542–7. Erasmus later made the same point in his *Lingua*, ASD IV-1a 93, and his *Apothegmata*, LB IV 162 D. Walter Kaiser also found it in Juan Luis Vives: *Praisers of Folly*, 40.

115 *Volpone*, Act 1.156–71: 'Fools they are the only nation / Worth mens envy or admiration; / Free from care, or sorrow-taking, / Selves, and others merry-making: / All they speake, or doe, is sterling, / Your Foole, he is your great mans darling, / And your ladies sport, and pleasure; / Tongue, and bable are his treasure. / E'ene his face begetteth laughter, / And he speakes truth, free from slaughter; / He's the grace of every feast, / And, sometimes, the chiefest guest; / Hath his trencher, and his stoole, / When wit waites upon the foole. / O, who would not bee / Hee, hee, hee?' *Ben Jonson*, IX 693 (with an attempt to find matching passages in the *Moriae encomium*). See also Kaiser, *Praisers of Folly*, 296 and passim; and for other Erasmian echoes in Jonson's work, D. Hayward Brock, *A Ben Jonson Companion* (Bloomington, IN, 1983), 90f.

116 It is true that Moria talks of monarchs willing to gain power at the cost of parricide and of theologians willing 'to think up means whereby it is possible for a man to draw a murderous sword and plunge it into his brother's vitals without loss of the supreme charity which ... every Christian owes his neighbour.' But these statements are isolated and no match for the foul language of Jonson's play, nor for one character's willingness to prostitute his own wife amid threats to butcher her, indeed to perform an anatomy on her corpse. Physicians are said to kill 'with as much licence as a judge.' On another count, a character is counselled: 'for your religion, profess none / But wonder at the diversity of all. Nick Machiavel and Monsieur Bodin both / Were of this mind.' See CWE 27.135, 139 and *Volpone*, I.332f., II iii, IV i.22f., 27f.

117 Frank McCombie, '*Hamlet* and the *Moriae encomium*,' 67. For a general survey see Rita Severi, 'Tracks: The Erasmian Legacy and Shakespeare,' in Corti, ed., *Silenos*, 87–113.

118 For example: 2 *Henry IV*, I ii 172f.: 'For my voice I have lost it with hallooing and singing of anthems' (Chaloner, 87.14–17). *Hamlet*, III iv 56–62: Jove, Mars, Mercury; and V ii 158: 'the fall of a sparrow' (Chaloner, 65f., 113.23). *Lear*, IV iv 3–6: 'nettles' and equivalents of 'furrow weeds,' 'hardocks,' 'cukoo-flowers,' and 'darnel' (Chaloner, 13). See Claudia Corti, 'Erasmus' Folly and Shakespeare's Fools,' in Corti, ed., *Silenos*, 13–40. McCombie, '*Hamlet* and the *Moriae encomium*.' Jürgen Schäfer, 'Falstaff's Voice,' *Notes and Queries* (April 1969): 135f.

119 ASD IV-3 104 (somewhat amplified in Chaloner's translation, 37f.), cf. 172.

120 See *Ecclesiastes* and *Purgatio adversus epistolam Lutheri*, LB V 937 C, X 1546 E.

121 CWE 27. 111. ASD IV-3 118.
122 CWE 27. 110. ASD IV-3 116.
123 For the following: Walter Naumann, *Die Dramen Shakespeares* (Darmstadt 1978), 243, 250, 261.
124 CWE 27. 153. ASD IV-3 194.
125 Kaiser, *Praisers of Folly*, 209.
126 CWE 27. 142. ASD IV-3 178f.
127 ASD IV-3 170. CWE 27.136f.
128 Kaiser, *Praisers of Folly*, 235.
129 'If it should come to the ear of the court how I have been ... washed and cudgelled, they would melt me out of my fat, drop by drop.' (IV v 77–80).

CONCLUSION

1 Augustijn, *Erasmus*, 192. Silvana Seidel Menchi, 'Érasme et son lecteur,' in *Colloque Érasmien de Liège*, (Paris 1987), 31–45, here 40f. Mansfield, *Erasmus in the Twentieth Century*, 203–5, 207f. Gilly, 'Erasmo, la Reforma radical,' 249f.
2 Rummel, *Annotations*, discusses a number of corrections Erasmus made in consecutive editions of his New Testament and the Annotations, e.g., in response to criticisms by Lee and Zúñiga (*Annotations* 123-35). In 1521 he admitted to Justus Jonas, referring to the advent of the Lutheran Reformation, 'had I known that a generation such as this would appear, I should either not have written at all some things, or should have written them differently' (CWE 8.209; Allen, IV, Ep. 1202.232f.). In 1526 Erasmus wrote much the same about the *Moria*: LB X 1559 F.
3 Note on Rom. 5:14, LB VI 591 C (added in 1527), CWE 56.163-7. The last note on Matthew (LB VI 148 D) shows that already by 1516 Erasmus had looked, and kept looking in vain, for further patristic commentaries on that passage that to him became uniquely relevant with regard to baptism. A confusing statement in Erasmus' note induced the Spanish monks to believe that he was questioning the resurrection of the flesh, but that was not his concern, as he could easily show by explaining the point more fully: LB IX 1079.
4 Erasmus, *De concordia*, LB V 505 C. 1 Cor. 1:14–16; Acts 16:14–15.
5 LB VII 855f.: 'Quum hodie satis esse putemus aquula modo tingi, ut subito fias absolutus Christianus.'
6 LB IX 1060f. The Spanish monks also quoted a similar and equally provocative statement in Erasmus' colloquy *Convivium religiosum*.
7 Coogan, *Erasmus, Lee*, 35-51. In *Hyperaspistes II* Erasmus argued against Luther that Rom. 5:12–21, like Luke 12:48, applied 'to the transgressions of mankind, not to what they call original sin': CWE 77.372, LB X 1354 F.
8 LB VI 584-91, here 591 C.

9 LB VI 148: 'Euntes ergo docete omnes gentes: baptizantes eos in nomine Patris et Filii et Spiritus Sancti; docentes eos servare omnia quaecunque praecepi vobis.' Cf. Mark 16:15–16 (LB VI 214): 'Et dicebat eis: ite in mundum universum et praedicate evangelium omni creaturae. Qui crediderit et baptizatus fuerit, salvus erit.'
10 LB VII 145f.
11 LB VII 672f., CWE 50.
12 LB VII 701f., CWE 50.
13 LB IX 497 D, 557-65, 1061f.
14 LB IX 558 C–D, 559 A.
15 Friesen, *Erasmus*, 20–42. Gilly, 'Erasmo, la Reforma radical,' 246–57. Cornelis Augustijn, *Erasmus: Der Humanist als Theologe und Kirchenreformer* (Leiden 1996), 325–51.
16 Abraham Friesen, *Thomas Müntzer, the Destroyer of the Godless: The Making of a Sixteenth-Century Revolutionary* (Berkeley 1990), 95, 122. Gilly, 'Erasmo, la Reforma radical,' 253f.
17 Zwingli, *Werke*, VII 440, 494, 499f. Allen, V, Ep. 1292, introd.
18 Zwingli, *Werke*, IV 578.
19 Zwingli, *Werke*, IV 578. *Briefe und Akten zum Leben Oekolampads*, ed. E. Staehelin (Leipzig 1927–34), I 343.
20 Zwingli, *Werke*, IV 292–337.
21 Hubmaier, 94f., 128-31.
22 *Quellen zur Geschichte der Täufer*, VII, *Elsass, I. Teil*, ed. M. Krebs et al. (Gütersloh 1959), 46 (letter from Hubmaier to Johannes Sapidus, 26 October 1521).
23 Zwingli, *Werke*, IV 577–647.
24 Zwingli, *Werke*, IV 622–4. Hubmaier, 139, 223f. Cf. LB VII 146 A–B, 674.
25 'Hier zaigt Erasmus offenlich an, das der Tauff für die unterrichten im glauben und nit für die iungen kindlen von Christo eingesetzt ist': Balthasar Hubmaier, *Schriften*, ed. G. Westin and T. Bergsten (*Quellen zur Geschichte der Täufer*, IX) (Gütersloh 1962), 231–3, cf. 209, 249, 267. Hubmaier, 252f., 255f.
26 Friesen, 53–75.
27 TRE 11.199f.
28 Servetus, *Christianismi restitutio*, 525-9, 537. For Franck, see above, 22f. Cf. Gilly, 'Erasmo, la Reforma radical', 253, 257.
29 See, e.g., Allen, V, Ep. 1369.38-41; VIII, Ep. 2134.212-27 (a most striking statement) and Ep. 2341; X, Ep. 2853.42-9. *De concordia*, LB V 505. In January 1528 a prominent Catholic, Johannes Cochlaeus, urged Erasmus to write a pamphlet against the Anabaptists, listing outrageous accusations against them: Allen, VII, Ep. 1928.
30 See above, 22.
31 See above, 202f. Erasmus, *De praeparatione ad mortem*, ASD V-1 354. CWE 70.407f.

32 See below, index to New Testament references. See also Rummel, *Annotations*, 132-4, and *Catholic Critics*, I 105, 128; II 91, 130, 132.
33 In 1520 he had replied to Lee's charge that he was reviving the Arian heresy: 'Cum nulla sit haeresis magis extincta quam Arrianorum, mirum unde sic metuat Leus' (LB IX 277 E).
34 LB VI 1079-81.
35 LB IX 275 B-C.
36 LB VI 1081 E: 'Non igitur constringit locus nisi compellat Orthodoxorum auctoritas et Ecclesiae praescriptio, docens hunc locum aliter exponi non posse. Pium autem est nostrum sensum semper Ecclesiae judicio submittere, simul atque claram illius sententiam audierimus. Nec interim tamen nefas est, citra contentionem scrutari verum, ut Deus aliis alia patefacit.'
37 'Non hoc ibi vertebatur in dubium, an Patris, Filii et Spirtu Sancti sit eadem essentia; nam id ubique mihi convenit cum his, qui locum hunc arroserunt, sed illud ventilabatur, utra lectio sit Apostolicae veriatis, nostra, quae nunc utimur vulgo, an Graecorum' (LB IX 1030 C-D).
38 Luther, *De servo arbitrio*, in WA 18.701, 741f. *Luther's Works*, 33.163, 224. *Hyperaspistes II*, LB X 1392 E, 1461 A. CWE 77.450, 587.
39 ASD IX-1 339 (*Epistola ad fratres inferioris Germaniae*).
40 ASD IX-1 427-83. WA, *Briefe*, 7.27-40, esp. 34f. On 22 May 1534 Nikolaus Koler wrote to Erasmus, reminding him how Luther had called him, amid other unflattering names, an Arian: Allen, X, Ep. 2936.62.
41 See, e.g., the questioning of the Anabaptist Herman van Flekwijk, 1569 (Coogan, *Erasmus, Lee*, 68-70), or the pamphlet *Le Jésuite sécularisé*, 1683, in *Formazione storica della alterità*, II 630.
42 See above, 37f.
43 LB VI 205 E-F, 716 E-F, cf. 316 E-F; IX 1064-6. Rummel, *Annotations*, 156-60.
44 Erasmus, *Enchiridion*, LB V 30 E-F, CWE 66.70f.; *De ecclesiae concordia*, ASD V-3 309.
45 Augustijn, *Erasmus*, 150-3, 189, 198.
46 In 1525, in a dramatic exchange of letters (Allen, VI, Epp. 1637-40), he swore solemn oaths that he had never supported the Swiss, but also admitted to ridding himself of 'fleeting thoughts' and conducting private conversations with learned friends, both apparently swaying from the Catholic position: CWE 11.347f.
47 'Nisi me moveret tantus Ecclesiae consensus, possim Oecolampadii sententiam pedibus discedere; nunc in eo persisto quod mihi tradidit Scripturarum interpres Ecclesia' (Allen, VIII, Ep. 2175, to Justus Decius, 8 June 1529).
48 Allen, VIII, Ep. 2133.64-8 (letter to Juan Vergara, 24 March 1529).
49 *Calvini opera*, 49.489, cf. 45.704-11.
50 Beza, *Novum Testamentum*, 215 (note on 1 Cor. 11:24).
51 See above, 19 n. 14.

52 See, e.g., Tracy, *Erasmus of the Low Countries*, 143f.
53 Arguments about Matt. 16:18 were at the centre of the first part of the Leipzig Disputation, 1519. Luther identified the rock with Christ, but on one occasion came close to Erasmus by also referring to the Christians at large: 'Ideo illud Ambrosii dicentis Petrum esse petram facile admitto, cum et quilibet Christianus sit petra propter Christum, in cuius soliditate firmatur et unum cum eo efficitur' (WA 59.465). See also WA 2.286, 70.78.
54 LB VI 88; cf. VII 92 F, 93 D.
55 LB IX 361f., 1066f.
56 Hubmaier, 290, cf. 352. Cf. Allen, VI, Ep. 1540.
57 *Calvini opera*, 45.476f.
58 CWE 11.xi–xii, 76.114. LB X 1256 D–F.
59 *Flugschriften der Bauernkriegszeit*, ed. A. Laube et al. (Berlin 1975), 27, 33, 48, 59, 65, 135.
60 Allen, IV, Ep. 1039.147–54. CWE 7.124. Cf. Allen, VI, Ep. 1653.29-33. The demand for elected priests comes first in the famous Twelve Articles manifesto of the German peasants.

Works Repeatedly Cited

Augustijn, Cornelis. *Erasmus: His Life, Works, and Influence.* Trans. J.C. Grayson. Toronto 1991.
Bainton, Roland H. *Hunted Heretic: The Life and Death of Michael Servetus, 1511–1553.* Boston 1953.
Baker-Smith, Dominic. *More's Utopia.* London 1991.
Belin, Christian. *L'œuvre de Pierre Charron, 1541–1603. Littérature et théologie de Montaigne à Port-Royal.* Paris 1995.
Best, Paul. *Mysteries discovered. Or a Mercuriall Picture pointing out the way from Babylon to the holy City ... by me Paul Best, Prisoner in the Gatehouse, Westminster,* n.p. 1647.
Beza, Theodore, ed. and trans. *Novum Jesu Christi Testamentum.* Geneva 1556.
Bietenholz, Peter G. *Daniel Zwicker, 1612–1678: Peace, Tolerance and God the One and Only.* Florence 1997.
– *Historia and Fabula. Myths and Legends in Historical Thought from Antiquity to the Modern Age.* Leiden 1994.
– *History and Biography in the Work of Erasmus of Rotterdam.* Geneva 1966.
Biondi, Albano. 'La giustificazione della simulazione nel Cinquecento.' In *Eresia e Riforma,* 5–68.
Brachin, Pierre. 'Vox clamantis in deserto: Réflexions sur le pacifisme d'Érasme.' In *Colloquia Turonensia,* I 247–75.
Bultot, R. 'Érasme, Épicure et le "De contemptu mundi".' *Scrinium Erasmianum,* II 205–38.
Burckhardt, Jacob. *The Civilization of the Renaissance in Italy.* Trans. S.C.G. Middlemore. London 1960.
Calvin, Jean. *Calvini opera quae supersunt omnia.* Ed. G. Baum et al. (Corpus Reformatorum). Brunswick–Berlin 1863–1900; repr. 1964.
Cantimori, Delio. *Eretici italiani del Cinquecento e altri scritti.* Ed. A. Prosperi. Turin 1992.
Cardano, Girolamo. *Opera omnia.* Lyon 1663; repr. with introduction by A. Buck 1966.

Castellio, Sebastianus. *Concerning Heretics ... A anonymous work attributed to Sebastian Castellio.* Trans. and ed. R.H. Bainton. 2nd ed. New York 1965.
- *De arte dubitandi et confidendi, ignorandi et sciendi.* Ed. E. Feist Hirsch. Leiden 1981.
- *De haereticis an sint persequendi et omnino quomodo sit cum eis agendum, Lutheri et Brentii aliorumque multorum tum veterum tum recentiorum sententiae. Réproduction en fac-simile de l'édition de 1554.* Ed. S. van der Woude. Geneva 1954.

Cavaillé, Jean-Pierre. *Dis/simulations. Jean-César Vanini, François La Mothe le Vayer, Gabriel Naudé, Louis Machon et Torquato Accetto. Religion, morale et politique au XVIIe siècle.* Paris 2002.

Celsi, Mino. *In haereticis coërcendis quatenus progredi liecat – Poems – Correspondence.* Ed. P.G. Bietenholz. Naples–Chicago 1982.

Cervantes, Miguel de. *The Ingenious Gentleman Don Quijote de la Mancha.* Trans. Samuel Putnam. New York 1949. (References are by part and chapter, with the volume and pages of the Putnam translation added in brackets.)

Chaloner, Thomas, trans. *The Praise of Folly.* Ed. H. Miller (Early English Text Society). London 1965.

Chillingworth, William. *The Works of William Chillingworth.* Oxford 1838.

Close, Anthony. *Cervantes and the Comic Mind of His Age.* Oxford 2000.

Coogan, Robert. *Erasmus, Lee and the Correction of the Vulgate: The Shaking of the Foundations.* Geneva 1992.

Corti, Claudia, ed. *Silenos: Erasmus in Elizabethan Literature.* Pacini Editore 1998.

Curione, Celio Secondo. *De amplitudine beati regni Dei dialogi sive libri duo.* Gouda 1614.

Darmon, Jean-Charles. *Philosophie épicurienne et littérature au XVIIe siècle en France.* Paris 1998.

De Breen, Daniel. *Breves in Vetus et Novum Testamentum annotationes.* Amsterdam 1664.
- *Compendium theologiae Erasmicae.* Rotterdam 1677.

Dejung, Christoph. 'Sebastian Franck.' In *Bibliotheca Dissidentium,* ed. A. Séguenny et al., VII. Baden-Baden 1986. 39–119.

DeWitt, Norman Wentworth. *Epicurus and His Philosophy.* Minneapolis 1954.

Di Rienzo, Eugenio, *L'Aquila e lo Scarabeo. Culture e conflitti nella Francia del Rinascimento e del Barocco.* Rome 1988.

Domański, Juliusz. 'Explicatio primae partis primi capitis Evangelii Ioannis de Fauste Socin et l'exégèse d'Érasme.' In *Movimenti ereticali in Italia e in Polonia nei secoli XVI-XVII,* Florence 1974. 77–102.

Falkland, Lucius Cary, Lord. *Discourse on Infallibility, with an Answer to it and his Lordship's Reply.* Ed. Thomas Triplet. London 1651.

Febvre, Lucien. *The Problem of Unbelief in the Sixteenth Century: The Religion of Rabelais.* Trans. Beatrice Gottlieb. Cambridge, MA, 1982 (first French ed. 1942).

Ferguson, John, and Jackson P. Hershbell. 'Epicureanism under the Roman Empire.' In *Aufstieg und Niedergang der Römischen Welt* 36-4, 2257–2327. Berlin–New York 1990.

Franck, Sebastian. *Chronica, Zeitbůch unnd Geschichtbibell*. Ulm 1536; repr. 1969.

– *Krieg Büchlin des Friedes*. Frankfurt am Main 1550; repr. 1975.

Friedrich, Hugo. *Montaigne*. Ed. and trans. Ph. Desan and D. Eng. Berkeley 1991.

Friesen, Abraham. *Erasmus, the Anabaptists, and the Great Commission*. Grand Rapids, MI, 1998.

Garin, Eugenio. *La cultura filosofica del Rinascimento italiano*. Florence 1961.

Gauss, Julia. 'Der junge Michael Servet.' *Zwingliana* 12 (1966): 410–59.

Gilly, Carlos. 'Erasmo, la Reforma radical y los heterodoxos radicales españoles.' In *Les Lletres hispàniques als segles XVI, XVII i XVIII*, ed. Tomàs Martínez Romero, Castelló de la Plana 2005. 225–376.

– *Spanien und der Basler Buchdruck bis 1600. Ein Querschnitt durch die spanische Geistesgeschichte aus der Sicht einer europäischen Buchdruckerstadt*. Basel 1985.

Gregory, Tullio. *Genèse de la raison classique de Charron à Descartes*, transl. M. Raiola. Paris 2000.

Grève, Marcel de. 'Rabelais et les libertins du XVIIe siècle.' *Études rabelaisiennes* I, 120–50. Geneva 1956.

Guggisberg, Hans R. *Sebastian Castellio, 1515–1563. Humanist und Verteidiger der religiösen Toleranz im konfessionellen Zeitalter*. Göttingen 1997.

Hexter, J.H. *The Vision of Politics on the Eve of the Reformation: More, Macchiavelli, and Seyssel*. New York 1973.

Hubmaier, Balthasar. *Balthasar Hubmaier, Theologian of Anabaptism*. Trans. and ed. H.W. Pipkin and J.H. Yoder. Scottdale, PA, 1989.

Israel, Jonathan I. *Radical Enlightenment. Philosophy and the Making of Modernity, 1650–1750*. Oxford 2001.

Jones, Howard. *The Epicurean Tradition*. London 1989.

Jonson, Ben. *Ben Jonson*. Ed. C.H. Herford, Percy Simpson, and Evelyn Simpson. Oxford 1925–52.

Kaiser, Walter. *Praisers of Folly: Erasmus, Rabelais, Shakespeare*. Cambridge, MA, 1963.

Kolakowski, Leszek. *Chrétiens sans Église. La conscience religieuse et le lien confessionel au XVIIe siècle*, transl. Anna Posner. 2nd ed. Paris 1987.

Kommoss, Rudolf. *Sebastian Franck und Erasmus von Rotterdam*. Berlin 1934; repr. 1967.

Kraye, Jill. 'Moral Philosophy.' In *The Cambridge History of Renaissance Philosophy*, ed. Charles B. Schmitt and Quentin Skinner, 303–86. Cambridge 1988.

Kutter, Markus. *Celio Secondo Curione. Sein Leben und sein Werk (1503–1569)*. Basel 1955.

Le Clerc, Jean. *Epistolario*. Ed. Maria Grazia and Mario Sina. Florence 1987–97.
Liebing, Heinz. 'Die Schriftauslegung Sebastian Castellios.' In Liebing, *Humanismus, Reformation, Konfession. Beiträge zur Kirchengeschichte*, ed. W. Bienert et al. Marburg 1986, 11–124.
Locke, John. *A Paraphrase and Notes on the Epistles of St. Paul to the Galatians, 1 and 2 Corinthians, Romans, Ephesians*. Ed. Arthur W. Wainwright. Oxford 1987.
Luther, Martin. *Luther's Works*. Ed. J. Pelikan et al. St Louis–Philadelphia 1955–.
Mansfield, Bruce. *Erasmus in the Twentieth Century: Interpretations c. 1920–2000*. Toronto 2003.
– *Phoenix of His Age: Interpretations of Erasmus c. 1550 – 1750*. Toronto 1979.
Margolin, Jean-Claude. 'Guy Patin, lecteur d'Érasme.' In *Colloquia Turonensia* I, 323–58.
McCombie, Frank. '*Hamlet* and the *Moriae encomium*.' *Shakespeare Survey* 27 (1974): 59–69.
McLachlan, H. John. *Socinianism in Seventeenth-Century England*. London 1951.
Milton, John. *Complete Prose Works of John Milton*. New Haven 1953–82.
Montaigne, Michel de. *The Complete Essays of Montaigne*. Trans. Donald.M. Frame. Stanford 1958.
More, Thomas. *The Yale Edition of the Works of St Thomas More*. New Haven, CT, 1963–76.
Murr, Sylvia. 'Gassendi's Scepticism as a Religious Attitude.' In *Scepticism and Irreligion in the Seventeenth and Eighteenth Centuries*, ed. R.H. Popkin et al. Leiden 1993. 12–30.
Newton, Isaac. *The Correspondence of Sir Isaac Newton*. Ed. H.W. Turnbull. London 1959–77.
– *Theological Manuscripts*. Ed. H. McLachlan. Liverpool 1950.
[Nye, Stephen], *A Brief History of the Unitarians Called also Socinians, in Four Letters Written to a Friend*. N.p. 1687.
Panizza, Letizia. 'Valla's *De voluptate ac de vero bono* and Erasmus' *Stultitiae laus*: Renewing Christian Ethics.' *Erasmus of Rotterdam Society Yearbook Fifteen* (1995): 1–25.
Patin, Guy. *Lettres choisies*. 5 vols. The Hague 1707; (*Nouveau recueil*) Rotterdam 1725.
– *Lettres du temps de la Fronde*. Ed. André Thérive. Paris 1921.
Penn, William. *A Collection of William Penn*. London 1726, with index, 1730; repr. 1974.
– *The Select Works of William Penn*. London 1825; repr. 1971.
Plattard, Jean. *L'Œuvre de Rabelais (Sources, Invention et Composition)*. Paris 1967 (first ed. 1909).
Popkin, Richard H. *The History of Scepticism: From Savonarola to Bayle*. Oxford 2002.

Quast, Bruno. *Sebastian Francks 'Kriegbüchlin des Frides.' Studien zum radikalreformatorischen Spiritualismus.* Tübingen–Basel, 1993.
Rabelais, François. *Œuvres completes.* Ed. Pierre Jourda. Paris 1962. (In view of the many fine editions of Rabelais, he will here be cited by the name of the writing and the number of the chapter.)
Renaudet, Augustin. *Érasme et l'Italie.* Geneva 1954.
Rotondò, Antonio. *Studi e ricerche di storia ereticale italiana del Cinquecento.* Turin 1974.
Rummel, Erika. *Erasmus and His Catholic Critics.* Nieuwkoop 1989.
– *Erasmus' Annotations on the New Testament: From Philologist to Theologian.* Toronto 1986.
Screech, Michael A. *Ecstasy and the Praise of Folly.* London 1980.
– *Rabelais.* Ithaca, NY, 1979.
Seidel Menchi, Silvana. *Erasmo in Italia, 1520–1580.* Turin 1987.
Servetus, Michael. *Christianismi restitutio.* [Vienne] 1553; repr. Frankfurt am Main 1966.
– *De Trinitatis erroribus libri septem.* [Haguenau] 1531; repr. Frankfurt am Main 1965.
– *The Two Treatises of Servetus on the Trinity.* Ed. and trans. E.M Wilbur. Cambridge, MA, 1932.
Shakespeare, William. *The Norton Shakespeare Based on the Oxford Edition.* Ed. St. Greenblatt et al. New York 1997.
Sozzini, Lelio. *Opere.* Ed. A. Rotondò. Florence 1986.
Surtz, Edward. *The Praise of Pleasure: Philosophy, Education, and Communism in More's Utopia.* Cambridge, MA, 1957.
Tenenti, Alberto. *Credenze, ideologie, libertinismi tra Medioevo ed Età moderna.* Bologna 1978.
Tracy, James D. *Erasmus of the Low Countries.* Berkeley 1996.
Trapman, Johannes 'Le millénariste Daniel Brenius (1594–1664) et le Socinianisme.' *Moreana* 35, nos. 135–6 (1998): 219–31.
Trevor-Roper, Hugh. *Catholics, Anglicans and Puritans: Seventeenth Century Essays.* Chicago 1988.
Valla, Lorenzo. *On Pleasure / De voluptate.* Intr. and trans. A. Kent Hieatt and Maristella de Panizza Lorch [with the Latin text established by the latter]. New York 1977.
Walker, D.P. *The Decline of Hell: Seventeenth-Century Discussions of Eternal Torment.* London 1964.
Williams, G.H. *The Radical Reformation.* 3rd ed. Kirksville 1992.
Wollgast, Siegfried, ed. *Zur Friedensidee der Reformationszeit. Texte von Erasmus, Paracelsus, Franck.* Berlin 1968.
Zagorin, Perez. *Ways of Lying: Dissimulation, Persecution, and Conformity in Early Modern Europe.* Cambridge, MA, 1990.
Zwicker, Daniel. *Novi Foederis Josias.* N.p. 1670.
Zwingli, Huldrych. *Huldreich Zwinglis sämtliche Werke.* Ed. E. Egli et al. Berlin–Leipzig–Zurich 1905–68; repr. 1981.

Index of Biblical References

Genesis	74, 83, 160f., 198f.	2:6	249n18
3:5	282n2	5:1–11	133, 280n141
		5:33–7	22, 179, 234f.
Exodus		5:38–42	263n21
3:14	207	5–7	87
		6:11	55
Deuteronomy	292n37	10:6–7	40
24:1–4	185	11:30	249n26
		12:46–8	248n10
2 Kings		13:24–30	22, 97f., 263n13
2:1–11	258n70	13:33	255n39
		13:36–43	22, 97f.
Psalms	84	13:55	297n48
46	86	16:16–19	17, 241–3
115 (116):11	141	16:20	40, 253n9
		17:2	132, 197
Ecclesiastes	139	19:3–9	185, 248n16
		19:13–15	232
Isaiah	84	19:17	293n53
7:14	60	21:23–7	285n56
		22:15–22	285n56
Hosea		23	173
14:9	57	24:23	249n23
		24:36	255n39, 293n59
Matthew		26:26–8	238
1:23	29, 248n10, 249n20, 294n76	27:8	249n18
		28:18–20	229–34, 253n9

Mark

1:2	249n18, 250n34
13:32	255n39
14:23–4	19n14, 238
16:15–16	229, 234

Luke

1:18–19	18
1:42	297n48
3:14	87, 260n94
4:8	249n20
6:27–31	263n21
11:3	55
12:15	260n99
12:48	302n7
16:19–31	25
22:17–20	238
22:36–8	27, 260n94, 262n1, 263n13
23:46	298n76

John

1	255n39
1:1–3	41, 49f., 64, 176, 186, 253n4, 255nn37, 39, 291n24
1:1–14	140f.
1:10	49, 261n120
1:14	39, 50, 64
1:15	178, 257n65, 261n120
1:30	253n9
3:13	51f., 178, 261n120
4:21	248n8
5:19–23	36
5:27	255n39
7:39	36
8.3–7	285n56
8:25–7	41, 253n4, 255n39
8:44	282n2
8:54	176
8:57	255n39
8:58	51, 253n9, 261nn120, 122
10:30	39, 60, 186, 255n39
14:1	176
14:16	294n76
14:27	82
14:28	255n37
17:3	50, 255n39
19:28–30	298n76
20:21	21, 27, 263n13
20:22–3	17
20:28	65
21:15	17

Acts

1:1	249n18
2:14–41	229, 233f.
2:20	178
5:1–11	104, 268n9
5:3	147
8.27–39	230, 233
13:12	262n124
13:33	260n103
15:18	257n57
16:14–15	302n4
17:22–31	144
17:31	253n9, 257n57
17:34	65f.
19:18	19
20:28	52, 60, 291n25, 292n31

Romans

1:3–4	253n4, 255n39, 261n120, 293n48
1:5	293n48
1:7	255n39

2:8–9	293n48	13:8	257n57
2:18	293n48	15:31	22
3:4	141		
3:20	293n48	**2 Corinthians**	
3:25	52, 293nn48, 50	1:6	293n48
3:27–8	248n8	2:1	293n48
4:12	293n48	2:5–8	268n9
4:19	293n48	2:10	292n37
5:7	257n57	2:13	249n18
5:12–21	28, 61, 65, 181, 229, 302n3	2:14	255n34
		3:18	293n48
6:6	54, 257n59	5:17–19	41, 176, 257n59, 293nn48, 50
7:7–25	55		
7:24	257n57	7:11	293n48
8:2	55	8:9	41
8:3	249n18	10:3–6	263n13
8:10–11	293n48	11:23–6	285n56
8:23	293n48	12:2	132, 258n70
8:30	181	13:1	293n48
9:5	50f., 60f., 178, 181, 250n34, 253n4, 255n39, 261nn120, 122, 293nn48, 59, 294n76	13:14	255n39
		13:15	292n37
		Galatians	
		1:7	293n48
		1:16	293n48
11:36	255n39	2:6	293n48
13:8	26	2:11–14	143–5
		2:16	248n8
1 Corinthians		3:5	293n48
1:14–16	302n4	3:19	257n57
2:8	258n70	3:20	293n48
4:3	249n18	4:4	60
5:11	268n9	4:12	293n48
7:31	293n48	4:19	257n59, 293n48
7:39	20, 185	5:6	257n57
8:6	181, 293n48	5:20	293n48
9:21	257n57	6:15	257n59
9:22	144	6:16	292n37, 293n48
11:23–5	238, 304n42		
12:10	271n48	**Ephesians**	
12:13	257n57	1:10	257n57

316 Index of Biblical References

1:17	255n39		255n39, 257n57,
2:8	206		294n76
2:15	41	6:15	255n39
3:9	41, 293n59		
4:9–10	293n48	**2 Timothy**	
5:5	255n39	2:24–6	268n9
6:5–7	26		
3:14	293n59	**Titus**	
		1:12	219
Philippians		2:11–13	13, 60, 250n34,
2:5–7	36, 39, 60, 64f.,		253n4, 255n39,
	250 n34,		294n76
	253n41, 255	3:4	253n4, 255n39
	n39, 261n122,	3:10–11	268n9
	293n59, 294n76		
3:3	255n39, 261n120,	**Hebrews**	291n17
	293n59	1:2–3	253n4, 255n39,
3:16	292n37		294n76
		1:7–9	60
Colossians		2:7	253n9, 255n39
1:15–17	253n4, 255n39,	2:10	255n 39, 257n57
	261n120	2:11–17	253n15
1:19–22	257n57	9:28	257n57
2:9	60, 250n34, 253n4,	11:1	199
	255n39		
2:20–3	56	**James**	
		5:12	179
1 Thessalonians			
3:11	176	**1 Peter**	
5:3	281n176	2:24	257n57, 271n48
5:13	281n176		
		2 Peter	
2 Thessalonians		1:19–21	179
2:7	175		
2:16	255n39	**1 John**	
		1:1	176
1 Timothy		2:27	292n37
1:1	255n39	4:2–3	41, 293n59
1:6	253n4	5:6–9	23, 34f., 48f., 60,
1:17	253n4, 255n39		178, 182f., 187,
1:19–20	104, 268n9		235–8, 253n4,
2:5	253n9		255n39, 291n25
3:16	46, 182, 253n4,	5:20	60f., 293n59

Revelation
1:11	293n59
7:9	291n26
13	293n59
9:14	291n26
16:12	291n26
20:14	297n57

General Index

Abélard, Pierre 140
Abraham 51, 147, 166
accommodation, exegetical theory
  of 56f., 146, 154, 164
Aconcio, Jacopo 182, 290nn6f.
Adam and Eve 28, 53, 65, 83, 184,
  198, 229
Adrian VI, pope 205
Aesop 69
Agricola, Rodolphus 119
Agrippa, Henricus Cornelius 46,
  71f., 83
Ailly, Pierre d' 46
Aleandro, Girolamo 120f., 227
Aleandro, Pietro 120
Ambrose, St 27, 71, 109, 304n45
Amy, Pierre 203
Anabaptists, Anabaptism 5f.,
  21–3, 39, 86, 96, 99, 102, 228,
  231–5
Andreae, Johann Valentin 5
Andreasi, Marsilio 103–5
Anne of Brittany, queen of France 79
Antenor 75
Antitrinitarians, Antitrinitarianism
  7, 33–67, 106, 175–8, 181f., 185f.,
  237

Arians, Arianism 23f., 34, 36f., 48,
  50, 54, 59, 100, 168, 172, 176f.,
  183, 186f., 236f., 303n27
Arias Montano, Benito 59
Ariosto, Ludovico 211
Aristotle, Aristotelianism 26, 47,
  109, 113, 116, 120, 135, 152–4,
  156, 159, 163
Arnobius 109
Ascia, Luca d' 148
Athanasius, St 33, 108
Augustijn, Cornelis 227
Augustine, St 3, 14, 17, 19, 26f., 36,
  47, 50, 61, 71, 87, 140, 145, 160,
  163, 206, 228, 293n57; *Commentary on Galatians* 143; *Confessiones* 111, 114; *De Trinitate* 45;
  letters 26, 99f., 143, 147; *Retractationes* 17; sermons 17

Bacon, Francis 151f.
Bade, Josse 120f.
Bainton, Roland H. 99
Basalù, Giulio 39
Basel 35, 38f., 47, 70, 95, 102–5, 108,
  111, 134, 147, 155, 197, 231, 241,
  276n62

Basil, St 45
Bayle, Pierre 9, 156, 166–8
Beatus Rhenanus (Beat Bild) 45, 290n15
Béda, Noël 97, 147, 231
Belin, Christian 160
Bellarmino, Roberto 5, 173
Bernard of Clairvaux, St 71, 113, 132, 200, 206
Bernard of Luxemburg 14
Best, Paul 175f., 178
Bèze, Théodore de 6, 48, 50, 52–4, 59f., 64, 97f., 106f., 241
Biandrata, Giorgio 43
Bidle, John 175, 177f., 186
Biel, Gabriel 239, 248n14
Boccaccio, Giovanni 111
Bodin, Jean 301n116
Bohemian Brethren 7, 61, 243
Bologna 39, 115f., 149
Borrhaus, Martin 38
Bracali, Mario 149
Brandenburg, Albrecht von, cardinal 30
Brant, Sebastian 133
Brenz, Johannes 96
Bruni, Leonardo 114, 121
Bruno, Giordano 5f.
Bucer, Martin 91
Budé, Guillaume 197
Bullinger, Heinrich 40, 105
Burckhardt, Jakob 116, 122, 148f., 272n6

Calvin, Jean 6, 24f., 38f., 96f., 100, 102, 105f., 147f., 172, 207, 241f.
Capito, Wolfgang 5, 38
Cardano, Girolamo 8f., 43, 141f., 148–57, 161, 165f.
Carvajal, Luis de 137

Castellio, Sebastian 8, 38f., 47f., 72, 95–103, 105–8, 182, 225, 292n38; Bible translations 48, 52f., 106f.; *De arte duitandi* 107f.; *De haereticis, an sint persequendi* 95–103; *Dialogi quatuor* 47, 107
Cecil, Robert, earl of Salisbury 217
Celsi, Mino 72, 98f., 259n94, 268n8
Cervantes, Miguel de 10, 184, 208–16, 219, 225
Chaloner, Thomas 216, 218
Charles V, emperor 14, 35, 70, 77, 81
Charron, Pierre 156, 160–2, 164
Chillingworth, William 171–5, 178, 290n6
Christian church, history of 14, 44–7, 59, 74, 100, 173, 182
Cicero 109f., 122, 128, 134, 142, 153; *Academica* 141; *De divination* 113; *De finibus* 113, 117, 121f., 138, 141; *De natura deorumi* 114, 117; *De officiis* 113f.
Clement VII, pope 204
Clement of Alexandria, St 109, 172
Cles, Bernhard von 30
Clichtove, Josse 137
Cochlaeus, Johannes 303n23
Colet, John 33, 132, 274nn33, 35
Constantine I, emperor 45, 165
Conway, Anne 178
councils, ecumenical: Fifth Lateran 116; Nicaea 33, 44, 252n2; Trent 229
Crell, Johannes 175
Crell, Samuel 182
Croy, Guillaume de, cardinal 132f.
Curcellaeus, Stephanus 5, 59
Curione, Celio Agostino 8, 39, 96, 102–6, 147f., 149, 296n39
Curione, Orazio Agostino 104

Cyprian, St 71, 241f.
Cyril of Alexandria, St 233

Dante Alighieri 111
Darmon, Jean-Charles 158f.
David 85
Dávid, Ferenc 43, 45f.
De Breen, Daniel 10, 61–7, 181
De falsa 42–6, 61
De Gouges, Olympe 4
Democritus 137, 161, 278n107
Demosthenes 142
Denis the Carthusian 71
Descartes, René 161, 163
DeWitt, Norman W. 139f.
Diogenes, Cynic philosopher 206, 273n29
Diogenes Laertius 109, 111f., 114, 117f., 140, 158
Di Rienzo, Eugenio 151
dissimulation and simulation 8, 40, 63, 66, 142–8, 151–6, 158, 168, 178, 217, 220f.
Dolet, Etienne 197
Domański, Juliusz 49, 55
Dorp, Maarten van 190, 217
Du Bellay, Guillaume, sieur de Langey 197
Du Bellay, Jean, cardinal 197
Dugard, William 186
Du Jon, François 59
Dunn-Lardeau, Brenda 10, 280n153

Eck, Johann 145
Elija 52
Elizabeth I, queen of England 290n6
Epictetus 202, 206
Epicurus, Epicureanism 8f., 109–40, 156, 159, 161, 164, 190–6, 208, 213, 222

Erasmus: *Acta academiae Lovaniensis* 227; *Adagia* 30, 49, 69, 73–9, 81, 84, 88, 96, 116–18, 157f., 163, 168, 184, 197f., 206, 210, 300n88; *Antibarbari* 110–12, 114, 282n1; *Apologia ad Caranzam* 52; *Apologia ad monachos Hispanos* 15–31, 33, 36, 54, 101, 186f., 228f., 234, 236–40, 242, 302n3; *Apophthegmata* 158, 202, 301n114; *Ciceronianus* 116; *Colloquia* 111, 134–50, 159f., 163f., 167f., 184, 197f., 200–2, 206, 210, 267n83, 271n5, 279n137, 298n75, 302n6; *De bello Turcico* 88, 92; *De concordia* 179, 240, 303n23; *De conscribendis epistolis* 134, 179; *De contemptu mundi* 112–14, 131, 135, 138–40, 191, 195, 279n136; *De copia* 282n1; *De immensa Dei misericordia concio* 103f; *De libero arbitrio* 28, 217; *De praeparatione ad mortem* 303n25; *De pueris instituendis* 118, 160f.; *De recta pronuntiatione* 161; *De vidua Christiana* 294n68; *Ecclesiastes* 66, 160, 259n87, 297n53, 301n120; *Enchiridion* (and dedicatory epistle to Paul Volz) 25f., 63, 70, 73, 160f., 173, 203f., 240, 263n13, 273n32; *Epistola ad fratres inferioris Germaniae* 303n31; *Epistola contra pseudevangelicos* 280n157; *Exomologesis* 19; *Exploratio symboli* 297n46; *Hyperaspistes I* 24, 243; *Hyperaspistes II* 202, 302n7, 303n30; *Institutio principis Christiani* 26, 88, 163, 267n81, 280n148; *Julius exclusus* 116, 204, 227; letters 81, 90, 102, 153, 163, 177, 196, 279n131, 280n152, 281n157, 290n10,

291n17, 302n2, 303nn13, 23, 304nn32, 38–40, 305nn48, 52; *Lingua* 142, 163, 300n88, 301n114; *Modus orandi Deum* 205, 297n46; *Moria (Moriae encomium)* 8, 10, 13, 30f., 70, 77, 109f., 116, 118, 121, 125–35, 140, 150, 157, 159, 161, 163, 171, 173, 183f., 187, 189f., 192–5, 208–13, 215–24, 270n43; *Novum Testamentum* (text, annotations, paraphrases): *see* Index of Biblical References; *Opera omnia* 6, 153, 163, 166, 168; *Panegyricus* 142; *Paraclesis* 135, 160; *Purgatio adversus epistolam Lutheri* 137, 237, 281n160, 301n120; *Querela pacis* 77–81, 84, 88, 90, 92f.; *Ratio verae theologiae* 17, 56, 144, 232, 258nn78, 80f.; Responses to Edward Lee 49; *Responsio ad Phimostomum de divortio* 294n66; *Spongia adversus Huttenum* 19
eschatological events, judgment day 24f., 64, 71, 89f., 176, 185
Eucharist 19, 21, 79, 207, 238–41, 243

Fabri, Johannes, bishop of Vienna 137
Falkland, Lucius Cary, Lord 9, 171–4, 181
Febvre, Lucien 197–9, 201f.
Ferdinand I, emperor 30, 69
Ficino, Marsilio 114f., 132
Filelfo, Francesco 114
Firmin, Thomas 176–9, 181f.
Fisher, John, St, cardinal 248n14, 291n18
Fisher, Samuel 178
Flekwijk, Herman van 304n33

Francis I, king of France 80f., 204
Francis, St 132, 194, 205
Franck, Sebastian 7, 9f., 13–31, 34, 67, 69–93, 225, 234, 241f.; *Chronica* or *Geshichtbibel* 14–31, 60, 69–72, 81, 83f., 96f., 233; *Krieg Büchlin des Friedes* 70–3, 82–93
François de Sales, St 162
Frederick III, emperor 70
free will 28, 47, 106f., 119
Freiburg 15, 30, 38, 111, 153f.
Friesen, Abraham 233
Froben, Johann 111, 117
Fubini, Riccardo 276n73

Galen 134, 150
Garasse, François 156, 161, 207
gardens 109–12, 190f.
Gassendi, Pierre 9, 162–4, 166
Gauss, Julia 35f
Geldenhouwer, Gerard 249n29
Genebrard, Gilbert 46
Geneva 8, 38f., 242
Gilly, Carlos 5, 35f.
Granada, Miguel A. 246nn6f.
Gratian 71
Gregory I, pope 71
Gribaldi, Matteo 106, 254n19
Grimani, Domenico, cardinal 116, 120
Grotius, Hugo 58, 60, 64, 67, 108, 162f., 177, 180, 185, 292n28
Gustavus Adolphus, king of Sweden 175

Hales, John 172f., 175
Hegius, Alexander 119
Henry VIII, king of England 81, 294n68
heresy, heterodoxy 14f., 44f., 95–101, 105, 149, 153, 167, 173, 184f.
Hesiod 105

Hexter, J.H. 195f.
Hobbes, Thomas 151, 178
Hoffmann, Melchior 21
Holcot, Robert 283n18
Homer 198
Horace 109, 114, 127, 131, 158, 208, 210, 222, 278n116
Hubmaier, Balthasar 231–4, 242
Huss, Jan 14
Hutten, Ulrich von 147

Ignatius, St 45
Ingegno, Alfonso 152
Inquisition, inquisitors 5, 16, 21, 25, 28f., 98, 101, 148f., 209
Irenaeus, St 253n9, 256n47
Israel, Jonathan 3

James II, king of England 177
Jerome, St 6, 28, 45, 71, 114, 143–5, 147, 177, 205, 233, 271n5, 293n57
Jesus Christ: views on his divinity 29, 35f., 39–42, 44– 6, 50–2, 54, 59f., 64f., 168, 175f., 180–2, 186f., 292n33
Joachim of Fiore 45
Joan, popess 204
John, evangelist 42, 44f.
John the Baptist 206
John Chrysostom, St 6, 45, 97, 101, 206, 283n21
Jonas, Justus 146
Jonson, Ben 10, 216–18
Jortin, John 175
Jovianus 28
Judith 147
Julius II, pope 79, 204
Justin Martyr, St 165, 172

Kaiser, Walter 115, 221, 223, 299n79
Karlstadt, Andreas 240

Károli, Péter 46
Kelley, Maurice 185f.

Lactantius 109, 114, 122, 140, 279n120
La Mothe le Vayer, François de 156, 162–5
Landino, Cristoforo 274n36
law: canon 87, 185, 204, 239; Mosaic 53, 72, 74, 86, 143; natural 75, 185; Roman 27, 74, 87
Le Clerc, Jean 6, 9, 25, 166–9, 180f., 183
Lee, Edward 34, 60, 229, 236, 303n27
Lefèvre d'Étaples, Jacques 33f.
Leo X, pope 77, 80, 204f.
Le Sauvage, Jean 77, 90
libertins 9, 148, 156–65, 207, 220, 290n7
Lips, Maarten 203
Lismanini, Francesco 42
Listrius, Gerardus 132, 279nn122, 134
Locke, John 9, 24, 175, 178–83, 187
London 114, 116, 125, 175, 178, 182f., 216
Louis XIV, king of France 164, 167
Louvain 49, 116, 134, 189, 276n62
Lubieniecki, Stanisław 255n37, 256n54
Lucian 109, 115, 120, 208, 277n99, 297n43
Lucretius 87, 109, 114f., 124, 127f., 140, 159, 161, 164, 191, 193, 208, 265n54, 273n24
Lushington, Thomas 175
Luther, Martin 8, 14, 21, 25, 47, 71f., 85, 91f., 137, 139, 145–8, 152, 174, 207, 240; Commentaries on Galatians, 1519 and 1535 145,

278n118; *De captivitate Babylonica* 146; *De servo arbitrio* 47, 106, 217, 229, 237; letters 237; Ninety-five Theses 4; *Resolutio ... de potestate papae* 241; Table talk 137, 204; *Von weltlicher Obrigkeit* 95f.

Machiavelli, Niccolò 153, 161, 166, 285n55, 301n116
Maclean, Ian 156
Manetti, Gianozzo 252n54, 265n54
Mansfield, Bruce 5, 167f., 171
Manuzio, Aldo 116f., 236
Margherita, duchess of Mantua 104
Martin, St 206
Mary, duchess of Burgundy 80
Mary, mother of Jesus 18, 40, 60, 122, 199–201
Mary I, queen of England 100
Maximilian I, emperor 81, 91
Mayer (Meyer), Georg, of Leeder 102
Mazarin, Jules, cardinal 162, 164f.
McLachlan, H. John 176f.
Mennonites 6, 61f.
Mersenne, Marin 58
Metsys, Quentin 298n69
millennium 8, 62, 64, 67, 105, 181f.
Milton, John 9, 171, 183–7
Montaigne, Michel de 9, 108, 155–62, 164, 167, 284n42
More, Thomas, St 10, 115, 125, 132, 167, 274n33, 291n18; *Utopia* 76f., 134, 172, 184, 190–6
Moses 85
Müntzer, Thomas 231

nature 73f., 78, 82, 124, 128f., 138, 141, 192–4, 202, 209, 264nn30f., 299n79

Naudé, Gabriel 155f., 162, 165f.
Newton, Isaac 9, 24, 166, 179, 181–3, 187
Nicodemism 105f., 148
Noah 83, 198f.
Nye, Stephen 176–8, 290n10

Ochino, Bernardino 46, 254n19, 287n12
Oecolampadius, Johannes 38, 71, 240, 298n61, 304n39
Oporinus, Johannes 101
Origen 17, 24, 27, 40, 45, 71, 109, 132, 140, 143, 145, 241f.
original sin 53f., 61, 65, 180, 265n55
Orléans 99, 153f.
Osiander, Andreas 59
Otto of Freising 14

Padua 39, 75, 116, 149
Palingenio, Marcello 286n68
Paracelsus, Theophrastus 101
Paris 114, 116, 119f., 134, 155, 197; University of 38, 162, 199
Patin, Guy 156, 162f., 165–7, 284n44
Paul, apostle 20, 26, 28, 36, 42, 52, 55, 60, 63, 66, 119, 130, 133, 142–6, 154, 228f.
peace and war 27, 59, 69–93
Pelagians, Pelagianism 28, 62, 229, 290n10
Pellicanus, Conrad 298n61
Pellicier, Guillaume, bishop of Montpellier 197
Pembroke, Thomas Herbert, count 180
Penn, William 178f.
Petau (Petavius), Denis 58, 177
Peter, apostle 17, 75, 86, 143–5, 154, 229f., 241f.

Peter Lombard 45
Petrarca, Franceso 111, 142
Pfefferkorn, Johann 203
Philip, duke of Burgundy 142
Phillips, Margaret Mann 157f.
Pistorius, Johannes 64
Plato, Platonism 25, 44–7, 110f., 113f., 131f., 135, 275n50; *Laws* 111, 195; *Phaedrus* 110, 274n35; *Republic* 195f., 209; *Symposium* 171; *Timaeus* 47
Plattard, Jean 206
Plautus 281n169
Pliny the Elder 111, 217
Pliny the Younger 275n50
Plotinus 132
Plutarch 8, 109, 121, 142, 272n22, 275n50
Popkin, Richard 160
Possevino, Antonio 5
Postel, Guillaume 207
predestination 47, 53, 103f., 180, 182
Przypkowski, Samuel 175

Quakers 9, 22, 178f., 241
Quast, Bruno 72
Quintana, Juan de 35

Rabelais, François 10, 136f., 156f., 161f., 184, 196–209, 225
Raimondi, Cosma 273n31
Raków 57–9; Racovian Catechism 58, 175, 186, 254n22
Raynaud, Théophile 156
Remonstrants (Arminians) 61f., 168, 175, 184
Renaudet, Augustin 116
Reuchlin, Johann 203, 271n5
Rex, Felix 136
Richard, Jean 180
Ricius, Paulus 47

Rome 116, 130, 155, 205, 279n122
Rotondi Secchi Tarugi, Luisa 10, 265n54, 270n38
Rotondò, Antonio 40f.
Ruar, Martin 58, 62

salvation, liberal access to 62, 103–5, 165
Sancho Panza 211, 213–15, 300nn89f.
Sandius, Christophorus 182
Scaliger, Julius Caesar 155f., 167, 287n16
Sceptics, scepticism 8f., 107f., 118, 141, 154, 158–60, 163–7, 172–5, 178
Schiner Matthaeus, cardinal 80
Schwenckfeld, Caspar 269n25
Screech, M.A. 197, 199, 203, 299n79
Seidel-Menchi, Silvana 5, 103, 148, 227
Seneca 8, 109, 112, 119, 122, 126, 158, 279n120
Servetus, Michael 8, 25, 33–40, 46, 48, 50–2, 55, 64, 95, 233, 237
Sextus Empiricus 172
Shakespeare, William 10, 218–25
Simon, Richard 168, 183
Simons, Menno 231
Socinians, Socinianism 4, 9, 24f., 42, 48f., 52, 57–9, 61, 64f., 67, 107, 163, 169, 172, 174–7, 180, 182f., 185f., 235, 290n7
Socrates 135, 138, 152
Solomon 165
Sommer, Johann 46f.
Sozzini, Fausto 10, 47–58, 60f., 64f., 107, 175, 177, 187, 225
Sozzini, Lelio 39–43, 47, 50f., 64, 106
Spinoza, Baruch 168
Spon, Charles 155
Stegmann, Joachim, senior 175

Stoa, Stoicism 8, 118, 121–7, 131, 133–5, 138, 140, 159, 190–2
Strasbourg 21, 30, 70, 231f., 237
Szczucki, Lech 10, 293n58
Szlichtyng, Jonasz 175

Tertullian 45f., 71
Theologia Germanica 82
Theophylact 233
Thomas Aquinas, St 160, 163, 239, 248n14
toleration, religious 59, 63, 95–102, 162, 165, 172, 180, 194, 263n13, 285n55
Torresani, Andrea 120
Transylvania 42–7, 50, 59, 176f.
Trapman, Johannes 64
Traversari, Ambrogio 117
Tremellio, Emmanuele 59f.
Trinity, dogma of the 7, 9, 20, 23, 29, 34–9, 43–9, 55, 59f., 62, 106, 108, 169, 175f., 180, 182f., 235–8
Triplet, Thomas 290nn5f.

Ulysses 152
Urquhart, Thomas 197
Utenheim, Christoph von, bishop of Basel 104

Valla, Lorenzo 8, 50, 110, 159; *Adnotationes in Novum Testamentum* 119; *De Constantini donatione* 119; *De voluptate* 119–30, 190–3; *Dialecticae disquisitions* 119; *Elegantiae* 122
Van Eyck, Jan 298n69
Venice 91, 116–18, 120, 296n39
Vesalius, Andreas 101
Vespasian, emperor 79
Vespucci, Amerigo 196
Vilanova, Antonio 209
Virgil 105, 109, 124, 128
Vitrier, Jean 132, 167, 203
Vives, Juan Luis 88, 135, 172, 301n114
Volz, Paul 203

Walpot, Peter 233
Wessel Gansfort, Jan 71, 85
Wier (Weyer), Johannes 101
Winstanley, Gerard 178
Wiszowaty, Benedykt 58
women 123, 131, 241
Wycliffe, John 14

Zúñiga, Francisco de 236, 242
Zurich 21, 39, 47, 105, 231–3, 237
Zwicker, Daniel 10, 58–62, 65
Zwingli, Huldrych 14, 200, 231–3, 240

www.ingramcontent.com/pod-product-compliance
Lightning Source LLC
Chambersburg PA
CBHW030304080526
44584CB00012B/430